A BRIEF HISTORY OF
THE ROMANS

A BRIEF
HISTORY
OF THE ROMANS

SECOND EDITION

Mary T. Boatwright

Daniel J. Gargola

Noel Lenski

Richard J. A. Talbert

NEW YORK   OXFORD
OXFORD UNIVERSITY PRESS

Oxford University Press is a department of the University of Oxford.
It furthers the University's objective of excellence in research,
scholarship, and education by publishing worldwide.

Oxford   New York
Auckland   Cape Town   Dar es Salaam   Hong Kong   Karachi
Kuala Lumpur   Madrid   Melbourne   Mexico City   Nairobi
New Delhi   Shanghai Taipei   Toronto

With offices in
Argentina   Austria   Brazil   Chile   Czech Republic   France   Greece
Guatemala   Hungary   Italy   Japan   Poland   Portugal   Singapore
South Korea   Switzerland   Thailand   Turkey   Ukraine   Vietnam

Copyright © 2014, 2006 by Oxford University Press

For titles covered by Section 112 of the US Higher Education
Opportunity Act, please visit www.oup.com/us/he for the latest
information about pricing and alternate formats.

Published by Oxford University Press
198 Madison Avenue, New York, New York 10016
http://www.oup.com

Oxford is a registered trademark of Oxford University Press

Library of Congress Cataloging-in-Publication Data

Boatwright, Mary Taliaferro.
  [Brief history of ancient Rome]
  A brief history of the Romans / Mary T. Boatwright, Daniel J. Gargola, Noel Lenski, Richard J. A.
Talbert. — Second edition.
    pages cm
  Revised edition of: A brief history of ancient Rome. New York : Oxford University Press, 2005.
  Includes bibliographical references and index.
  ISBN 978-0-19-998755-9 (acid-free paper) 1. Rome—History. I. Gargola, Daniel J. II. Lenski,
Noel Emmanuel, 1965- III. Talbert, Richard J. A., 1947- IV. Title.
  DG209.B582   2013
  937—dc23

                                                                                    2013014883

Cover: Basilica cistern, Istanbul, Turkey (Turkish, Yerebatan Sarayı). Cisterns for storing water were a
distinctive and remarkable feature of Constantinople, the New Rome. During the fifth century A.D.,
three vast open ones were dug in the area between the Constantinian and Theodosian Walls (see Map 14.2).
Within the city, more than 150 covered cisterns have been recorded. The largest, close to the Great
Palace, was dug under a basilica (great hall) by the emperor Justinian in the mid-sixth century. It
measures approximately 453 ft/138 m by 212 ft/64.5 m, with a vaulted brick roof supported by 336
marble columns—most of them taken from elsewhere and reused here—30 ft/9 m high. This cistern
is capable of holding about 2.8 million cubic ft of water (80,000 cubic m). Because water had to be
brought to the city from its western hinterland through exceptionally extended aqueduct lines,
emperors always feared interruptions to the flow, not to mention a siege or blockade: hence their
concern to maintain ample reservoirs of water within the city.

Printing number: 9 8 7 6 5 4 3 2

Printed in the United States of America
on acid-free paper

CONTENTS

2   Republican Rome and the Conquest of Italy

 ## 3   The Beginnings of a Mediterranean Empire

6   The Domination of Sulla and Its Legacy

 7   End of the Republic: Caesar's Dictatorship

12   The Third-Century Crisis and the Tetrarchic Restabilization

13   The Rise of Christianity and the Growth of the Barbarian Threat (324–395)

MAPS

FIGURES

PLATES

PREFACE TO THE
SECOND EDITION

This second edition reflects the changes made in the second edition of *The Romans from Village to Empire*, published in 2012. In particular, the coverage now continues for a further two centuries, to around A.D. 500. For this purpose, Noel Lenski has rewritten the final chapter of the first edition and has added two fresh chapters. In the meantime, the opening five chapters of the first edition have been reworked and trimmed to become four, so that there is now only one more chapter than before (fourteen instead of thirteen). Another distinctive and enriching feature of the second edition is the inclusion of eight pages of color plates. As a result, it has been possible to present in color some illustrations that previously could only appear in grayscale, and to expand the range of pictures. There is fuller discussion of some aspects of social, cultural, and religious history. Considerable changes have been made to Boxes (now Sources), Suggested Readings, and the presentation of maps. At the end, the Gazetteer now precedes the Index.

New to This Edition

- Timeline of the book has been expanded by about 200 years, down at least to the fall of the western empire in the late fifth century.
- Chapters One and Two have been combined into Chapter One, "Archaic Italy and the Origins of Rome."

- There are two new chapters: Chapter Thirteen, "The Rise of Christianity and the Growth of the Barbarian Threat (324–395)," and Chapter Fourteen, "The Final Years of the Western Empire and Rome's Revival in the East."
- The edition features an eight-page full-color insert.

Mary T. Boatwright, Durham, North Carolina
Daniel J. Gargola, Lexington, Kentucky
Noel Lenski, Boulder, Colorado
Richard J. A. Talbert, Chapel Hill, North Carolina

PREFACE TO THE
FIRST EDITION

Shortly after *The Romans from Village to Empire* appeared in 2004, our editor, Robert Miller, asked if we would be willing to create a shorter version of it, much as our colleagues S. B. Pomeroy, S. M. Burstein, W. Donlan, and J. T. Roberts had already done with such skill for their *Ancient Greece*. Intrigued by the challenge of reducing what is itself only an introduction to more than a millennium, we have striven to craft here a coherent, satisfying overview. We anticipate that it will be in greatest demand among readers whose knowledge and interest in ancient Rome are cultural and artistic. Accordingly, we have chosen to focus on Rome's historical growth as a state and community. We recognize that neither this choice nor any other can meet with universal approval; the hard fact remains that the shorter the book, the more selective its coverage must be.

The approach adopted and the nature of the presentation resemble those of *The Romans from Village to Empire*. We draw attention to some very recent books of special value for further reading, and we have taken the welcome opportunity to enhance our treatment of certain fundamental topics—the place of religion and of slavery in Roman society, for example.

We have also expanded the scope of the final chapter to extend into the early fifth century A.D.

It would have been impossible to produce this book without once again drawing upon all the assistance we received in completing its larger predecessor. We are more grateful than ever, therefore, for this widespread support from colleagues, students, and others. Dr. Tom Elliott, Director of the Ancient World Mapping Center at UNC, Chapel Hill, merits fresh thanks for his willingness to adapt some maps that now appear in a slightly different form than before. We three partners have worked together as closely and amicably as ever. This shorter book, we hope, will equip readers with an informed basic insight into Roman history while attracting them to a closer engagement with the Romans, because there is much more—of absorbing interest—to be explored.

Mary T. Boatwright, Durham, North Carolina
Daniel J. Gargola, Lexington, Kentucky
Richard J. A. Talbert, Chapel Hill, North Carolina

ACKNOWLEDGMENTS

Our original editor has been succeeded by Charles Cavaliere, and we thank him warmly for steering this second edition to publication. Faith Orlebeke's editorial assistance was invaluable to Noel Lenski in drafting the new chapters. Staff at the Ancient World Mapping Center most ably made, or remade, all the maps: Dr. Brian Turner, Dr. Jeffrey Becker, Ray Belanger, Steve Burges, and Ashley Lee. The terrain depiction on all the maps (except city plans) is calculated from Environmental Systems Research Institute SRTM Shaded Relief, on ESRI Data & Maps 2006 [DVD-ROM], Redlands, California.

We would also like to thank the many professors who have made valuable comments regarding *The Romans* and *A Brief History of the Romans*. They include, but are not limited to

David Cherry, Montana State University
Andrew Gallia, University of Minnesota
Vanessa B. Gorman, University of Nebraska–Lincoln
Robert L. Hohlfelder, University of Colorado, Boulder
Ralph Mathisen, University of Illinois at Urbana-Champaign
Brian McGing, Trinity College Dublin

M. Gwyn Morgan, University of Texas at Austin
Carlos F. Noreña, University of California, Berkeley
Debra L. Nousek, University of Western Ontario
Guy MacLean Rogers, Wellesley College and Western Connecticut State University
Michael Wolfe, St. John's University

NOTES TO THE READER

To assist further investigation of the themes introduced by this book, suggested readings are listed at the end of each chapter. In addition, two works to be referred to throughout are the fourth edition of the *Oxford Classical Dictionary* (*OCD*) edited by Simon Hornblower and Antony Spawforth (Oxford: Oxford University Press, 2012), and Roger Bagnall et al. (eds.), *The Encyclopedia of Ancient History* (13 vols., Malden, Mass., and Oxford: Wiley-Blackwell, 2013). For the fourth century A.D. onwards, a further invaluable work of reference is Alexander P. Kazhdan et al. (eds.), *The Oxford Dictionary of Byzantium* (3 vols., Oxford: Oxford University Press, 1991). Expanded coverage of Rome's entire history is offered by *The Edinburgh History of Ancient Rome* (8 vols., Edinburgh: Edinburgh University Press, 2012–2014).

A timeline, a glossary, a gazetteer for the maps, and an index are to be found at the end.

The Ancient World Mapping Center at the University of North Carolina, Chapel Hill, offers free digital copies of each map that it produced for this book: visit awmc .unc.edu/wordpress/free-maps.

Some "Sources" translate Latin texts to be found in the periodical *L'Année Epigraphique* (*AE*) and in Hermann Dessau (ed.), *Inscriptiones Latinae Selectae* (Berlin: Weidmann, 1892–1916) (*ILS*).

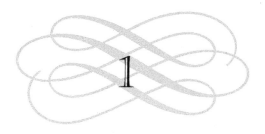

ARCHAIC ITALY AND
THE ORIGINS OF ROME

For centuries before the formation of cities, Italy was a land of villages and the outside world impinged on life only fitfully. Urban life appeared here long after it had emerged in other parts of the Mediterranean basin. Over time, some settlements slowly became larger and more complex socially, economically, and politically, and the leaders of these more highly structured towns and villages gloried in their connections with the wider Mediterranean world. In the seventh and sixth centuries B.C., some communities achieved the status of cities, with elaborate social systems, monumental buildings and temples, and formal public spaces; others would follow in later centuries. These urban centers would long remain the chief centers of power in Italy (Map 1.1).

ITALY AND THE MEDITERRANEAN WORLD

Italy (Italia in Latin) is a long peninsula, encompassing slightly less than 100,000 square miles (260,000 sq km), that juts out from the northern or European coast of the Mediterranean Sea (Latin, Internum Mare). In the far north, the Alps (Latin, Alpes) divide Italy from the rest of Europe. To their south, the valley of the Po (Latin, Padus)—Italy's largest river—contains land with great agricultural potential. Except for the plains along the eastern coast, the Apennine mountains separate the Po Valley from the rest of Italy. Peninsular Italy begins south of the Po Valley. The peninsula is about 650 miles in length (1,040 km), and it never is more than 125 miles wide (200 km); the sea is always fairly close. The Apennines dominate the peninsula. From their northwestern end, where they meet the western Alps and the sea, these mountains run almost due east in a narrow and virtually

1

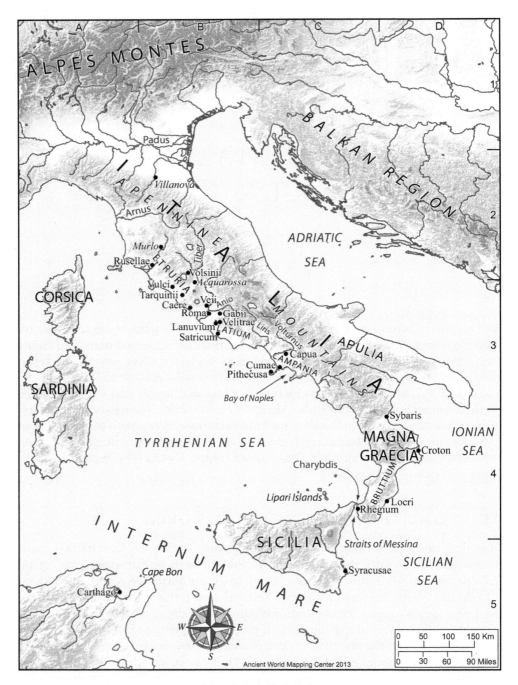

Map 1.1 *Archaic Italy*

unbroken line that nearly reaches the Adriatic Sea; this portion of the chain separates the Po Valley from Etruria, an early center of urban life. As they approach the eastern coast, the mountains turn sharply to the south, running in a series of parallel ridges that in places reach almost 10,000 feet in height (3,000 m). In its northern half, the main chain lies much nearer to the Adriatic than it does to the Tyrrhenian Sea on the western side of the peninsula. South of Rome, however, the mountain chain gradually leaves the eastern coast and approaches the western, ending in the southwestern promontory of Bruttium. The mountains on the island of Sicily (Latin, Sicilia), separated from the mainland only by a narrow strait, are a continuation of this chain, which ultimately reappears in the mountains of Tunisia, Algeria, and Morocco in North Africa.

The first great centers of population and civilization arose in the coastal regions. The Adriatic coast, with few harbors and little space for large-scale settlement, was for a long time backward. For much of their length, the Apennines leave no more than a narrow coastal plain. Only in the south, where the mountains approach the Tyrrhenian coast more closely than they do the Adriatic, are there broad plains. Much of the plateau of Apulia, however, is semiarid; only a few river valleys here were sufficiently fertile and well-watered to support substantial populations. The peninsula's southern (Ionian) shore also has narrow plains or semiarid ones. The mountains of Bruttium closely confined some coastal communities. Even so, in some more favored areas, sufficient land and water could be found for large settlements. Towns appeared early here, and some became wealthy and important.

The west coast was the most favored. Here, well-watered and fertile lands proved capable of supporting large populations, many harbors gave access to the sea, and four rivers—the Arnus (modern, Arno), Tiberis (modern English, Tiber), Liris, and Volturnus—all navigable in small boats, barges, and rafts for some distance, gave easy passage to the interior. Three of the regions facing the Tyrrhenian Sea had especially prominent places in the history of ancient Italy. Etruria, the land of the ancient Etruscans, is the northernmost; this region of fertile hills, forests, and lakes, roughly bounded by the Arno and Tiber rivers, saw some of the earliest centers of urban life. Next, two regions each with an important plain occupy the coast to the south of Etruria. First comes Latium. East to west, the Latin plain ran from the sea to the foothills of the Apennines. North to south, it covered the stretch of coast between the lower Tiber River and the northern limits of Campania. Rome itself (Latin, Roma) would rise here on the banks of the Tiber, just across the river from the southernmost Etruscan centers. Centering on the Bay of Naples and its hinterland, the Campanian plain is the southernmost of the three regions.

The surrounding mountains and seas did not isolate the peninsula. Although the Alps seem quite formidable from the Italian side, large-scale movement across them has always been possible, and the inhabitants of the Po Valley have often had closer cultural links and firmer and friendlier relations with groups across the northern mountains than they have with peoples to their south. From an early period, ships traveled from Italy across the Mediterranean, moving goods, people, ideas, and institutions. Much of this traffic was only local, but at times long-distance commerce developed and flourished. Before Rome succeeded in dominating the peninsula, seaborne connections flourished only fitfully along the Adriatic, although the mouth of the Po River on occasion received much trade. The peninsula's southern and western shores were more open. Good harbors could be found along the coasts of the Ionian and Tyrrhenian seas, and the richer and more extensive plains provided valuable hinterlands.

Italy occupies a strategic point in the Mediterranean world. The island of Sicily, off the southwest tip of the peninsula, divides the Mediterranean Sea in two, and maritime traffic between east and west necessarily passes by the island. Ships seeking to enter the Tyrrhenian Sea from the Ionian and Sicilian seas had to pass through the narrow Straits of Messina before they could proceed north along the Italian coast or west along the north shore of Sicily. This passage could be dangerous: Greek writers would place there the whirlpool Charybdis and the monster Scylla, who fed on ships' crews. Other important routes passed to the south of the island, eventually funneling through the passage between western Sicily and Cape Bon in modern Tunisia, about 100 miles away (160 km). The island could also serve as a virtual bridge between Italy and North Africa, facilitating north–south traffic across the central Mediterranean.

ITALY BEFORE THE CITY

The basic pattern of social and economic life in peninsular Italy was established early. For centuries after the first appearance of agriculture around 4000 B.C., Italy was a land of villages with simple forms of economic and social organization. Settlements were very small, usually with no more than a few huts and outbuildings and less than one hundred inhabitants. Villagers planted barley and several types of wheat, and they raised sheep, goats, cattle, and pigs. Their technology was simple, and signs of occupational specialization are few. Tools necessary in everyday life were generally made of wood, bone, or stone. The use of metals provides the only clear example of more sophisticated techniques and some craft specialization. Around 2000, copper tools and ornaments appear in the material remains. In the succeeding Early (c. 1800–1600) and Middle (c. 1600–1300) Bronze Ages, a limited range of tools, weapons, and ornaments were made of bronze, an alloy of copper and tin. Metal working was a task for specialists, since it requires both expertise and organization: materials must be acquired, often from great distances, and the processes of refining the ore and casting the metal require knowledge and skill.

Beginning in the ninth century, there occurred a series of developments in Italy leading, by the seventh century, to the appearance of the cities that would turn out to dominate Italian history. Archeologists refer to the years between the start of the ninth century and the last third of the eighth as the Iron Age. The extraction of metal from the ore and the working of the iron require complex and sophisticated techniques, and the making of steel is an even more elaborate process. Iron has important advantages over bronze. Iron ore is relatively common, so that the acquisition of this metal is a much simpler and cheaper process; when used in the form of steel, tools and weapons can be made harder and better able to retain an edge. Eventually, the use of iron would lead to cheaper products. For centuries after its introduction, however, a wide range of objects, utilitarian and otherwise, continued to be made of bronze, wood, bone, and stone.

In the ninth and eighth centuries, Etruria, Latium, and Campania saw the rise of an interrelated group of cultures that would eventually develop into major centers of power and wealth. In Etruria, the Iron Age culture of these centuries is known as "Villanovan" from the estate near modern Bologna where archeologists first found traces of its material culture. One of Villanovan culture's most significant traits was the greatly increased size of its settlements—over one thousand inhabitants in some instances. Beginning around 900, certain ones began to grow larger, typically situated on easily defended plateaus where the natural features of the site formed the primary defense. In their internal organization, these new and larger settlements remained relatively simple, consisting of clusters of huts without elaborate social systems, clearly identifiable distinctions in wealth, formal layouts, or public buildings. Placed between Villanovan Etruria and Campania, Latium developed its own regional culture around 1000, with smaller settlements located on hills or on spurs that projected from the Apennines into the plain.

Greeks and Phoenicians in the Central Mediterranean

Outside contacts markedly affected both the pace and the nature of change in the centers of the Villanovan and Latial cultures. In the late ninth century, as well as in the eighth, maritime contact with the eastern Mediterranean became a prominent factor in the development of central Italian societies. The Phoenicians led the way. The coastal regions of the modern states of Syria and Lebanon on the eastern shore of the Mediterranean were their homeland. Their world centered on a number of cities. Long-distance trade by land and by sea was important in the social and political order of a Phoenician city-state; kings and temple priesthoods participated, as did associations of rich and powerful merchants. Around 1000, these cities, especially Tyre and Sidon, began to send out settlers and trading expeditions, first to the nearby coast of Cyprus, but soon as far away as Spain. Eventually, Phoenician settlers would establish a series of new cities along the coasts of western Sicily, Sardinia, northern Africa, and southern Spain. Carthage (Latin, Carthago), probably founded around 800 in the territory of modern Tunisia, would become the most powerful of these new settlements—and Rome's great rival.

Greeks followed shortly afterward. By 775, some Greeks had established a settlement on the island of Pithecusa in the Bay of Naples, and a few Phoenicians may also have settled there. In this new community, and in others that would be founded later, trade and access to metals played an important role—Pithecusa shows signs of ironworking on a large scale—but the search for farmland was vital, too, and before long would become the most important factor. Greek settlements on the mainland soon sprang up. Cumae, founded around 750, was the first. Eventually the eastern, southeastern, and northern coasts of Sicily would be dotted with Greek city-states, as would the southern and western coasts of Italy as far north as Campania. Later, Romans would call these mainland areas of Greek settlement "Great Greece" (Latin, *Magna Graecia*).

THE RISE OF CITIES

Beginning in the middle of the eighth century and continuing over the next three centuries, Etruria, Latium, and Campania witnessed a series of political, social, and cultural innovations that would result in the formation of the first central Italian city-states. The appearance of this new form of social and political life was a broad phenomenon that characterized many Mediterranean regions and ethnic groups. In Italy, city-states became the dominant form of organization in Etruria, Latium, Campania, and the Greek regions of Sicily and southern Italy. Similarities in form, however, should not mask the great diversity in detail and the many local variations that could be found in important aspects of urban life.

A city-state was both a kind of settlement and a form of political, military, and social organization. Fully developed city-states usually possessed a clearly defined urban core, with special areas designated for elite and for communal activities, and cemeteries encircling it. Beyond, the surrounding territory contained scattered shrines, hamlets, and farmsteads. The scale of these city-states varied greatly. In the contemporary Greek world, a "typical" one may have had approximately one thousand inhabitants and perhaps a territory of around 40 square miles (100 sq km); its army would have numbered no more than a few hundred men. In central Italy, many of the emerging city-states would have been somewhat larger; by the end of the sixth century, some had populations of several tens of thousands.

Some formal political organization was essential. In a typical city-state, elite residences, political life, and communal religious activity were all concentrated in and about the center. Here, members of elite families displayed their status, competed with their peers, and exercised leadership over their own followers. At first, aristocratic families and their retainers dominated most emerging city-states. In the seventh and sixth centuries, kings reigned in some. By the early fifth century certain cities possessed formal offices and priesthoods, filled by a process of election and held for terms of one year. Arrangements such as these would eventually become standard. In central Italy, scholars divide the formative age of the city-state into two broad phases: the Orientalizing Period (c. 725–580) and the Archaic Period (c. 580–480).

Beginning of Writing

During the eighth century, writing came to Italy, and written texts now supplement the archeological evidence. The Greek language and script were to have a long life in Italy and would exert great influence there. By 700, texts in one or another of the languages of Italy itself appear, written in scripts derived from the Greek. The earliest known Etruscan documents date from the very beginning of the seventh century; known texts of the seventh and sixth centuries now number in the many hundreds. Early documents in Latin are less common.

The surviving texts of the eighth through the fifth centuries are generally short, difficult to interpret, hard to date, and not very informative. Inscribed on stone, bronze, or pottery, the languages in which they are written are often not well understood today. Some identify the occupants of tombs, or the owner or maker of an object; others are dedications of gifts placed in temples and shrines. No evidence survives of a bureaucratic use for writing, such as occurs in some other Mediterranean societies.

Appearance of an Elite

Toward the end of the eighth century, some families in the coastal regions of Etruria, Latium, and Campania began to demonstrate that they possessed wealth, status, and power on a scale far greater than others in their communities had attained. These emerging elite families sought to distinguish themselves through a distinctive way of life with the appropriate marks of status. Many of the objects, and the imagery associated with them, had their origins in Greece and the Near East. Tombs provide the earliest signs of elite families and their pretensions. In the eighth century, rich deposits of grave goods become more common. Associated with these ways of death was a way of life that marked off aristocrats from the mass of the population and often united them with the leading families in other communities (Fig. 1.1). Again, evidence from tombs is central, since mourners deposited there objects that played a prominent role in an aristocratic self-image: horse tack, chariots, rich armor and weapons, personal ornaments, and the equipment for feasting and drinking (Fig. 1.2). Extravagance was a prominent feature of elite burials of the eighth and seventh centuries, but their sixth- and fifth-century successors were on a much-reduced level.

Cities and Monumental Architecture

In the ninth and eighth centuries, settlements in Etruria, Latium, and Campania consisted of collections of huts with no traces of planning, formal organization, or public buildings, let alone private dwellings on a significantly larger scale than their neighbors. From the beginning of the seventh century, however, members of elite families began to construct larger structures in the main centers of population. They also began to lay out the public spaces that would define communal life for centuries—all signs of their ability to muster resources and labor on an increasing scale.

Figure 1.1 *Banquet scenes were common in the art of archaic Italy. This drawing reproduces such a scene on a terracotta frieze from the palace at Murlo. The artist shows the guests reclining on couches (as was customary in the Greek world too), attended by four servants. A mixing bowl of the kind often found in aristocratic tombs rests on a stand between the two couches. One of the guests plays a lyre. Hunting dogs crouch beneath tables laden with food.*

As part of this development, the ruling elites of central Italy made the cult places of their communities grander and grander. From around 600, some cities began to build large, elaborate temples to their gods. These edifices were often located on the central square of a settlement or on a hill overlooking it, where they would dominate the city's physical appearance. Temples in central Italy generally were built upon a high platform or *podium*, fronted by a porch with columns; crowning the structure was a peaked roof of terracotta tiles with terracotta decorations (Fig. 1.3). In later periods, these structures had an important place in communal identity, and they served functions beyond the strictly religious. In Rome, for example, officials performed many of their duties here, and speakers addressed their audience from a temple podium, where they would be highly visible.

As wealth came to concentrate in cities and towns, many communities began to expend resources on their defense. For centuries, villages were often located on easily defensible hills or plateaus, which the inhabitants might strengthen with ditches, dikes, and palisades. From the eighth century, some communities began to construct more elaborate and expensive defensive systems. Many fortified themselves by first digging a deep, broad ditch (*fossa*) and then using the excavated earth to construct a thick, high mound (*agger*) inside it (note Fig. 2.1). However, such defenses seldom extended completely around the settlement.

Warfare in the Orientalizing and Archaic Periods

The eighth, seventh, and sixth centuries saw major changes in the frequency of warfare, as well as in its scale and degree of organization. The new ways of making war affected not only relations between the emerging cities, but also the role and power of aristocracies, the political and social organization of the communities themselves, and their physical layouts. At first, there were few or no set battles. Quick raids for cattle and other loot predominated. Warriors served not as members of the community, but rather as followers of an aristocratic leader who had organized the enterprise. The transition to a more formal mode of warfare was gradual, although the stages and the timing of the shift are very obscure.

In the Greek world, which was the source of important innovations, the new way of war-making centered on hoplite infantry, who were protected by body armor or corselets (made either of metal or of leather reinforced with metal), bronze greaves (leg armor), and bronze helmets (Fig. 1.4). These hoplites carried a large circular shield or *hoplon* and were armed with both a spear and a sword or dagger. This new equipment was better suited to close combat than to fighting at a distance with weapons that were thrown. At the same time it made combatants less mobile in the field, so that hoplites fought in a dense formation, or *phalanx*, where men were protected and reinforced by those on either side. The new tactic emphasized formal battles over raid and counterraid. It also favored the larger formation over the smaller, so that communities had a positive incentive to increase the number of men serving in their armies (Fig. 1.5).

Social and Economic Organization

Elite families dominated the social and economic life of their cities just as they did their political, religious, and

Figure 1.2 *Chariots occupied a prominent place in public displays of status, and they were often highly decorated for that purpose. This bronze panel covered the front of a chariot-body interred in a grave high in the Apennines around 550. The two sides of the chariot were similarly decorated. The relief depicts what is probably an arming scene, where the woman on the left hands the man on the right his shield and helmet. The birds flying over their heads may represent good omens. The chariot was probably produced in an Etruscan workshop.*

military organization. The wealth and power of the upper classes rested upon their control over their followers and other dependents as well as over land. Prominent individuals mobilized groups of men for war, led them in battle, and, if successful, distributed the fruits of victory: land, cattle, captives, and the movable

Figure 1.3 *This reconstruction of the so-called Portonaccio Temple at Etruscan Veii (built c. 500) illustrates some of the typical features of a central Italian temple. It was built upon a high platform or* podium. *In front was a deep colonnaded porch, and behind was the chamber or* cella *where the cult statue of the god was sited. Along the ridge and edges of the roof, terracotta sculptures were placed (see Fig. 1.6). The altar would have been somewhere in front of the temple; most ceremonies here would have been outside (not inside) and public.*

goods of the defeated. In peacetime, leading families also assembled dependents to farm their land, guard their herds and flocks, and attend to household tasks.

Long-term ties of dependency bound many of the inhabitants of the new cities to aristocratic leaders. Links between members of the elite and their followers could be defined in terms of "patrons" and "clients." Ideally, the patron granted protection to his clients, who followed this protector in war and in politics and served him in other ways when appropriate. In some cases, a powerful family may have controlled entire villages or clusters of dwellings in a larger settlement. The communities of central Italy possessed what has been called a "gentile" organization. Romans, for example, belonged to a clan or *gens* (plural, *gentes*). At first, a gens consisted of an aristocratic lineage or group of lineages and some of their lesser followers and dependents. A special system of nomenclature characterized groups formed in this fashion. Members were identified by a name or *nomen* (plural, *nomina*) that identified their gens, and they also had a first or personal name, the *praenomen*. Names in this style appear on inscriptions from the seventh century, although it is unclear whether that is a recent development or just the first appearance in writing of an already established practice. All of a city's residents need not have been either aristocrats or dependents of some aristocratic family. In some cities, independent elements of the population could certainly be found.

Eventually, they too came to be organized into gentes, so that every member of a community would belong to a gens.

For many, dependence on the rich and powerful was unavoidable. So long as communal organizations were relatively weak, only powerful families, with their many armed retainers, could offer protection from war and other forms of violence. Debt formed another route to dependency. In many societies of the ancient Mediterranean world, debt established—and was intended to establish—a long-term relationship between borrower and lender. Farmers who possessed only a small plot of land were highly vulnerable to crop failure, and they had great difficulty in assembling a surplus that would see them through bad years. In the semiarid environment of much of the Mediterranean basin, crop failures or low yields because of drought were fairly frequent, a circumstance that regular warfare could only aggravate. Many men were forced to turn to their wealthier neighbors for assistance, borrowing to feed their families or to plant their next crop. Debt incurred in this fashion, it should be noted, would probably never be repaid; debtors would never gain enough wealth to repay in full, and they would continue to need further assistance in lean years. Instead, debt created a permanent relationship in which debtors lost control of their land and their labor, while creditors gained followers and a permanent workforce. In many early city-states of Greece and Italy, debt formed one of the chief sources of social conflict.

GREEKS AND ETRUSCANS

The seventh, sixth, and fifth centuries were the great age of the Etruscan and Greek cities of Italy and Sicily. In addition to the evidence provided by archeology and occasionally by inscriptions, the histories of these societies are illuminated by a few literary texts in Greek. Some of them are even contemporary with the last stages of the Archaic Period; they identify major figures and events and shed light on social and political organization. All these texts, however, were composed at a considerable distance from the communities themselves. Unlike the Greeks, the Etruscans are largely silent. Some probably did write histories and chronicles of their own cities,

Figure 1.4 This Umbrian bronze votive figure of a warrior wears some of the equipment of a hoplite, including a helmet with a high, very prominent crest. It probably dates from the fifth century.

but only a few, slight traces of these works remain. The cities of coastal Etruria sometimes appear in the writings of later Greek and Roman historians. In the Greek texts, the Etruscans appear as enemies, competitors, and pirates, cruel and faithless. The Roman writers were less hostile, but no less ethnocentric.

By the end of the eighth century, some of the Greek colonies of Sicily and southern Italy began to take on the forms of city-states (Greek, *polis*). Several became

Figure 1.5 *This mid-sixth-century terracotta frieze from the palace at Acquarossa depicts two warriors equipped as hoplites on the far left, following in procession behind a man with a bull and a chariot with two riders. The winged horses signify that the procession belongs in the realm of myth. The man with the bull may be identified as the Greek hero Heracles, the Latin Hercules.*

notably powerful, dominating extensive hinterlands and large populations—only a fraction of whom, however, would have been citizens of the polis, because these Greek cities made sharp distinctions between citizens and noncitizens. They also typically suffered from bitter internal divisions. Narrow oligarchies, composed of the descendants of the first settlers, for a long time controlled the best land and the public offices. Strife between oligarchs and the mass of citizens, as well as the sharper divide between Greek and non-Greek, made the internal stability of many cities precarious. Civil wars and coups were common and could result in the establishment of a tyranny, the personal rule of a single individual backed by an armed following.

From the middle of the sixth century, these Greek city-states, already disturbed by internal problems, entered into a period of wider, more serious conflict. The more powerful cities, able to dominate the native populations in their hinterlands, began to press on the territories of others. During the sixth century Sybaris was the most powerful Greek city in Italy; in 510, however, after being weakened by civil strife, it was defeated and destroyed by its neighbor Croton. Then in the fifth century, Rhegium and Locri (both farther west) ended Croton's preeminence. During this century, Syracuse successfully dominated many of its smaller Greek neighbors.

Beginning in the late eighth century, a number of communities in southern Etruria—Caere, Tarquinii, Vulci, and Veii—began to develop rapidly into city-states (Map 1.2). By the end of the seventh century, others could be found in northern Etruria, at Populonia, Rusellae, and Volaterrae, as well as inland in the valleys of the Tiber and Arno rivers. These cities possessed a common language, and many features of their government, social organization, and religion were similar; they also had some sense of a shared identity. Yet Etruscan city-states were never united politically, and frequently they were rivals and even enemies.

In the Archaic Period, Etruscan elites were among the most active in Italy, but the nature of their interaction with non-Etruscan communities is not always clear. It has been suggested that Etruscan practices spread with the movement of elites and their followers, who would come to dominate a preexisting community. Some of the Etruscan centers in the north may have begun in just this way: Hatria, from which the Adriatic Sea received its name, and Spina, a major trading center from the closing decades of the sixth century, may originally have been Greek cities. Roman writers of a later date thought that two of Rome's last three kings were of

Map 1.2 *Northern Italy*

Etruscan descent, and they believed that some of Rome's core institutions and practices were of Etruscan origin. Even so, it is by no means clear how far the emergence of cities in regions such as Latium is to be credited to Etruscans. In the seventh and sixth centuries, the chief Etruscan communities were among Italy's richest and most powerful urban centers; as such, they would plainly have had marked influence, either imposed directly through the power they exerted over their neighbors or indirectly through the models they provided for others. The similarity in material culture that many scholars regard as signifying the undoubted presence of an Etruscan elite may rather be due to the formation of an international elite style—one that crossed ethnic boundaries and was shared by numerous local elites imitating each other to increase their own prestige. By the same token, the presence of Etruscan speakers may indicate only that the newly forming city-states in many regions were for a time open to outsiders. The Romans, it should be noted, thought that Lucius Tarquinius Priscus—the first Etruscan king of Rome and father of the second—came to Rome from Tarquinii as an immigrant, not as a conqueror.

THE EMERGENCE OF ROME

Rome occupied a group of hills overlooking the Tiber River (Map 1.3). The location was a favorable one: water was plentiful, and defense easy. Two of the most important routes in central Italy passed by the site, one from the salt pans at the mouth of the Tiber along the banks of the river into the interior, and the other the coastal road from Etruria to Campania, which crossed the Tiber by a ford here, the closest place to the sea where this was possible. A small stream running through a marshy valley separated three of the hills that proved especially important in early Rome: the Capitol, the Palatine, and the Velia. When drained in the seventh and sixth centuries, this valley would become the *Forum Romanum* (Roman Forum), the city's political and religious center. Along the banks of the Tiber, where the stream that drained the Forum valley joined the river, a small plain gave access to the Tiber ford; this plain would become the *Forum Boarium*, the chief market and harbor of urban Rome.

The hills and valleys here were inhabited for centuries before Rome became a city. Finds show that several small clusters of huts occupied the hills and perhaps also the valleys between them and the plain by the river. Some of these hamlets shared cemeteries, but it would seem that no sense of common identity linked all the hamlets on the hills. In this respect, early Rome was little different from other Latin centers, although it may have been more populous than most. After c. 800, signs appear that a larger and more highly organized community was emerging. Burials began to concentrate at a few large cemeteries on the margins of the settled area; meanwhile the scattered cemeteries, each shared by a few hamlets, began to fall into disuse.

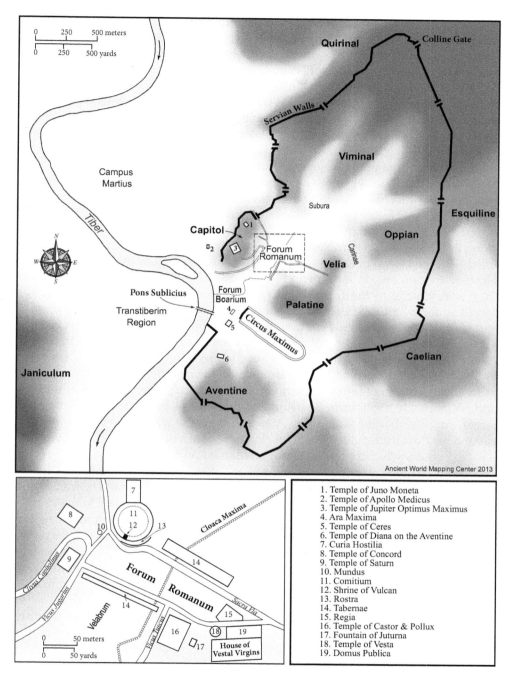

1. Temple of Juno Moneta
2. Temple of Apollo Medicus
3. Temple of Jupiter Optimus Maximus
4. Ara Maxima
5. Temple of Ceres
6. Temple of Diana on the Aventine
7. Curia Hostilia
8. Temple of Concord
9. Temple of Saturn
10. Mundus
11. Comitium
12. Shrine of Vulcan
13. Rostra
14. Tabernae
15. Regia
16. Temple of Castor & Pollux
17. Fountain of Juturna
18. Temple of Vesta
19. Domus Publica

Map 1.3 *Rome in the Early Republic (before 300 B.C.)*

From the middle of the seventh century, the Romans began to transform the valley separating the hills into the civic and religious center of the city, the Forum Romanum. Earlier, this valley—much of which was marshy and liable to flooding—held no more than a few clusters of huts and some cemeteries. The first phase of construction, which began around 650, turned part of the valley into a place where Romans could gather for communal events; for this purpose, the huts were cleared, the valley's lowest areas were drained and filled, and a rough surface of beaten earth was laid. A quarter of a century later, this pavement was refurbished and extended by filling in more wetlands. Henceforth the Forum would serve as the chief place for large public assemblies and ceremonies in the city.

As the political center of the city, the Forum also became Rome's most prominent building site. Near the end of the seventh century, the *Regia* (see below, Politics and Society Under the Kings) was erected along its edge. At the end of that century, builders laid out another public space, later known as the *Comitium*, and along its edges they constructed a large stone building that is probably to be identified with the later *Curia Hostilia*. The original uses of the Comitium and the Curia Hostilia are obscure. In later periods at least (and possibly from the outset too), they were crucial to the functioning of the Roman state. The Comitium was a sacred space where officials would summon citizens to vote, to hear legal cases, and to make (or be informed about) important public decisions; the Curia Hostilia served as one of the meeting places for the council of elders known as the *senate*. Around the beginning of the fifth century, temples to Saturn and to Castor and Pollux were constructed on the south side of the Forum.

In addition to the Forum Romanum, two other major centers of Rome's civic and religious life, the Forum Boarium and the Capitol, began to be adorned with larger, more elaborate structures. At the end of the seventh century, builders cleared the huts from part of the plain along the banks of the Tiber and established a sacred space, which in all likelihood contained an altar. The first temple here, probably dedicated to Fortuna, was built in the second quarter of the sixth century; it was rebuilt a generation later and decorated with terracotta friezes and statues of the Greek hero Heracles and the Greek goddess Athena. On the Capitoline hill, the Romans began to construct the temple of Jupiter Best and Greatest (Jupiter Optimus Maximus) around the beginning of the sixth century; when completed toward the end of the century, this structure was one of the largest temples in Italy. Roman authors later claimed that it was adorned with sculptures produced by an artist from the nearby city of Veii, who may also have decorated at least one of the temples there (see Fig. 1.6).

A wealthy and powerful elite lived in the city. Goods deposited in seventh-century tombs reveal the presence of aristocratic families able to expend resources in large-scale displays of their status. Wealthy Romans also constructed buildings for their personal use. By 625, houses built of stone and roofed with tiles had replaced some of the huts on the Velia. By the end of the sixth century, dwellings spread over most of the hills, making Rome one of the largest cities in Italy.

THE ROMANS AND THEIR EARLY HISTORY

The evidence of archeology and the brief, fragmentary texts of archaic inscriptions are eventually supplemented for us by an active tradition of history writing at Rome. It merged myths of Rome's origins with detailed accounts of the achievements of prominent individuals who may once have lived. According to this tradition, Rome was founded as a result of a conflict in the ruling family of the mythical city of Alba Longa. The king, Numitor, was deposed by his brother Amulius, who

forced Numitor's daughter Rhea Silvia to become a virgin priestess of the goddess Vesta ("Vestal virgin"). However, the god Mars made her pregnant, and she gave birth to twin sons, Romulus and Remus. Amulius gave orders for them to be drowned in the Tiber, but the basket carrying them washed ashore at the foot of the Palatine hill. There, a she-wolf suckled them and, later, a shepherd rescued them. Once adult, they overthrew Amulius, restored Numitor to his throne, and decided to found a city where they had been saved. The brothers quarreled, however, and Remus was killed, so that Romulus became Rome's sole founder (Source 1.1) and (Rome's historians believed) the first of seven kings.

Romulus founded the city and established its most important political institutions (Table 1.1). His successor, Numa Pompilius, set the pattern for Rome's religious life. The kings who followed built temples, founded further institutions, and, like their predecessors, waged war on Rome's neighbors. Servius Tullius, the sixth king, was virtually a second founder of the city. Accounts of the reign of Tarquinius Superbus, Rome's last king, justify his fall and the end of the monarchy. The dates that Roman scholars gave to Romulus' foundation of the city vary widely. Marcus Terentius Varro (116–27 B.C.) opted for 753, a date that came to be generally adopted.

The reliability of these histories is far from certain. Their authors wrote centuries after the events they recounted; they filled their works with anachronisms and patriotic mythmaking; they regarded the city as unchanging in many important ways; and they presented its history in a fashion that often

Figure 1.6 *This terracotta statue of the Greek god Apollo decorated the roof of the Portonaccio Temple at Veii, which was probably dedicated to the goddess Minerva (see Fig. 1.3). Other statues attached to the temple represent Heracles and possibly Hermes.*

TABLE 1.1 Dates of Rome's Kings According to Varro

Romulus, 753–715
Numa Pompilius, 715–673
Tullus Hostilius, 673–642
Ancus Marcius, 642–617
Lucius Tarquinius Priscus (Tarquin the Elder), 616–579
Servius Tullius, 578–535
Lucius Tarquinius Superbus (Tarquin the Proud), 534–510

SOURCE 1.1: *When recounting Rome's early history, both Roman and (later) Greek historians often imagined the city's first leaders as initiating and performing practices that later would be typical of its officials. Here Plutarch presents Romulus as founding Rome with just the same rites that the founders of Rome's own colonies used later (see Chapter Two).*

Romulus buried Remus in the Remonia, together with the servants who had reared him. He then began to build his city, after summoning experts in sacred customs and writings from Etruria, who taught him everything as if in a religious rite. A trench was dug around what is now the *Comitium*, and in it were deposited first fruits of whatever was considered good by custom and necessary by nature. And finally, each man brought a small portion of their native soil and threw it in, where it mixed together. They call this trench the *mundus*, as they do the heavens. Then, they marked out the city in a circle around this center. And the founder, after placing a bronze ploughshare on the plough and yoking to it a bull and a cow, ploughed a deep furrow around the boundary lines, while those who followed behind turned the clods thrown up by the plough inwards toward the city, leaving none to face outward. With this line, they mark out the course of the wall, and it is called by contraction the *pomerium*, in other words "behind the wall" (*post murum*). And where they intended to place a gate, they lifted the plough and left an empty space. And this is why they regard the entire wall as sacred except for the gates. (*Life of Romulus* 11)

ignored or minimized the influence of neighbors and allies. It was the Greeks who taught the Romans to write histories. Between them, Greek and Roman historians came to develop clear ideas about how one should do so and why. Proper histories should glorify one's city, as well as entertain and instruct one's readers. Thus, historians offered quantities of vivid and dramatic stories full of colorful details. To instruct, they focused on leading individuals, the situations that these faced, and the effects of their actions on their city. Such accounts, it was hoped, would provide memorable examples of actions that good citizens should either imitate or avoid.

Our knowledge of this historiographical tradition of early Rome derives from two Roman writers in particular—Marcus Tullius Cicero (106–43) and Livy (Titus Livius, 59 B.C. to A.D. 17)—as well as from such Greek authors as Diodorus Siculus (mid- to late first century B.C.), Dionysius of Halicarnassus (late first century B.C.), Plutarch (before A.D. 50–after 120), and Cassius Dio (late second and early third centuries A.D.).

POLITICS AND SOCIETY UNDER THE KINGS

Kings certainly once ruled in Rome. *Rex*, the Latin word for king, appears in two fragmentary sixth-century texts. And kingship persisted in Rome in the form of a priestly office, the *rex sacrorum*, that continued the king's religious functions long after the political and military powers had been lost. Rome was not the only Italian city with a king, but it is far from clear how common monarchy was. According to Rome's historians, their monarchy had not been hereditary, so that each king had to establish his right to rule. In the traditional list of seven kings, it should be noted, there is only one instance where a father and his son both held the throne, although even here the reign of another intervened.

Romans of a later date associated their kings with leadership in war, the construction of temples and other public buildings, the performance of religious rites, and the granting of judgments in legal disputes. These early rulers, we are told, defeated many of the surrounding towns and villages, forcing some of their inhabitants to move to Rome, while others were permitted to remain in what would become no more than small rural centers without much civic life. Archeologists have found the remains of towns near Rome, some of which were wealthy and powerful in the seventh century but no more than fortified villages in the sixth. In later periods, the Romans regularly celebrated rites that marked the boundaries of their territory centuries earlier. They preserved the memory of a time when Roman territory encompassed only about 75 square miles (190 sq km), and Rome's frontiers were no more than 5 miles (8 km) from the city in any direction. By the end of the sixth century, however, Roman territory probably covered almost 300 square miles (780 sq km), while the population may have been as high as 35,000.

The area around the Forum Romanum contained a number of places linked to rites and activities that Rome's historians later associated with kingship. Around 625, the Regia, a group of small chambers surrounding a central courtyard, was constructed; it had a clear religious function. In the sixth century, the Regia probably formed part of a larger complex that included the temple of Vesta, containing the sacred hearth of the city, and the *domus publica*, later the house of the leader of an important group of priests and quite possibly the sixth-century dwelling of the kings.

The aristocracy, too, had its own political, religious, and military roles in the city. Roman historians later held that the leaders of the city's aristocratic families met in a council of elders known as the senate, which chose the kings, helped them make policy, and on occasion resisted their initiatives as they saw fit. Aristocratic councils were common in the world of the city-state. Like kings, prominent members of the Roman elite also had their own religious roles. Later Romans believed that certain aristocratic families enjoyed especially close relations with the gods; in time, too, prominent families certainly did come to monopolize the most important priestly offices.

Like other cities of central Italy, Rome seems to have witnessed a certain mobility of elite families during the seventh, sixth, and early fifth centuries. Some aristocrats and their followers moved from city to city, taking up in the new place the position they had abandoned in the old. The Elder Tarquin was thought to have moved to Rome from the Etruscan city of Tarquinii. Around 500, the aristocratic family of the Claudii, which centuries later would provide emperors for Rome, first came to the city with a great body of clients, having left its native Sabine country to the northeast after suffering political setbacks there. A few leaders of private armies gained an especially prominent place in the history of central Italy during the sixth and early fifth centuries. Some dominated their own cities, while others sought wealth and power away from home. Romans of a later age liked to believe that their kings had ruled with the consent of the leading families and the people. In practice, however, the entry of powerful individuals and their followers into a new city may have been tantamount to conquest.

One of the chief characteristics of a fully formed city-state was a citizenry organized communally to fulfill its roles in politics, religion, and war. In Rome, the mass of adult male citizens was known as the *populus Romanus*. At some indeterminate point, this populus gained the right to give assent to officeholders and their policies, a practice that would eventually become formalized as a vote. The bulk of Rome's population was integrated into the city's institutions through intermediary groups known as *curiae* (singular, *curia*). These curiae, supposedly thirty in number, came together to form three tribes. The tribes had an essential role in Rome's political and military organization. When the city made war, its army—the followers of the king and of powerful members of the elite, along with some sort of general levy—was organized by tribes, with each one providing its own unit of cavalry and of infantry. Aristocratic families probably dominated their tribal contingents just as they did the curiae.

During the sixth century, a reform superseded this organization of tribes and curiae but did not eliminate it. The sixth king, Servius Tullius, supposedly created new forms of classifying and organizing the population—the beginnings of the Roman *census*, in other words, which in later periods would be one of the central institutions of the city (see Chapter Two). The core of the new arrangement was the regular compilation of a list of adult male Romans, in which they were classified by wealth and by residence, rather than by kinship. In the world of the city-state, citizens provided their own arms and armor when serving in the army. Aristocrats clearly possessed the resources to equip themselves in this manner, and they may have supplied weapons and armor to their followers too. Tullius' census divided Romans into those who could afford to equip themselves for service on foot (known as the *classis*, "those summoned") and those who could not (*infra classem*, "below those summoned"). Citizens who belonged to the classis were further subdivided into units known as centuries (*centuriae*; singular, *centuria*). In the strictest sense, the term centuria should denote a group of exactly one hundred men; however, in later periods at least, the size of a centuria could be quite different from this supposed norm.

Units likewise termed centuriae also occupied a primary position in the organization of Rome's armies in the field. Commanders raised armies by summoning citizens to gatherings where they chose their soldiers from those eligible to serve. The force raised in this way was called a legion (*legio*; plural, *legiones*), which signified that it stemmed from a selection process—the verb *legere* meaning either "to collect" or "to pick." Under the kings, the legion selected each year was the army of the city. In later centuries, the term came to denote a unit of several thousand men serving under one of the commanders who held office for the year (see Chapter Two). From the earliest period for which we have information, a legion was always subdivided into sixty centuries. The centuries of the census, however, were not the same as the centuries of the legion. Later, for certain, the former came to comprise voting units in one type of citizen assembly (see Chapter Two), and this function may even have been original, so that from the outset this "assembly of centuries" represented the citizenry under arms.

Although it may not have been part of the original census, citizens soon came to be assigned to tribes that received their members from defined territories. Servius Tullius supposedly divided the city itself into four "urban" tribes for its residents, and this number was never increased. At the same time or shortly after, "rural" tribes were added for the inhabitants of the countryside, and their number was to grow as Roman territory expanded. Tullius' creation of these tribes did not require the elimination of the three original ones, which continued to perform some of their old functions. Consequently, Roman citizens now belonged to two tribes in two different tribal systems. Over time, however, the new tribes came to be considerably more important than the old, and membership in one became a mark of citizenship.

ROME AND THE LATINS

A shared identity linked the cities of Latium. Much later, Roman writers would maintain that the ancestor of all Latins was Aeneas, a noble Trojan who escaped from Troy as it fell to the besieging Greeks. After many adventures, Aeneas landed in Latium near the future city of Lavinium, where he formed a new people from his own followers and from the aboriginal inhabitants of the area (Fig. 1.7a, b). His son would found Alba Longa, the seat of kings who would rule Latium and found the other Latin cities. This tale certainly does not depict historical events: Latins were not Trojans, and Alba Longa probably never existed as a city and as the seat of a powerful dynasty of kings. But the myth does serve a distinct purpose: it expresses an unmistakable sense of a perceived relationship between the cities of Latium, and it also connects them to one of the most important "events" in Greek myth, celebrated in the epic poems, Homer's *Iliad* and *Odyssey*, that were so central

Figure 1.7 *In the 1960s an open-air sanctuary with a row of thirteen monumental stone altars [a] was discovered by Italian archeologists just outside the walls of Lavinium, a Latin city not far south of Rome. The altars—never all in use simultaneously—seem to have been built at various times between the sixth and fourth centuries, and the sanctuary remained in use to the end of the third century. The likelihood is that different Latin cities each commissioned an altar and sacrificed to the Penates here. Nearby, also just outside the city walls, a temple of the goddess Minerva was built around 500. In the third century, the temple was apparently cleaned and remodeled, and over one hundred terracotta statues were placed in a votive deposit. The statue shown [b] was found there, and represents Minerva in armor, probably the temple's original cult statue, an imposing 6.5 ft tall (2 m).*

to Greek culture. Moreover, the inhabitants of Latium did have much in common. They shared the name of Latin (*nomen Latinum*), and they used variants of the Latin language. From the beginnings of the "Latial culture" around 1000, they also possessed a common material culture.

The belief in an identity that transcended the separate communities of Latium received clear expression in religious ritual. At certain festivals, they came together for the performance of communal rites. The Latin Festival, or *Latiar*, held in honor of Jupiter Latiaris (Jupiter of the great feast of the Latins), was the most prominent. Latins' sense of a shared identity also found expression in other ways. In the Greek world, the ideal city-state or *polis* was a closed community; few outsiders became citizens, intermarriage with noncitizens was sometimes discouraged, and the right to own land was restricted to citizens. Latin cities were less exclusive—at least with other Latins. Later, all Latins possessed the right of *conubium*, permitting them to make a lawful marriage with a resident of any other Latin city (children of the marriage gained the citizenship status of the father; children born outside marriage received their mother's status). Equally, the right of *commercium* allowed Latins to own land in any of the Latin cities and to make legally enforceable contracts with their citizens. In addition, all Latins had the right to take up citizenship in any other Latin city merely by establishing residence there. These rights achieved formal expression no later than the fourth century, although it is likely that they were, in some form, much older.

Despite all this sharing, the Latins were not politically unified. Their communities waged war against one other, and the largest and most powerful of them competed for primacy, often at the expense of the weaker. Hence, cities grew by war; the political institutions that would later unite the Latin communities resulted from the domination of a few, and eventually from the leadership of just one, Rome. Roman authors later thought that their city, under its kings, had led the other Latins. Although the extent of Rome's power remains uncertain, this claim is to some degree correct. The terms of a treaty made around 500 between Rome and the North African city of Carthage clearly illustrate Rome's claim to leadership of the Latins and also show that its rule was contested or resisted by some Latin cities.

SUGGESTED READINGS

Grandazzi, Alexandre. 1997. *The Foundations of Rome: Myth & History*. Ithaca and London: Cornell University Press.

Smith, Christopher J. 1996. *Early Rome and Latium: Economy and Society c. 1000–500* B.C. Oxford: Oxford University Press.

Smith, Christopher J. 2006. *The Roman Clan: The Gens from Ancient Ideology to Modern Anthropology*. Cambridge: Cambridge University Press.

Spivey, Nigel. 1997. *Etruscan Art*. London: Thames and Hudson. This work is broader than its title indicates, covering art throughout central Italy and placing it in its social context.

REPUBLICAN ROME AND
THE CONQUEST OF ITALY

In the sixth century, Rome was one of the largest and wealthiest cities in Italy. At the end of the century, however, Rome and many of its neighbors entered into a period of great turbulence. In Rome itself, this coincided with an important shift in rule with the end of the monarchy and the beginning of the Roman Republic.

THE EARLY REPUBLIC

Rome's monarchy ended in the midst of decades of strife that seem to have shaken many of the cities of Italy. Rome's historians later described the expulsion of the last king, Tarquinius Superbus, in terms that justified his fall, presenting him in the conventional garb of a tyrant and providing the details appropriate to such a figure and to his family. The central episode was an assault by his son, Sextus Tarquinius, on Lucretia, the wife of Lucius Tarquinius Collatinus, and her subsequent suicide. Because of this and other crimes, we are told, prominent members of the Roman elite, especially Lucius Junius Brutus, Collatinus, and Publius Valerius Publicola (or Poplicola), exploited the king's absence to take over the city and begin the Republic. Romans of a later date believed that the end of the monarchy marked the beginnings of the major political institutions of the Republic, but the transition was definitely not so sharp and clear. Powerful leaders still possessed armed followings, and it may have seemed an open question to contemporaries whether or not a new king appeared.

In the Roman Republic, magistrates took the king's place. Magistracies spread power more widely among the rich and powerful, which is perhaps why so many cities eventually discarded their kings. The frequent replacement of kings by elected officials, moreover, may well be a sign that the aristocratic families of many Italian cities had never become fully reconciled to the rule of one man; in later periods, at least, resistance to monarchy and tyranny would be a central element in their ideology. Rome would eventually possess a hierarchy of offices, each with its own tasks and powers. Each office was annual—its occupants served only for a year—and collegial; more than one individual shared the powers of the position at the same time, and each could check improper actions by a colleague. Later, limited terms and shared tenure in office would be seen as a chief prop of liberty, and this may well have been true from an early date.

For much of the fifth century, there was some instability and experimentation in Rome's offices and in the rules surrounding them. Roman historians later would identify the Republic with the two consuls who were elected yearly (see below). The predominance of the consulship, however, would not become fixed until the fourth century. During the second half of the fifth and early in the fourth centuries, the Romans chose military tribunes with consular powers (*tribuni militum consulari potestate*). At first these tribunes served in groups of three or four, but eventually six would be chosen in most years. Later Roman historians thought that the consular tribunate was inferior to the office of consul in its powers and its religious prerogatives; why the Romans resorted to it for a period remains obscure. Perhaps having a larger number of officeholders was occasionally more important than having fewer, but more powerful, magistrates.

In times of emergency, the Romans resorted to the dictatorship, an office with extraordinary powers. The practice during the fourth and third centuries was for magistrates to appoint one man to serve as dictator in emergencies or in a major war when a unified command seemed desirable. Dictators were not elected. Instead, a consul designated a single man for the post in a ceremony that took place in the dead of night. The new dictator then appointed a "master of cavalry" (*magister equitum*) as second-in-command to assist him. Dictators were thought to possess the undivided authority of the old kings of the city, and they surrounded themselves with symbols of royal power; perhaps for this reason, they were bound by a series of ritual prohibitions limiting their conduct. A dictator remained in office for six months or for the duration of the emergency, whichever was shorter; in the meantime, the consuls remained in office but served under the dictator's command. The roots of this office certainly lie in the wars and civic disturbances of the fifth century.

Annual magistracies require a process of selection. Citizen assemblies certainly fulfilled this function during the fifth century, and they may even have done so under Rome's kings, but little is known of their powers and mode of operation then. In later periods, the "Centuriate" assembly chose the highest officials and rendered judgments in important cases. It is uncertain when it gained these functions, but the mid-fifth-century law code of the Twelve Tables does mention a "greatest assembly" that gave judicial rulings in the same kinds of cases later judged by the centuries. The adjective "greatest" itself demonstrates that this was not the only citizen assembly at the time.

Some fifth-century laws give a glimpse of contemporary Roman society. According to Rome's historians much later, popular agitation to limit the consuls' power and to make the laws public by writing them down for the first time led to the creation in 450 of a special commission of ten men or "decemvirs" (*decemviri*). They were to hold supreme power for one year, superseding the consuls, and by the end of this year they were to produce a body of laws to regulate the Republic. In some accounts, a second such commission was chosen for the following year to complete the task. The final result was the "Laws of the Twelve Tables," which served for centuries as the fundamental text in Roman law. These laws were not a code in the modern sense. Instead, they were a collection of specific, detailed, and narrowly focused provisions. They best fit a society where the family and the household are the fundamental units of social life, and agriculture and animal rearing the primary economic activities. The authors of the laws addressed aspects of marriage and divorce, inheritance, and the rights of a father over members of his household. They attempted to regulate disputes over the ownership of land and its boundaries, farm buildings and fences, livestock, fruit-bearing trees, and slaves, as well as conflicts that arose over injuries to persons or property. Procedural matters loom large. Plaintiffs themselves were responsible for notifying the other parties, for ensuring their attendance in person for trial in the Forum or Comitium, and for collecting any judgments awarded. When defendants did not appear for trial, the Twelve Tables authorized plaintiffs, after summoning witnesses, to seize defendants by force and bring them to court.

Debt and its consequences were among the lawmakers' central concerns. At Rome, as in other cities of the ancient Mediterranean world, debt could force small-scale farmers into a state of permanent dependency (see Chapter One). The Twelve Tables prescribed that creditors must ensure the debtor's appearance in court and must carry out all judgments. Debtors had thirty days to pay a debt in default or to satisfy a judgment against them.

Rome and Its Neighbors in the Fifth Century

The circumstances in which the Romans found themselves changed dramatically around 500. In consequence, the fifth century seems to have been a difficult time for the inhabitants of Latium, Campania, and the Greek cities of the south. The settled coastal plains of the west and south were disturbed by the movements of peoples and bands of warriors beyond their margins. The inhabitants of the valleys and plateaus of the central Italian highlands did not live in an urbanized social environment. Villages were the chief settlements here, and in their economies the herding of animals seems to have been more important than agriculture. Raiding may well have been ubiquitous; some villages shared fortified hilltop places of refuge. By the beginning of the fifth century, ruling elites had begun to form federations. Although these combinations did not result in cities and the more highly organized life associated with them, they were capable of collective action on a larger scale than before, especially when it came to raiding, warfare, and self-defense.

By the beginning of the fifth century, the highlanders had begun to press on the coastal plains. Latium suffered, and very severely in the case of some cities. Sabines, Volsci, and Aequi emerged from the hills that bordered Latium in an arc from northeast to southeast (Map 2.1). Rome may well have led the other Latins in the common defense, and by the end of the fifth century together they had the upper hand. Steadily, the highlanders were first repelled and then pushed back. In the process, Latin cities that had fallen or been abandoned were reoccupied as colonies (*coloniae*; singular, *colonia*). Here the victors established new settlers to serve as garrisons, gave them land around the town that had been freed by the victory, and organized it as a city-state with officials of its own. Last but not least, the new foundation was assigned a recognized place as an ally of Rome and the other Latin cities.

Roman tradition associated model figures with these wars. Gnaeus Marcius Coriolanus, who earned his third name or *cognomen* from his leadership of the army that captured the Volscian town of Corioli (its exact location is no longer known), left Rome because of his unpopularity there and took refuge with the Volsci he had previously defeated. Coriolanus then led their armies against the Romans with great success and (we are told) failed to capture Rome only because he heeded the pleas of his mother Veturia and his wife Volumnia, models of the virtuous Roman matron. Lucius Quinctius Cincinnatus provides a more positive example. In 458, he was summoned from his fields to serve as dictator after the Aequi had trapped a Roman army in the mountains. Within sixteen days, he had gathered an army, defeated the Aequi, rescued the beleaguered Roman army, resigned his dictatorship, and returned to his farm. There could be no better model of the modest and dutiful citizen. Although there is much embellishment in these stories, which undoubtedly grew in the telling, real people and situations may lie behind them.

Struggle of the Orders

In the fifth and early fourth centuries, Rome also faced severe internal conflicts that accompanied its foreign wars. Roman historians later recorded frequent reports of famine and of strife over land and debt. But there were deeper divisions too, reflecting aspects of the basic organization of the Republic and of Roman society in general. Modern scholars call this conflict the "Struggle of the Orders."

Certain kinds of conflict were endemic in the archaic city-states of both Italy and the Greek world. One concerned access to magistracies because, after the expulsion of a king, leading families often tried to monopolize the new offices in their communities. A second area of conflict concerned the ability of officials to punish at will. A third and final one involved the roles of magistrates and citizen assemblies, in particular the ability of such assemblies to choose officeholders freely and to make laws requiring or forbidding certain actions by magistrates. Each of these sources of strife was present in Rome during the fifth and fourth centuries, although all need not have been matters of controversy simultaneously.

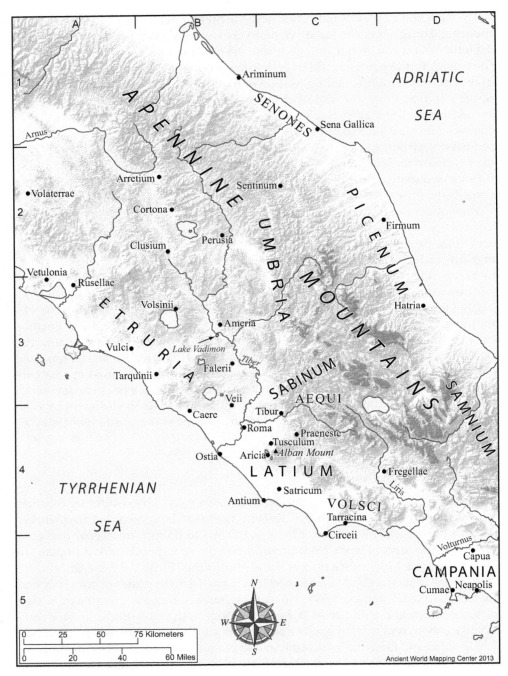

Map 2.1 *Latium and Southern Etruria*

Roman historians of a later date believed that a long conflict between two opposing groups, *patricians* and *plebeians*, characterized the first centuries of the Republic. To be a patrician, a Roman had to belong to one of a very few families. The origins of the patriciate are unknown. From the eighth century, in Rome and elsewhere, wealthy, powerful families assumed leading roles in their communities, and some, or most, of those that made up the Roman patriciate may have had their origins here. At any rate, Roman patricians claimed privileges that ensured their leadership. Later, Rome's historians thought that patricians enjoyed the exclusive right to hold high office under the Republic. This belief can only be accepted with modifications, however.

Patricians also claimed to have exclusive rights over the religious life of Rome, a central aspect of communal life. It is true that priestly offices long remained the prerogative of the patriciate, and claims to secular offices also rested on a religious foundation. Roman kings and the magistrates who succeeded them possessed as a mark of their office the right to take the auspices (*auspicium*), rites by which an officeholder sought the approval of the gods to take up his office for the first time and, while serving, divine consent for all of his official actions (see Plate 1a). Patricians regarded the auspices as their own possession.

The plebeians are much more shadowy than the patricians. Plebeians certainly far outnumbered patricians, but they need not have encompassed all of the inhabitants of Rome outside the patrician group. It remains possible, for example, that the clients of the great families counted as neither patricians nor plebeians. The Roman plebs was not a very homogenous group, since it contained individuals with a range of statuses and roles in the city. Some were not even poor, although most probably were. In the fifth and early fourth centuries, plebeians were able to supply leaders from their own ranks, so that some plebeians clearly had standing in the community. As a result, the mass of plebeians may not have been very unified in their concerns. Matters of land distribution and of debt would probably have concerned the poor more than the well-to-do, while access to office may have interested the leaders more than the bulk of their followers. In these circumstances, the leadership may have been more capable of mustering followers at times when debt, high food prices, and poverty were proving especially burdensome. Roman historians later believed that the plebeians' main weapon was the "secession," a kind of strike in time of war, and that their major successes derived from this. In a secession, plebeian members of an army would withdraw to a hill outside of Rome, choose their own leaders, and refuse to cooperate with the magistrates of the city until their grievances had been addressed.

Successes by the plebeians created a dual organization in the city. Consuls and military tribunes were seen as leaders of the Roman people as a whole, the populus Romanus, and they were expected to provide political, military, and religious leadership in matters of general concern. In the meantime, the plebeians created a parallel organization of officials and cults that addressed only matters specific to the plebs. The plebeians' first major gain (in the 490s) was the right to choose their own leaders, the tribunes of the plebs (*tribuni plebis*); their title may have been intended to provide a clear contrast with the military tribunes (*tribuni militum,* literally "tribunes of the soldiers"), who were, in many of these years, the Republic's chief officials. At the same time, plebeian tribunes, and the plebeian *aediles* who assisted them, established their own cult site at the temple of Ceres, the goddess of grain, on the Aventine hill. In later periods, the Roman plebs met in tribes to elect tribunes, and this may well have been the case in the fifth century too.

Much of the early history of the tribunate is obscure. Roman historians later believed that the powers of the office all began with the elections of the first tribunes, but this almost certainly would not have been the case. By the second century, the tribunes of the plebs held a wide range of functions—protecting individuals, blocking official actions they considered improper, convening the senate, proposing legislation—but they did not acquire them all at once. At first, their responsibilities may have been limited to providing leadership, and to protecting individuals threatened with severe treatment by magistrates. Roman historians later agreed that a key complaint by plebeians concerned their vulnerability to arbitrary actions by magistrates. *Auxilium,* the giving of aid, was central to the tribunes' office. They even had the right to intervene physically between an official and the targets of his wrath, freeing the victims or preventing the official and his attendants from seizing them. The authority of their physical presence was reinforced by their "sacrosanctity." Plebeians took an oath to regard anyone who laid hands on a tribune as an outlaw liable to be killed without penalty.

Fall of Veii and the Sack of Rome

Early in the fourth century, a Roman victory made the city preeminent in its region. Around 396, the Romans succeeded in capturing the Etruscan city of Veii after a siege. Veii, about ten miles (16 km) from Rome, was a wealthy and powerful city-state, which, like Rome, dominated some of its smaller neighbors. In the fifth century, Rome and Veii had fought over land and over the leadership of smaller cities, without either gaining a distinct advantage. Now the Romans marked their victory by eliminating Veii as an autonomous city-state. Veii's land became Roman territory, and some of its citizens became Roman citizens. Rome enslaved or expelled the remainder of the population, and settled some Roman citizens on parts of Veii's territory that were made vacant as a result.

Rome's victory was matched by a defeat. Around 387, a large army of Gauls that had been plundering in the upper Tiber Valley moved down the river toward Rome, defeated a Roman army, and entered the city. In the opening decades of the fourth century, Gauls dominated the valley of the Po River and the northern portion of the plains along the eastern coast of the Italian peninsula. Their origins lie across the Alps in central Europe, and their advance into northern Italy formed part of a larger movement that would carry Gallic tribes to the margins of the Greek world, and even (in the third century) into Asia Minor. By the end of the fifth century, the Etruscan cities north of the Apennines were hard-pressed by Gauls, and some may already have been wiped out.

The Gauls did not have an urban culture and the social and political organization that went with it. Instead, their political life centered on aristocratic families and their armed retainers. Prominent leaders could assemble large forces, and they faced relatively few communal restraints on their actions. Gallic warbands, some apparently fairly large, would often raid across the Apennines. Cities of northeast Etruria and the upper Tiber Valley were especially vulnerable to them, but their southern neighbors were not immune either. Such Gallic raids would persist, with decreasing frequency, well into the third century. Greeks and Romans would long continue to regard Gauls as uncivilized, warlike, predatory, and expansionistic.

Roman historians would later make Marcus Furius Camillus the hero both of the final war against Veii and of the recovery after the sack of Rome (Fig. 2.1). As dictator, he commanded the Roman army that captured Veii. After the Gauls had entered Rome, Camillus was supposedly once again made dictator, defeated the Gallic army, and recovered the treasure that the Gauls had taken from the city. As dictator yet again, he was reported to have had a central role in opening the highest offices to plebeians in 367, a crucial event in the Struggle of the Orders (see page 27). In all, Rome's historians thought that he had been military tribune with consular powers six times and dictator five times, and he came to be regarded as virtually a second founder of the city. However, to tease out his actual accomplishments from the myth may well be impossible.

Figure 2.1 *This stretch of wall on Rome's Esquiline hill formed part of defense works built to encircle the city and attributed to King Servius Tullius in the sixth century. While Rome may well have had some defenses at that early date, the encircling wall, of which several stretches survive today, is more likely to have been constructed after the Gallic sack of the city around 387. The tufa blocks for the wall were cut from a quarry near Veii, Rome's nearby rival until its capture around 396. Even though the wall as it stands today is up to 13 ft thick (4 m), and can rise to over 30 ft high (10 m), it in fact formed just one component in a more complex construction which included a massive* agger *(rampart) of earth reinforcing the wall on its city side, and a deep* fossa *(ditch) beyond it.*

THE CITY AND ITS INSTITUTIONS
IN THE FOURTH CENTURY

The political order that would govern Rome in later, better-documented centuries emerged in a series of reforms and reorganizations that began during the mid-fourth century and continued into the early third century. Roman government required the direct participation of citizens, although all did not have equal responsibilities. Officials, priests, senators, and citizens performed their roles in and around the temples, public squares, and processional routes of the city. Most official actions took place in the open, under the gaze of others. Because Rome lacked a bureaucracy, officials dealt directly with those they were in the process of governing. Roman assumptions about government were markedly hierarchical, and, in all periods, a few leading families dominated public life. In the fourth century, magistracies and priesthoods formed the focus of conflicts and competition. These conflicts over offices, priesthoods, and the powers of citizen assemblies were part of the larger Struggle of the Orders. Plebeians sought eligibility for the highest offices, and many patricians resisted such demands.

Officials

A small number of officeholders occupied the center of public life. At the top, beginning in 366, military tribunes with consular powers were no longer elected, and instead two consuls were chosen each year. During their year in office, the consuls served primarily as generals in Rome's wars. When they were present in the city, they made sacrifices and performed other rites of the public cults, presided over meetings of the senate, addressed assemblies of citizens, listened to complaints, and rendered judgments.

Consuls could be identified at a glance. The Roman citizen's robe (*toga*) that they wore was a special one bordered in purple, the *toga praetexta*, and they sat on a distinctive chair inlaid with ivory, the *sella curulis* or "curule" chair. Generally, a consul was surrounded by attendants of various kinds, most notably twelve lictors, who maintained order in his presence and carried the *fasces*, double-headed axes bound in rods. The fasces were old marks of royal power in Rome and in Etruscan cities; they symbolized quite starkly the consuls' power to punish. In public, consuls often took their places on elevated platforms, and their movements within the city resembled processions.

Roman historians later would connect the replacement of military tribunes by consuls with an important episode in the Struggle of the Orders. After years of conflict, two tribunes of the plebs, Gaius Licinius Stolo and Lucius Sextius Lateranus, had a series of laws passed known as the Licinian-Sextian Laws. Some of their provisions allegedly addressed matters of land use and debt, but the most important ones (we are told) fixed the office of consul as the highest in the city and permitted plebeians to compete for it. Even though many of the stories surrounding the Licinian-Sextian reforms are improbable, it is quite clear that the Roman political order did shift around this time. Over two decades later, another tribune, Lucius Genucius, had a law passed requiring that at least one of the two consuls chosen each year be a plebeian. The practical result of the reforms, it should be noted, was not the opening of offices to the entire citizen body, but rather the creation of a new political elite, composed of some patrician families and some plebeian ones (see Chapter Three).

The Licinian-Sextian reforms also created the new office of *praetor* (initially, one elected to hold office each year). Praetors were the leading officials in Rome when the consuls were absent on campaign. When necessary, a praetor could himself command an army. Because of their regular presence in the city, holders of this office often heard testimony and issued judgments against those thought to have injured the community. Praetors would come to exercise a great deal of influence over the ways in which private disputes between citizens were resolved; thereby, they would assume a major role in the development of Roman law. Plebeians would successfully gain access to this office, too; a plebeian was praetor for the first time in 337. Almost a century later, in 242, the Romans would add a second praetor, who divided responsibilities in the city with the first. In the decades thereafter, the number would be increased to meet the needs of Rome's developing empire outside of Italy (see Chapter Three). Like the consuls, praetors were surrounded by visible signs of their power. However, it was deemed inferior to that of the consuls, and in the presence of the higher official, they were expected to give way.

Both consuls and praetors possessed a wide range of powers and functions that were regarded as dependent upon their *imperium* and *auspicium*. Auspicium denoted their right to seek the approval of the gods for their tenure in office, and for their official actions, through the rituals of divination known as the auspices. Along with a dictator and his second-in-command, the *magister equitum*, every consul and praetor possessed a special right to command known as imperium, a term that is related to the verb *imperare*, meaning "to order" or "to command." For Romans, imperium had strong religious associations, and its possession was what provided the essential basis for a higher magistrate's authority to lead armies and to punish offenders.

This said, a consul's or praetor's powers varied according to the place where he chose to exercise them. Whenever he headed an army, his right to command was virtually unlimited, and the special nature of his imperium at these times was indicated by addition of the noun *militiae* ("on campaign"). Within the *pomerium*, the sacred boundary of the city of Rome,* however, consuls and praetors possessed only a more limited kind of imperium, qualified by the term *domi* ("at home"); here, they had no authority to command troops, or to ignore or brush aside all lesser officials.

In addition to consuls and praetors, the Romans also filled a number of lesser positions. From 366, they elected two *curule aediles* annually, an office created as the counterpart to the two plebeian aediles. Between them, the four aediles

---

*Its actual course is too poorly known to mark on a map.

maintained temples and the city's streets, and they also supervised its markets, where they judged disputes arising from business there. *Quaestors*—an office that apparently dated back to the mid-fifth century—took care of public money. In particular, this responsibility required them to supervise the treasury (later, at least, located in the temple of Saturn), as well as to oversee the funds that generals took on campaign.

The ten tribunes of the plebs were the most important of the lesser officehold-ers. Like consuls and praetors, they possessed the right to summon citizens to vote. However, many of their most important powers were essentially negative, because it was they who—through their ability to block public actions that they considered unlawful or inappropriate—guaranteed the rights of citizens against ill treatment by other magistrates. Tribunes were very much officials of the city, and, in later periods at least, they were prohibited from spending much time out-side of it. Beyond the first milestone outside the pomerium, tribunes no longer possessed the ability to prevent consuls and praetors from acting as they wished, so that they could not interfere with a general on campaign.

Later, in the third and second centuries, it was tribunes of the plebs who se-cured the passage of nearly all laws, but the early history of Roman legislation remains controversial. Roman laws or *leges* (singular, *lex*) were usually limited in scope, instructing or permitting officials to take certain actions, or setting up rules to regulate officeholders. A law was generally known by the name of the one or more officials who placed it before the citizens for a vote. Thus, a law proposed by Gaius Licinius and Lucius Sextius would be a *lex Licinia-Sextia*. During the last secession of the plebs, which took place sometime around 287, the dictator Quintus Hortensius sponsored a law, the *lex Hortensia*, that supposedly gave to citizen as-semblies meeting under the presidency of a tribune of the plebs the right to enact laws binding on the entire community, rather than just on the plebs. At a very early date, patricians had possessed the right to approve all legislation before it was presented to the people, but the senate subsequently claimed this as its exclu-sive prerogative. Later, only tribunes and the Plebeian assembly were exempted from having to seek senatorial approval.

The two *censors* held the only office that was not annual. From 443, these cen-sors replaced the consuls as supervisors of the *census*; usually elections would be held every five years, and the successful candidates would hold office for around eighteen months. The census counted only Roman citizens. However, beyond enumerating them it developed into an elaborate operation that assigned them to their proper places in the city (see further below). Censors were important figures, therefore, and this importance only increased after they began to choose the senate from the last decades of the fourth century.

Senate

This collection of officials did not form a government on the modern pattern; there need be little coordination among them, and there was no central direction of policies. Officials were at least expected to consult others before acting (see Source 2.1). In Rome itself, the senate filled this advisory role. It met only when called together by a consul or a praetor, or later, by a tribune of the plebs, and in the presence of that official. By strict rule, it could meet only in a place dedicated to the gods, usually in a temple. When conferring with a consul who had already taken up his military command and was thus barred from entering the city itself, the senate would meet in a consecrated place on the *Campus Martius*, just beyond the pomerium.

The senate's role would change greatly over the course of the fourth and third centuries. In theory, it was merely advisory, and senators should discuss only the matters put to them by the official who called them together. However, the senate would gradually assume a much more active role. In particular, it came to make decisions in matters of religion, supervise public finances, receive embassies from both allies and enemies, and determine military assignments for consuls and praetors. This shift in the senate's place in the Roman order did not go uncontested, and it sometimes led to conflicts between the senate and individual officeholders.

In part, the shift may have been due to changes in how the senate's members were chosen. During the third and second centuries, every five years the censors compiled a ranked list of around 300 senators; the member placed at the head of the list gained the honorific title *princeps senatus*. Censors eventually included everyone who had held elected office, from quaestors to former praetors and consuls; exclusion of any former officeholder was a mark of disgrace. In these circumstances, therefore, membership in the senate effectively became lifelong, and officeholders would spend the bulk of their political careers there. As a result, senators had a strong sense of belonging to a well-defined and honored group in society, and, on occasion, they could be quite willing to assert the senate's power and prestige against magistrates and assemblies.

At the same time, the Roman elite seems to have asserted itself against its more powerful and popular members. In the fourth century, a very small number of individuals dominated officeholding in Rome. Consequently, in the years between 366 and 291, fourteen men between them held fifty-four consulships, over one-third of the total, and eight of these fourteen held the office as many as thirty-eight times. These same men also held other offices, some more than once. Such concentration of power in a very few hands did meet resistance. In 342, Lucius Genucius, a tribune of the plebs, had a law passed that prohibited the holding of more than one office at the same time, or of the same office more than once in any ten-year period, a practice known as "iteration." For two decades or so, this law proved effective, with few men holding the consulship more than once. In the 320s, however, when Rome was under pressure from war, some again held further consulships within ten years. The goal of restricting iteration would ultimately be attained, showing that opposition to the practice was strong, at least among the Roman elite. After 290, Romans who achieved success in their political careers were rarely consul more than once: only a few gained the office twice, and no more than a handful more than twice.

This limitation on multiple officeholding had important consequences. First, it spread the available offices over a slightly larger group, enabling some individuals to rise higher now than they had previously been able. Second, it meant that virtually every holder of an office was now inexperienced in it and thus in need of advice. Finally, it lessened, although it did not eliminate, the importance of popularity; for anyone to court popularity in the hope of staying in office over an extended period was now pointless. As a result, in the course of their career, politically active individuals were more likely to focus their attention on the senate; its importance rose as a result, and senators were more prone than ever to be very supportive of its claims to privilege.

Assemblies of Citizens

Underpinning offices and the senate were assemblies of citizens who chose new officeholders and authorized important public actions (Table 2.1). Roman assemblies, however, were not representative bodies of the kind found in modern states. Instead, elections, the enactment of laws, decisions on war and peace, trials for public crimes, and discussions of other state business all took place in large, open-air meetings where citizens, by their votes, chose officeholders, accepted (or rejected) policies and laws, and issued verdicts in trials. These gatherings were open to any citizen who wished to come, so that attendance could vary markedly from one occasion to another, and the composition of no two assembly meetings would ever have been exactly the same. No seating was provided.

Officials of the city kept a firm control over the agenda. Only holders of certain offices—consuls, praetors, and tribunes of the plebs—possessed the power to summon citizens to meetings to elect new officeholders, to discuss matters of importance, and to decide on laws and policies. *Contiones* (singular, *contio*) were

Table 2.1 Roman Assemblies

	Centuriate assembly	Tribal assembly	Plebeian assembly
Composition	All citizens	All citizens	Only plebeians
Voting Units	193 centuries	35 tribes (after 241 B.C., 31 rural and 4 urban)	35 tribes
Presiding Officials	Consul or praetor	Consul or praetor	Tribune of the plebs
Elections	Elects consuls, praetors, and censors	Elects curule aediles and quaestors	Elects tribunes of the plebs and plebeian aediles
Legislative Powers	Normally votes only on issues of war and peace	Votes on proposals made by a consul or praetor	Votes on proposals made by a tribune of the plebs
Judicial Powers	Hears citizens' appeals on capital charges	Issues verdicts in trials	Issues verdicts in trials

occasions just for discussion and debate. The official who had called the meeting addressed the crowd himself and also brought forward others whose opinions he wished citizens to hear. *Comitia* and *concilia* were assemblies where they actually voted. These assemblies met only at Rome—so that any citizen resident elsewhere who wished to vote had to come to the city to do so—and the voting had to be completed within a single day. Once again, the official who called the meeting controlled the agenda, and the assembled voters could do no more than accept or reject the candidates or the proposals put before them. When assemblies gathered for a discussion or a vote, the senate met at the same time nearby to provide advice. At any assembly, therefore, ordinary citizens had little freedom of speech or initiative. In practice, however, they could still register dissatisfaction with the proceedings informally, through demonstrations, heckling, and occasionally even by destroying an official's insignia of office, such as his fasces or his official chair.

The fact that Roman citizens did not cast their votes in a mass made the census one of the city's vital political institutions. By the fourth century, the census had become highly complex and had come to serve a larger range of functions than when it was instituted. Property, reputation, and place of residence remained fundamental to the operation of the developed census. Once new censors were chosen, all citizens made declarations to them, in which they identified themselves and their places of residence and listed their property and their dependents. From these declarations, and on their assessment of each citizen's character, the censors assigned men to centuries and tribes and also made distinctions of age. Censors assigned the wealthiest to the centuries of the cavalry, while they placed those who were too poor to serve in the army in the single century of the *proletarii*. All those considered eligible for service in the infantry were placed in a further group of centuries, ones that were now arranged in a series of finely gradated classes (even so, there was no longer necessarily a strict correspondence between a citizen's century and whatever military service he performed). Throughout this entire process, it should be remembered, censors maintained the right to examine any citizen's physical condition and way of life. They could express their disapproval of a citizen in various ways—by rebuking him publicly, by registering a cause for complaint in a "note" (*nota*) attached to his name in the roster of citizens, or by imposing penalties.

The categories established at regular intervals in the census were the basis of all assemblies. The Centuriate assembly (*comitia centuriata*), which only an official with imperium could summon, was organized like the army, with the presiding official acting as a commander and the voters as soldiers. For this reason, it met outside the sacred limits or pomerium of the city, since commanders could not issue binding orders to their soldiers within Rome. Voting was oral, and each citizen, when summoned to vote, signified his acceptance or rejection of any candidate or proposal by word of mouth. This voting was organized and tallied by centuries, which voted in turn. Each century possessed one vote, which was itself determined by the votes of a majority of the century's members who were present. Victory in a straight majority of centuries determined the outcome. In general, the Centuriate assembly elected new consuls, praetors, and censors, and voted on matters of war and peace.

Procedures in this assembly favored any presiding official, and also the wealthiest citizens. In elections, the former was entitled to accept or reject the names of would-be candidates, although it is unclear how freely this right was exercised in practice. The votes of the rich carried far more weight than those of the poor, since the rich occupied a large number of small centuries. The eighteen equestrian centuries voted first, and, as each finished voting in turn, the results were publicly proclaimed to guide the vote of the remaining citizens. Next, the richest centuries of the infantry voted, followed in turn by those who were progressively poorer. As the vote went down the scale, moreover, the number of centuries diminished, so that many more voters were crammed into fewer voting units. The *proletarii*, who were too poor to be eligible for military service, all occupied the single century which was slated to vote last. In any case, voting always ceased as soon as a sufficient number of centuries had voted to settle the outcome for or against. Frequently, therefore, the lower centuries, which contained the great mass of citizens, would never have been called upon to vote at all, in particular whenever the rich showed themselves to be in broad agreement.

Assemblies of tribes were neither as complex nor so blatantly weighted toward the rich as was the Centuriate assembly, although poorer citizens, especially if they lived far from the city, may have found it hard to attend these assemblies, too. As we have seen, every Roman citizen belonged to a tribe determined by place of residence. Those who lived in Rome itself filled four "urban" tribes, while those resident elsewhere belonged to one of the "rural" tribes whose number was slowly increased as Rome's power expanded; by 241 that number had reached thirty-one, where it remained. Potentially, therefore, the votes of members of "rural" tribes could carry more weight in these assemblies, if those members could afford to be present.

Tribunes of the plebs summoned citizens by tribes to elect their successors as tribunes or to accept or reject proposed laws; whenever a tribune did this, the assembly was known as the Plebeian assembly or *concilium plebis*. On other occasions, consuls or praetors summoned the tribes to fill certain minor offices (they probably did not preside over assemblies to vote on legislation until much later). In the tribal assemblies, citizens cast their votes one tribe after another. The voting order was determined on every occasion by lot, with each tribe in turn accepting or rejecting the candidates or the proposals under consideration. The first candidates acceptable to a majority of the tribes filled the offices. A law, too, passed (or was rejected) as soon as the bare majority of tribes for or against was attained; voting ceased at that point. In these assemblies, therefore, many of the citizens present could not know until well into the day itself whether or not they would in fact be called upon to vote.

The City, Its Gods, and Its Priests

Religion formed an important part of Rome's organization, and the prominent remains of cult places show that this was true from the beginning of the city. Roman religion cannot be separated from the city and its public institutions or from the social groups and settlements that made up the Roman people; all these had their own divinities, which they worshipped in their own ways. Thus, Rome itself had its protecting divinities, and the city's officials and priests took the lead in cultivating them. Households contained shrines to the *lares*, ancestral spirits, and the *penates*, the protective divinities of the house, while old aristocratic families maintained their special relations with major gods. Away from Rome, the towns and villages inhabited by Roman citizens had their temples, shrines, and cult activities. In the countryside, some forms of religious activity concentrated around crossroads.

Other practices centered on individuals and their concerns, and they were not as bounded by family, neighborhood, or even citizenship as were the cults of the Roman people. When confronted with difficult choices or stressful situations, many people made vows to favored deities, to be fulfilled if and when the desired outcome should be achieved. Those about to undertake journeys or projects could try to determine the attitude of the gods towards their plans through rites of divination. Some especially prominent shrines, even outside of Roman territory, drew such pilgrims from considerable distances. The temple of Fortuna Primigenia in the allied city of Praeneste, for example, drew many seeking good fortune in their activities (see Fig. 5.3). Healing shrines dotted much of rural central Italy; at many, archeologists have found terracotta feet, hands, limbs, eyes, and other anatomical models left by worshippers as tokens of their vows (Fig. 2.2).

In general, the chief elected officials of Rome performed the major rites of the city. Consuls, praetors, censors, and other officials each had their own religious programs (compare Fig. 2.3). In these matters, magistrates were often assisted and advised by priests, who came from many of the same families as the city's political leaders, and sometimes held elective offices themselves.

"Colleges" or groups of priests sharing the same function had an important role in Roman public life. The pontiffs (*pontifices*, singular, *pontifex*), headed by the *pontifex maximus*, exercised a general supervision. They could give an opinion on whether a ritual had been properly performed (if it had not,

Figure 2.2 *In the case of some terracotta anatomical models left at Italian shrines, it is hard to be sure just which organ is meant, and even whether it is intended to be human or animal. No such doubt attaches, however, to human uteri, which are rendered oval, flat on one side, and with transverse ridges on the other. Even so, the additional pear-shaped feature sometimes found extending down from the mouth—either to the left, or to the right (as here, a votive recovered from the Tiber River)—remains a puzzle. There is no agreement on whether this feature represents some defect in need of healing, say, or a plea for a child of a particular sex. At least, any explanation which presupposes a confident grasp of gynecology should be treated with caution, because in all likelihood the human body was not well understood.*

Figure 2.3 *In this fifth-century relief from Clusium, officials on the left observe contestants in ludi. The farthest left of the participants in these games is probably an armed dancer, while a female dancer and flute player are immediately to his right. The figures on the platform are clearly officials, since the one in the middle carries a curved staff or* lituus *(compare Plate 1a). The seated figure to his right is a scribe, writing the results of the games (or of the judges' decisions) on a tablet.*

they could recommend that it be performed again until satisfactory, a procedure known as *instauratio*). Their supervision of the calendar empowered them to identify the days when it was permissible for magistrates to conduct public business or hold assemblies. Originally, the pontiffs numbered three, and only patricians could serve. By the end of the fourth century, the number had increased to nine and plebeians now made up about half the total; the number would be further increased to fifteen in the first century B.C. Pontiffs served for life. When a vacancy occurred, the surviving pontiffs chose the new priest, who was often a relative of the man he replaced. From the third century, seventeen of the tribes, chosen by lot, elected the pontifex maximus from among the serving pontiffs—a limited assertion of control by the citizen body.

The "augurs" were at least as important. Like the pontiffs, they possessed their own areas of expertise, central to the political organization of the city. The first of these were the auspices, essential to an official's power. Before taking office or before beginning any public action, an official was expected to consult Jupiter, the god of the auspices. This could be done by watching the flight of birds or by observing the feeding of chickens kept for the purpose (compare Plate 1a). Although magistrates performed the rite, it was the augurs who were thought to be the experts in its proper forms and in the interpretation of the results. Augurs also possessed knowledge of the rituals necessary to "inaugurate" certain places.

Consequently, magistrates and pontiffs could dedicate sacred sites, such as temples and shrines, only after the augurs had prepared the location. At first, there were only three augurs, but by the end of the fourth century their number had been increased to nine; at this time, plebeians were permitted to serve, filling about half of the positions. Like the pontiffs, the augurs too were increased to fifteen in the first century B.C.

Women possessed a more prominent place in the religious life of the city than they did in politics. The six Vestal virgins performed the rites of Vesta, the Roman goddess of the hearth, from her shrine near the Regia in the Forum Romanum. Among their tasks was to tend the sacred flame; its extinction would endanger the city itself. The wives of the pontifex maximus and of the *flamen* or priest of Jupiter (the *flamen Dialis*) shared in some of their husbands' ritual responsibilities. Women of elite families, moreover, were thought to have dedicated the temple of the Fortune of Women (*Fortuna Muliebris*) early in the Republic, and it long served as a center for their religious activities. Women and girls had defined places in processions and in other celebrations.

ROME AND CENTRAL ITALY

During the fourth century and the opening decades of the third, Rome became the dominant city in Italy. Wars, battles, victories, and defeats—all illustrated by acts of Roman heroism and the perfidy of Rome's enemies—fill Roman accounts of this century. Despite this wealth of detail, however, a clear narrative of the wars is not possible. There is the usual problem of exaggerated victory claims, not to mention a desire to blame Rome's enemies for all conflicts. Furthermore, the changing alliances of the period confused later authors, and Roman opportunism among these shifts may have embarrassed some. In addition, Roman families descended from the commanders in these wars occasionally made claims for their ancestors that were unjustified.

Warfare and the Civic Order

War occupied a central place in the civic and religious structure of many city-states, but this was especially true of Rome. By the fourth century, Rome had evolved a pattern of warfare that centered on campaigns undertaken almost every year, a level of intensity and regularity that is unique among ancient city-states. In the process, warfare came to be deeply entrenched in Roman political and religious life, shaping the highest offices as well as the lives and careers both of the community's leaders and of its citizens. Military service was one of the central duties of the citizen body. The boundaries between citizen and soldier were neither firm nor long-lasting, and each year large numbers of adult males performed both roles. Soon after the new consuls had entered office, citizens eligible for military service came to Rome for the levy, or *dilectus*, in which some were chosen to be soldiers in the consuls' armies in the upcoming season. After a season's campaigning, soldiers were discharged, returning to their places in civil life.

Warfare followed a clear seasonal pattern. Direct attacks on cities or long sieges of fortified places were relatively rare. Instead, commanders of invading armies more often sought to interfere with the ability of the inhabitants of the targeted city to cultivate their lands and feed their families. Even successful wars could have few permanent results. Some wars were encompassed within a single summer's campaigning, while others consisted of a series of annual campaigns, each with a different commander and army. Sometimes, campaigns ended in truces that could run for several years; on other occasions, defeated cities might accept the dominance of the victor. It was the belief of Rome's leaders that a formal surrender established a permanent relationship of subordination (Source 2.1). However, certain defeated communities plainly did not share this view, and Roman armies sometimes had to force them into submission repeatedly. Altogether in ancient Italy, none but the strongest of cities was able to exert long-term dominance over a substantial number of others. During the fourth century, Rome became just such an exceptional city.

Rome in Latium and Campania

Rome's victory over Veii around 396 profoundly changed relations among the cities of central Italy. Rome, already a relatively large and populous city, came to overshadow its neighbors even more starkly. Strength in war was closely related

---

SOURCE 2.1: *The formal procedure for total, unconditional surrender* (deditio in fidem) *that Rome might traditionally demand from a defeated enemy is well known from Rome's historians. Only a single documentary record of an actual instance survives, however, on a partially preserved bronze tablet. This deditio was made by an otherwise unknown people in Spain (the end of their name is lost too) in 104 and can be reckoned to reflect typical Roman practice.*

In the consulship of G. Marius and G. Flavius: The people of Seano . . . gave up themselves and theirs to L. Caesius, son of Gaius, *imperator* [commander]. L. Caesius, son of Gaius, imperator, after he accepted them into his trust, referred to his *consilium* [council] what orders they considered should be issued to them. On the advice of his consilium he ordered that they hand over their arms, deserters, captives, stallions, and mares that they had taken. All these they handed over. Then L. Caesius, son of Gaius, imperator, ordered that they be free; he handed back to them the lands and buildings, laws and everything else such as then existed which had been theirs on the day before they gave themselves up, insofar as it should be the wish of the Roman people and senate, and he ordered that envoys should go [to somewhere: Rome?] concerning this matter. Crenus, son of . . . , and Arco, son of Cantonus, were the envoys. . . . (*AE* 1986. 304)

to a city's population and to the numbers of its adult males who could afford to serve in its army. Rome's treatment of Veii enlarged its own citizen body, and in addition the land then distributed to poorer citizens gave still more Romans the necessary means to equip themselves as soldiers. These new circumstances affected Rome's relations with other cities in turn.

In the third quarter of the fourth century, Roman commanders proceeded to wage wars and make alliances with states that were more powerful than their nearest Latin or Etruscan neighbors; in the process, they succeeded in extending Roman power over all of Latium and northern Campania, where Capua was the largest city (Map 2.2). At this date the Samnites were the strongest group in the central highlands (see Fig. 5.2). In the valleys of Samnium, archeological evidence reveals a dense pattern of rural settlement with the inhabitants living in scattered villages, where they raised crops, vines, and livestock. City-states had not taken root here, but a powerful military confederacy of tribes had emerged. The Samnites were very aggressive, and they possessed a formidable military reputation.

During the late 340s and early 330s, Roman armies fought Latins, Volsci, Campanians, and possibly Samnites, while Campanians and Samnites also conducted wars of their own. In what later authors would call the First Samnite War (343–341), it is far from clear how much fighting between Romans and Samnites actually took place. At about the same time, the Latin War (341–338) marked the end of any autonomy for the Latin cities. The actions of one of the consuls in command went into legend. Titus Manlius Torquatus, this consul's son, killed an enemy soldier in single combat but was then put to death by his father for disobeying the explicit order given that no Roman should engage in single combat—an example of the virtuous official placing the welfare of the city and its laws above family. By 338, the war essentially had ended, although scattered communities did continue to resist for a few years afterwards.

After the Latin War, most Latin communities were incorporated into the Roman state, just as Veii had been over half a century earlier; their citizens became Roman citizens and their land Roman territory. Their urban centers continued to exist as units of no more than local government with restricted freedom of action. Such towns were styled *municipia* (singular, *municipium*). They retained much of their old civic organization, electing officials, maintaining the local equivalent of a senate, and performing their traditional religious rites. They could not make war or peace on their own, however, and their citizens, when drafted, served in the Roman army. They could vote in Roman assemblies if they were present in Rome. A few Latin communities—in particular Tibur and Praeneste, the largest ones—did maintain a formal independence and were not absorbed directly into the Roman citizen body. Even so, they became Roman allies, were completely surrounded by Roman territory, and were no longer capable of any independent action (Fig. 2.4).

Some defeated communities were treated in ways that did disrupt their social and political arrangements. Victorious Roman armies plundered them, and Rome often imposed penalties on communities that had fought too hard or resisted too

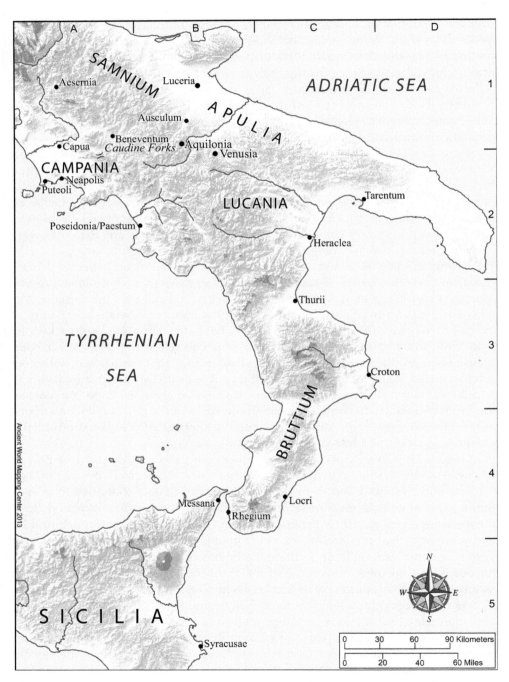

Map 2.2 *Southern Italy*

Figure 2.4 *This bone plaque (8 × 2 in / 20 × 5 cm), originally attached to a wooden box as decoration, was found at the Latin city of Praeneste. It depicts a warrior in the panoply of a hoplite; his shield can be seen behind his left leg. The plaque was carved in the late fourth century, when Praeneste was firmly an ally of Rome.*

long, confiscating land and displacing or enslaving the inhabitants. Roman citizens, as individuals, could take up small allotments of some of this captured land in what are known as "viritane" assignments. Other substantial tracts of it went to groups of settlers in colonies.

Seeking to hold new territory or allies by founding colonies was an old Roman and Latin practice, but now the process became more formalized and came under Rome's exclusive control. Colonies were to be fully functioning city-states with their own fighting forces and capable of their own defense. In some colonies, the settlers remained Roman citizens and were enrolled in a tribe. Such citizen colonies were small—300 adult men—and they were generally situated along the coast, at harbors, or at the mouths of rivers. Most colonies were larger, however, with 2,500, 4,000, or 6,000 adult male settlers; colonists in these new communities lost Roman citizenship, but they received instead the privileges enjoyed by the citizens of towns with Latin status. From the late fourth to the early second century, the Romans established at least fifty-three colonies in Italy at locations open to enemy attack, in recently subjugated regions liable to revolt, at strategic river crossings and road junctions, and on vulnerable sections of coastline (see Source 1.1).

The resulting system of alliances and incorporated communities was primarily military in nature. After the actual conquest, the Roman state did not seek any financial benefit from the defeated, since it imposed no taxes or tribute. Instead, the Romans sought to exercise their leadership primarily in war. Colonies, municipia, and allies were expected to defer to Rome, to follow its leadership in war and peace, and to provide soldiers for its wars. Such an assemblage of communities could field formidable military forces, and it could be expanded indefinitely.

Samnite Wars

The late fourth and early third centuries were dominated by the Second and Third Samnite Wars. Both powers were expansionist, and they were now neighbors with nearly equivalent forces, so that the Roman–Samnite wars really did determine which would be the leading power in Italy.

The Second Samnite War (326–304) was a long struggle for dominance. It began over the Roman foundation of a colony at Fregellae, on the eastern bank of the Liris River, in territory that the Samnites apparently considered their own. This phase of the war ended at the Battle of the Caudine Forks (Latin, *Furculae Caudinae*) in 321, when Samnite forces succeeded in ambushing a Roman army in a mountain valley and forcing its surrender (see Map 2.2). In the resulting peace, the Romans gave up their colony at Fregellae. Fighting resumed on a large scale in 316. For the next few years, Roman historians record Samnite invasions of Latium and Campania, but Rome's armies did recover and would then invade Samnium yearly until peace was made in 304. During this war, Rome founded several colonies in southern Campania, and one, Luceria, far away in Apulia, in an apparent attempt to create bases for further operations against Samnium.

The Third Samnite War (298–290) secured Rome's leadership. Hostilities seem to have begun over Roman activities in Lucania. By the end of 297, a coalition of Samnites, Etruscans, Umbrians, and Gauls formed, although its actions were not well-coordinated. In 295, the two consuls of the year decisively defeated a force of Samnites, Umbrians, and Gauls in a great battle at Sentinum in Umbria. This victory was later to be closely associated with the consul P. Decius Mus, who lost his life in the same act of self-sacrifice that his father had made in a battle against the Latins in 340. Like his father, at a crucial point in the fighting the son "devoted" or pledged his life to the gods if they would claim the enemy too; he then rode alone into the enemy ranks, causing his own death, but also theirs so as to ensure their defeat. In 291, another Roman consul defeated the Samnites at Aquilonia; soon afterwards, the Romans would establish the colony of Venusia south of there. After this defeat, the Samnites again made peace.

Wars in Central and Northern Italy

Rome's success did not end its wars. In 290, just after the Roman victory in the Third Samnite War, the consul Manius Curius Dentatus ravaged the land of the Sabines, who lived in scattered villages, and then reached the Adriatic Sea. As a result of this campaign, the Romans established a Latin colony at Hatria, and made the Sabines Roman citizens without the right to vote. Roman armies also conducted regular campaigns into Etruria and Umbria, especially along the valley of the Tiber. These wars were complicated, with shifting alliances between states, and they often involved Gauls. In 284, the Gallic Senones defeated a Roman army at Arretium in northern Etruria. In the following year, by contrast, another Roman army defeated the Gallic Boii and some of their Etruscan allies at Lake Vadimon, about fifty miles (80 km) north of Rome. By 283, the Romans had expelled the Senones from a portion of their territory, which would become known as the *ager Gallicus*. There, the Romans would establish colonies at Sena Gallica (in 283) and Ariminum (in 268; modern Rimini). In the 280s and 270s, Roman armies forced most of the cities of Etruria and Umbria into a dependent status. By the 260s, few, if any, communities there or in Picenum possessed any real independence. Attempts to reassert it were severely punished. The Picentes revolted in 269. When defeated, they lost territory—a Roman colony was established at Firmum—and they were made citizens without the vote. In Etruria, the revolt of Falerii in 241 was the last.

Conquest of the South

After the Third Samnite War, Roman officials quickly involved themselves in the affairs of the Greek cities of southern Italy. This growing Roman presence now alarmed the citizens of Tarentum, the largest Greek city in the region and often ambitious to lead the others. In 281, the Tarentines sought assistance from Pyrrhus, king of the Molossians in Epirus across the Adriatic (see Map 3.4). Pyrrhus was a typical monarch of his time (the "Hellenistic" period) in the Greek world. His power base was his kingship over the Molossians, an office with traditional limitations. Pyrrhus also controlled cities and districts in his own name, which were administered by his personal officials and commanders; here he was able to raise revenue and soldiers outside the limits of Molossian law and custom. Altogether these territories provided the means for pursuing greater ambitions than had traditionally been within reach of the Molossian king, and Pyrrhus would spend much of his reign doing just this on an increasing scale. Accordingly, when he received the Tarentines' invitation in 281, he resolved to seek opportunities in the West.

For a time, Pyrrhus and his Tarentine allies were successful. In 280, Pyrrhus' army, accompanied by elephants (note Fig. 3.2) and reinforced by the Tarentines' citizen army, engaged a Roman consular army at Heraclea, southwest of Tarentum. Pyrrhus won, but with immense loss of life, giving rise to the expression "Pyrrhic victory" for a battle won at such cost that it almost amounted to a defeat. The war then spread, and a number of Rome's allies—the Samnites were the most important—decided to join Pyrrhus. The king then invaded Campania, but without capturing any major community or inspiring any to desert Rome and join him. Next he turned towards Rome itself, approaching to within fifty miles (80 km) of the city. By this time, however, another Roman army that had been campaigning in Etruria returned to protect Rome, and Pyrrhus led his army back to Tarentum, where he began offering harsh peace terms, which the elderly, blind senator, Appius Claudius Caecus (censor in 312), persuaded the Romans not to accept.

In the following year (279), Pyrrhus brought over reinforcements from Epirus. He met the Romans at Ausculum, and another lengthy, fearsome clash ensued. Once again, Pyrrhus proved victorious in battle, but at terrible cost. At this point, therefore, he decided to respond to a call for help against the Carthaginians from Syracuse, the leading Greek city in Sicily. In 275, Pyrrhus returned to Italy, prompted perhaps by renewed appeals from his Italian allies as well as increasing dissatisfaction with his leadership in Sicily. Later that year, Pyrrhus' army fought the Romans at Beneventum in Samnium, and this time the Roman army won. By the end of the year, Pyrrhus had crossed the Adriatic and returned home. There he would achieve some success for a time, only to be killed during street fighting at Argos in southern Greece in 272.

Pyrrhus' failure proved disastrous for many of his allies, who in consequence would lose their independence to Rome and suffer Rome's vengeance. In 272, Tarentum became a Roman ally. Wars with the Samnites continued into the 260s. By this time, the Romans had reduced to the status of allies, voluntarily or otherwise, around 150 once-independent communities. Another important consequence of Rome's war with Pyrrhus and the associated involvement in the affairs of the Greek cities of the south was an altogether closer engagement with the wider Greek world and its culture.

WAR AND THE ROMAN STATE

In over a century of virtually continuous warfare, Roman officials and armies established their city as the most powerful in Italy, and they erected around it a network of alliances that made Rome a key participant in the larger politics of the Mediterranean world. This pattern of regular warfare merits explanation, although no single element or cause can serve to account for all of Rome's wars.

Several features of Roman society and politics encouraged acceptance of, and perhaps the active search for, frequent wars. Possession of the military virtues was central to the self-image of the Roman elite, to the ways its members competed among themselves for offices and honors, and to their claims to leadership in their city and elsewhere (see Chapter Three). Regular warfare provided ambitious Romans with the opportunity to display their bravery and skill memorably—vital achievements for those who wished to reach high office. Indeed, the highest Roman office of consul was itself substantially military in nature, and its occupants would have expected, and probably desired, to command armies in the field.

Decisions over war and peace were not just for the most prominent members of Rome's elite to take. The Roman practice of campaigning virtually every year required consensus among the populace too. Successful warfare brought loot and other tangible benefits to many Roman citizens (see Source 4.1). Distribution of captured land would have enabled many poorer Romans to receive a plot that was sufficient to support their families. Demands from the poor for land redistribution were not the cause of turmoil at Rome, therefore, that they often were elsewhere. In the last decades of the fourth century, moreover, mass enslavements of defeated enemies occurred frequently. Some of the newly enslaved probably were sold outside of Italy. Others were put to work on the lands and in the households of Roman citizens, beginning a gradual shift away from the labor systems of archaic Rome, which had been based on dependent clients and debt-slaves. Altogether, the acquisition of wealth through regular campaigns no doubt reduced the level of internal conflicts in the city.

Internal factors are not the whole picture, however. Roman historians later regarded these wars as essentially defensive in nature, aimed at restraining aggression by others or at punishing disloyalty by cities that had supposedly accepted Roman leadership. From this perspective, therefore, Roman expansion was a successful response to the aggressive actions of others. Such a viewpoint may indeed plausibly explain some campaigns against some enemies, but it is unlikely to apply universally. Even so, it is important to recognize that other states, whether friend or foe of Rome, had their own agendas, ambitions, and military traditions. Some of these states were themselves aggressive and expansionist, and they may, on occasion, have forced the Romans to respond to their initiatives. Unfortunately, the surviving evidence, which focuses so strongly on Rome itself, does not permit the full recovery of these other, less successful histories.

SUGGESTED READINGS

Eckstein, Arthur M. 2006. *Mediterranean Anarchy, Interstate War, and the Rise of Rome.* Berkeley, Los Angeles, London: University of California Press.

Harris, William V. 1979. *War and Imperialism in Republican Rome, 327–70 B.C.* Oxford: Oxford University Press. A controversial examination of Roman attitudes toward war and the ways that they shaped Roman actions.

Lintott, Andrew. 1999. *The Constitution of the Roman Republic.* Oxford: Oxford University Press. A clear guide to the institutions of the Republic and their development, workings, and interaction.

Salmon, E. Togo. 1967. *Samnium and the Samnites.* Cambridge: Cambridge University Press.

THE BEGINNINGS OF A MEDITERRANEAN EMPIRE

In the 130 years following the end of the war with Pyrrhus (275), the Roman Republic became the dominant state in the Mediterranean. In the city itself, moreover, a new elite group, the nobility, emerged to take the lead in Rome's political structure; at the same time its foremost members became some of the wealthiest and most powerful individuals in the Mediterranean world. Participation in wars over a far wider geographical area, together with the consequent expansion of Roman power beyond the Italian peninsula, would now put major strains on the Republic's traditional structure and on its customary ways of making war and forging alliances.

THE NOBILITY AND THE CITY OF ROME

The opening of offices and priesthoods to plebeians that occurred during the fourth and third centuries resulted in the formation of a new governing elite in Rome with a distinctive way of life. This elite, collectively known as the "nobles" or *nobiles*, would govern Rome and its empire throughout the period of expansion in the third, second, and first centuries. Archaic Rome had been governed by relatively few individuals from a small group of families. However, the city's new leadership, also a group of limited size, would differ from the old in significant ways. The patriciate was always an aristocracy of birth; in addition, certain leaders of the archaic period possessed personal military followings that made them important regardless of whether they held an office. Although some patrician families would achieve prominent places in the new elite, too, it was not an aristocracy of birth, nor did its leading members possess significant military forces of their own. Instead, individuals and families had to establish and maintain their place in the city.

Officeholding was central. The new nobility rested on its members' ability to win offices and gain priesthoods. In this context, it was above all the magistracies that a man held which defined him as well as his family. Indeed, the Latin word *nobilis*, in its most restricted sense, designates an individual with an ancestor who had been chosen consul. By its very nature, this new order was highly competitive. More contestants, patricians as well as plebeians, now sought a limited number of positions. In Rome, as in other city-states, offices in practice were open only to the rich and, more particularly, only to those rich who maintained a respectable way of life—whose wealth, in other words, derived primarily from landholding, and not from trade or from the practice of a "sordid" profession, such as auctioneer or scribe or trader. The position of the new elite families, however, was less secure than that of the patriciate of the past. In each generation, they had to provide new and successful seekers of offices; families that failed to do so could otherwise drop out of the governing elite. Meanwhile a few men from families that had never held office did succeed in gaining at least lower magistracies; these individuals were termed "new men" (*novi homines*). If their descendants maintained and improved upon this success, they could become new members of the nobility.

The rise of the nobility accompanied, and reinforced, other developments in Roman public life. The emphasis on offices—especially the office of consul—would result in the gradual creation of a hierarchy of positions, each of which conferred on its holders a successively higher status. In its developed form, these offices, from lowest to highest, would be quaestor, tribune of the plebs, aedile, praetor, and consul. The prohibition against holding the consulship more than once or twice became firmly established in the third century, and enabled two men to hold this office each year who had never done so before. The other offices tended to be held earlier, and because there was a greater number of openings for them, more families were able to compete successfully at this level. Some families in fact gained the lower offices for generations without ever achieving a consulship. The tribunate of the plebs now came to serve not only as an office of value in its own right, but also as a desirable early stage in the career of members of prominent plebeian families. As a result, the tribunate lost much of its radical nature—although it retained the powers for this to return later—and tribunes became part of the established order, as did the Plebeian assembly over which they presided.

It was during the third and second centuries that the senate took on its leading role in the city, and these centuries in many ways marked its high point. This was the period when the senate's "influence" or *auctoritas* peaked, in other words when its direction of affairs won highest respect. The censors began to enroll primarily former officeholders, who in practice would serve for life. At some point in these centuries, tribunes of the plebs gained the right to summon meetings of the senate; they also came to be enrolled in it after holding office. These two developments (which cannot be dated precisely) mark the integration of plebeian officials into the official order of the city. As a gathering of former officeholders, the senate came to be organized internally in the same hierarchical fashion as were the magistracies. Former consuls tended to lead in the senate because they had held the highest office. The senate came to be seen as a store of virtues, prestige, and experience.

In this competitive and hierarchical environment, prominent individuals could be very protective and assertive of their claims to status. Members of Rome's elite liked to think that the pursuit of praise or fame (*laus*) and glory (*gloria*) was integral to their way of life. The Roman public virtues were primarily military—indeed, the primary meaning of the Latin noun *virtus* is "manly courage"—and they were closely linked to the holding of offices. It was above all military success that led to laus and gloria. The higher offices earned a man greater esteem or *dignitas* than the lower. In the late second and first centuries, other forms of elite activity, such as skill in public speaking or in the law, also came to be seen as praiseworthy, but never to the same extent as holding magistracies. Officeholders wished their term of office to stand out in some way. Leading Romans missed no opportunity to proclaim their merits and accomplishments, and often asserted their superiority over the achievements of their competitors. Failure to recognize someone's accomplishments to the degree he expected—to be disrespectful to his dignitas, therefore—could provide a cause for lasting enmity.

The great pressure to assert a man's claims changed not only public life, but also Rome's physical appearance. The third and second centuries saw increasing elaboration of the city's ceremonial and religious life in ways that emphasized the power and glory of the official who staged the rites. Displays of wealth, luxury, and military power were at first limited to officeholders, but other members of wealthy and powerful families would eventually mount them, too, so as to add to the collective glory of their families.

Because war was the chief arena in which members of the elite could exhibit their virtue and gain fame and glory, leading citizens craved public recognition of their military accomplishments. The chief celebration of victory was the triumph, a formal procession of a victorious general and his army through the city. The triumph was in fact an old ceremony in Rome. At first, the triumphal procession was primarily a rite intended to purify an army returning from battle or to thank the gods for a victory. In the late fourth and third centuries, however, under the influence of the elaborate ceremonies of the Greek kingdoms to the east, the Roman triumph became less a celebration by the community and the army than a glorification of the officeholder who had commanded the army. In the triumph, the victorious general or *triumphator*, accompanied by senators and other officials, led his army through the city together with prisoners, displays of captured property, and tableaux and paintings depicting key episodes in his victory (Source 3.1). The figure of the triumphator stood out clearly, because he wore the gold and purple costume of the old kings, he painted his face to resemble the cult statue of Jupiter Best and Greatest in the temple on the Capitoline hill, and he rode a four-horse chariot, just as did representations of the god.

SOURCE 3.1: *The triumph of Scipio Africanus in 201 as described by the historian Appian (Punic Wars 66). Note that mocking rituals formed a part of the triumph, just as they did of the processions that marked the Roman Games.*

Everyone in the procession wore crowns. Trumpeters led the advance, and wagons laden with spoils. Towers were borne along representing the captured cities, and pictures illustrating the campaigns; then gold and silver coin and bullion, and similar captured materials; then came the crowns presented to the general as a reward for his bravery by cities, by allies, or by the army itself. White oxen came next, and after them elephants and the captive Carthaginian and Numidian leaders. Lictors wearing purple tunics preceded the general; also a chorus of harpists and pipers—in imitation of an Etruscan procession—wearing belts and golden crowns, and marching in regular order, keeping step with song and dance. One member of the chorus, in the middle of the procession, wearing a body-length purple cloak as well as gold bracelets and necklace, caused laughter by making various gesticulations, as though he were dancing in triumph over the enemy. Next came a number of incense-bearers, and after them the general himself in a richly decorated chariot. He wore a crown of gold and precious stones, and was dressed, in traditional fashion, in a purple toga woven with golden stars. He carried a scepter of ivory, and a laurel branch, which is invariably the Roman symbol of victory. . . . The army itself was marshalled in squadrons and cohorts, all of them crowned and carrying laurel branches, the bravest of them bearing their military prizes. The men praised some of their officers, and ridiculed or criticized others; during a triumph there are no restrictions.

The triumph was the single most important ceremony that any Roman in public life could hope to perform. Eventually a list of triumph-winners, the *fasti triumphales*, would be put on prominent display in the city to mark their accomplishments for all time. The decision over whether or not a victory warranted a triumph was too important to be left to the commander alone. At some point, the senate asserted its control. In consequence, victorious commanders and their armies waited outside the *pomerium* while the senate debated their accomplishments. Because a triumph was so prestigious, conflicts were common.

A public figure was particularly concerned to preserve the memory of his accomplishments. By their very nature, victories were ephemeral. Hence, from the last decades of the fourth century, leading Romans sought to enshrine the memory of their accomplishments in prominent monuments; the Latin word *monumenta* (singular, *monumentum*) is actually related to the verb meaning "to remind" or "to instruct." Often, initiatives of this type involved the official religion of the city. When beginning a campaign or preparing for battle, for example, Roman commanders made vows in which they promised new temples to favored deities should they prove successful. As a result, dozens of temples came to be built in prominent places. In addition to statues of the gods and altars for their worship, temples often housed statues of the victor and associated inscriptions. By the end

Figure 3.1 *Because wax is a far from robust material, no imagines of a prominent Roman family's ancestors survive. All the same, the impact made by such commemorative objects is vividly recalled by this marble statue (5.5 ft/1.7 m tall)—the so-called "Togato Barberini"—where a dignified male figure wearing a toga stands proudly holding a bust of one man in his left hand, while resting his right hand on the bust of another man placed atop a column. The two busts seem realistic renderings of individuals rather than idealized ones, and the men portrayed may be family members, possibly of different generations. The statue is difficult to date, but stylistic criteria point to the late first century B.C.*

of the third century, monuments to past leaders surrounded the places where magistrates performed their tasks, where the senate held its meetings, and where assemblies of citizens gathered to hear debates and to vote.

Advancement of a family's claims to status came to involve remembering and celebrating the specific offices held by its members in earlier generations and their notable achievements in those capacities. Certain types of display were designed simply to encourage family members to imitate or outclass their ancestors. Other types were more public, because the successes of famous ancestors helped advance the claims to office made by their descendants, who supposedly had inherited their virtues. This desire to proclaim the glory of one's ancestors led some aristocrats to stress an additional name, the *cognomen*, which, when added to their *praenomen* and *nomen*, announced their descent from a particular member of their *gens*; thus, the Cornelii Scipiones used the cognomen Scipio to identify themselves as lineal descendants of a common ancestor within the larger gens Cornelia. Some families were not entirely honest in their claims.

Portrait masks of wax, or *imagines* (singular, *imago*), offered another means of proclaiming the greatness of a family's ancestors (Fig. 3.1). Prominent Romans kept masks of those ancestors who had held high offices or performed famous exploits in the *atria* or reception halls of their houses, where they would be visible to visitors and passersby. Funerals provided an especially important occasion for such families to display the imagines of officeholders in their past, and to proclaim their versions of the family history. Like other public ceremonies, these funerals became more elaborate over time. From the middle of the third century, combats between pairs of gladiators also formed part of the proceedings. The first known gladiatorial games were staged during the funeral of Decimus Junius Brutus in 264; by the end of the third century, the sons of Marcus Aemilius Lepidus would put on combats with twenty-two pairs of gladiators.

WARS WITH CARTHAGE

Wars with Carthage—called Punic from the Latin adjective *punicus* meaning "Phoenician"—dominate Roman history in the middle and late third century.

Carthage was the most powerful of the cities that had emerged from the Phoenician colonization of the ninth through sixth centuries (see Chapter One). Carthage came to control, directly or indirectly, a considerable territory in North Africa (Map 3.1). By one means or another, the city of Carthage and members of its elite also exploited subordinate communities of their territory's original population. By the end of the fourth century, the Carthaginians controlled an area almost equivalent to Latium and Campania combined, although they restricted their citizenship much more than did the Romans. Still farther away, Carthage exercised some leadership, if only intermittently, over rulers of various tribes and confederacies; the Numidians, in modern Algeria, were the most important.

Carthage also expanded its power and influence by sea. From the end of the seventh century, the Phoenician settlements of western Sicily, Sardinia, and the Balearic Islands were subordinate to Carthage in some way. By the end of the sixth century, the Carthaginians controlled the coasts of Sardinia, where they established colonies of their own and controlled mines in the interior. In the sixth, fifth, and fourth centuries, Carthaginian armies fought, with varying degrees of success, against the Greek cities of Sicily. Carthage also had contacts, if sometimes distant and indirect, with cities in Italy. As part of their struggles with the Sicilian Greeks and to protect their trade, the Carthaginians concluded treaties with some central Italian communities, including Rome. The first of these Roman–Carthaginian agreements was probably made as early as c. 500, and others followed, although the precise number made thereafter is uncertain.

First Punic War (264–241)

In 264, war broke out between the Romans and the Carthaginians as a result of a three-way struggle between Carthage, Rome, and Syracuse over the strategic city of Messana (modern Messina), which controlled the straits between Italy and Sicily. Syracuse, the weakest of the three contending states, soon became an ally of Rome. In 262, a Roman army advanced into western Sicily and besieged the Greek city of Agrigentum (modern Agrigento), where the Carthaginians had concentrated their forces. It fell to the Romans, however, and was brutally sacked. A period of stalemate followed. Both sides faced extraordinary difficulties. Carthage possessed one of the most powerful war fleets in the Mediterranean, but it depended upon mercenaries to fill out its armies. Because of this strength at sea, Carthaginian forces were able to hold towns on the coast, where reinforcements could easily be landed. Rome, on the other hand, had a large army, though only a small fleet. Roman commanders were able to bring armies across the narrow straits between Sicily and Italy, but the Carthaginian fleet made it impossible for them to expel Carthaginian forces from Sicily.

The Romans responded by building warships to challenge Carthage at sea. Shipbuilding was complex and expensive. Commanding fleets, moreover, was a specialist operation, and warships by definition required large numbers of

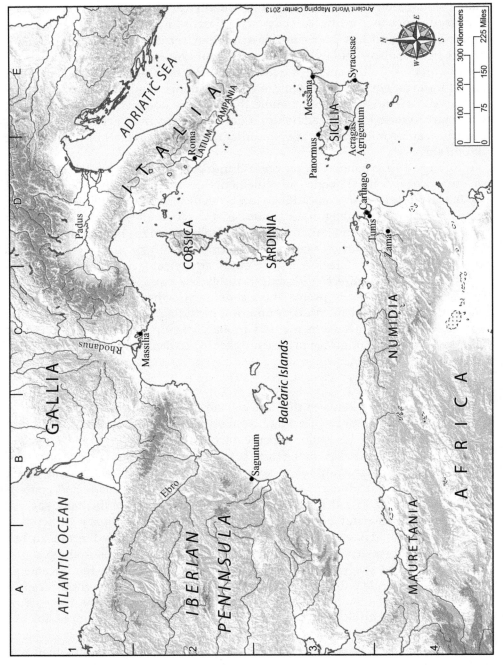

Map 3.1 *Western Mediterranean in the Mid-Third Century*

skilled oarsmen. Here, the Carthaginians had a great advantage, but the Romans adapted remarkably quickly. Copying Carthaginian methods of construction, they began by building about one hundred large warships; over the course of the war, they would build many more. For sailors and oarsmen, they turned to their allies and also recruited Roman citizens too poor to serve in the army. Roman fleets soon began to win battles at sea, although they also lost many ships.

For a time, neither side could gain a decisive advantage. In 256, both consuls took the further initiative of crossing to North Africa with an army and a fleet to attack Carthage itself. One of these consuls, Marcus Atilius Regulus, at first proved successful, but was defeated and captured in 255. Roman writers would later turn this humiliation into a patriotic myth that contrasted the supposed virtues of the consul and the vices of his captors. Later, according to the tale, the Carthaginians allowed Regulus to go to Rome in order to negotiate either a peace or an exchange of prisoners, making him promise to return if his efforts were to prove unsuccessful. When the senate refused to negotiate, Regulus returned to Carthage, where he died, exhibiting in the process characteristic Roman good faith (*fides*).

After the failed invasion of North Africa, warfare continued on land and sea for fifteen years. In Sicily, Roman commanders slowly gained the advantage. In the process, much of Sicily was devastated. In 241, the Carthaginians gave Hamilcar, their commander in Sicily, authority to negotiate a peace. The result was that they agreed to leave Sicily and to pay Rome a large indemnity. Hostilities did not end here, however. At the end of the war, Carthage had insufficient funds to pay its mercenaries, who were owed for many years of service. So the large mercenary army assembled in North Africa mounted a revolt, which soon spread to some of Carthage's Libyan and Numidian allies. During this crisis Roman officials, ignoring earlier agreements, forced Carthage to abandon the strategic island of Sardinia. The Carthaginians, beset on all sides, agreed.

It was in fact victory in the First Punic War that led to the creation of Rome's first permanent commitments outside Italy. By 227, the decision had been made to station a commander and troops permanently in Sicily, Sardinia, and Corsica. In that year, the Centuriate assembly elected four praetors for the first time, with the intention that one of them should regularly be sent to Sicily and another to Sardinia-Corsica. Thus these islands became the first of Rome's "provinces" outside the Italian peninsula (see A Mediterranean Empire).

The First Punic War, and to a lesser degree the war with Pyrrhus that preceded it, marked an important stage in how Rome waged war. The traditional pattern was for consuls and praetors to raise armies each spring and discharge them in the fall after the end of the campaigning season. Consequently, Roman soldiers could be self-supporting, because they always returned home in time to plant their crops and provide for themselves and their families in the following year. In several wars of the third century, however, this long-established practice no longer met Roman needs. Now, it was sometimes necessary to keep armies in the field over the winter and to maintain garrisons in distant locations.

In response to the new forms of warfare, Roman practices underwent some adjustment. Traditionally, Roman commanders had for the most part sought to supply their armies either by living off the land or by demanding the necessary funds and provisions from nearby allies and subjects. Rome's administrative organization, like that of most city-states, was rudimentary, and its ability to direct a range of activities was correspondingly limited. To be sure, from time to time the state needed supplies and labor for rituals, for building projects, and for the army. In these circumstances, however, officials would typically turn to private contractors or *publicani* (singular, *publicanus*). Some publicani were undoubtedly involved in equipping and supplying Roman fleets and armies.

By the middle of the third century, there are clear signs that the Romans were expending public funds on a larger scale than they had in the past (Fig. 3.2). It was when ancient communities faced the necessity of making regular payments on a large scale—either for war or for other public projects—that they usually began to mint coins in silver. When the Romans first made use of such high-value coins, late in the fourth century, they relied on ones produced at irregular intervals by Campanian mints. During the Pyrrhic War, however, they began to mint their own, using Greek weights and designs. Eventually, in the last two decades of the third century, they introduced a complete range of denominations with Roman weights and designs (Fig. 3.3).

Second Punic War (218–201)

The Second Punic War broke out over Spain. Leadership of the Phoenician cities of the Iberian peninsula, together with influence in the interior there, had long

Figure 3.2 *In addition to silver coins—which at first appear to have circulated primarily in southern Italy, where the use of money was long established—the Romans began to cast bronze in the form of ingots or coins; these circulated more locally and may have been intended for distribution to soldiers. This bronze ingot, dating between 275 and 242, bears an elephant on one side and a sow on the other; the elephant is probably a reference to the war with Pyrrhus (see Chapter Two).*

been a major prop of Carthaginian power. The Carthaginians used Iberian mercenaries to fight in their wars; Iberian gold, silver, and other metals to pay and equip their soldiers and sailors; and Iberian timber to build their ships. After the end of the First Punic War, they attempted to extend their power in the peninsula and increase their access to its rich resources. In 237, Hamilcar Barca, previously Carthage's general in Sicily, landed in Spain; from then on, he regularly conducted military operations and extended Carthaginian power there until his death in 229. At that point he was succeeded by Hasdrubal, his son-in-law, who governed and campaigned until he, too, died in 221. After Hasdrubal's death, Hannibal Barca, Hamilcar's own son born in 247, became the chief Carthaginian commander in Spain.

Figure 3.3 *From around 211, the Roman state began to mint silver coins known as* denarii *with their own original designs and with Latin inscriptions. The denarius would long remain the most common silver coin. This early example bears a helmeted image of the goddess Roma on the obverse, and the Dioscuri (Castor and Pollux, twin sons of Jupiter) on the reverse. These designs, too, would long remain standard.*

This increase in Carthage's power provided the occasion for a new clash with Rome. In 218, after Hannibal had provocatively besieged and captured Saguntum—a town that Rome claimed to be under its protection—Rome declared war. Hannibal surprised Rome by daring to attempt the long march to Italy. Despite difficulties and much loss of life, he and his forces successfully crossed the Alps into Italy. Here, at the Trebia River, he virtually destroyed a Roman army that confronted him in December 218 (Map 3.2).

Despite these remarkable achievements by Hannibal, however, the Romans still possessed most of the advantages. Rome's fleet far outclassed that of Carthage. For this reason, Rome's leaders had apparently expected to be able to fight the war in Africa and Spain, both of which they could reach by sea. At the same time, Rome's control of the sea meant that Hannibal could receive only limited reinforcements by ship while in Italy. Here, the Romans possessed great reserves of manpower—upwards of half a million potential recruits—although they could not mobilize all of them at one time. There can be no question that Hannibal had far fewer soldiers. A bronze tablet that he later erected in the south of Italy supposedly claimed that he had 12,000 African and 8,000 Iberian infantry, and no more than 6,000 cavalry, when he entered Italy. He may have hoped to win victories that would be sufficiently impressive to encourage the Romans to make peace, or Rome's allies to revolt. Any such aims proved only partially successful.

When Hannibal crossed the Alps, he entered a region disturbed by warfare between Romans and Gauls. The Gauls made common cause with him, and some would join his army. His successes continued in 217. When he crossed the

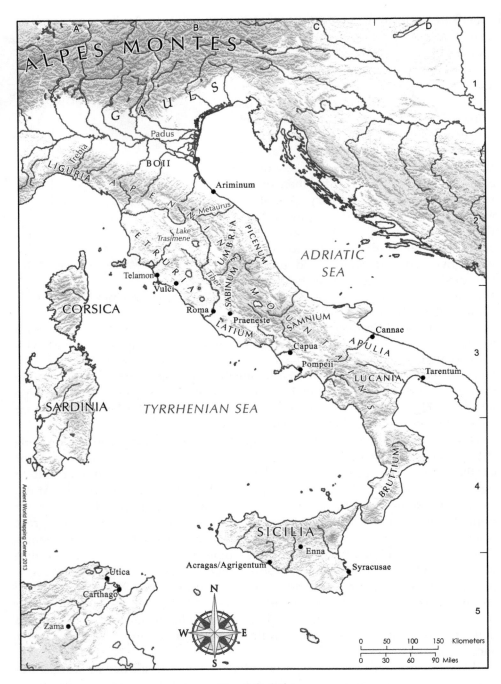

Map 3.2 *Italy*

Apennines and invaded Etruria, Gaius Flaminius marched to block him, but Hannibal succeeded in ambushing and destroying this consul's army at Lake Trasimene. At this critical juncture for Rome, Quintus Fabius Maximus, already twice a consul, was appointed dictator. He adopted a firm strategy of avoiding battle with the Carthaginians unless there were conditions especially favorable for the Romans. Instead, he harassed Hannibal's army on the march, attacked detachments foraging for supplies, and looked for any opportunity to exploit some advantage. For this reason, he was mockingly dubbed "the Delayer" (*Cunctator*). Fabius' strategy was most unpopular and incurred sharp criticism.

The consuls of 216 did not follow Fabius' strategy either. Instead, they marched against Hannibal with a combined army of Romans and allies that may have numbered as many as 80,000 soldiers. The battle they fought at Cannae in Apulia was a further Roman disaster; one of the consuls lost his life, and only a small fraction of the army escaped. Afterwards, some of Rome's allies began to change sides. The cities of Sabinum, Etruria, and Umbria largely remained Roman allies. In the south, however, many Samnites, Lucanians, and Bruttii either served as soldiers in Hannibal's army, or provided supplies for it, or fought against the Romans on their own. Capua in Campania, one of the largest cities in Italy and a Roman *municipium* for the past century, also joined Hannibal's alliance. In Sicily, Syracuse declared for Hannibal. In 212, he captured Tarentum, although a Roman garrison held out in a fort on the harbor, preventing the use of the only major port he would gain.

After the defeat at Cannae Rome remained resolute (Source 3.2), but its commanders reverted to avoiding battle with Hannibal's army, while harassing it and limiting its freedom of movement. At the same time, other Roman forces attacked disloyal cities and allies, too many in number for Hannibal to protect. In Sicily, Marcus Claudius Marcellus captured Syracuse in 213. Two years later, Capua fell, and the Roman commander then ordered the executions of the city's leading citizens and sold much of the population into slavery. In 209, the Romans recaptured Tarentum too, sacked it, and enslaved its inhabitants. After this date, Hannibal and his depleted army were more or less confined to Bruttium in the extreme south of Italy.

In the midst of the war in Italy, the magistrates and the senate searched for signs of divine disfavor and for ways to bring better fortune to Rome. They sought to introduce new gods to the city and gain their protection. In 205, after a series of distressing portents, the senate consulted Roman priests and the Greek oracle at Delphi. Both recommended bringing the Great Mother (*Magna Mater*) from her sanctuary in Asia Minor to Rome. So, in the following year, the goddess' cult image—a black meteorite—and some of her priests arrived in the city. However, the senate seems not to have realized what her worship entailed. The cult of the Magna Mater centered on self-castrated priests, ecstatic rites, and wild singing and dancing. In consequence, shocked Roman officials then saw to it that citizens were prevented from participating in the more disturbing forms of the cult.

SOURCE 3.2: *The second-century Greek historian Polybius offers this episode as a perfect illustration of Rome's extraordinary strength:*

After winning the battle of Cannae [in 216], Hannibal gained control of the 8,000 Romans guarding the camp. He made them all prisoners, and agreed to a deputation being sent home to discuss their ransom and release. . . . However, despite the major setbacks which the Romans had suffered on the battlefield, as well as the prospect that they were now losing in effect all their allies, together with the likelihood that Rome itself was in imminent peril, they did not react to what the delegation said by losing their dignity in the face of calamity, nor did they omit to consider all the appropriate concerns. They grasped that Hannibal's object was the desire to gain funds in this way, and at the same time to reduce his opponents' ardor for battle by demonstrating that the defeated still had a hope of release. They were so opposed to acting upon any of the delegation's requests that they even discounted sympathy for the men's relatives as well as their potential value to the Roman cause. Rather, they overturned both Hannibal's calculations and the hopes he based on them. They rejected ransom for the captives, and laid down the rule that in battle Rome's soldiers must either win or die, with no other hope of rescue if defeated. . . . Consequently, Hannibal's satisfaction at having defeated the Romans in battle was surpassed by his dismay at the steady resolve these men displayed in their discussions. (6.58.2–13)

A "second front" that Rome opened in Spain proved decisive, even though the effort to support armies and fleets there soon strained Roman resources (Map 3.3). Two brothers, Publius Scipio and Gnaeus Scipio, held command there from the opening year of the war until their deaths in battle in 211. Roman voters then assigned the Spanish command to another Publius Cornelius Scipio, in fact the son of Publius and the nephew of Gnaeus. In 209, he captured Carthago Nova, one of the chief centers of Carthaginian power (see Source 4.1). In the next year, he succeeded in crossing the mountains between the coast south of Saguntum and the headwaters of the Baetis River. In the latter area—a valley of vital importance to the Carthaginians—the remaining major battles of the war in Spain were fought. However, even though Hasdrubal, Hannibal's brother, was defeated by Scipio, he was then able to follow his brother's route into Italy and attempt to join their two armies. But in 207, at the Metaurus River along the Adriatic coast of Italy, his army was stopped and beaten, and he lost his own life, thus extinguishing any hope that significant reinforcements might reach Hannibal. By the end of 206, the Romans had overcome virtually all Carthaginian forces in Spain.

As consul in 205, Scipio had the task of preparing for the invasion of North Africa. In the following year, his army landed outside the city of Utica, not far north of Carthage, and with the help of the Numidian ruler Masinissa defeated the Carthaginians in battle. The Carthaginian leaders then summoned Hannibal back to Africa, and he obeyed even though he had to leave his army behind in Italy.

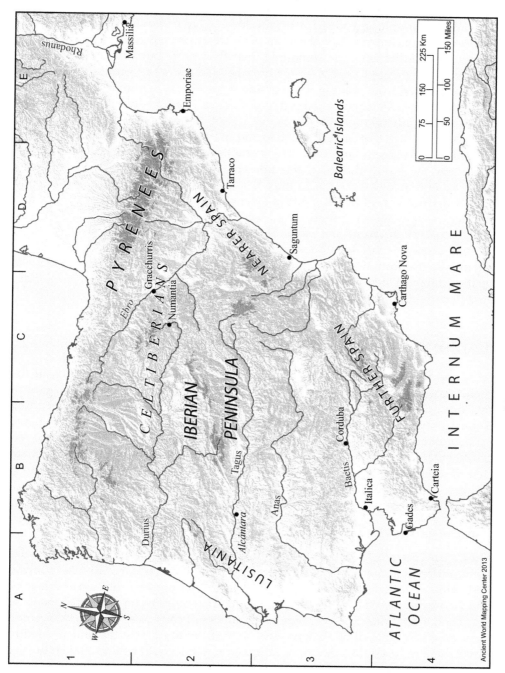

Map 3.3 *Iberian Peninsula*

Ancient World Mapping Center 2013

The decisive encounter between the Roman and Carthaginian forces occurred in 202 at Zama, where Scipio won another victory (see Map 3.1). He then returned to Rome for a lavish triumph, and added Africanus to his other names (see Source 3.1).

Peace was concluded in 201. The terms of the treaty severely restricted Carthaginian power. The Carthaginians surrendered their fleet, were burdened with crippling indemnity payments, lost all their territory beyond the core around Carthage, and were prohibited from waging war outside this territory without Roman permission. Meantime, Masinissa emerged as a staunch Roman ally with control of an enlarged Numidian kingdom.

Altogether, this prolonged war had imposed grave strains upon the Roman authorities, its citizens, and the citizens of allied states. Much of Italy was devastated. For the entire duration, the Romans had to maintain armies in Spain, Sardinia, and Sicily, as well as in Italy. The consequent need for numerous commands disrupted traditional political arrangements, while the many armies and the high casualty rates required an unusually large percentage of the male population to be drafted. To fill the ranks, Rome drafted even criminals and slaves. At Cannae, around eighty senators were said to have been killed; this depletion of the senate was so substantial that men who had never held office were chosen to make up its numbers. Despite all the setbacks, Rome emerged from the war with a dominant position in the central and western Mediterranean.

A MEDITERRANEAN EMPIRE

After the Second Punic War, Roman power soon spread through much of the Mediterranean world. Once again, no single cause explains all the wars waged at this date. The governing elite seems to have had no clear plan for expanding Rome's power or for establishing its authority. Instead, it just seems to have made arrangements piecemeal as it responded to the unfolding of events. Moreover, despite the Roman state's need for funds, there appears to have been no desire at first to promote the systematic exploitation of conquered communities' economic resources, although awareness of this type of potential would slowly gain ground.

Governors, Provinces, and Empire

During the Second Punic War and in the decades that followed, Roman armies were stationed in many places, often distant from Rome. Because Roman political and military leadership was closely tied to the tenure of a limited number of annual offices, these far-flung campaigns put great burdens on officeholders. First, the number of armies often exceeded the number of consuls and praetors. Second, some assigned areas of operations were so far from Rome that the time needed to travel there reduced the amount of campaigning that could be undertaken during the magistrate's year in office. Last but not least, generals operating in ever more distant theaters of operation effectively gained greater freedom of action.

Some of these difficulties were met by increasing the number of high officials. After the Second Punic War it became the practice to elect four praetors one year, then six the next, alternately. In fact this number, in addition to the two consuls annually, still did not suffice to provide commanders for all Rome's armies; nevertheless, expansion of the number of officeholders ceased until the first century B.C. Tenure in these offices, after all, was the primary route to fame and glory, and to continue increasing the number of occupants meant diluting their prestige.

To meet the increased demand for commanders, the Romans also resorted to extending the terms of some officials, a procedure known as "prorogation." In the late fourth century and during the First Punic War, a few officials with a limited task to complete had occasionally continued in office for a short time after their magistracies had expired. In their additional period of service, such officeholders were known as *proconsul* or *propraetor*, because each served in place of a consul or a praetor. During the Second Punic War, when the need for commanders was high, the practice became more common, and commands were sometimes extended for a year or more. After this war, prorogation became a regular practice. Prorogued officials had a different legal status from those actually in their year of office, and they had no authority in Rome itself. Commands were extended in one of two ways. On some occasions, voting assemblies extended the commands of serving officials or even assigned provinces to private citizens, where they were to serve as promagistrates; on other occasions, the senate did likewise on its own authority. During and after the Second Punic War, it was most common for the senate to act.

More generally, the senate took the lead in the conduct of wars and diplomacy. It received ambassadors from other states. It also took the primary responsibility for assigning duties to officials. Each year, senators decided the tasks that would be divided among the new consuls and praetors. After the election, the new consuls cast lots to determine the assignment each would have, while the new praetors shared out their tasks in the same fashion. Alternatively, the members of each group could determine assignments by mutual agreement before lots were cast, a process known as *comparatio*.

Roman officials abroad often had considerable freedom of action to wage war, make alliances, and set the terms of peace—perhaps greater freedom than many senators found desirable. Sometimes the senate refused to accept treaties that a commander had negotiated, leaving his successor to establish new arrangements. The most persistent problem, however, concerned charges of extortion and corruption. In the late third and second centuries, prosecutions for official misconduct, such as cowardice, incompetence, and corruption, served as the primary means of controlling an official's behavior in office (see Chapter Four), but such prosecutions could take place only after an official had returned to Rome and laid down his office.

Engagement beyond Italy grew steadily during the second century, but still this extension of Roman power and influence developed very unevenly and with much variation, as officials and the senate responded to events. The Roman elite did not believe its leadership to be restricted to the regions—more or less well-defined—where Rome happened to be maintaining armies. Whenever a community surrendered or put itself under Rome's protection (see Source 2.1), magistrates and the senate thought that it thereby became part of the *imperium* of the Roman people. Although this word is the root of the English "empire," the Latin term does not denote a clearly delimited territory, nor does it imply any administrative responsibilities by the victors or prescribed duties by the defeated.

The creation of "provinces" was the main vehicle for Roman expansion. In modern English, a province usually denotes a subdivision of a larger state or country with well-defined borders and a capital of its own. In time, the Latin term *provincia* would gain this meaning too, but for a long period it did not denote anything so fixed. In the late third and early second centuries, and probably earlier, the term merely denoted the sphere of operations given to a Roman official, defined by task and location. Provinciae could be short-lived and ill-defined. A consul's or praetor's provincia was primarily military in character, although gradually, in the longer-lasting provinces, commanders took on other tasks, such as arbitrating disputes between cities and hearing legal cases.

At the beginning of the second century, the Roman state lacked the institutions or the administrative apparatus needed to exploit thoroughly the regions that were in some way its dependencies. Outside of Italy, the Romans slowly adopted different practices as they began to develop more financial sophistication. To gain necessary supplies and funds, governors would now impose payments of tribute on some communities and individuals, and require the contribution of supplies by others; any funds or items demanded had to be gathered together by the communities themselves. Meantime, certain especially favored cities and persons would be freed from all but the most extraordinary demands. In addition, state contractors or *publicani* were active outside of Italy, although the extent of their operation is unclear. From at least the 170s, Roman magistrates, acting on decrees of the senate, leased to private contractors the exploitation of certain lands and resources. Towards the end of the second century, officials in Rome would also arrange contracts for the collection of taxes and rents from entire provinces and cities; this was to become the most prominent and controversial function of publicani in the first century.

Spain

To judge from its actions, the senate seems to have had no well-defined notion of how to proceed in Spain following the end of the Second Punic War. Some senators may have wished to disengage, but Rome had become too entangled in the affairs of the peninsula to leave easily. Other senators were evidently eager to punish communities that they thought had betrayed Rome or had proven to be especially bitter enemies; Roman commanders did in fact take such punitive action over several years. Roman officials also had allies and interests to protect, and these allies often attempted to persuade Rome to intervene in struggles with their neighbors. Towards the end of his time in Spain, Scipio Africanus had settled some of his wounded veterans at Italica—not far from modern Seville in the lower valley of the Baetis River—probably to guard against any return by the Carthaginians. This town would become a major center of Roman power. From the start, it was a mixed settlement with firm local roots. The Roman and Italian veterans who formed the core of its population sought wives locally. For almost forty years, Spain received praetors as commanders. The senate usually assigned two provinciae: Nearer Spain (*Hispania Citerior*), centered on Tarraco and the lower Ebro Valley; and Further Spain (*Hispania Ulterior*), the valley of the Baetis River. Away from the coast and the Baetis Valley, Roman commanders found it difficult to establish control over the scattered population or to form any lasting ties of alliance and subordination. Some attempted to found settled communities as a means of gaining control.

From the middle of the 150s, warfare became more serious and larger in scale, and the senate often assigned provinciae to consuls. These wars centered on two groups, the Lusitanians and the Celtiberians. The Lusitanians inhabited the region to the northwest of the Baetis Valley and to the southwest of the central plateau crossed by the Tagus and Anas rivers (modern Tejo and Guadiana). In 150, Servius Sulpicius Galba, invading from Further Spain, persuaded some Lusitanians to surrender, but he then massacred thousands and sold the survivors as slaves. This treachery helped Viriathus (who had escaped the massacre) to emerge as a powerful leader of both his fellow Lusitanians and other disaffected groups in Spain. He defeated several Roman armies. Eventually in 139, Quintus Servilius Caepio arranged for Viriathus' assassination. As a result, peace was made with the Lusitanians the following year.

At about the same time, the Romans also entered into a lengthy series of wars with the Celtiberians. Their settlement at Numantia occupied a strong position on a high ridge in the upper reaches of the valley of the Durius River (modern Douro). In the 150s, 140s, and 130s, no less than five Roman consuls commanding in Nearer Spain made unsuccessful attacks on it, and two of them had to negotiate peace terms, which the senate later rejected, in order to secure the safe withdrawal of their armies. Publius Cornelius Scipio Aemilianus, the victor over Carthage in the Third Punic War (see North Africa section) and chosen consul for the second time for 134, finally put an end to this war. After an eight-month siege, the Numantines—reported as numbering 4,000—surrendered to Scipio in 133.

Through all these wars, Roman arrangements in Spain were becoming more settled and more profitable to the Roman state. Parts of Spain became the home of Romans and Italians, not to mention others who claimed Roman or Italian ancestry. Around 160, Marcus Claudius Marcellus founded Corduba (modern Córdoba), another mixed settlement like Italica, farther up the Baetis River. In the decades immediately following the end of the Second Punic War, Roman financial arrangements in Spain had been haphazard at best. Earlier, in 180, Tiberius Sempronius Gracchus in Nearer Spain tried to specify more clearly the obligations of allied communities under his authority and to regularize their financial contributions. By mid-century, some communities in both provinces provided 5 percent of their grain each year, while others paid a fixed sum of money. Even so, there was no single system that regulated all of Rome's Spanish subjects.

Over time, the Romans also began to exploit Spain's mineral resources more systematically. Mines on the fringes of the Baetis Valley and in the hills behind Carthago Nova certainly proved lucrative. The latter mines are said to have extended over an area of about one hundred square miles (260 sq km), where 40,000 miners recovered enough silver each day to provide the Roman state with as much as 10,800 pounds (4,900 kg) of ore annually. We are told that Italians exploited these mines, using a vast workforce of slaves who toiled day and night under horrific conditions and frequently died from exhaustion.

Greece and Asia Minor

After the end of the Second Punic War, the Romans also began to intervene more regularly in the politics and diplomacy of the Balkans and Asia Minor (Map 3.4). The eastern Mediterranean was a bewildering mix of kingdoms, tribal states, cities, and leagues of cities, all with shifting alliances and enmities. Three kingdoms tended to dominate. First, the kings of Macedon had long sought to extend their power over the Greek cities of the south, the islands of the Aegean, and neighboring kingdoms in the Balkans. Second, the Seleucids of Syria had once ruled an extensive state that reached from the Mediterranean to the frontiers of India, but by now much of it had fallen away from them. Third, the Ptolemies of Egypt fought Syria for control over Palestine; with their powerful fleet, they also dominated and protected some of the islands in the Aegean, and they often intervened in the affairs of cities on the Greek mainland. Around these three great monarchies, there were many lesser states, sometimes allied with larger ones and commonly on the lookout to pursue their own advantage. Unlike in Spain, the Romans would employ elaborate diplomatic and administrative protocol to confront these well-established and powerful states to the east; consequently this gave Roman intervention here a very different character.

The First Macedonian War (215–205) grew out of the Second Punic War. After Rome's defeat at Cannae in 216, Philip V, the Macedonian king, probably suspicious of Roman interventions across the Adriatic, began to negotiate with Hannibal. Discovery of their alliance led to war between Rome and Macedon. Rome gradually assembled a coalition of cities, leagues, and kings. The two most important were the Aetolian League—communities in western Greece that elected leaders, made war as a group, and were feared as pillagers—and Pergamum in western Asia Minor, a long-time enemy and rival of Macedon, ruled by King Attalus I. This coalition of allies did not make war according to a common strategy, nor did the Romans, with so many commitments elsewhere, pursue the war vigorously. In 206, Philip and the Romans made peace, the so-called Peace of Phoenice, in which both sides essentially kept what they held.

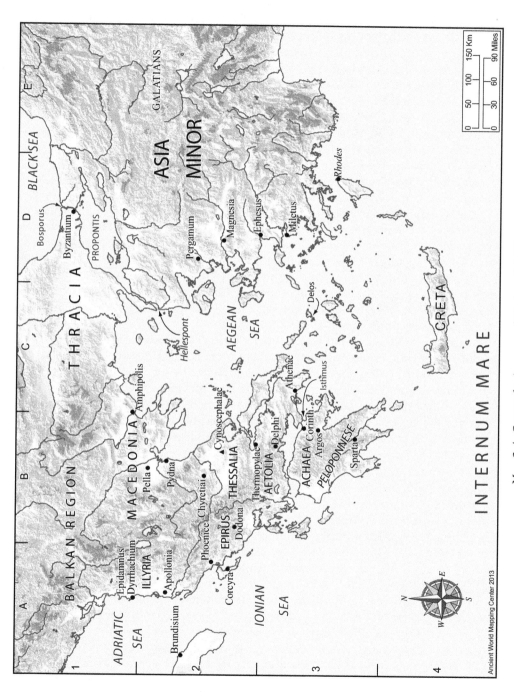

Map 3.4 *Greece, the Aegean, and Western Asia Minor*

The Second Macedonian War (200–196) marked the beginning of the next stage of Roman intervention. Immediately after the end of the war with Carthage, Rome's former ally Attalus of Pergamum, together with some Greek cities, successfully urged intervention in Greece, a plea that must have gained strength from resentment among the Roman elite over Philip's earlier alliance with Hannibal. Titus Quinctius Flamininus, consul in 198 and proconsul for several years after, was able to defeat Philip's army at Cynoscephalae in 197. In the peace that followed, Philip agreed to withdraw his garrisons from Greek cities, surrender most of his fleet, and pay Rome a large indemnity. Shortly afterwards, the senate ceased assigning *provinciae* in this area.

Unlike in Spain, the Roman senate could be thought to have had no desire for a permanent military presence among the Greeks. It would be a mistake, however, to infer that consequently Rome's leaders did not regard themselves as preeminent here. After his victory, Flamininus proclaimed the freedom of a number of Greek cities at the Isthmian Games, where thousands had gathered for the festival. Proclamations of freedom had a long and honored place in Hellenistic diplomacy, and Flamininus' decree shows how Romans adapted themselves to local practices while maintaining their own leadership. Such "freedom" usually meant no foreign garrisons, no tribute, and no change to existing laws; however, it did not mean that the newly freed city could also omit to acknowledge the leadership of a larger and more powerful state.

Subsequent events would reveal how seriously the senate took its claims to leadership. The first major military intervention following the Second Macedonian War came shortly after the withdrawal of Roman armies. Antiochus III, king of Syria, had restored much of the grandeur and power of the Seleucid dynasty. While Rome was engaged with Philip V, Antiochus had extended his power in Asia Minor, largely surrounding the small kingdom of Pergamum. The Syrian War (192–189) began when Antiochus sent a small force across the Aegean Sea to Greece. In 191, one of the consuls defeated Antiochus and his allies at Thermopylae. In the next year, the senate sent a commander with an army and a fleet across the Aegean, where they joined forces with Eumenes, who had succeeded Attalus as king of Pergamum. Finally in 189, Lucius Cornelius Scipio, the brother of Africanus, defeated Antiochus' army at Magnesia. Antiochus had to abandon all his claims to Asia Minor, refrain from making alliances in and around the Aegean, surrender most of his ships, and pay an exceptionally large indemnity. In Asia Minor, Roman officials then divided Antiochus' territory among Eumenes and other allies.

The Romans followed this victory with a campaign against the Galatians, Gallic migrants who had entered Asia Minor in the previous century and had for decades posed a threat to the kings of Pergamum as well as to settled communities throughout the region. The campaign was highly successful, devastating many of the communities of the Galatians and forcing them to accept peace on Roman terms. Within a few years, the senate again assigned no more *provinciae* in Greece, the Balkans, and Asia Minor for some time.

A primary goal in these wars was stability in Greece, together with preservation of Rome's position in the Greek world. Roman forces returned to Greece because Antiochus III appeared to be challenging Rome's leadership there, and because some of Rome's allies seemed to be willing to join him. Such a desire to lead, but not necessarily to rule or to exploit systematically, evidently lay behind other Roman actions in the area. At first, it would seem, the senate attempted to assert Roman preeminence largely through diplomatic means in line with the Greek world's complicated political and diplomatic culture.

The Third Macedonian War (171–168) ended the Macedonian monarchy. For years, prominent Romans had distrusted Philip's son and successor, Perseus, and were willing to listen to complaints against him. Perseus' marriage to a daughter of Seleucus IV, Antiochus' successor as king of Syria, no doubt increased their suspicions. In 172, Eumenes of Pergamum came to Rome with a long list of complaints against Perseus, and, with these as pretexts, the senate decided on war. The result was that in 168 Lucius Aemilius Paullus defeated Perseus at Pydna, where he had concentrated his army. The terms of the peace were severe. Perseus was transported to Rome, where he was paraded in Paullus' triumph. Macedon was divided into four regions, each with its own assembly and elected officials. The king's lands and mines became Rome's property. Altogether, Roman preeminence was forcefully asserted (Source 3.3).

At this period the small island of Delos emerged as one of the great commercial centers of the Aegean and the chief place of business for many Italian *negotiatores* (singular, *negotiator*), individuals who were at once speculators, merchants, and financiers. At the end of the Third Macedonian War, Roman officials punished the city of Rhodes by removing Delos—sacred to the god Apollo and the site of an important sanctuary—from its control and transferring it to Athens. Merchants, ship owners, and bankers began to concentrate on the island, and their number increased sharply after the destruction of Corinth in 146 (see below). Later in the century, the merchants of Delos took a pivotal role in the transshipment of slaves—captured by pirates, often with the connivance of kings—from the eastern Mediterranean to Italy.

Roman armies intervened again less than twenty years after the end of the Third Macedonian War. In 149, Andriscus, who claimed to be a son of Perseus, declared himself king of Macedon. In the next year, Quintus Caecilius Metellus (later known as Macedonicus) defeated the self-proclaimed monarch and ended his reign. From this time onwards, the senate regularly assigned Macedon as a *provincia*. Roman commanders there spent much of their time guarding against incursions made by Balkan peoples to the north; these were wars that Rome now inherited from Macedonian monarchs. By contrast, the commanders in Macedon probably did not intervene much in the affairs of the Greek cities to their south and east. In 148, however, the senate did assert itself against the Achaean League to the south, ordering it to give independence to some cities under its control. When the Achaeans refused to comply, war began. In 146, Lucius Mummius defeated the League's army and captured Corinth, one of the richest and most famous cities in

---

SOURCE 3.3: *A memorable act of diplomatic bravado in 168 by the Roman senate's envoy Gaius Popillius Laenas sufficed to forestall an invasion of Egypt (under the rule of King Ptolemy VI) launched by King Antiochus IV of Syria. Strictly speaking, Rome had no right to intervene here, but by this date the senate had become concerned with relations between the states of the entire eastern Mediterranean and the balance of power there. In the aftermath of Rome's shocking defeat of King Perseus of Macedon at Pydna earlier the same year, Antiochus could only acknowledge that it would be suicidal for him to persist with his invasion of Egypt against the senate's wishes. Polybius narrates:*

Just as Antiochus was approaching Ptolemy in order to gain possession of Pelusium [entry-point to Egypt at the eastern end of the Nile delta], the Roman commander Popillius—being hailed with a greeting by the king, who held out his hand—had the document containing the senate's decree ready and so passed it to him, directing Antiochus to read it first. . . . The king, having read the decree, said that he would like to communicate the circumstances to his advisers. Popillius' reaction was to do something that seemed severe and utterly outrageous. Taking a stick of vine-wood that he had in his hand, he used it to draw a line around Antiochus and instructed him to give his reply to the document from within this circle. The king was amazed at such assertion of authority by this means, but after brief hesitation declared that he would comply with all the Romans' demands. With handshakes Popillius' entire entourage then greeted him warmly. The document ordered him to abandon his war against Ptolemy at once. So, within the period that he was permitted, he led his forces back to Syria, aggrieved and protesting, but for the time being submitting to the situation. (29.27.1–9)

Greece. As a dire warning to other Greeks, he then plundered and destroyed it, and sold many of its citizens into slavery.

North Africa

To the west, Roman armies and fleets were waging war against Carthage at the same time. The Third Punic War (149–146) began as a result of longstanding quarrels between the Carthaginians and Masinissa, king of the Numidians. For years, he had been making provocative demands of the Carthaginians, and in the resulting arbitrations, Roman ambassadors had generally supported the Numidian king. For equally long, too, some leading Romans had not hesitated to voice the enmity and suspicion they felt towards Carthage. In particular, according to one tradition, for several years before Rome finally declared war, Cato the Elder ended every speech he made in the senate with the demand that Carthage must be destroyed. Eventually, the exasperated Carthaginians used force to resist Numidian claims, and the senate made this step the cause for war in 149.

For over two years, Roman forces besieged the city. It was not until early in 146 that, under the leadership of Scipio Aemilianus (grandson through adoption of Scipio Africanus), they were able to force their way inside. In days of street fighting, they killed thousands of Carthaginians, enslaved many thousands more, and completely destroyed the city. Afterwards, Scipio and his senatorial advisors imposed heavy penalties on the Punic cities that had remained loyal to Carthage, while rewarding those that had changed sides. From now onwards too, the senate regularly assigned Carthage's former territory here as a provincia called "Africa." This destruction of Corinth and Carthage during the same year marked the end of an era in Roman expansion; Roman historians later would believe that both events also signaled the beginning of Rome's moral decline.

SUGGESTED READINGS

Erskine, Andrew. 2010. *Roman Imperialism*. Edinburgh: Edinburgh University Press. Concise analysis with marked attention to the second century B.C., followed by extracts from key sources in translation.

Gruen, Erich S. 1984. *The Hellenistic World and the Coming of Rome*. Berkeley, Los Angeles, London: University of California Press.

Hoyos, Dexter (ed.). 2011. *A Companion to the Punic Wars*. Malden, Mass.: Wiley-Blackwell.

Richardson, J. S. 1986. *Hispaniae: Spain and the Development of Roman Imperialism, 218–82 B.C.* Cambridge: Cambridge University Press.

4

ITALY AND EMPIRE

After the Second Punic War, Roman power spread throughout much of the Mediterranean world. This expansion was accompanied by major changes in the social, political, and cultural life of Rome and many other Italian communities, as a result of the burdens of military service, the great wealth acquired through conquest, the consequent movements of people, and the deeper exposure to foreign ideas and practices. The first half of the second century marked the high point of the domination of the state by the senate and the nobility. Thereafter, in the third quarter of the century, a steady accumulation of political tensions and divisions would lead to the emergence of new forms of political activity that would undermine the senate's leadership.

SENATORS, OFFICIALS, AND CITIZEN ASSEMBLIES

During this heyday of power and prestige for the senate and the nobility, it was the norm for members of a relatively few families to hold the offices of consul and censor. At the same time, the consensus of senators, expressed in the form of decrees, exercised a strong influence over policy making. In the second century, the 300 senators were chosen from former officeholders, and each senator, once chosen, served for life unless he was convicted in court, or unless a subsequent pair of censors dropped him from the senatorial roll for some moral failing. When an officeholder consulted the senate, senators registered their opinion in the form of an advisory decree or *senatus consultum*, rather than an order, because the formal role of the senate was to advise. Senatorial decrees were not determined by a strict majority vote. Instead, leading senators or *principes* (singular, *princeps*)—the members who generally had held the highest offices, belonged to the leading families, and had acquired the greatest fame and glory—sought to create a broad consensus for or against policies and individuals.

Since the late fourth century, the senate had taken for itself a wide range of rights and privileges that enabled its members to exercise considerable influence over public affairs. In the years following the Second Punic War, the senate determined the tasks that magistrates would perform, fixed the funds that governors would receive to finance their operations, selected the magistrates whose terms in office would be extended, and ruled on the acceptability of treaties that generals in the field had negotiated. Altogether, the senate's place in the Roman political order rested on its great prestige and authority. At the same time, however, the fact is that the senate lacked any specific power to command, to punish, to enact laws, or to implement policies.

By law and by custom, Rome's "government" corresponded to the officeholders who were elected to fill specific posts for limited periods of time. Only they could call meetings of the senate and of citizen assemblies, hear legal cases and issue judgments, command armies, and perform public ceremonies. In the city, their ability to act could be obstructed by certain other officials and priests. Higher magistrates did not command or instruct lesser magistrates in Rome, although they could forbid them to act in specific cases. Consuls and praetors could each block the actions of colleagues who held the same office and possessed identical powers, but they could do this only when present personally on the spot. Within the city, tribunes of the plebs could likewise block any magistrate's action, but once again personal intervention was a requirement.

In the city, too, state religion forced many magistrates to adhere closely to established procedures; on occasion, religion could equally serve to check their activities. In particular, when consuls and praetors were in Rome, a wide range of mandatory rituals surrounded their public actions. Moreover, omissions or flaws could have serious consequences. If colleges of priests found fault, and if the senate concurred, the official's act would be declared invalid. On other occasions, even a single augur could order the postponement of a public meeting, for example, if he announced that he had seen signs that the gods desired such a delay. This right of priests and the senate to nullify magisterial actions in the city did not extend to the tribunes of the plebs.

However, the tribunes of the plebs, who had once mobilized citizens against the governing elite during the Struggle of the Orders (see Chapter Two), had become more a part of the established order. In the early second century tribunes generally put forward proposals that had already met with senatorial approval, or blocked actions by magistrates in the city that were known to displease many senators. Few officials defied a senatorial consensus for long. To be sure, the senate's decrees were only advisory, and it could not formally compel obedience, yet still the great majority of officials largely followed its wishes. The senate collectively, and leading senators individually, could obstruct the political advancement of senators who had isolated themselves too much from the majority of members.

Only the senate could grant triumphs, for example—essential distinctions to maintain a commander's fame and glory (see Chapter Three). Candidates for office, moreover, required allies in the senate at election time, and the more prestigious these allies were, the better. Last but not least, the senate's assumption of the power to assign tasks to each group of officials annually allowed it to exercise great influence.

Meantime it should not be forgotten that some of the governing elite were concerned to prevent popular senators from overshadowing their peers by too wide a margin. Senators after all, especially the most prominent among them, were participants in a constant competition for fame and glory. Officials made attempts therefore—probably with the support of most senators—to limit an individual's ability to stand out too far above his peers (see Chapter Two). Limits on the number of times that anyone could hold high office were clearly a key restriction in this respect.

However, during the decades following the Second Punic War a series of laws did now attempt to force senators' careers into a more regular, obligatory pattern. It became a formal requirement that anyone who stood for election as quaestor (the lowest senatorial office) had to have already completed ten years of military service. Moreover, the offices were formed into a fixed hierarchy, within which individuals had to advance step by step from lesser offices to higher. A law enacted after the Second Macedonian War made it mandatory that anyone seeking election as consul must have already served as praetor. In 180, a tribune, Lucius Villius, successfully proposed the first law fixing the minimum age at which the offices of praetor and consul could be held, and requiring that at least ten years must elapse before a holder of either office should be able to hold the same one again. Later, after this interval had not been observed when Marcus Claudius Marcellus gained the consulship for the third time in 152, further legislation prohibited holding the office of consul more than once. Altogether, the eventual result was the development of a standard *cursus honorum* or hierarchy of senatorial offices within which contemporaries competed against one another to move up from quaestor to praetor to consul, and even censor. At each stage, of course, more competitors would fail to advance, because successively fewer positions were available.

Threats of prosecution were the sole check on the actions of officials when away from the city of Rome. In practice, only a limited number of perceived offenses against public order were investigated. In the late third and second centuries, prosecutions for official misconduct—charges such as cowardice, incompetence, and corruption—generally took place before assemblies of citizens, who would vote on the fate of the defendants. From the second century onwards, prosecutions of former officials in fact became a common feature of the Roman political order. Trial hearings offered a natural opportunity for a prominent citizen's rivals to try to damage his prestige, and many leading senators faced multiple prosecutions in the course of their careers. Even Scipio Africanus eventually withdrew from public life to avoid further such harassment.

From 149, a series of laws began to create permanent courts—so-called *quaestiones perpetuae*—to try certain specific offenses by magistrates and senators.

In that year, a tribune, Lucius Calpurnius Piso, carried a law establishing such a court to hear charges of extortion in the provinces (see Chapter Five): accusers presented their cases to juries chosen from members of the senate, who would then issue verdicts that could not be appealed. Later, similar permanent courts for other offenses would be established, in some of which it was permissible to prosecute non-senators, too. In time, as we shall see, the question of who should make up the juries of all the permanent courts would become a contentious political issue.

ITALY AND THE CONSEQUENCES OF EMPIRE

Italy had long been a land with marked regional differences in language, economic and social organization, and political and religious life. By the end of the Second Punic War, communities with Roman citizenship were concentrated in Latium, Campania, southernmost Etruria, Sabinum, and a few adjacent areas along the Adriatic coast; those cities possessing full citizenship were mostly nearer to Rome than those with only partial citizen rights. Both levels of citizen community still also maintained much of their original culture, although they did adapt themselves to some Roman forms and procedures. Citizen communities aside, substantial regions of Italy—for example, most of Etruria, Umbria, Lucania, Samnium, Bruttium, and the Greek cities of the south—all remained as allies with their own customs and practices, but no Roman citizen rights.

During the second century, however, much of Italy experienced profound changes that disrupted long-established political and social practices. Some of the changes stemmed from wartime devastation and from the harsh peace that Rome forced on disloyal allies. Others derived from the movements of people within the peninsula made possible by the greater integration of Italian communities. Still others were consequences of the vast influx of wealth stemming from Rome's wars outside of Italy. At the same time, as the result of warfare, diplomacy, and business dealings, members of the elite throughout Italy gained a closer familiarity with Greece and Asia Minor; the societies they encountered here were older, wealthier, and more complex, and offered attractive models to emulate in many respects.

Changing Relations Between Rome, Its *Municipia*, and Allies

The Second Punic War and its aftermath imposed severe strain on Rome's network of alliances and cities with shared citizenship. Some remained loyal, but at great cost in lost lives, devastated land, and increased internal political tensions. Others abandoned their relationship with Rome, and sought greater freedom of action in an alliance with Hannibal and Carthage. When Rome recaptured the cities of former allies, its commanders unflinchingly ordered the executions of leading citizens and the enslavement of many others. In the course of the arrangements made after the end of the war, moreover, many communities in southern Italy suffered massive confiscations of land, which badly hurt their citizens and

Figure 4.1 *Late in the second century, a number of objects associated with the worship of Dionysus were placed in a votive deposit just outside the north gate of the Etruscan city of Vulci. Among them were a terracotta statue of a seated Dionysus and a small terracotta model of a temple. The two reclining figures in the pediment of the temple represent Dionysus and Ariadne in a sacred union.*

their economies. In the Po Valley and in peninsular Italy, Roman officials conducted large-scale settlement projects after the Second Punic War, in particular settling veterans of campaigns in Spain, Sicily, and North Africa on some of the land confiscated from allies who had rebelled or were considered untrustworthy.

During the war with Hannibal and for two decades after its end, the senate had regularly instructed Roman officials to search out signs of disloyalty in some allied cities and to punish those suspected of it. This task was by definition intrusive, and, on occasion, such officials' actions may well have been harsh. Attempts to search out perceived threats to good order wherever they might be found were not limited to charges of assisting Rome's enemies. Three times between 184 and 179, the senate assigned to praetors the task of investigating the many poisonings said to be taking place. For the Romans, the crime of poisoning (*veneficium*) included not only doing harm through drugs or potions, but also causing injuries through magic and the casting of spells; it was, thus, a category of offense readily open to rumor and panic.

Another series of investigations may have been even more intrusive and extensive. In 186, Roman officials and senators became disturbed by the practices and wide diffusion of the cult of the god Bacchus, the Greek Dionysus. This Bacchic cult was deeply entrenched in the cities of Campania and the south, but its devotees could also be found in Rome and other cities (Fig. 4.1). Worship of Bacchus often involved groups with no official sanction, outside of a city's normal religious and political framework. Moreover, in these rites there could be shouting, frenzied dancing, the use of cymbals and drums, drinking, and some sexual license. In Rome itself, the cult may have become more active in recent years, mixing men and women, some from prominent families, and performing nocturnal rites in secret.

Spurius Postumius Albinus, one of the consuls of 186, began the investigation after receiving reports that worshippers included ritual murders and poisonings in their nocturnal rites. The senate then issued a decree ordering a search for Bacchic priests in both Rome and the rest of Italy, forbidding initiates to gather for rites, and instructing investigators to seek out criminals and performers of immoral acts. Lesser officials were to guard against nocturnal meetings and fire, always a danger in a crowded city such as Rome. Other provisions of this decree ordered the dismantling of shrines, prohibited the mixing of men and women on ritual occasions, forbade men to be priests, and banned secret rites and the swearing of oaths.

An expansion of full Roman citizenship and a hardening of the distinctions between Romans and non-Romans accompanied greater Roman surveillance over local affairs in Italy. Among Romans, the chief division had been between residents of municipia with the right to vote in Roman elections and residents of communities without this right. Over much of the third and second centuries, full citizenship with voting rights was gradually extended to more cities that had not previously possessed it. By the end of the second century, in all probability only a few citizen communities would still not have gained the right to vote. Early in the same century, the right of Latins to take up Roman citizenship by moving to Rome was progressively restricted. One remarkable incident exposes changed perceptions of the relationship between Rome and its Italian allies. In 173, the consul Lucius Postumius Albinus, while traveling to Campania on official business, sent a message ahead to Praeneste (an allied city in Latium) instructing its officials to come out to meet him (a mark of special honor), to prepare to accommodate and entertain him at their own expense, and to provide pack animals for his baggage. This was unprecedented arrogance.

At the same time, the Romans seem to have gradually shifted more of the burdens and fewer of the benefits of waging war to the Latins and other Italian allies. No doubt the Romans had always apportioned the burdens and benefits of warfare unequally, but there are signs now that allied communities were carrying more of the burdens for a smaller share of the profits. During the second century, the ratio of Roman citizens to Latins and other allies in Rome's armies varied between rough equality and two allies for each Roman. By the end of the century, however, allied contingents seem to have regularly outnumbered Roman ones. Increased differentiation between Rome and its Italian allies was accompanied by a greater imitation of Roman institutions and practices. Latin colonies, founded by Roman officials, had long been organized in a Roman manner. Now, some allied communities began to imitate Rome more closely. Especially in the south of Italy, more communities began to use Latin in official inscriptions, and the use of Roman law and Roman titles for offices increased.

Roman and Italian Elites

The political and social orders of Rome and its municipia and allies each rested on small groups of wealthy, prominent families who held magistracies and priesthoods and who filled out the ranks of the senate or its equivalent in the many smaller cities of Italy. In the second century, these ruling elites of Rome and of many other Italian cities grew richer through the profits of empire. They began to beautify their cities and to proclaim their position in them through public building projects on an ever-larger scale. They also came to adopt an increasingly similar way of life, strongly influenced by Hellenistic Greece.

SOURCE 4.1: *Plunder was a major source of wealth for commanders and soldiers alike, and the Romans developed highly formalized ways of acquiring it and distributing it. This passage from Polybius describes the manner in which the army of Scipio Africanus looted Carthago Nova in 209.*

When Scipio thought that a sufficient number of soldiers had entered the city, he sent most of them—as is the Roman custom—in pursuit of the inhabitants, with orders to kill everyone they encountered, sparing nobody, and not to start pillaging until the order was given. They do this, I think, to inspire terror, so that when cities are taken by the Romans, one may see not only the bodies of human beings, but also dogs, cut in half and the dismembered limbs of other animals. On this occasion, these scenes were many, because of the number of people in the city. . . . After this, once the signal was given, the massacre stopped and they began to plunder. At nightfall, those Romans who had received orders to remain in the camp did so, while Scipio with his thousand men camped in the citadel. Through the military tribunes he ordered the rest of the troops to leave the houses, and then instructed them to collect their plunder in the forum, unit by unit, and to guard it by sleeping there. . . . On the next day, the plunder collected in the forum was divided among the legions in the usual way. After capturing a city, the Romans deal with this matter as follows. Depending on the city's size, on some occasions a certain part of each unit and, on others, whole units are assigned to collect plunder, but never more than half of the army does this, the rest remaining under arms either inside the city or outside, ready for any trouble. . . . All the men who are ordered to plunder bring back what they have taken, each to his own legion, and, after this has been done, the military tribunes distribute the loot equally among everyone, including not only those in the protecting force, but also those guarding the camp, the sick, and anyone absent on a special assignment. (10.15.4–16.9)

The social orders of Italian towns and cities were complicated and hierarchical. Not all forms of wealth were considered equally honorable or desirable. The holders of magistracies based their wealth on land, on government, and on the profits of war (Source 4.1); by contrast, direct participation in trade, even on a fairly large scale, could threaten their status. Successful merchants sometimes sought to improve their own position and that of their descendants by abandoning trade and becoming landowners themselves. In Rome, moreover, senators were specifically barred from participating in trade and in holding public contracts as *publicani*. Even so, ways could be found around the limits imposed by law and custom. Finance, for example, was honorable if undertaken on a sufficiently large scale, and if the lending of money was divorced from any direct participation in the activities funded.

Status certainly affected the ways in which individuals could profit from Roman expansion. Roman magistrates and senators had the greatest opportunities and the greatest benefits. In Italy, transfers of wealth had long accompanied Roman warfare. The wars outside of Italy, in Greece and Asia Minor especially, resulted in seizures of property and enslavements on a scale that the Romans had never experienced before.

The vast influx of wealth into Italy changed the appearance of many cities and the ways of life of their leading families. Wealthy Romans now built elaborate private houses and financed the construction of temples, public buildings, and monuments in prominent locales (Fig. 4.2). Many members of the local elites that dominated the other cities (both citizen and allied) of the peninsula behaved in a similar manner, building houses—some of which rivaled royal palaces in size—and adorning their cities (Fig. 4.3). For many of these projects, architects and builders imitated a Hellenistic style of building in both private houses and public structures.

Imitation of the Greek world was not limited to styles of building. In the third and early second centuries, magistrates staging festivals had come to favor playwrights who imitated Greek styles. Later, participation in a Hellenizing literary and philosophical culture came to be a mark of elite status that linked individuals across communities. By the end of the Second Punic War, some members of Rome's elite were writing histories, at first in Greek and later in Latin too. During the second century, members of the leading families in Rome and many other Italian cities, eager for political careers, sought training in Greek rhetoric, the highly formal art of public speaking. Some more restricted circles began to find the study of Greek philosophy stimulating.

Greater wealth, more lavish lifestyles, and closer familiarity with Greek culture provoked a response among certain members of the

Figure 4.2 *The innovative design and costly materials of this temple in Rome dating to the late second century/ early first century* B.C. *reflect the growing fascination for Greek culture felt by many upper-class Romans. Neither the Roman who commissioned the temple, nor the deity to whom it was dedicated, can be identified, although the latter is likely to be Hercules with his links to commerce among other attributes. The temple—about 48 ft (14.8 m) in diameter—is situated in the Forum Boarium area of Rome (see Chapter One), close to the Tiber, and is the city's oldest surviving building in marble. In this instance it was specially imported from Greece, and was used both for facing the entire exterior of the circular structure and for its twenty Corinthian columns, 35 ft (10.6 m) in height. The temple suffered damage in antiquity as well as later, but owes its survival to conversion into a church; the roof and many of the columns are not original.*

Roman senate. Some—Cato the Elder was the most prominent—denounced luxury and, when in office, sought to limit it. Others were unsettled by Greek philosophy, which encouraged the questioning of fundamental truths, or by Greek rhetoric, since its techniques could be used to persuade without apparent regard for the moral value of a position. From time to time, therefore, magistrates and the senate ordered the expulsion of philosophers and teachers of rhetoric. Other prominent members of the Roman elite, however, clearly desired their presence, so that the expulsion of learned Greeks had little permanent effect.

Demographic and Economic Changes

The wars that established Roman leadership of the Italian peninsula had been accompanied by serious disruptions to population levels and settlement patterns. In the midst of this upheaval, Rome and a few other cities grew much larger. Firm statistics for Rome's population do not exist, and modern estimates have large margins for error, but it seems likely that, in the second century, several hundreds of thousands of people inhabited the city. They were highly diverse in class, in legal status, and in place of origin. Despite the prospect of advancement for some, much of Rome's population was still ill-housed and led only a marginal existence. Tensions between rich and poor seem to have become more pronounced.

The constant wars outside the peninsula added to the mobility of the population of Italy. Some sought opportunities in Spain or the east, while many served in Rome's armies there. Wars in distant places made military service more burdensome for some Romans and allies—perhaps 120,000 men in a typical year and, on occasion, even more. Absences of four to six years probably were common, with some men serving for over a decade. Military service on this scale and of this duration disrupted communal life and the organization of labor. Most of the soldiers in Rome's armies were small-scale farmers, and prolonged absences must have weakened their ability to maintain themselves and their families. Indeed, the pressures of

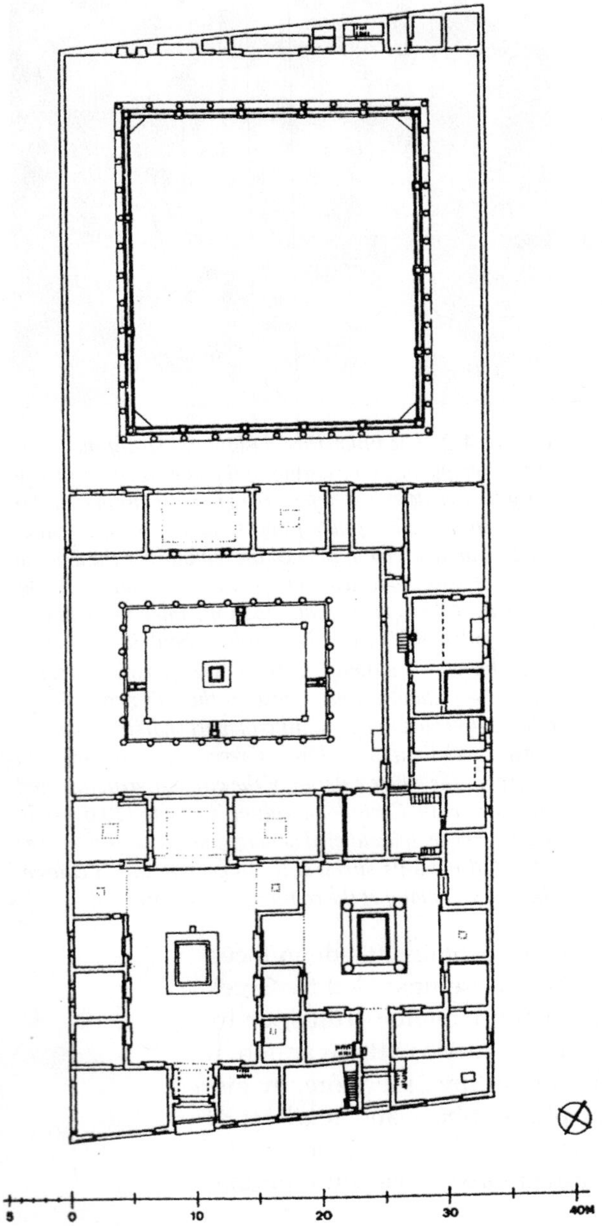

Figure 4.3 *The "House of the Faun" at Pompeii in Campania is one of the most elaborate second-century houses known in Italy. Later extended, it covers about 31,000 sq ft (2,800 sq m). The only known residences of comparable size at this date are royal ones, such as at Pella in Macedon. The lower part of the plan shows the house's two reception halls or atria; above them are its two peristyle courtyards. In all, this house, which probably belonged to a member of the local elite, is more reminiscent of Greek palaces and public buildings than of the earlier dwellings of central Italian aristocrats.*

military service may well have encouraged some to abandon the land and move to the cities.

Landowning on any scale is always dependent on the availability of labor to farm it. In the fourth and early third centuries, Rome's elite increasingly turned to slaves (who were not subject to conscription), either born and raised in the household, or taken in large numbers in Roman wars, or purchased from abroad, the victims of piracy and other people's wars. In addition, from the beginning of the second century, if not earlier, Roman landowners employed tenant farmers, sharecroppers, and occasional free laborers. In the second century, slavery in Italy became larger in scale and importance as Roman armies abroad forced larger numbers into slavery, and as more slaves became available.

Slavery in Italy was a complex phenomenon. Some slaves worked in the fields or guarded the herds and flocks of their owners. Others were servants in the households of the wealthy. Still others served as managers, accountants, and teachers. Masters typically employed skilled slave craftsmen to make products for domestic use and for sale in the market. For the more able or more fortunate, slavery might be only a temporary condition, although whether or not to free (or "manumit") a slave was always a decision for the owner alone. By Roman law, slaves were merely chattels with no rights; in practice, owners in Italy often permitted slaves to acquire personal property, and some purchased their freedom by this means. For others, freedom could come as a reward for services. In either case, freedmen—often employed as managers or business agents—and freedwomen were obligated to continue assisting and honoring their former owners. Very remarkably, according to Roman law, most slaves of Roman owners who gained manumission also acquired the status of Roman citizen at the same time, which could help to assimilate them and their children (if any) into the community.

During the second century, there are signs that the Roman elite, and perhaps also certain leading families of cities elsewhere in Italy, came to control more land than they had in the past and in more distant locations. Some land they gained by purchase or by marriage, or by taking for themselves land that the Romans had confiscated from their former enemies but had not yet assigned to any public purpose. On other occasions, these wealthy families expropriated the holdings of small-scale farmers who had moved to the city or were absent for long periods on campaign. The result was an agricultural economy with marked regional variations in crops, land tenure, and labor systems.

The use of slaves on a large scale had the potential to reduce Rome's grip on Italy. Hence in 185, Lucius Postumius Tempsanus was assigned to suppress an uprising in Apulia, where groups of slave shepherds were robbing people in the countryside; he is said to have condemned around 7,000 men to death, although many may have escaped execution. In the Roman world, pastoral slavery often was associated with brigandage. Slave shepherds, whose occupation made them difficult to supervise, were generally armed to protect their charges from carnivorous animals and thieves, and sometimes it was only by resorting to force that they could assert their right to use pastures and springs.

a   *b*

Figure 4.4 *There have been many random finds of lead slingshots used in Roman wars. Typically, such shots measure about 1.3 in (3.5 cm) long, and weigh 1.5 to 2 oz (40–60 g). They often carry brief inscriptions in relief—a war-cry, for example, a leader's name, or some insult to the enemy; these were incised in the clay molds within which the shots were made. The two shots illustrated were found in Sicily, both of them likely to have been fired by slaves resisting Roman armies in the two Slave Wars of the late second century B.C. Their inscriptions are in Greek: the first [a] proclaims NIKH ('Victory'); the second [b] is the name of a slave leader in the second war, in the genitive, with a qualifying noun to be understood: "Athenion's [shot]." See Chapter Five for this second war.*

The most alarming instance of the danger created by extensive use of slaves occurred in Sicily, in full view of the Roman elite. The First Slave War began around the city of Enna in the middle of the island. Eunus, its leader, a slave from Apamea-on-the-Orontes in Syria and a wonderworker who claimed the patronage of the Syrian goddess Atargatis, recruited a number of slave shepherds. One night in 136, he gathered them outside the city and encouraged them to break into the slave barracks on the estates that surrounded it, freeing the field slaves housed there, who were usually kept shackled. With this force of several hundred, he then broke into Enna, and began a massacre in which some slaves resident in the city joined. The next day, he declared himself to be king. A month later, another rebellion began around the city of Agrigentum, where more massacres took place. Eventually the rebellion spread to include about half of the island. Its suppression proved a long, hard task that was only completed in 132 (Fig. 4.4).

ROMAN POLITICS FROM THE MID-SECOND CENTURY

In the third quarter of the second century, a few members of Rome's governing elite began to base their position in the city more on their ability to court popularity and to mobilize crowds than on their standing with their fellow senators. Some of these men were charismatic military figures, eager to reach new offices and fresh heights of glory; others were more confrontational tribunes. In many ways, the shift they initiated represents a return to an older style of leadership, before the reforms of the late fourth and early third centuries began to elevate the senate above any individual officeholder. Both the growth of the city of Rome and the changes in the Italian countryside may have fueled the new development. The population of the city was now disturbed by starker contrasts between rich and poor, as well as by the presence of many people who had been forced through changes in the countryside to migrate to the city. As a result, crowds in Rome would have been larger, and their emotions more easily stirred.

In many ways, the institutional basis of the senate's position was weak. Its leadership depended on its high prestige and on the willingness of officeholders and candidates to abide by senatorial consensus in important matters. At the same time, by law officeholders possessed considerable powers of self-assertion, and, if they sought popular support, there was little to restrain them. Tribunes in particular possessed formidable powers to act, as well as to block the actions of others, should they wish to exercise this authority. From the late 150s, a few tribunes became notably more active. In 139, Aulus Gabinius enacted the first law requiring secret ballots, rather than having citizens declare their votes in full view of the city's leaders. Two years later, another tribune's proposal instituted the use of secret ballot for trial verdicts. During this period, figures such as Scipio Aemilianus and Tiberius and Gaius Gracchus would develop new styles of popular leadership, ones that would be much imitated in succeeding generations.

Scipio Aemilianus

Scipio Aemilianus was born in 185 or 184. His father was Lucius Aemilius Paullus, the victor over Perseus at Pydna, and his grandfather was one of the consuls defeated at Cannae in 216. He was adopted by Publius Cornelius Scipio, the son of Scipio Africanus, who had defeated Hannibal. Scipio Aemilianus first served as consul in 147. In the previous year, he had initially sought election as aedile. However, popular discontent over the failure of Rome's generals to win a quick victory in the Third Punic War created an opportunity that he exploited, and he switched his candidacy to the consular election, where his success was extraordinary. He was considerably below the minimum age for consul, and he had yet to hold the office of praetor; he was, in other words, just the kind of candidate that the laws sought to bar.

With the backing of the senate, the consul who presided over the elections duly sought to bar Scipio's candidacy. Widespread protests were then voiced in the assembly, and some in the crowd asserted that the people possessed the right to elect whomever they wished. When one of the tribunes announced his intention to prevent any vote unless the consul permitted Scipio to stand for office, the senate gave way, instructing the tribunes to put forward a law permitting this, on the understanding that the regular requirements would once again be upheld the following year. After the election, Gaius Livius Drusus, who was chosen to fill the other consular position, requested that lots be cast to determine their *provinciae*, the normal procedure. Again, a tribune intervened, proposing that a citizen vote determine the assignment of provinces. Accordingly, in this exceptional way Scipio was assigned the war against Carthage. There, he would prove very successful, destroying the city in 146 and earning the cognomen Africanus.

This election reveals some of the weaknesses of the senate's rule. Restrictions on eligibility for office—a vital means by which senators sought to protect themselves against their more popular peers—had force only so long as no one mobilized mass outrage against them and no tribune asserted the citizens' right to vote as they wished; in that event, angry crowds and obstinate tribunes could force magistrates and the senate to yield. Scipio's reputation for bravery and military skill, gained in Macedon, Spain, and North Africa, may have been the source of much of his popularity; but popular support, to be effective, must be organized and directed, as Scipio and his associates somehow achieved.

In 135, Scipio again sought election as consul. When he first stood for this office, Roman armies had proven unsuccessful against Carthage. Now, a series of Roman commanders had failed against Numantia in Spain. Once again, his tremendous military prestige helped him gain office. As in his first bid for the consulship, he also had to overcome a legal prohibition on his candidacy. After Marcus Claudius Marcellus had been consul for the third time in 152, a new law prohibited holding the office more than once. Scipio somehow found a way around the prohibition, and he was chosen consul for 134. The majority of senators then showed their dissatisfaction by refusing to vote him funds for the campaign in Spain, and by prohibiting him from drafting new soldiers. Scipio's spirited reaction was evidently to raise 4,000 men through voluntary contributions of troops by allied cities and by foreign kings who wished to gain or hold his favor; at the same time wealthy friends offered him funds. His campaign against Numantia was successful, increasing his prestige and glory still further.

In Scipio's day, a successful political career usually rested on the goodwill of one's fellow senators (gained largely through the exchange of favors), on some display of military prowess, and on popularity among the voters of the city. Individual senators were likely to possess such qualities in different proportions of course. Scipio proved to be one who often seemed indifferent to the wishes of a majority of his fellows. As a result, his career provoked sharp responses among his ostensible peers in the senate.

Tiberius Gracchus

Tiberius Sempronius Gracchus' tribunate in 133 marked a sharp break in Roman political development. Cicero, an orator and political figure of the next century, would later claim that his death divided the Roman people into two camps. Tiberius Gracchus came from a wealthy and powerful family. The Sempronii Gracchi had served as consuls from the mid-third century, and the tribune's father, the elder Tiberius Sempronius Gracchus, held the office twice (a rare honor at this time), triumphed twice, and served as censor. His wife, the mother of the later tribune, was Cornelia, the daughter of Scipio Africanus, the victor over Hannibal in the Second Punic War. After her husband's death around 150, she never remarried, and raised her two sons and a daughter alone. Some accused her of instilling in her sons great ambition and a love of fame, but these were traits that were widely admired among Rome's elite.

Soon after he began his term as tribune, Tiberius Gracchus introduced a law regulating the use of the "public lands of the Roman people" (*ager publicus populi Romani*), in other words, lands seized in Rome's various wars, but not yet distributed to settlers or leased to provide revenue. The core of the measure was an old law, long ignored, that limited to 500 *iugera* (about 300 acres or 120 hectares) the amount of "public" land that a single individual could exploit merely by occupying it. Use of such land in this manner was legal, but occupiers never legally gained ownership, and Roman magistrates and assemblies had the right, rarely exercised, to reclaim it if the state had need of it. Tiberius proposed to enforce this limit and confiscate the excess, which would then be distributed in small allotments to landless Roman citizens. As compensation for lost holdings, the law made the remaining portions of occupiers' holdings their private property and thus immune from further seizures and distributions.

The law's most innovative feature was also its most controversial. In the past, when senate and assemblies decided to found colonies or make assignments of captured land, they had chosen special magistrates who were to travel to the scene, supervise personally the division of the land into small plots, and assign them directly to the beneficiaries. Under this arrangement, such commissioners had limited powers of discretion. Tiberius' proposal likewise gave responsibility for enforcing its provisions to a group of three, but with wider powers. These commissioners were to be able to assign land to as many recipients as they could; at the same time, they possessed the power to determine themselves which lands were "public" and which private.

The Gracchan agrarian law aimed at resolving serious problems that the reformer and his associates thought threatened the state. He may well have considered the increase in the size and the number of slave-run estates to be both an injustice and a danger. The flight of small-scale farmers from the land lowered the number of potential recruits for Rome's army and increased the burdens of conscription—and the desire to resist them too—among those who remained on the land. The large number of slaves there was itself a threat, as the war with the slaves in Sicily so clearly indicated. Tiberius' proposal addressed both of these problems by breaking up certain estates and by settling the poor on small plots of land. At the same time, it should be noted, his reform would also remove large numbers of poor people from Rome, lessening the strain on urban institutions and removing a source of tension and instability. Other accounts, less friendly to the reformer, insist that he was motivated by a desire for fame and by rivalry with some of his contemporaries. The different versions are not incompatible.

Tiberius' reform attracted important supporters and intense opposition. Some accounts attribute this to a desire on the part of many senators to preserve their own landholdings. Political considerations may also have had a role. Securing the passage of welcome reforms would have increased Tiberius' popularity and prestige, and that could only irk his rivals for office (Source 4.2). In the face of senatorial opposition, Tiberius submitted his measure to the Plebeian assembly without first consulting the senate.

In the meetings that Tiberius called to explain his law and to mobilize support for it, another tribune, Marcus Octavius, emerged as his chief opponent. Octavius announced his intention to use his power as tribune to prevent a vote. In the past,

SOURCE 4.2: *From the specimen of Tiberius Gracchus' oratory that Plutarch preserves here, we gain a vivid glimpse of his skill in appealing to the emotions of the crowd at a time of tremendous tension in Rome.*

[Tiberius] certainly did not draft the law just by himself, but consulted citizens of outstanding merit and reputation, including Crassus the (future) *pontifex maximus*, the jurist (and consul at the time) Mucius Scaevola, and his own father-in-law Appius Claudius. Never, one might think, was a law aimed at such injustice and greed drafted more mildly and delicately. . . . But despite the tact with which matters were made right, and the readiness of the people to put the past behind them provided these wrongs would not recur, greed nonetheless led the men of wealth and property to detest the law and—in their rage and rivalry—its proposer. They attempted to change the minds of the people by arguing that Tiberius was introducing land redistribution to throw the state into turmoil and stir up revolution. Their efforts failed, however. The fact was that Tiberius—battling for a worthy, just cause with an eloquence capable of enhancing far less reputable ones—proved formidable enough to outclass any opponent whenever he took his position on the rostra and spoke about the poor, with the people thronging around him: "Every wild creature that lives in Italy has its own den and place to sleep and shelter. But the men who fight and die for Italy have a share in nothing more than its air and light. With their wives and children they roam homeless and unsettled. It's a lie when the commanders urge soldiers in battle to protect their graves and shrines from the enemy. Not one of them has a family altar, none of these Romans has an ancestral tomb. They go to war and die, rather, for the sake of others' wealth and luxury. 'Lords of the earth' they're hailed, but not one clod of it is theirs." (*Life of Tiberius Gracchus* 9)

tribunes had generally used their vetoes against consuls and praetors. A tribune's interference with the actions of another tribune was relatively rare, and the tribune who sought to veto a proposal of a colleague usually gave way if the colleague was able to muster support against the obstruction. In dramatic confrontations, Tiberius sought unsuccessfully to persuade or to pressure Octavius to withdraw his veto. He even attempted to increase the pressure by blocking other public business himself and by locking the public treasury. Finally, he sought to remove his intransigent colleague from office—a step that was also unprecedented—seeking to justify the action by claiming that a tribune who attempted to obstruct citizens' ability to vote had failed in his duty to protect their rights. Here, he was successful, and the Plebeian assembly did remove Octavius from office and then replaced him with another tribune. Soon after, the assembly enacted the agrarian law. In a later assembly, voters chose Tiberius himself, his brother Gaius, and his father-in-law, Appius Claudius Pulcher, to be agrarian commissioners.

Tiberius' efforts to enact his law and the attempts of his opponents to block it had escalated through a series of unprecedented actions, which must have increased tensions between the participants and among the citizen body as a whole. This escalation and the rancor accompanying it did not end with the law's passage.

The senate had long had the right to determine the amount of public funds that magistrates would receive to perform their duties. Now, senators voted the Gracchan commissioners only a trivial sum. At this time, by coincidence, news arrived of the death of Attalus III, king of Pergamum, who had no heirs and had left his kingdom to the Romans in his will. In consequence, Tiberius acted in a way that undercut the senate's claims to manage Rome's foreign affairs and its finances. He successfully brought to the Plebeian assembly a new proposal assigning Attalus' treasure to the commissioners, so that they could finance their operations.

Tiberius then announced that he would run for reelection as tribune, another act without apparent precedent. His motive, we are told, was fear that his enemies would seek to prosecute him when he left office, and that they would attempt in some way to nullify his agrarian law. In the electoral assembly, after the first two tribes had voted for Tiberius, his opponents began to assert that it was illegal for him to seek reelection, and, amid arguments, the assembly was adjourned. As the day for the new vote approached, crowds began to gather around the Capitol, where the vote would be held, while the senate met in the nearby Temple of Fides. Here, Tiberius' opponents apparently argued that he was seeking to make himself tyrant, and they sought unsuccessfully to persuade the presiding consul, Scaevola, to authorize the use of force against him. Then, Scipio Nasica, the *pontifex maximus*, with a number of other senators and their retainers, left the meeting of the senate and attacked Tiberius and his supporters with wooden cudgels, killing, according to one account, two to three hundred. One of Tiberius' colleagues as tribune beat him to death with the leg of a stool.

In the following year, 132, the senate assigned both consuls the task of conducting a formal investigation into the conduct of Tiberius' supporters. Their investigation was harsh, and they are reported to have ordered executions, although no other senators seem to have suffered. Tiberius' murder did not result in the clear triumph of his opponents. The land commission, in particular, continued to operate, although it encountered much resistance, and some disorder may have accompanied its judgments and settlements. In 129, however, Scipio Aemilianus succeeded in blocking further action by claiming that the commission was interfering with the rights of allied communities.

Gaius Gracchus

When Gaius Gracchus sought the tribunate for 123, his candidacy was much anticipated by opponents and supporters alike. In the years after his brother's death, lines of conflict had hardened; many hoped for a revival of reform, while others feared it. As quaestor in 126, Gaius had been assigned to accompany the consul Lucius Aurelius Orestes to Sardinia. The senate prorogued Orestes' governorship three times, perhaps to keep Gaius out of Rome. In 124, however, he returned without waiting for an end to the consul's promagistracy. He received a hero's welcome in the city, where many expected him to be the new advocate for the citizenry. Despite attempts to undermine his popularity, Gaius' candidacy was successful. In 123, he even gained reelection as tribune, an action that had led to his brother's death. His associate Marcus Fulvius Flaccus—a member of the agrarian commission and former consul—also sought and won election as tribune for 122, an unprecedented act for a man of his rank.

Gaius Gracchus appears a more complex and more confrontational figure than his brother. Tiberius' reform had limited goals at first; he became more controversial as opposition grew. Gaius introduced a large number of laws, covering a wide range of matters, which suggests that he had a clear legislative agenda. His laws are the only direct evidence for his plans, and their provisions and sequence are often unclear. Analysis of this legislation, moreover, can support different views of his goals. One unfriendly account claims that Gaius Gracchus sought to bring down the senate, and for this reason tried to rally others against it. More probably, Gaius merely wished to curb some of the excesses of the senate's rule, rather than to eliminate it altogether.

As tribune, Gaius began a long, fast-moving series of actions that must have greatly encouraged his supporters, but aroused the fears of his opponents. He is reported to have been an electrifying speaker, perhaps the best of his day, capable of moving crowds with tremendous displays of enthusiasm and emotion. The frequent meetings of the citizen body necessary to enact his many laws would have created a constant feeling of excitement. Like his brother, he probably did not bring his proposals to the senate for discussion. Even so, he too had supporters among his fellow senators, although they seem a more shadowy group and on the whole less senior than Tiberius' had been.

Among Gaius' earliest measures were laws aimed against the investigations that had led to the execution of so many of his brother's supporters. In the past, the senate had authorized most investigations and, by extension, the punishments that followed. Gaius now enacted a measure stipulating that any capital sentence imposed in such circumstances must be authorized by a citizen assembly. After the passage of this law, Publius Popillius Laenas, who as consul in 132 had presided over the executions of Tiberius' supporters, went into exile, probably to avoid prosecution.

Gaius also introduced a range of laws that he probably expected to be popular among the bulk of the city's population. He renewed his brother's land law, but with some modifications. Later, he would secure the passage of laws authorizing the foundation of several colonies in Italy and one—to be named Junonia—in North Africa on the site of Carthage. Another early measure would also have contributed to his popularity in Rome. In all likelihood the city's poorer residents often faced difficulty in obtaining sufficient grain at a price they could afford. Gaius therefore now guaranteed citizens the right to purchase in Rome a set amount of grain each month at a fixed price. Thus the state had to arrange for a regular supply of grain, and to make up the difference whenever the fixed price for citizens turned out to be lower than the market price; it also had to construct granaries and improve harbor facilities.

Certain measures may have been crafted to define and limit some of the senate's most important prerogatives, although it is possible that they were merely aimed against prominent abuses. One law required that senators decide before elections the provinces that would be allocated between the new consuls. Gaius may have intended this law—which remained in effect after his death—to free the process of determining provinces from intrigue. Another law prescribed that taxes in the new province of Asia (formed out of the old kingdom of Pergamum) should be collected by Roman *publicani* bidding for contracts at Rome—the first known instance when these state contractors collected the revenues from an entire province. Some have seen this measure as a sign that Gaius wished to mobilize the *publicani* against the senate, but it may have been aimed simply against official corruption in the province.

Perhaps the most important limitation of the senate's role concerned membership on the juries of the standing courts. As we have seen, in 149, a tribunician law had determined that juries made up of senators would judge cases involving corruption in the provinces. Since only former officeholders and senators could be defendants in these cases, the result was that in these matters senators judged other senators. Gaius' jury law now created a new list of jurors that probably excluded senators altogether, perhaps a response to the lax way in which senatorial jurors had handled prominent trials. Instead, lists of potential jurors were in the future to be chosen from the class of citizens called *equites* (singular, *eques*).

The equites formed an important part of the Roman elite, and, in the late second century, they became more clearly distinguished from the members of the senate. *Eques* literally meant "cavalryman." Originally, officials conducting the *census* had enrolled those eligible to serve in Rome's cavalry in the equestrian centuries. Later, probably during the fourth century, others who possessed sufficient wealth to supply their own horses were also expected to serve in the cavalry, although censors did not enroll them in the equestrian centuries; they too came to be called equites, but they did not possess the voting privileges held by those who were actually enrolled in the designated centuries. Much later, one ancient writer claimed, with some exaggeration, that Gaius had made the equites "rulers over the senate and the senators virtually their subjects."

Probably in Gaius' second term, he and Fulvius Flaccus unsuccessfully proposed a law that would give Roman citizenship to all Latins, and the privileges of Latins to all the Italian allies. This measure, which is unlikely to have been popular among the citizens of Rome, may have begun the decline in Gaius' popularity that would result in his death. Gaius' opponents did not confront him in the same manner that their predecessors had opposed his brother Tiberius. No tribune seems to have dared to block his laws, as Octavius had done a decade earlier. The most successful opponent was Marcus Livius Drusus the Elder, tribune in 122. Like Gaius, he was an effective speaker and was often surrounded by crowds of enthusiastic supporters. In particular, he proposed to found a series of colonies in which land would be given to more people. While Drusus campaigned for his measure, Gaius Gracchus and Fulvius Flaccus left Rome to direct the foundation of the colony at Carthage. When they returned, the political situation had changed drastically, and their popular following was not as large or as secure as before.

After his return, Gaius sought a third term as tribune for 121. This time, he was unsuccessful. In 121, when Gaius was now out of office, the consul Lucius Opimius and several of the tribunes began to try to revoke some of his laws. An attempt to repeal the one that founded the colony at Carthage began the final confrontation. Gaius Gracchus and Fulvius Flaccus, with a large following, attended the meeting where one of the tribunes was seeking to marshal support for the proposed repeal. Here, in a confrontation between the supporters of both sides, a herald of the consul Opimius was killed. Opimius treated the death as a deliberate attack against the state, and he summoned Gaius and Flaccus to the senate to defend themselves. After the two failed to appear, Opimius called on wealthy citizens to gather with their servants to defend the state. Gaius, Flaccus, and their supporters then withdrew to the Aventine hill, a spot long associated with the Roman plebs. Opimius then ordered an attack. Flaccus was killed in the fighting, and Gaius committed suicide. Three thousand of their supporters are reported to have died in the fighting and in the prosecutions that followed.

Opimius based his actions on what came to be called the "Final Decree of the Senate" (*senatus consultum ultimum*), in which senators instructed the consul "to take care that the state suffered no harm"—that is, to do what he considered necessary to preserve the political and social order without regard for the normal protections and rights due to citizens. These events leading up to Gaius' death were the first occasion on which the senate passed such a decree, and its legality would long be contested. In this "ultimate decree" (the SCU), senators asserted their ability to authorize investigations and punishments as they had done after the death of Tiberius Gracchus, and just as Gaius Gracchus had tried to prevent.

The tribunates of Tiberius and Gaius Gracchus were to begin a tumultuous period in Rome's domestic politics, and their careers and their fates illustrate both the strengths and the weaknesses of their office. As long as a popular leader could muster a large following, as they did, he could exercise considerable power in the city. This popularity had to be constantly reinforced, however. Some of the laws and issues of these years—land and grain distributions, control of the courts, and extensions of citizenship—would long remain prominent in the programs of ambitious tribunes. At the same time, opponents had little ability to block popular tribunes through normal means, so that resorting to violence would also remain an option.

In the following decades, a sharp division in political styles would develop among members of the Roman governing elite. Some would follow the traditional methods of competition within the senatorial order, making the traditional alliances and building coalitions of senators to back their plans and their ambitions. Those who furthered their careers in this manner came to be known as *optimates*, a term that marks their self-identification as the best people in the city. Others sought wider popularity among the citizen body as a way to advance careers and agendas, and the term *popularis* (plural, *populares*) identified them. In some cases, it should be noted, ambitious Romans could behave as optimates or as populares at different times in their careers.

SUGGESTED READINGS

Astin, Alan E. 1967. *Scipio Aemilianus*. Oxford: Oxford University Press. Despite Scipio's absence from Rome in 133, this book includes two admirably clear, full chapters on the tribunate of Tiberius Gracchus.

Bradley, Keith R. 1989. *Slavery and Rebellion in the Roman World, 140 B.C.–70 B.C.* Bloomington: Indiana University Press.

Flower, Harriet I. (ed.). 2004. *The Cambridge Companion to the Roman Republic*. Cambridge: Cambridge University Press. Fifteen accessible overviews of political, military, social, and cultural topics.

Stockton, David. 1979. *The Gracchi*. Oxford: Oxford University Press.

ITALY THREATENED, ENFRANCHISED, DIVIDED

Any Romans who had hoped that the brutal elimination of Gaius Gracchus and his associates in 121 might mark an end to violence and turmoil were to be sadly disappointed by the outcome of events during the following twenty years or so. Unfortunately, the surviving ancient accounts of this period (and well beyond) are for the most part too sketchy for us to monitor the unfolding of events in depth, let alone offer satisfactory explanations for many of them.

CHANGES IN ROMAN SOCIETY

The transformation of Roman society and politics that began in the second century and continued into the first also altered Roman private life and the roles and status of Roman women. Our grasp of these changes is by no means firm, and it is really only from the second century that we gain any knowledge of individual named Roman women; even then they are so few that it is hard to assess the representativeness of someone like Cornelia, the mother of the Gracchi brothers (see Chapter Four). Nevertheless, by assembling and analyzing literary, documentary, visual, and legal evidence, we can gain important insights into Roman social history of the mid- to late Republic.

The basic unit of Roman society was the "house" or extended family, conceived of as a tightly knit unit obedient to the "father of the family" (*pater familias*) and under his authority. The conceptual family was the husband and wife, and all their children, slaves, freedmen and freedwomen, and other dependents such as young orphaned relatives who had been entrusted by a court of law to the pater familias. He controlled all property, and all transactions were to be authorized by him. Even grown sons—who advanced to manhood and liability for military duty when they assumed the *toga virilis* between the ages of fourteen and sixteen—were under their father's authority until he died or they were otherwise "freed" by him. If a woman passed into her husband's control at her wedding (in what is termed a *cum manu* marriage), she, too, could make no legally binding decisions without her husband and owned no major property of her own. In an alternative form of Roman marriage (*sine manu*), however, the wife nominally remained under the power of her father, which meant that "her" property did not become her husband's.

Women, like men, were expected to marry and to bear and raise children. Respectable opinion expected a first-time bride to be a virgin, and Roman law in fact allowed her to be as young as twelve (and her husband fourteen). Even so, in practice it would be more typical for a woman to marry during her late teens to a man in his late twenties, except at the top social level, where the ages of both bride and groom might well be a few years younger. Marriages are prominent in at least some of Rome's political alliances during the second century, linking together the Scipio and the Gracchus families, for example. But it is probably a mistake to see women simply as pawns here. Despite the traditional power of the pater familias, we know of no instances of a woman being forced into a marriage, and by the first century women such as Cicero's daughter Tullia definitely had a say in the choice of their husbands.

The ideal of the pater familias was not only reinforced by Roman law beginning with the Twelve Tables, but was also tied to the equally powerful Roman ideal of the farmer-citizen who remained on his property except for periodic skirmishing with hostile neighbors, voting in Rome, or otherwise fulfilling civic duties. Although women could also be classified as citizens and could play a role in Roman religion, only citizen men could participate in most activities that clearly defined a Roman: military service, voting, and holding an elective position or judicial office. As Rome expanded, however, the ideal of the farmer-citizen became increasingly hard to maintain, in particular when overseas wars kept many men away from home for years on end. Such prolonged absence of a pater familias must have been especially shocking to families in which the wife and other relatives were under the husband's control. Roman women were usually not educated in a way that might prepare them for involvement in property and business transactions or in legal and ethical deliberations. Women were expected to help run the household, educate their children (as did Cornelia), and undertake many religious duties. They must have consulted with their husbands and other family members in the normal Roman way; long-term absence on the part of their spouses added to their burdens. Such strain may be one reason why very few Roman women were married *cum manu* by the first century. This change, which can be dated only generally, could have given a wife more agency during the times that her husband was away, because the property of a wife married *sine manu* was not subsumed to that of his, although legally she was still under the control of her father. In any case, the change is one among several that suggest the emergence of a little more individuality, independence, and respect for women, at least at the top of Rome's society.

Map 5.1 *Rome's Wars, 113–82*

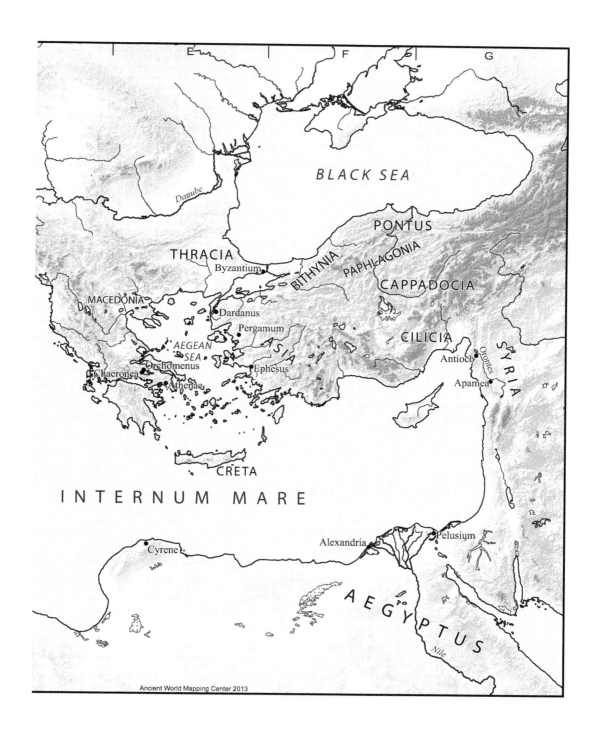

Whether the prospects for poorer Roman women likewise improved in the same period is doubtful, however. It was households headed by men, not women, that stood to benefit from the new schemes that offered land and a fresh start in the countryside. Meantime, poor rural families evidently migrated in large numbers to Rome and other cities, but no industries were to be found there, and very few occupations were open to women. If a woman were fortunate enough to possess the appropriate skills or education, she could work as a nurse or midwife, or at some craft or trade. Less training was needed to eke out a living as a musical entertainer, barmaid, or prostitute—professions that the law grouped together. Freeborn women might also work as a wet-nurse, nanny, servant, or personal attendant, although in rich households slaves usually held these positions.

Richer, more politically active families used the growing cities as showcases, and women increasingly played a part in the exhibition of prestige. Rome's first sumptuary law, the *Lex Oppia*, was passed in 215 when the severe losses in the Second Punic War demanded extraordinary measures. This law debarred women from having more than a small amount of gold, wearing multicolored clothes, or using vehicles drawn by an animal within a city, except during public religious festivals. These measures demonstrate that wealthy women were by no means confined to their homes, that they customarily took part in their community's religious ceremonies, and that their style of dress could attract attention. Moreover, to judge by surviving representations, there is no cause to think that women's clothing covered their faces or otherwise masked their appearance. By 195, six years after the end of the Second Punic War, the Lex Oppia was repealed. During the second century the female relatives of the Scipios became well known for the opulence of their dress and carriages, their sacrificial utensils, and the crowds of their attendants during festivals. A public funeral for a woman was held in the Forum for the first time around 102. There can be no doubt that this greater visibility of wealthy women stems from the increasingly competitive politics of the period.

WAR WITH JUGURTHA (112–105)

Despite our uneven understanding, two developments in the years after Gaius Gracchus' death emerge clearly enough as special challenges for the state and the source of lasting change. Both were external, and both took Rome by surprise (Map 5.1). At the center of the first was a Numidian named Jugurtha, who had been adopted by his uncle King Micipsa, the son and (since 148) successor to Rome's long-standing ally Masinissa. Micipsa, however, also had two sons of his own, both younger than Jugurtha. So on Micipsa's death, around 118, the kingdom was left jointly to all three. But any hopes of a working partnership were soon dashed, especially after Micipsa's sons had complained of Jugurtha's prominence. When Jugurtha had one (Hiempsal) murdered and the other (Adherbal) driven out of Numidia altogether, Adherbal begged for help from Rome. In 116, the senate dispatched a commission of inquiry headed by Lucius Opimius, the brutal consul of 121; it divided the kingdom, assigning the west to Jugurtha and the more developed east to Adherbal. Jugurtha's acceptance of this settlement is notable, as is the senate's willingness to intervene so deeply in the affairs of a foreign state. To be sure, Numidia was an old ally of Rome, it now had a long common border with the Roman province of Africa, and Rome naturally wanted a stable neighbor there. Perhaps the senate's hope was that this degree of intervention would suffice to ensure long-term stability.

If so, Jugurtha soon demonstrated otherwise by invading Adherbal's territory; by 112 he had him trapped in his capital Cirta (modern Qacentina/Constantine, in eastern Algeria). The senate's protests left Jugurtha unmoved. Eventually Adherbal surrendered, and Jugurtha executed him along with some Italian businessmen in Cirta who had been Adherbal's supporters. Romans' sharp reaction to these outrages now impelled the senate to send forces to discipline Jugurtha, though their campaigns had limited success at best. Diplomacy was tried again, too, but proved futile, especially in 111 when Jugurtha even came to Rome, only to be required by a tribune's veto not to speak there at all. In 110, the senate rejected a treaty made by a Roman commander in the field, and general dissatisfaction with its whole handling of the Numidian problem came to a head.

The effectiveness of the Roman forces in Numidia improved under Quintus Caecilius Metellus in 109–108, and likewise from 107 onwards under the commander who displaced him (in circumstances treated below), Gaius Marius. Only in 105, however, was the war at last brought to an end when Marius' quaestor, Lucius Cornelius Sulla (another figure we shall return to), successfully persuaded Jugurtha's ally, King Bocchus of Mauretania, to betray him to the Romans. Jugurtha was then executed after being paraded in Marius' triumph the following year. Meantime, Bocchus was granted part of Numidia to add to his own kingdom, while a brother of Jugurtha was made ruler of the rest. Roman honor was thereby restored, and an unreliable neighbor to the province of Africa was removed. Otherwise, however, it is striking how minimally the settlement of 105/104 differs from what Opimius' commission had determined just over a decade earlier. Rome exacted no direct permanent gain from this costly, prolonged series of embarrassments; there was no wish to annex Numidia. The fundamental shortcoming—as in some previous instances—was the senate's lack of capacity for determining the extent and the timing of any Roman intervention in the affairs of a foreign state.

ITALY THREATENED FROM THE NORTH (113–101)

The second development that surprised and challenged the Roman state towards the end of the second century was a migration south by groups of German peoples, principally the Cimbri and Teutoni. Why they left their homeland in north Jutland is not certain. By 113 they had drifted as far as the eastern Alps, where they defeated a Roman consul and his army who had been sent to observe them. Next, by entering the Rhone River Valley (Latin, Rhodanus), they naturally posed a threat to Rome's province of Transalpine Gaul (formed in 121), in particular after they had defeated another consul and his army in 109. Further Roman defeats followed in 107, and again most seriously of all at Arausio (modern Orange) in 105, where the catastrophic losses stemmed in part from the refusal of Quintus Servilius Caepio (a noble who had been consul in 106) to cooperate with his superior, the *novus homo* consul Gnaeus Mallius Maximus.

The tribes' next move was evidently northwards, rather than south towards Italy, but in Rome, understandably, panic prevailed. News of the disaster at Arausio came not long after confirmation of Jugurtha's capture. So at the elections for the consulship of 104, with the war in Numidia now known to be over, Marius was elected in his absence and assigned the command in Gaul. For this purpose, the law of the late 150s permitting no more than a single tenure of the consulship also had to be somehow set aside. Even more remarkable is Marius' subsequent reelection as consul every year through 100, by which date he had held the office for five years consecutively and six in total. These reelections are a puzzle insofar as he might just as well have been continued in his command as proconsul. In all likelihood, however, there was an overwhelming desire on the part of voters to guard against any repetition of the standoff between Caepio and Mallius at Arausio.

In the event, the German tribes' movement north in 105 gave Marius the precious breathing space he needed to restore the Roman army's strength with recruitment, training, and new equipment. By the time that the tribes did eventually turn south, he was able to defeat the Teutoni at Aquae Sextiae (modern Aix-en-Provence in southern France) in 102, and the Cimbri at Vercellae in northern Italy the following year. With the threat from the tribes thus removed, Marius was appropriately hailed as Rome's savior and offered two triumphs (he took only one); his reelection as consul for 100 reflected popular gratitude.

CHANGES IN THE ROMAN ARMY

Without question, the end of the second century saw changes not only to the recruitment of the Roman army (see next section), but also to its equipment, training, and battle formation (for training, see Fig. 6.1). More problematic, however, is just how extensive and sudden these changes were, as well as how far they were initiated by Marius himself (as our sources maintain). It may have been he who made the eagle a legion's principal standard and who had javelins (*pila*; singular, *pilum*) produced with a weak rivet; once thrown, the shaft would buckle on landing and become useless to the enemy. It was evidently Marius, too, who required soldiers to carry more of their gear themselves than had been regular practice; hence the description of them as "Marius' mules" (*muli Mariani*). Less clear is the degree to which Marius reformed the army's battle formation. Certainly, by the mid-first century there were no longer the traditional three distinct ranks of infantry identifiable by age and equipment, nor did Romans serve as cavalry or light-armed troops at this date. Instead, the two latter roles were now filled by allied auxiliaries, while the heavy infantry had become a uniform body of Romans grouped in larger formations (cohorts of four to five hundred men) than had been the norm a century earlier. Given Marius' urgent need to recruit widely and provide inexperienced men with fast, effective training to meet the threatened invasion of Italy from the north, it is tempting to speculate that he played some part in advancing these important changes, even if their introduction began earlier. What the army lost by them in flexibility, it gained in cohesive fighting power, and this was a vital boost after its series of demoralizing recent defeats.

MARIUS' CAREER IN ROMAN POLITICS

In the competitive atmosphere of Roman politics, multiple triumphs and consulships represented enviable distinction even for a noble. For a novus homo like Marius, they were honors beyond his wildest dreams. Now is the point, therefore, to review Marius' political career, with particular reference to appreciating its relationship to his military success and the resulting impact on the Roman state. Marius was born about 157 near Arpinum, a town sixty miles (96 km) southeast of Rome. His family had equestrian status but was otherwise only prominent locally; even so, he was somehow able to serve under Scipio Aemilianus at Numantia, and he distinguished himself there. Not until after further military service, however, did he attempt to stand for office at Rome, and then only with the backing of a leading noble family, the Metelli. With this help he gained the quaestorship sometime in the late 120s, followed by the tribunate in 119. Thereafter he failed in his attempt to become aedile and only just secured election as praetor in 115. His prospects for further political advancement were bleak; to build up the necessary wealth and influential support was a hard struggle. He did proceed to benefit financially, however, from a governorship in Further Spain and was then able to make an advantageous marriage to Julia, whose family—the Julii Caesares—was an ancient patrician one, though not notably distinguished in the recent past (the famous Julius Caesar, born in 100, was to be her nephew).

In Spain, Marius had revealed a talent for guerrilla warfare. This, and the family's previous relationship, prompted Quintus Metellus to make him his second-in-command when he set out against Jugurtha in 109. The two of them quarreled the following year, however, when Metellus denied Marius leave to go to Rome and stand for the consulship of 107. Allegedly, with a noble's condescension towards a novus homo (compare Source 5.1), Metellus recommended the fifty-year-old Marius to wait until his own twenty-year-old son was ready to be a candidate too. Marius returned to Rome and ran for the office regardless, tapping his links with the equites (see Chapter Four) and stressing the need for a change from so much corrupt, ineffectual leadership by nobles. When the senate tried to thwart

SOURCE 5.1: *This sketch by the Roman historian Sallust of how Marius advanced until he eventually dared to stand for the consulship may be uncritical, not to say exaggerated and inaccurate in certain respects. However, its tone is still instructive, as are the aspects selected for attention.*

Even prior to this stage [in 108], Marius had been obsessed by a powerful longing for the consulship, an office which he was amply qualified in every way to fill, except that he did not come from an old family. He was a hard worker, a man of integrity, and a highly capable soldier. He devoted his energies to warfare. His private life was unremarkable, and he was no slave to passion or riches; all he craved was glory. His birthplace was Arpinum, where he had spent all his boyhood. As soon as he reached the age to enlist, he had gone on active service, training himself in this way rather than by any course of Greek rhetoric or city polish. With this fine education his sound character soon matured. So on the first occasion that he stood for election as military tribune, even though many citizens did not know him by sight, they were sufficiently aware of his record that all the tribes voted for him. Thereafter he won one office after another, invariably shouldering his responsibilities in such a way that he was thought to merit the next higher one. Even so, despite the worth he had demonstrated thus far, he never—and I say this of a man who later would be ruined by overambition—dared to aspire to the consulship. This was still a time when plebeians might win other offices, but the consulship was handed down by the nobles from one of their own number to the next. For this distinction, a "new man" (*novus homo*)—no matter how famous he might be, or how outstanding his record—was considered unworthy, and even tainted. (*Jugurthine War* 63)

him by reappointing Metellus as commander in Numidia, the Plebeian assembly overruled it and appointed Marius.

Although authorized to draft men for his campaign in 107, Marius was wary of the difficulties he was likely to encounter if he attempted this. Instead, therefore, he limited himself to calling for volunteers, promising them rewards. He was even willing to take men of the lowest census rating, who would normally not be recruited because of their lack of property. With hindsight, this step has been seen as the source of lasting harm, and Marius has been criticized for not anticipating the difficulties of rewarding his volunteers, as well as for not grasping how they might prove willing to advance the political ambitions of their commander. Even so, to expect such foresight of Marius or anyone else in 107 is hardly realistic. In the event, despite opposition, generous plots of land in Africa were readily assigned to the surviving volunteers as a reward in 103. The magistrate whom Marius had to thank for arranging this legislation was an ambitious tribune, Lucius Appuleius Saturninus; he was at odds with the senatorial establishment and clearly drew inspiration from the example of the Gracchi. At the same time, he was even less afraid of confrontation than they, and he cultivated Marius as a potentially valuable patron who would be able to provide military backing in a crisis, if required.

SIXTH CONSULSHIP OF MARIUS AND SECOND TRIBUNATE OF SATURNINUS (100)

In 100, Marius again needed help in rewarding veterans—this time those who had defeated the Cimbri and Teutoni—and he was again willing for Saturninus to act on his behalf. Saturninus was no less a controversial figure than before. By now he had also developed a working partnership with Gaius Servilius Glaucia, who was praetor in 100, while Saturninus was tribune. Saturninus' legislative proposals were both wide-ranging and provocative. It was not just Marius' veterans whom he wanted to settle (on land in Transalpine Gaul). He also proposed the foundation of colonies and allocation of land in Greece and Sicily for veterans of campaigns that had recently ended there, as well as allocation of land in Cisalpine Gaul for Roman civilians. Such sweeping initiatives, if approved, were sure to make him highly influential.

If this were not provocation enough, his opponents were offended by a clause that required all senators to take an oath to respect the law within five days of its passage. The opposition also found fault with the right that Marius was granted to confer Roman citizenship on a small number of the settlers in each of the new colonies. Popular hostility to the extension of citizenship was again stirred up, just as it had been against Gaius Gracchus. The opposition did everything possible to prevent a vote on the proposals. Tribunes imposed vetoes, and calls were made to disband the assembly on religious grounds because thunder had been heard. Saturninus brushed all these obstacles aside. Once it was clear that the proposals were likely to be rejected, Marius' veterans were deployed to keep hostile voters away by force, and they in turn reacted violently. In the event, the veterans won the confrontation, but it took this ugly use of force to ram the proposals through. The immediate need for senators to take the oath embarrassed Marius and raised the tension still further; only Quintus Metellus refused, and he left Rome as soon as Saturninus proposed his exile.

Next Saturninus achieved his own reelection as tribune for 99, but he then overstretched himself in working to have Glaucia made consul. Marius as the presiding magistrate rejected Glaucia's candidacy because it did not meet the legal requirements. Saturninus then had his followers beat a rival candidate to death and tried to have a law passed permitting Glaucia's candidacy, but even with further resort to violence this attempt failed. The senate was now thoroughly alarmed by such disorder and for the second time passed its "ultimate decree" (the SCU) instructing the consuls to secure the safety of the state. That step forced Marius to decide whether or not to remain loyal to his associates. He chose to take the lead in pursuing them, and their group soon surrendered to him after receiving an assurance that they would not be summarily executed. When Marius did no more than confine them in the senate house, however, a lynch mob quickly formed to take revenge for their violent treatment of fellow citizens. Men from the mob then climbed to the roof, tore off the tiles, and battered Saturninus, Glaucia, and the others to a gruesome death.

Subsequently, it would seem that the land assignments enacted by Saturninus were respected, but most of his colonies were never founded. The degree to which he was a sincere Popularis politician as opposed to a manipulative self-seeker is hard to judge. Even so, there can be no question that his impact on political life at Rome was a damaging one. He had proved even more domineering a tribune than Gaius Gracchus, not least because he had grasped how effectively Marius' poor volunteer veterans could be deployed in political struggles; he thereby introduced a new and disturbing level of violence to Rome's public affairs. Where Saturninus perhaps proved naive was in expecting Marius' continued support as alarm mounted within the senate. Marius, for his part, had no plans for reform. Rather, even as a novus homo of unique distinction, what he craved most deeply was confirmation that the nobles now respected him as one of themselves rather than as still the outsider whom Quintus Metellus had so crushingly rebuffed in 108. The senate's gratitude to Marius for decisive implementation of the SCU proved to be short-lived, however. He was not prominent again until an extraordinary turn of events early in the 80s.

ADMINISTRATION OF THE PROVINCES

As explained in Chapter Three, Rome's annexation of territories beyond Italy—which eventually made up an "empire" of "provinces"—was a gradual, haphazard process. It is equally important to appreciate that the individual circumstances of an annexation, or the established character of particular communities and their administration, could lead to striking, permanent variations in their treatment. Even so, by the late second century norms for the administration of the provinces had taken shape and can be outlined. The underlying concerns were similar to those for Italy at an earlier stage in Rome's growth. Consequently, each provincial community or people was to continue locally autonomous, staying free from internal strife as well as from warfare with others. Tax (often agricultural produce rather than money) was normally payable to Rome, but there was no regular obligation to furnish manpower for the army. The fundamental components of a province and its organization were encapsulated in a "law of the province" (*lex provinciae*), which defined each community's form of constitution, its boundaries, its relationship with Rome, and its tax obligations. This law could be amended, but only by the senate and people in Rome. To address matters of immediate concern, the governor issued his own edict (often merely repeating what one or other of his predecessors had prescribed).

Each governor had a quaestor assigned to him by the senate, whose special responsibility was to oversee Rome's financial interests in the province. It was for the governor himself to choose a handful of "legates" (*legati*), who were then officially recognized by the senate. Such men would be upper-class associates, or even relatives, of the governor, on whom he conferred authority as his deputies. Because their assistance could be of the greatest value, they were often chosen for some special skill or experience—in warfare, for instance. In addition, a governor would usually invite other friends (*amici*) or relatives to join his entourage (*cohors*) unofficially. A governor was supreme in his province. Everyone—civilian or soldier, Roman citizen or alien—was bound to obey his orders. In principle, Roman citizens had some right of appeal; in practice, however, this might prove difficult to exercise. The governor alone had the right of execution, so that cases liable to require a capital sentence had to be referred to him, along with certain other types of major charges. In addition, he could order instant execution, especially if he suspected a serious threat to Rome's main concern, the peace and security of the province.

Unless he was deterred by bad weather or diverted by the need to go on campaign, a governor's customary routine would be to move from one major community to the next, quickly checking as best he could on the welfare of each, and adjudicating the cases, petitions, and other matters brought to him. For even the most conscientious of governors, this tour was a daunting challenge—encountering regions and cultures with which in all likelihood he had little or no prior acquaintance, and engaging with populations who were not necessarily well disposed to Rome. Because most provincials understood neither Latin nor Greek, and Roman interest in learning other languages was minimal, reliance upon interpreters was frequently essential. Appropriate behavior within societies where the giving and receiving of gifts were standard practice (as in the Greek East especially) posed a real dilemma for fair-minded governors; to accept all gifts (or bribes) was clearly criminal, but to refuse everything might only cause offense.

Less responsible governors felt no such anxiety, and instead—with varying degrees of greed—exploited the opportunities that their situation offered. Although the temptations were infinite, the term of office in which to indulge them was unlikely to exceed a single year. Many a governor had heavy debts to pay off, often ones incurred on the latest occasion that he had competed for office in Rome. Although the senate allocated an ample lump sum for a governor's expenses, he received no salary. His orders and verdicts were not to be questioned, Rome was far away (from a distant province, messages could take weeks), and for the most part provincial news attracted little attention there, so long as Roman interests were not under threat.

Some of the most painful dilemmas for fair-minded governors were likely to be created not by provincial subjects, but by the syndicates (*societates*) of private contractors, or *publicani*, who collected taxes on Rome's behalf. Whenever the tax contract for a major province was auctioned (Asia's five-year contract was the largest), a huge capital outlay was required to secure the winning bid. To operate effectively, a large tax-collecting syndicate had to maintain ships and branch offices, employ hundreds of staff (predominantly slaves or freedmen), and in many respects function as a bank. In addition, because it existed to deliver a profit to the partners who provided the capital, it could hardly afford to be patient or indulgent in its dealings with taxpayers. A governor too ready to lend a sympathetic ear to their complaints was most unwelcome to a syndicate, and it would not hesitate to pressure him into rethinking his attitude. Worst of all for provincials was their plight in those instances where a governor unashamedly collaborated with a syndicate in fleecing taxpayers.

The senate, for its part, was acutely aware of Rome's dependence upon the tax-collecting syndicates for providing revenue; in consequence, efforts to discipline their operations too strictly would only prove self-defeating. This said, we should recognize that there was an influential body of opinion in the senate eager to see members on a provincial assignment held to a high standard of conduct. As noted in Chapter Four, in 149 the novel step was taken of instituting a special jury court to hear complaints lodged against such senators. Subsequently, Gaius Gracchus as tribune in 123 and 122, a member of the Cato family around 100, Sulla as dictator in 82–81, and Julius Caesar in his first consulship (59) were all responsible for legislation that sought to discipline governors and make them more accountable. Even so, adequate means of enforcement could not be found, while general principles that seemed admirable when advocated in Rome might well turn out more awkward to uphold under specific conditions in a province. The convictions that Rome as a responsible ruler had obligations to the provinces, and that leading provincials who supported Roman rule should be treated as partners rather than mere subjects, were still not widely shared among senators at the end of the Republican period.

It is hard to determine how effectively the jury court acted to reduce misconduct. The plain fact that no more than a limited number of the cases heard there led to conviction must have been heartening to those governors willing to risk prosecution. There was much else to give a defendant hope. A governor could be charged only after his term of office had ended. The court only sat in Rome, and its proceedings were all in Latin. Its jury comprised upper-class Romans exclusively (at different periods, senators or equites, or both), who would readily sympathize with a fellow Roman and might also prove corruptible. Meantime the provincials laying charges had to bear all the difficulty, risk, and expense of engaging advocates, assembling evidence, and producing witnesses. Even should they secure a conviction, there would be further uncertainty over whether they could successfully reclaim the cash or stolen items awarded to them; for example, it was easy enough for a convicted defendant to remove himself into comfortable, self-imposed exile beyond the reach of Roman jurisdiction.

We can surely conclude, then, that the prospect of a trial was little or no deterrent to those governors willing to risk prosecution. Less easily quantifiable, by definition, is the proportion of governors averse to incurring the personal strain and exposure of a trial, no matter how favorable the prospects for evading conviction. Even so, it would be wrong to imagine that such men all governed honestly in consequence. One practical safeguard was to identify the most powerful provincials and then simply follow their guidance. In gaining protection of this sort, such a governor might well have to abandon any higher sense of responsibility to the province as a whole. But in all likelihood he had only been assigned there randomly by the lot, lacked any sense of commitment to the area, and saw no value in jeopardizing his own future prospects during a mere year's tenure.

TRIBUNATE OF LIVIUS DRUSUS (91)

Surviving accounts of the 90s are too fragmentary to give us adequate insight into the unfolding of developments during that decade. At least it is plain that the existing tensions remained high. In 91, however, there emerged a tribune, Marcus Livius Drusus, with a wide-ranging program designed to overcome several of the principal difficulties. He was the son of the Livius Drusus who had opposed Gaius Gracchus, and like his father he acted in the interests of the Optimates. To resolve the issue of whether the members of the jury courts should be senators or equites, he proposed that they all be senators, but that 300 equites be made senators. He further proposed the foundation of colonies and the distribution of "public" land to poor citizens, and finally a grant of Roman citizenship to all Latins and Italians. Although some of these proposals seem to have been passed by the Plebeian assembly, each of the groups most affected by Drusus' program soon began to question whether its prospective gains would outweigh its losses. Some Optimate senators were not sure that they wanted the senate to be doubled in size. Equites regretted the loss of their distinctive role on the jury courts, and of their broader influence as a class which would now be permanently undermined. Rome's allies generally welcomed the grant of citizenship, to be sure, but at the same time the larger holders of "public" land among them did not relish the prospect of having to lose some of it to settle the poor. Eventually the opposition to Drusus' legislation gained the upper hand and successfully maneuvered to have all of it declared invalid. Shortly afterwards, Drusus died at the hands of an unknown assassin.

SOCIAL WAR (91–87)

By seeking to please everyone, in the event Drusus pleased no one. Worse still, his efforts to reduce tension only raised it. In particular, many Italians—with their hopes of being awarded Roman citizenship dashed yet again—now began organizing to claim by force the status that Rome would not offer through legislation. Almost at once Rome was faced by just the threat that the structure of its alliance had been designed to eliminate, namely a confederation of member-states turning against their leader. The conflict came to be known as the Social or Allies' War (in Latin *socius* signifies ally). The peoples of the central and southern Apennines formed the largest concentration of rebels. In a display of remarkable speed and efficiency they established a confederate capital at Corfinium—renamed Italica— with magistrates on the Roman model and a senate of 500 representatives from member-states (Fig. 5.1). Their forces totaled perhaps 100,000 men, well acquainted with Roman methods of warfare.

  It is important to recognize that many communities either joined only briefly at the outset (as in Etruria and Umbria, for example), or not at all. In particular, the Latin communities never joined (theirs was already the most privileged allied

Figure 5.1 *It was not yet typical Roman practice to refer to contemporary events on coins, as the rebels did on these two during the Social War. Note the personification of "Italia," as well as the vignettes of eight warriors swearing an oath in front of a standard, and the (Italian) bull mounting and goring the (Roman) wolf. The language used on the lower coin is Oscan, which was widely spoken in southern Italy.*

status), nor did central Campania; moreover, even within predominantly rebel areas, certain communities chose to stay loyal to Rome. Loyalist forces always outnumbered those of the rebels, and in the longer term, too, the financial and material resources that Rome could draw upon would prove superior. Even so, the rebels caught Rome by surprise. During 90 they succeeded in capturing several Roman strongholds and inflicting some severe defeats before Roman commanders were able to regain the upper hand. A vital lesson for each side emerged from the operations of this year. To the rebels, it was plain that their ultimate defeat by Rome was inevitable. Any hope of overthrowing the Roman state was just unrealistic. It would seem that only a minority of the rebels were so extreme in their thinking, notably the Samnites and Lucanians (Fig. 5.2); the majority were fighting mainly for higher status within the Roman alliance. To Rome, on the

Figure 5.2 *At modern Pietrabbondante—a superb site with a panoramic outlook in Italy's Molise region—the Samnites established a sanctuary to a god of war as early as the fifth century B.C. Laid out along two mountainside terraces, it reached its most developed form during the second century, boasting two temples and the (restored) Greek-style theater seen here. In all likelihood this sanctuary became a meeting place of the entire Samnite confederacy (see Chapter Two). Following the Social War, however, and Sulla's massacre of Samnites, the site came to be abandoned.*

other hand, the rebels' effectiveness during 90 demonstrated that they had to be granted the advancement they had long sought. This realization made the tragedy of the war all the more poignant, because it was exposed as an entirely avoidable conflict provoked by the Romans' persistent inability to overcome their own shortsightedness.

During fall 90 Rome did in fact offer citizenship to all communities of allies that had remained loyal, as well as to those that had joined the rebels but either had already abandoned hostilities or would do so by a specified date. This offer was not enough to prevent continued hard fighting during 89. Corfinium fell to the Romans, however, and eventually (in November) the rebels' last major stronghold at Asculum. After 89, only a few rebel communities continued to hold out, including Nola in Campania. Meantime, a second law was passed at Rome, which seems to have extended the offer of citizenship to those allies who were ineligible at the time of the previous grant in 90. Also in 89, communities directly north of the Padus River (in the "Transpadane" region, part of Rome's newly formed province of Cisalpine Gaul) were awarded Latin status.

It would be hard to overstate the importance of the Social War as a turning point, with consequences stretching over the next several decades. It was Italy's first, sudden exposure to the traumas of full-scale civil conflict, a prelude (as it turned out) to successive, more prolonged bouts of similar horror over the next sixty years. It changed the administrative, political, and cultural complexion of Italy from the Padus River southwards. Communities that had run their affairs in accordance with a wide variety of constitutions of their own making now gradually abandoned these in order to become Roman municipia. Urbanization was encouraged for this purpose. At the same time, members of all allied communities gained the right to vote, and to run for office, in Rome itself. Last but not least, these changes fostered the spread of Latin and the disappearance of regional languages such as Etruscan, Oscan, Umbrian, and Messapic.

TRIBUNATE OF SULPICIUS RUFUS (88)

As we have seen, when Rome finally offered citizenship to the allies, this was done only under duress. There was a further respect in which the award can be regarded as either grudging or cautious, and in consequence the cause of violent reactions for several years to come. This was the restriction of the new citizens to a small number of newly created tribes (perhaps eight), which would all be called upon to vote only after the existing thirty-five tribes had voted. In other words, this arrangement would limit the influence that the new citizens could exert upon elections and legislation at Rome as a body.

One of the tribunes for 88, Publius Sulpicius Rufus, inspired by the ideals of his predecessor Livius Drusus in 91, pledged himself to gaining full voting rights for the new citizens. This would mean abandoning the creation of new tribes for them, and instead distributing them throughout the existing thirty-five tribes. Although Sulpicius naturally anticipated opposition to such a proposal, he never expected that either consul would stand in his way. After all, one was a friend of his, and he had helped the other (Sulla) win the election.

Lucius Cornelius Sulla had advanced far since we first encountered him in 107 as Marius' quaestor in the campaign against Jugurtha. He came from an old, but not recently distinguished, patrician family, and it was perhaps partly this background that had influenced the novus homo Marius to choose him. Certainly he served Marius well both in Africa and then against the German tribes, although later he increasingly provoked him by representing that he alone (and not Marius his commander) was responsible for contriving Jugurtha's capture. Recently, Sulla had been one of Rome's most successful generals in the Social War, and deserved his election as consul for 88. It was also appropriate that he was allotted a command against King Mithridates of Pontus, who (as we shall see in Chapter Six) was now posing a serious threat to Roman interests in Asia Minor.

In 88, when Sulpicius introduced his proposal to redistribute the new citizens among the thirty-five tribes, he was shocked to encounter fierce opposition, not just from the old citizens, but also from both consuls. He therefore cast around for alternative powerful support. Marius—who could rally influential equites in particular—was willing to provide this. But he also demanded an extraordinarily high price, which he and Sulpicius kept secret for the time being: Sulla's command against Mithridates must be reassigned to him. This maneuver would bring Marius double satisfaction: it would humiliate Sulla, and it would give Marius himself the chance to regain the military glory that his political ineptitude had so badly tarnished during his sixth consulship in 100.

It is a further puzzle that Sulpicius, like Saturninus in 100, offered no proposal designed to make voters more favorably disposed to his principal concern, the redistribution of the new citizens throughout the thirty-five tribes. Instead, he tried to use violence and intimidation to force this measure through, forming a bodyguard for the purpose. The consuls reacted by declaring a *iustitium* or suspension of public business. Sulpicius countered with a threat to use force against them if this ban were not lifted. Street fighting broke out, in the course of which Sulla found himself driven to seek sudden refuge in, of all places, Marius' house. In all likelihood, to save his own skin Sulla was then obliged to agree that the iustitium would be lifted. It was, and at the same time Sulla left for Campania to join his army, which was still besieging Nola, a holdout from the Social War.

After these developments, when Sulpicius put his redistribution proposal to the vote, it passed; he was also able to reassign the command against Mithridates from Sulla to Marius. Sulpicius had thereby fulfilled his bargain with Marius, but at the same time he also presented Sulla with an impossible dilemma. If Sulla accepted the reassignment, then he ruined all his hard-earned political prospects. On the other hand, if he attempted to fight it, he would be forced to take the law into his own hands. Personal interest aside, he was at least entitled to regard his predicament as insufferable. True, his reassignment had been legally enacted, but still there was no crisis at this date to justify a tribune arranging to take the Mithridatic command from a consul who was qualified for it in every way, and to bestow it upon a seventy-year-old private citizen.

SULLA'S FIRST MARCH ON ROME (88)

Because only the use or the threat of force had allowed Sulpicius to pass his measures, it was natural enough for Sulla at this stage to contemplate introducing force on his own behalf. The means were ready to hand—the army of six legions now besieging Nola, which he had been due to lead against Mithridates. As he knew, from a constitutional viewpoint the very thought of bringing an army to Rome to seize by force what he could not secure by the appropriate vote in a citizen assembly was heinous; it was unheard of, and struck at one of the vital foundations of the Republic. All politically active citizens in Rome were sure to be adamantly opposed to such a crime. Sulla himself realized the risk he ran in even broaching the possibility to his men. But he also had a sound appreciation of where their priorities lay, pointing out that if he simply accepted his removal from the command, then in all likelihood his replacement Marius would recruit other forces to take to Asia Minor, and these would become the ones to enjoy the rewards of victory there. So when officers sent by Marius arrived to take over command of the army, the men stoned them to death. All of Sulla's own officers, on the other hand, except one, deserted him: they were fully conscious of the illegality of a march on Rome.

Sulla's anticipation of the reaction that his fateful step would provoke was largely accurate. There was never much doubt that he would gain control of Rome, because Sulpicius, Marius, and the senate were taken completely by surprise. Once in control of the city, Sulla immediately prevailed on the senate to declare a group of twelve—Sulpicius, Marius, his son of the same name aged about twenty-two, and nine others—enemies of the state because of their violent, seditious behavior. This maneuver created the impression that by contrast Sulla's own no less violent, seditious reaction was legitimate. It also—very disturbingly—made instant outlaws of Roman citizens without any trial, and let them be hunted down and killed. Next, Sulla cancelled all the measures passed by Sulpicius after the imposition of the iustitium. This meant that Sulla himself was now restored to the Mithridatic command; it also meant, however, that the new citizens were not to be redistributed among the thirty-five tribes. At the elections that followed, however, voters could articulate their hostility. Neither of the candidates elected to the consulship for 87 was supported by Sulla, although afterwards he did persuade both to swear that they would leave his measures intact. That done, he departed to the East with his army. Meantime, of the group outlawed by him, only Sulpicius had met his death as he fled. Marius and his son had managed to reach Africa, where many of his veterans were settled.

CINNA'S RULE (87–84)

With Sulpicius now dead and Sulla departed to the East, there was some hope that 87 might turn out a less traumatic year than 88 had been. In fact it was not, because one of the consuls, Lucius Cornelius Cinna, was somehow persuaded to take up the cause of redistributing the new citizens among the thirty-five tribes. Evidently during the course of his election he had not declared any such concern, but he now became an implacable advocate of the cause. His fellow consul Gnaeus Octavius remained opposed to it, the tribunes were divided (some vetoed the proposal), and rioting ensued. Cinna then left Rome and traveled through Italy rallying support—behavior for which the senate removed him from office and declared him an enemy or *hostis*. Marius seized the opportunity to return from Africa and offer Cinna his assistance, which was accepted. Both sides took desperate measures to raise troops; slaves were offered their freedom in return for serving; and the Samnites (who were still stubbornly at war) in the end agreed to support Cinna. Eventually, late in the year, after a siege, Rome fell to Cinna and Marius. The consul Octavius was killed. Cinna and Marius embarked on a bloody purge of their enemies. Sulla was outlawed in his absence.

By some irregular means Cinna and Marius had themselves made consuls for 86 and duly entered office on January 1. By mid-month, however, Marius was dead, perhaps of pneumonia. It was a tragic end for a man who had both saved the

Republic and then in old age done much to undermine it. It is impossible to justify the way in which he exploited the opportunity offered to him by Sulpicius in 88. To be sure, he was not solely to blame for the damage done to the Republic then, just as earlier in 107 he cannot be expected to have foreseen the disruptive political potential that his recruitment of poor volunteers would unlock. The fact is, however, that from 88 he discarded all sense of responsibility towards the state.

Marius was replaced as consul by Lucius Valerius Flaccus, but leadership of the state remained with Cinna. The extent to which he formulated plans for the longer term is unclear. All he could manage immediately was to tackle pressing crises, among which he did *not* include redistribution of the new citizens throughout the thirty-five tribes; they were still kept waiting. A financial crisis did receive attention, however. We know only the outcome, which was a law allowing debtors to pay back no more than one-quarter of what they owed at that date—a devastating blow, in other words, to creditors, whose loan capital was drastically diminished. At least the law underlines for us the disruption and massive loss of confidence that affected everyone financially and economically.

Meantime, despite being outlawed by Cinna, Sulla was not deterred from pursuing Mithridates with marked success (see Chapter Six). By 85, however, he believed that it suited his purpose better to let Mithridates escape for the time being and to make peace with him. It is true that Mithridates was still a formidable foe, but had he been eliminated then there was no one on his side of comparable stature to replace him. Really, we have to see Sulla's preference for missing this opportunity, and instead terminating hostilities, as the product of his own selfish ambition to return to Rome with a minimum of delay.

Once news of Sulla's preparations for return reached Rome, Cinna and his handpicked colleague for the consulship of 85, Gnaeus Papirius Carbo, began rallying troops and resources against him. Both had themselves reelected consuls for 84. Their plan was to face Sulla in Greece, and they had already dispatched some advance contingents when Cinna was killed in the course of a mutiny at the port of Ancona on the Adriatic. Afterwards, in consequence, Carbo recalled the contingents and decided that any stand against Sulla should be made in Italy, not abroad. It was probably he, too, who at this critical juncture finally had a law passed providing for the redistribution of the new citizens among the thirty-five tribes.

SULLA'S SECOND MARCH ON ROME (83–82)

As soon as Sulla landed at Brundisium with his five legions in spring 83, he was joined by two men who both had reason to keep out of Cinna's way: Marcus Licinius Crassus, aged thirty-two and son of the consul of 97, and Gnaeus Pompeius, aged twenty-three and son of the consul of 89. Pompey had coolly raised three legions from his father's former supporters in Picenum, and now placed this private army at Sulla's disposal. In general, Rome and most of Italy were initially hostile to Sulla. Although this resistance at first suffered from divisiveness, it was strengthened in 82

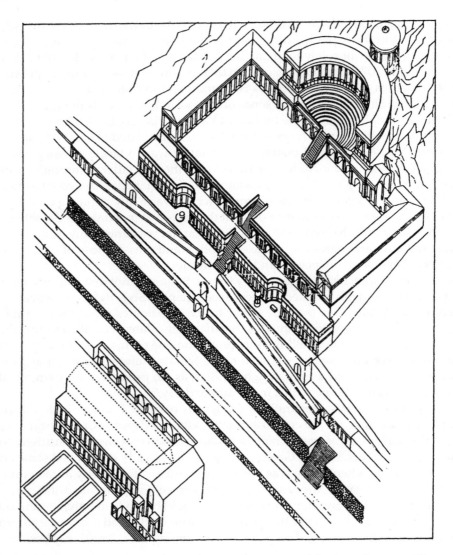

Figure 5.3 *Praeneste (modern Palestrina), situated on a spur of the Apennines east of Rome, was always appreciated as a cool refuge from summer heat in the city, and many wealthy Roman families had villas in its vicinity. It was also the site of an important sanctuary, the largest in Italy, dedicated to Fortuna Primigenia ("Firstborn Fortune"). The massive surviving remains reflect construction of the late second century B.C., with an amazing series of barrel-vaulted terraces ascending a steep hillside on which the modern town is also built; ramps link the terraces. Architectural inspiration came from famous sanctuaries of the Greek world. The cult of the goddess drew not only men from Rome, Italy, and farther afield—especially those seeking success in politics or warfare—but also women eager for children. An additional attraction at Praeneste was an oracle associated with the cult; the responses made to those who consulted it took the form of inscribed wooden* sortes *(literally "lots").*

with the election of Carbo as consul again (he had not been consul in 83), alongside Gaius Marius, the son of Rome's savior. Even the potency of Marius' name, however, could not prevent the city itself from falling into Sulla's hands. "Young" Marius escaped to make a stand at Praeneste, twenty-three miles (36 km) to the east (modern Palestrina; Fig. 5.3). Gradually the fighting that raged all over northern and central Italy during 82 came to center on this stronghold, from which "Young" Marius could be neither relieved nor dislodged. Eventually, fellow commanders of his sought to relax Sulla's grip on the siege by making a diversionary attack on Rome from the north. On November 1, 82, they took up a position one mile outside the Colline Gate. Sulla dashed from Praeneste to confront them. When the battle began in the late afternoon, the left wing under his own command collapsed, but the right under Crassus broke the enemy. Very gradually, after a period of despair, the two men's forces at last gained the upper hand after nightfall.

With Sulla's narrowly won victory at the Colline Gate, effective resistance to him in Italy came to an end. Praeneste soon surrendered, and "Young" Marius was killed. Elsewhere, Sicily and Africa were still in the hands of Sulla's opponents, but Pompey was sent to each of these provinces in turn, winning them back with a devastating efficiency that gained him the nickname "Young Butcher." One of his victims was Carbo, who had fled to Sicily after Sulla's victory at the Colline Gate. After these campaigns Sulla, who had already given his stepdaughter in marriage to Pompey, now instructed him to discharge almost all his forces. Pompey wanted the further reward of a triumph, however, despite not being a senator. Sulla eventually granted this wish and even addressed him by the name conferred by the troops in Africa, Magnus or "The Great."

Meantime, from November 82 Rome and Italy were at Sulla's mercy, resigned to whatever fate he had in store for them. Thanks to all the bloodshed, their conqueror in this latest bout of civil war now enjoyed a far tighter grip than Cinna or Marius had ever achieved. In addition, unlike his predecessors, he possessed a clear vision of the reforms required in his opinion to return the state to its old stability, as well as a steely determination to put them into effect.

SUGGESTED READINGS

Dillon, Matthew, and Lynda Garland. 2005. *Ancient Rome from the Early Republic to the Assassination of Julius Caesar.* London and New York: Routledge. This extensive sourcebook, with its informed commentary, includes valuable chapters on women, Marius, and the Social War.

Flower, Harriet I. 2010. *Roman Republics.* Princeton: Princeton University Press. A short book valuable for its sharp analysis of the pressures and dilemmas that assailed the Republic from the second century.

Knapp, Robert. 2011. *Invisible Romans.* Cambridge, Mass.: Harvard University Press. An engaging study of men and women, mostly poor and ordinary, and such livelihoods as slave, soldier, prostitute, and bandit.

Lintott, Andrew. 1993. *Imperium Romanum: Politics and Administration.* London and New York: Routledge. Informative outline and discussion of provincial government.

THE DOMINATION OF
SULLA AND ITS LEGACY

SULLA'S PROSCRIPTIONS (82–81)

For Sulla, victory at the Colline Gate on November 1, 82, was not enough. After so much fierce resistance, he needed to be confident of gaining undisputed control of Rome and Italy. For this purpose he instituted "proscriptions." In other words, he published lists of individuals who were thus automatically condemned to death without trial. Anyone could kill them and then claim a reward. There were rewards, too, for informers and penalties for those who helped the proscribed evade detection. A proscribed person's property was confiscated and auctioned off by the state, and his sons and grandsons were barred from seeking any public office. The first proscription list was published very early in November 82, two more soon followed, and June 1, 81, was eventually set as the final day for publishing further names. Officially, Sulla's purpose in instituting proscriptions was to root out those prominent individuals—senators and *equites* especially—who had taken sides against him. The total number of individuals killed in this way is unclear; 500 seems the minimum figure, and it could have been two, or even three, times that. Of all the forms of violence that Sulla unleashed against his fellow citizens in the course of his career, it was the proscriptions that were remembered with the most lasting horror and revulsion. Moreover, by targeting men of wealth and initiative, as well as excluding their sons and grandsons from public office, the proscriptions caused severe social and economic disruption, and for too long deprived the state of talent that it could ill afford to lose. Not until 49, as it turned out, would the exclusion from public office be lifted.

SULLA THE DICTATOR AND HIS PROGRAM (82–81)

Also in November 82, the senate recognized as legal all Sulla's past actions as both consul and proconsul. It officially conferred on him an additional name, Felix or "fortunate"; Sulla had always believed in his personal luck. Most important of all, the senate initiated the procedure, which led to Sulla's immediate appointment as dictator charged with bringing order back to the state and formulating laws. The name and style of the office purposely recalled the traditional office of dictator, which remained familiar to Romans, although in fact no appointment had been made to it since the end of the Second Punic War. In vital respects, however, Sulla's dictatorship departed from the traditional model. His appointment to it specifically validated all his actions in advance; he could execute anyone without trial and was not required to submit any legislative proposal to a citizen assembly. In addition, there was no time limit to his tenure of this office.

The absence of such a limit, however, should not be taken as a sign that Sulla envisaged remaining dictator indefinitely. Far from it. Instead, he was committed to restoring the state to the stable condition which, in his view, it had enjoyed under the guidance of the senate until Tiberius Gracchus and a succession of other ambitious leaders proceeded to upset its balance with increasingly damaging consequences. The senate's persistent weakness, as Sulla saw it, was that its predominance could readily be challenged. Moreover, most recently its numbers had been badly depleted in all the civil strife; perhaps no more than about 150 members still survived out of the normal total of around 300. Sulla therefore made up this total and also introduced around 300 further members, so that altogether the senate now became double its traditional size, and its meeting place (the *curia*) on the north side of the Forum Romanum was enlarged. By definition, the new members came from the equestrian class, because this was the group of wealthiest Roman citizens outside the senate. Many equites had opposed Sulla, and had been proscribed. On the other hand, the most loyal of those who had supported him now gained this reward, at the same time further weakening equestrian identity and influence. Even so, that was hardly a matter of regret to Sulla.

To maintain a total of around 600 senators, Sulla doubled the number of quaestors (the lowest senatorial magistracy) to twenty. At the same time, advancement through the *cursus honorum* inevitably became a more competitive struggle, because Sulla only increased the number of praetorships annually from six to eight, and he left the number of consuls at two. Orderly competition for office seemed essential to him, and to this end he revived certain old restrictions which had been either ignored or set aside in recent decades. These were, first, that only ex-quaestors were eligible for the praetorship, and likewise only ex-praetors for the consulship; and second, that these successive offices could not be held before the ages of thirty, thirty-nine, and forty-two respectively. Third, there must be a ten-year interval between holding any particular office again. This restriction would make it impossible to repeat the electoral successes of Marius and Cinna above all.

The tribunate was the one magistracy that Sulla modified significantly, because he regarded the challenges to the senate mounted through it as particularly harmful. A man who served as tribune was now automatically barred from standing for any further office, and tribunes' authority was drastically curtailed. The only legislative proposals they might now bring to the Plebeian assembly were ones already approved by the senate. However, the tribunes' traditional right of exercising a veto may have remained intact. Even so, no office could now be less attractive to anyone with political ambitions.

Equites, as we have seen, lost much of their identity and influence as a class thanks to the violent deaths of many and the promotion of others to the senate. Sulla struck equites a further blow by excluding them entirely from membership of the juries in the jury courts and restricting these juries to senators only. The dominance of senators in this important sphere was made all the greater by Sulla's establishment of seven such courts on a permanent basis.

In order to gain support, Sulla had promised that he would redistribute among the thirty-five tribes everyone awarded Roman citizenship as a result of the Social War, and this promise he kept. Meantime, citizen residents of Rome and its environs stood to lose by his abolition of the grain distributions instituted by Gaius Gracchus. Sulla viewed subsidizing these as an unwarranted drain on the treasury. Elsewhere in Italy, his two principal concerns were to find land for settling his veterans and to discipline those areas, which had opposed him. He addressed both concerns by widespread confiscations from communities and reallocation of the land to his veterans. The program's sheer size was unprecedented—there were perhaps 80,000 men to settle—and its impact harsh and disruptive (Fig. 6.1).

Outside Italy, in Sulla's view, the state had most to fear from the commander who could persuade his troops to join him in attacking Rome, just as Sulla himself had done twice. The shorter a commander's term, the less time he would gain to cultivate his troops. Accordingly, Sulla's hope was that at the end of their original term of office as many consuls and praetors as possible would accept one-year provincial governorships, with their *imperium* extended as proconsul or propraetor. There was no law requiring such acceptance, however.

Sulla revived, and perhaps added to, the existing restrictions on a governor's activity, which, like so much else, had been ignored in the recent past. These were that only with prior authorization from Rome could a governor make war or leave his province, either alone or at the head of his troops. In addition, he must leave the province within thirty days of his successor's arrival there.

VERDICTS ON SULLA'S PROGRAM

Sulla resigned the dictatorship by the end of 81, was elected consul for 80, and thereafter retired to a villa near Puteoli, where he died early in 78. Because much of his program was to be dismantled so rapidly, its shortcomings tend to engage

Figure 6.1 *Pompeii, famous as one of the Campanian cities overwhelmed by the volcanic eruption of Mt. Vesuvius in* A.D. *79, preserves an amphitheater seating perhaps 20,000 spectators in thirty-five rows, surrounding an arena measuring 220 × 115 ft (67 × 35 m). An inscription dates the dedication of the structure to about 70* B.C., *thus making it one of the earliest known amphitheaters to be erected in permanent stone form, and a marked advance on the temporary wooden structures, which continued to be used in the forum at Rome and elsewhere. In addition, the dedication specifically identifies Pompeii's amphitheater as a structure commissioned for their own benefit by the veteran colonists who were settled there by Sulla within the previous decade, and who were for a long time resented by the established members of the community. Evidently the new, tougher military training associated with Marius (see Chapter Five) incorporated gladiators' fighting techniques. The veterans at Pompeii might well have been eager to maintain an interest in gladiatorial combat. Their amphitheater stood as a stark warning to any hostile citizen that they were here to stay.*

our attention more than its strengths. The latter, however, are real and should not be dismissed out of hand. Most striking is Sulla's reinforcement of certain Republican ideals as he saw them. The opportunity to subject Rome permanently to a sole ruler was easier for him to seize than it had been for Marius or Cinna. Like them, however, he had no intention of going to this extreme; later, Julius Caesar would mock him for this restraint (see Chapter Seven). Sulla wanted to equip the state with stable, undisputed leadership, and he continued to regard the senate as the best agent for this key role by law.

For all its cohesion and its adherence to Republican ideals, however, his program also reflected serious limitations, which he evidently overlooked or chose to ignore. Many groups of individuals, not to mention most of the controversial political and social issues of the past half-century, were simply set aside. At a stroke the equites and the tribunate were eliminated as political forces along with the

Figure 6.2 *Bust, possibly Sulla.*

Plebeian assembly, and the monthly grain distributions in Rome were terminated. Proscriptions, as well as widespread land confiscation and resettlement, created huge social dislocation.

Any hopes for the future could only be fulfilled by the enlarged senate. From the outset, however, there must have been grave doubt whether its members were capable of maintaining sufficient unity and sense of responsibility to provide the self-denying collegial leadership that Sulla somehow expected of them (Source 6.1). When it came to a choice between resorting to force or respecting constitutional principle, his own example was quite appalling. It would be remarkable if his new senators—themselves likewise the winners in civil strife—could prove consistently more restrained, especially when there was now sure to be increased competition for the top magistracies. As to the danger of another march on Rome, Sulla's legal restrictions on governors could offer no more than paper protection.

LEPIDUS' RISING AND ITS AFTERMATH (78–77)

Sulla left election procedures unchanged, so candidates opposed to his program could stand and win. This occurred even while he was still alive, when Marcus

---

SOURCE 6.1: *Cicero's successful defense of Sextus Roscius of Ameria in southern Umbria was one of his first major cases, conducted in 80 when he was twenty-six. Chrysogonus, a freedman of Sulla, accused Roscius of parricide. In fact his father had been murdered by others, and his name then added by Chrysogonus to a proscription list (after these had been closed) in order to justify the disposal of his property. Cicero gives his defense of the son broader significance by boldly arguing to the jury of senators that Sulla's new senate will lose public confidence if it tolerates the continuation of such disrespect for the law.*

There was a period, of course, when the situation called for one man [Sulla] to be in complete personal control. But he has now re-appointed magistrates and passed laws restoring to each their traditional tasks and powers. And if the men appointed want to keep these powers, they can, for ever—but not if they indulge or acquiesce in acts of robbery and murder, or in such lavish expenditures as I have described. I do not want to bring bad luck to anyone by saying anything too harshly critical, gentlemen of the jury, but I must insist that unless the nobles show themselves the true guardians of the state, brave and merciful, they will be obliged to surrender the very powers they have so recently acquired to men who do have such merits. (139)

Aemilius Lepidus was elected consul for 78, despite Sulla's open disapproval of his candidacy. Lepidus soon advocated increasingly sweeping measures—the repeal of Sulla's acts, the return of confiscated land, the reintroduction of the grain distributions, and finally the restoration of tribunes' powers and a second consulship for himself. This crescendo motivated former owners in Etruria to attack the settlers placed on their land by Sulla. The senate sent both consuls to restore order, but Lepidus then proceeded to join the attackers and lead them. Dreading the prospect of new civil strife, the senate sought to placate him, but he would not be deflected from marching on Rome early in 77. The senate conferred a command upon Pompey and prepared to make a stand. In the event, Lepidus' ill-prepared assault was repulsed, his followers were pursued, and many of them were killed; he himself died soon after in Sardinia.

Even so, Lepidus had exposed bitter discontent with Sulla's program, as well as the senate's vulnerability in such a crisis. He also turned out to fulfill Pompey's wish for further opportunities because now, when ordered to discharge his troops, Pompey declined. In all likelihood, Metellus in Spain had already requested help to defeat Sertorius, the sole remaining opponent of Sulla and his regime outside Italy (see below). Neither of the consuls finally elected for 77 after Lepidus' defeat wanted such a dangerous and thankless assignment. Moreover, since Pompey already had a body of troops, it seemed only right to send him, even though he was only a young private citizen; there was no other practical option anyway.

Over the next few years the restoration of tribunes' powers seems to have been the most fiercely argued political issue, although the only concession made by the senate (in 75) was to remove the ban, which prevented tribunes from holding any further office. In 73, the grain distributions were reinstated. Finally, we know that towards the end of the 70s the regulation of governors' behavior and the restriction of juries in the jury courts to senators again claimed attention, but no measures were taken yet. Instead, throughout the 70s, the state had to be more preoccupied with a formidable range of threats that emerged, or reemerged, both in Italy and in various areas of the Mediterranean.

CHALLENGE FROM SERTORIUS IN SPAIN (80–73)

Among these threats, we may note first Quintus Sertorius. An associate of Cinna, then Carbo, as ex-praetor he took up the governorship of Nearer Spain at the end of 83, but in 81 he was proscribed and expelled from there, and fled to the independent kingdom of Mauretania in Africa (Map 6.1). The following year, however, the Lusitanians in the west of the Iberian peninsula, along with other anti-Sullan Roman exiles, invited him back to lead the rising, which they had begun. He accepted, and his rapid defeat of the governor of Further Spain prompted Sulla to dispatch there his consular colleague of 80, Quintus Caecilius Metellus Pius. Sertorius, however, continued to be so successful that by 77 almost all of Roman Spain, except the south, was under his control. At this stage, he was joined by the

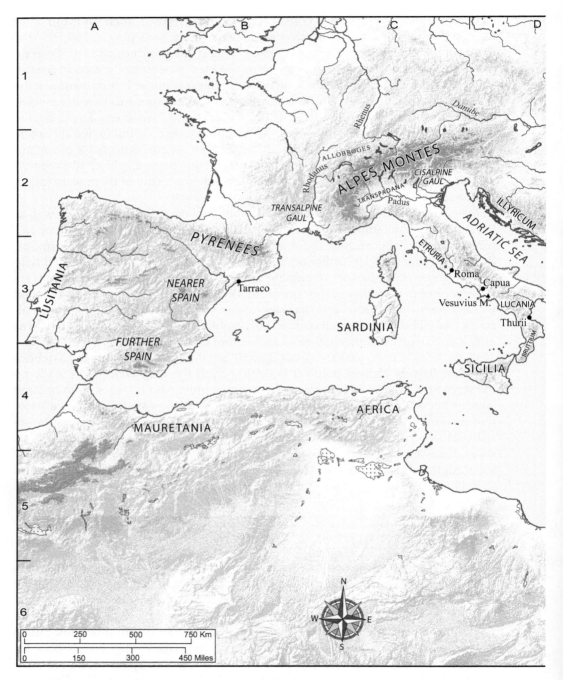

Map 6.1 *Rome's Wars, 78–63*

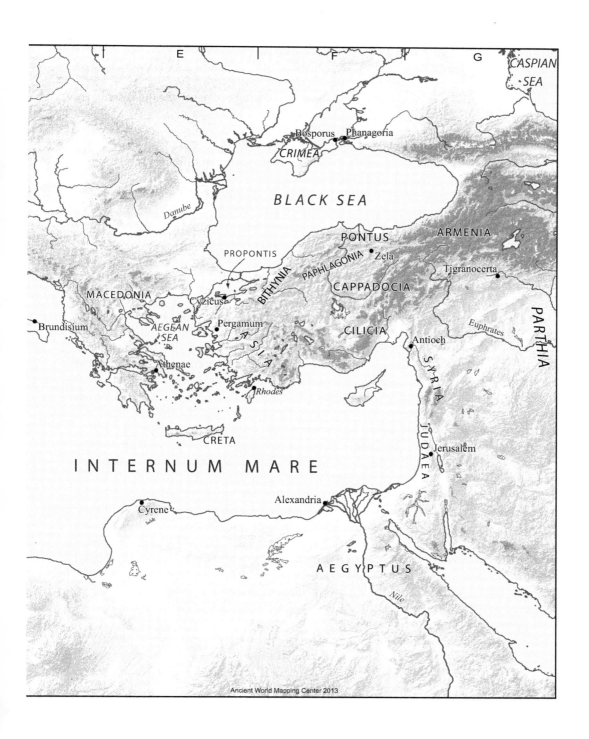

E F G

CASPIAN
SEA

Bosporus Phanagoria
CRIMEA

BLACK SEA

PONTUS ARMENIA

PROPONTIS PAPHLAGONIA Zela

MACEDONIA BITHYNIA CAPPADOCIA Tigranocerta

Cyzicus

Pergamum CILICIA PARTHIA

AEGEAN A S I A Euphrates
SEA Antioch

Brundisium

SYRIA

Athenae

Rhodes

JUDAEA

CRETA

Jerusalem

INTERNUM MARE

Cyrene Alexandria

AEGYPTUS

Nile

Ancient World Mapping Center 2013

survivors of Lepidus' rising in Italy, led by Marcus Perperna Veiento; soon afterwards, on the other side, Pompey arrived to reinforce Metellus. For the next two years the struggle remained intense and inconclusive, with both sides gaining victories but also suffering defeats. Pompey in fact very nearly met his match in Sertorius.

Meantime, Sertorius persuaded Mithridates to send him money and ships. Yet, by the time these arrived in 73, Pompey and Metellus had begun to gain the upper hand. Much of Sertorius' Spanish following fell away; finally his officers, led by Perperna, turned traitor and assassinated him. Soon afterwards (still in 73), Perperna in turn was easily defeated and then executed by Pompey; with his death, the prolonged rising in Spain came to an end. What Perperna and his fellow officers had expected to gain by their disloyalty to Sertorius remains a puzzle; just possibly they imagined that Pompey would reward them.

SPARTACUS' SLAVE REVOLT (73–71)

With the elimination of Sertorius and Perperna in 73, the senate was relieved of one crisis at least. It was fortunate, therefore, that another developed only now. This occurred in Italy itself, when a group of seventy-four slaves led by a Thracian, Spartacus, and a Gaul, Crixus, escaped from a gladiatorial training school at Capua. In no time, the stronghold they established on Mt. Vesuvius attracted not only runaway slaves, but also free workers on rural estates—eventually 70,000 men and more. At first, the Roman forces hurriedly sent against them were defeated. Spartacus urged his followers to head north out of Italy and to disperse back to their different lands of origin before Rome could prepare a major assault. Crixus countered by proposing that they loot southern Italy first, and this they proceeded to do until he and the force with him were wiped out by a Roman army in 72. Spartacus in the meantime did head north, but for some unknown reason he turned back after he had won a victory in Cisalpine Gaul, made for Rome itself but then thought better of it, and finally seized Thurii in the south.

At this stage, after further Roman defeats, the senate decided to put Crassus—who had won the battle at the Colline Gate for Sulla in November 82 and had been praetor in 73—in sole charge of the offensive against Spartacus; he took over the consuls' four legions and raised six more. Since the senate was still short of funds, he may have been chosen partly for his wealth; "rich" in his view was a description applicable only to someone with the means to maintain a legion out of his own pocket. With the forces he raised, Crassus drove Spartacus' force still farther south. Meantime, the senate in its continuing alarm had summoned Pompey back from Spain. Crassus naturally hoped that he could finish off the war alone, and he almost did so, winning a battle in Lucania in which Spartacus was killed. However, 5,000 slaves who managed to escape and flee northwards were caught and slaughtered by Pompey, who was therefore able to claim to the senate that *he* was responsible for finally ending the war.

CONSULSHIP OF CRASSUS AND POMPEY (70)

This claim by Pompey did nothing to reduce Crassus' long-standing jealousy of him. Even so, now in 71, when both men contemplated running for the consulship, Crassus took the precaution of soliciting Pompey's support. Crassus' candidacy was unimpeachable; he was old enough, and he had been praetor. Pompey, by contrast, was too young (only thirty-five), and he was not even a senator. He, like Crassus, had an army at his disposal in Italy and could have used it to demand high office. But it looks as if there was no difficulty over first securing exemption from the law for Pompey and then electing both men consuls for 70. That way, at least, Pompey's position was finally regularized. By this stage, nothing less than a consulship would be an appropriate reward for his service to the state, even if it did require the strict rules revived by Sulla to be swept aside.

Once in office, Crassus and Pompey were soon on bad terms. They did cooperate, however, in proposing that the tribunate's full powers be restored, and evidently the law passed without disturbance. This need not mean that all opposition to the traditional powers of the office had evaporated since Sulla's dictatorship; it was more perhaps that doubters acknowledged the futility of making a stand on the issue at this date. Another, lesser blow to Sulla's program in 70 was the passage of a proposal to make equites two-thirds of the jury members in the jury courts; the other third remained senators. Inevitably, the change further impaired the supremacy of the senate as established by Sulla, but it does at least seem to have ended the long-standing contention on this issue of jury membership.

POMPEY FREES THE MEDITERRANEAN OF PIRATES (67)

At the end of 70, Crassus and Pompey staged a public reconciliation, but both ignored Sulla's hope that as senior magistrates they would agree to take up a command of some kind after their year in office. An attractive opportunity did arise for Pompey, however, in 67. By that date the widespread frustration felt throughout the Mediterranean at the Roman authorities' incapacity to suppress piracy had reached a breaking point. The problem itself was not new, nor had Roman efforts to control it been lacking. On the other hand, they had for long proven largely ineffectual, and pirates' depredations were becoming ever more damaging and outrageous. Grain supplies to Rome itself were interrupted, and the maritime trade routes of the entire eastern Mediterranean had become altogether unsafe. There were no longer any strong powers there to keep piracy in check; Rhodes, Syria, and Egypt were now all weak.

So in early 67 the tribune Aulus Gabinius proposed a three-year command that would equip Pompey with the authority and resources to tackle the problem comprehensively. Pompey would be a proconsul with authority throughout the Mediterranean and up to fifty miles beyond, equal but not superior to all other proconsuls; he would also have as many as twenty subordinate commanders or "legates," each with the rank of propraetor. Gabinius' proposal aroused furious opposition from the substantial body of senators who asserted Sulla's principle that it was both unconstitutional and irresponsible to place so much authority in the hands of one individual. While recognizing Pompey's extraordinary generalship, at the same time they were naturally both jealous and fearful of him.

Once the proposal had been pushed through, Pompey wasted no time. He divided the entire Mediterranean into zones, each of them the responsibility of a legate, so that when their simultaneous offensive began there was nowhere left for pirates to run. Pompey himself tackled Cilicia, the coast with the greatest concentration of them. Thanks to this comprehensive strategy, the pirate menace was removed within three months. Rather than butchering the survivors, Pompey then found land in Cilicia (now claimed as a Roman province) and elsewhere for them to settle. During the next unstable forty years or so, piracy did return to the Mediterranean, but never again did it attain the level of the early 60s.

THREAT FROM KING MITHRIDATES VI OF PONTUS AND SULLA'S RESPONSE (87–85)

Once again Pompey had been offered the opportunity to deal with a major threat and had succeeded where others before him had failed. His unexpectedly rapid completion of this task in 67 meant that he seemed the obvious choice the following year when there was renewed pressure to appoint a commander who could end intolerably prolonged hostilities with a decisive victory. The opponent in this instance was the formidable King Mithridates VI of Pontus, the coastal region towards the southeast corner of the Black Sea. He now needs to be properly introduced at last, and his previous engagements with Rome reviewed.

Mithridates, the older of two sons, was only eleven when his father was assassinated in 120. His mother Laodice then ruled as regent, favoring her younger son, until around 113, when Mithridates (aged about eighteen) managed to oust them both and assert sole, personal control. His next concern was to raise both his personal standing and that of his kingdom, which he did dramatically over the next few years by bringing the Crimea and the northern shores of the Black Sea under his control; these areas gave him immense material resources and manpower. He also pressed farther and more aggressively than any of his predecessors into Paphlagonia and Cappadocia, eventually (about 101) even making his eight-year-old son nominal king of Cappadocia. After a rebellion there in the mid-90s, Rome ordered Mithridates to abandon Cappadocia and sent a governor (Sulla, in fact) to install a new ruler. Mithridates acquiesced in this instance, preferring to postpone the clash that seemed increasingly unavoidable. Around the same time (mid-90s), as it happened, he gained the notable advantage of an alliance with the major kingdom of Armenia to the southeast of his own; his daughter married its new king, Tigranes I. Then in 90, when Rome was preoccupied with the Social War in Italy, Mithridates caused the king of Cappadocia to flee and expelled the young king Nicomedes from Bithynia, west of Paphlagonia. But, surprisingly, when a force of five Roman legions arrived, he agreed to withdraw.

At that point, however, the Roman commanders fatally miscalculated. They urged the newly restored kings of Cappadocia and Bithynia to take revenge, and to recoup their financial losses, by invading Pontus. Nicomedes did so, thus finally provoking Mithridates to action, which he began to take in 89. That year and into the following summer of 88, Mithridates' westward sweep proved invincible. He soon had all of western Asia Minor under his control (Fig. 6.3). In what had been the Roman province of Asia for the previous forty years, he was for the most part welcomed as a liberator. He sought both to allow expression of hatred for Roman rule and to reinforce his own position there by secretly arranging for a massacre of all resident Romans or Italians. This occurred early in 88; the death toll was said to have been around 80,000.

By 88 Rome was less preoccupied than before by crises in Italy. The Social War was largely won, and so war was declared against Mithridates, to be waged by Sulla with five legions. As we have seen, however, he encountered unusual difficulties in claiming this command and then arranging for his departure from Rome. This prolonged delay left Mithridates free to consider advancing still farther west, which he decided to do in 88 when invited to occupy Athens by opponents of Rome there. Once Sulla and his army finally set out in 87, therefore, it was Greece they made for. They did successfully take Athens and its port, the Piraeus, by siege, but Mithridates in the meantime dispatched to central Greece an army under his general Archelaus that was perhaps three times larger than Sulla's. So it was here that the two decisive battles were fought in summer 86, at Chaeronea and Or-

Figure 6.3 *After King Mithridates VI of Pontus had occupied the Roman province of Asia in 89, he showed no hesitation in issuing coins there with his image (modeled on Alexander the Great) on one side and his name, title, and associated symbols on the other. The language used is Greek, and this example carries the date "Year 2" of the new era.*

chomenus. Both were clear victories for Sulla, and as a result almost all of Archelaus' forces were wiped out. Sulla then offered lenient terms.

At this point, despite all the setbacks in Greece, Mithridates was disinclined to accept terms, and it was hard for Sulla to pursue him further without a fleet, which he was only now beginning to assemble. In fall 85, however, as the threats to his control escalated, Mithridates finally agreed to accept the terms that Sulla had offered a year before. The two men met and reached agreement at Dardanus, on the Asian shore of the Hellespont. Both had much to gain by abandoning the struggle at this point. Mithridates welcomed the chance to revive his strength and await another opportunity to exploit some future crisis facing Rome. It was precisely because of the current atmosphere of crisis there that Sulla, for his part, wanted to make peace and return home as soon as possible. It was not at all in his immediate interests to pursue Mithridates further. All he wanted to do first was to reestablish the Roman province of Asia. This he did with unwavering harshness, demanding tax arrears and a huge indemnity from the cities there. After doing terrible harm, Sulla and his army eventually left Asia in 84, spent the winter in Athens, and sailed to Italy in spring 83.

CAMPAIGNS OF LUCULLUS AND POMPEY AGAINST MITHRIDATES (74–63)

In 75, when Nicomedes of Bithynia died and bequeathed his kingdom to Rome, Rome's decision was both to accept the bequest and to resume the fight against Mithridates, regardless of the agreement reached at Dardanus. Lucullus, consul in 74, was made governor of Asia and Cilicia jointly, with five legions at his disposal. In 73, however, Mithridates struck first by moving west from Pontus, through Paphlagonia, into Bithynia, where he laid siege to the key port city of Cyzicus on the Propontis. Surprisingly, the city held out, reinforced by Lucullus, even though Mithridates had larger forces, but with the onset of winter he was no longer able to supply them and so had to withdraw back to Pontus.

Lucullus, on the other hand, had achieved victory in 73 without risking a major battle. The following year he was bold enough to advance into Pontus and penetrated more deeply there in 71. When Mithridates' cavalry attacked, the Romans repulsed it with heavy losses. Subsequently, when the king decided upon a withdrawal to the mountainous kingdom of Armenia, his infantry no longer had the cavalry's protection and so incurred severe casualties from Roman pursuers. Tigranes, king of Armenia, respected his long-standing alliance with Mithridates to the extent of giving him refuge, but otherwise disappointed him by refusing to be drawn into the conflict between Pontus and Rome. Lucullus in the meantime, in his determination to overcome Mithridates, resolved to cross the Euphrates River and invade Armenia. This was a momentous and unauthorized step, because he had no instructions for extending his campaign in this way, and Armenia was a state, which had previously been quite outside Rome's orbit.

The further risk that an invasion of Armenia might in turn provoke its more powerful neighbor to the east, the Parthian empire, hardly seems to have struck Lucullus. In the event, he invaded Armenia in 69 and after a great battle captured and razed its southern capital, Tigranocerta. Parthia—a huge kingdom extending beyond the Caspian Sea, but often unstable—declined to intervene. Tigranes and Mithridates both eluded capture, however, and the failure of Lucullus' energetic operations to pursue them finally provoked his exhausted troops to mutiny by late 68. By chance just at the time of the mutiny, Mithridates managed to make his way back to Pontus with a small force. He stirred up revolt and wiped out the main body of Roman troops stationed there at a battle near Zela in summer 67. Lucullus had already withdrawn from Armenia but did not reach Pontus in time to prevent this unraveling of what he had achieved there; equally, he was unable to campaign further because of his men's refusal to cooperate.

During summer 67, two new commanders arrived from Rome to take over Lucullus' huge sphere of command between them, but they had never expected to be faced by such a crisis, and it soon became clear that they were not equal to retrieving Rome's position. All of Lucullus' success seemed to be reversed. Mithridates had recovered Pontus, and Tigranes had invaded Cappadocia. At Rome, it is no surprise that dismay and frustration led to pressure for more decisive action. One of the tribunes for 66, Gaius Manilius, consequently proposed that all the Roman forces in Asia Minor and the entire conduct of the war be handed to Pompey. Given his swift and total success against the pirates the previous year, this solution seemed unarguable, and there was none of the fierce opposition that had resisted Gabinius' proposal the previous year. Yet again, therefore, Pompey was invited to take an extraordinary command to retrieve a situation where others had failed. This outcome left Lucullus embittered, because he had come so close to eliminating Mithridates. Looking further back, we may reflect that this opportunity for Pompey, and the difficulties associated with it, need never have arisen in the first place had Sulla set himself different priorities in the mid-80s.

In 66, Pompey moved fast, as usual, to restore the Roman position. He now persuaded the king of Parthia not to help Mithridates or Tigranes, but instead to attack Armenia, a key development, which forced Tigranes to abandon his invasion of Cappadocia. Pompey himself drove Mithridates to the far east of Pontus and defeated him there. In consequence, the king finally abandoned Pontus and made his way to the Crimean Bosporus, the last secure part of his realm. Pompey chose not to pursue him, but instead to enforce the submission of Tigranes, which he did without difficulty by late 66. Pompey then took the year 65 to suppress resistance in this distant region altogether, marching almost as far as the Caspian Sea; the region was mostly divided among dependent rulers, however, rather than being annexed. In 64 Pompey was preoccupied with reorganizing part of Pontus as a Roman province, but late in the year he marched south to annex Syria and then proceeded on to Judaea, where he captured Jerusalem after a three-month siege in 63. His justification for all this further invasion and annexation was that effective, reliable rulers in the Roman interest were simply lacking here. In addition, although Parthia was not yet the obvious threat that it would later become, Pompey may have welcomed the chance to block the possible growth of its influence.

Pompey was criticized at Rome for taking these other initiatives while Mithridates was still free. If Pompey had assumed that the king would be a spent force after he fled from Pontus, that may have been a mistake, because in fact Mithridates did set about vigorously building up power in the Crimean Bosporus once he reached there in 65 (Fig. 6.4). His troops, however, no longer shared his zeal, and it was a revolt by them that led to his death in 63, either by suicide or possibly assassination; his son Pharnaces succeeded him. So finally died a king whose relentless struggle against Rome over a period of about thirty years forms an episode of exceptional importance for Rome's development.

Figure 6.4 *The manly qualities—as a horse rider especially—shown by a concubine, later wife, of Mithridates were so outstanding that he was said to have called her by the masculine form of her name, Hypsicrates, rather than by the feminine Hypsicrateia. As a remarkable corroboration of this tale preserved by Plutarch, Russian underwater archeologists diving at Phanagoria have recovered this impressive marble base for a statue inscribed in Greek "Hypsicrates, wife of Mithridates Eupator Dionysus, hail!" Phanagoria was an important city situated on an island on the eastern side of the Crimean Bosporus (modern Straits of Kerch), where the sea level has risen since ancient times.*

ROLES OF CRASSUS AND CICERO IN ROME (65–63)

Pompey's unbroken success and luck in the East aroused envy at home, as well as concern for how he might act on his return. In particular, would he seek sole power like Sulla, bringing further bloodshed and terror? No one brooded over these issues with greater jealousy and apprehension than Crassus. After his consulship in 70, we know next to nothing of his activities until he became censor in 65, but from then onwards we can detect him searching desperately to secure some kind of influence or authority with which to stand up to his former colleague. The elections conducted in 64 for the two consuls who would hold office during 63 were to have a particularly significant outcome. We know that seven candidates stood, but three dominated the race. Two were "nobles"—Gaius Antonius Hybrida, whose father had been consul in 99, and the patrician Lucius Sergius Catilina, better known today as Catiline. Both were suspect figures who had served under Sulla and in very dubious circumstances had escaped conviction for major offenses; both were also in the typical senator's predicament of having seriously overspent in their competition for political office. At least they settled on cooperating against their main rival, the exceptional figure of Marcus Tullius Cicero. It was potentially to his disadvantage that he was a *novus homo*. He was born in 106 to a wealthy family of Arpinum, southeast of Rome (Marius' birthplace, too), and made his mark as a brilliant advocate and orator. His most memorable case to date had been in 70, when against all the odds he had secured the conviction of Gaius Verres for extortion during his governorship of Sicily. In 66 he had spoken in support of Manilius' proposal to give Pompey the command against Mithridates, and he continued to make Pompey's interests one of his principal political concerns.

The two noble candidates stressed that their background should favor them above the novus homo. But this claim was not enough to dispel widespread doubt about their personal records. Cicero, by contrast, was a popular figure with a high reputation, as well as being a skilled electioneer who had cultivated widespread support. So he came out on top of the poll, a remarkable achievement. Antonius narrowly beat Catiline for the other consulship of 63. Cicero, as the leading figure, could hardly expect a calm year in office, and this became clear at once when a tribune, Publius Servilius Rullus, proposed the establishment of a major commission to take exclusive charge of the distribution of "public" land throughout Italy and the provinces. The

Figure 6.5 *Bust of Cicero.*

commission would have funds to buy more land as required, rather than resorting to confiscation (as Sulla had done), and to found colonies. In this way it could help relieve unemployment among the poor in the city of Rome by resettling them, as well as offer a fresh start to the huge number of people in distress throughout the Italian countryside. These included not only the many Sullan veterans who had failed as farmers and were now deep in debt, but also the landholders they had displaced in the first place. One clear reflection of this predicament dating to 64 is the senate's disbandment of all associations (*collegia*) in Rome. Normally there was no objection to peaceful groups of any kind; neighborhood, religious, or trade associations were the most common types. Recently, however, such groups in the city had been adding an unacceptable element of organized violence to political activity. This was a frightening development in a community, like almost all ancient ones, with no regular police.

In principle, therefore, the proposed land commission could do much to restore stability by reducing distress and the dangers it posed. There was also a less attractive side to the scheme, however. The ten senators elected to head the commission would become powerful figures, because they were to hold imperium for five years. With large funds at their disposal, they would have every opportunity for financial gain. Most ominous of all, Pompey on his return would have to apply to the commission if he was to secure land for his veterans. These possibilities prompted Cicero to set aside any social concern he may have had and instead to argue vehemently against Rullus' proposal. One danger for Cicero was a clash with Antonius over the whole matter, but he bought his fellow consul's silence by offering to exchange the provinces that they had each drawn in the lot, so Antonius now had the more lucrative opportunity to become governor of Macedonia rather than of Cisalpine Gaul. In the end, Rullus withdrew his proposal.

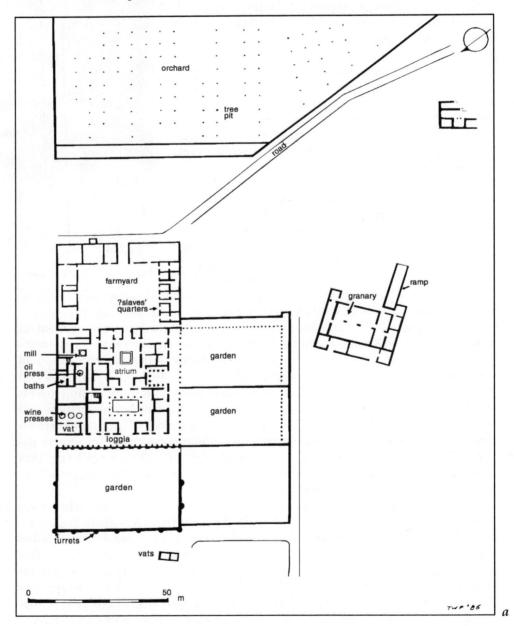

Figure 6.6a, b

b

Figure 6.6a, b *Settefinestre is the modern name for a grand villa in Etruria, not far inland from Cosa. Excavations here have provided exceptionally important insight into the rural economy. The villa's construction dates to the mid/late first century* B.C., *and reflects to an uncanny degree the recommendations of Roman writers on estate management. It is both a country residence and a working farm [a]. The owner's opulent living quarters—square in shape—were elegantly decorated, and the loggia, which extends along one entire side (145 ft/44 m long), overlooked an elaborate garden enclosed by a turreted wall (bottom left), resembling that of a city [b]. In addition, there was accommodation for an estate manager, and for slaves. The farm establishment included further gardens, a walled orchard, presses for wine and oil, a large wine vat, and an even more impressive granary. A port from which produce could be shipped out was close (below Cosa), and it is quite possible that the grain was grown specifically for the city of Rome. The villa's owners may have been a senatorial family, the Sestii.*

Two elections during the year 63 produced notable results. First, by chance, this was the time at which a new holder of the lifetime office of *pontifex maximus*— elected by seventeen of the thirty-five tribes—was required. The competition for such a venerable, prestigious position was normally just between elderly senators of the highest standing. Two such ex-consuls put themselves forward in this instance, but Gaius Julius Caesar (who was already a pontifex) had the nerve to compete also, and, thanks to heavy bribery, which drove him deep into debt, he won. This was really the first achievement in his career that marked him out as exceptional. He was born in 100 into the most ancient of patrician families, but not one that had shown much distinction in the recent past, though it had gained some by association after Marius married into it. Caesar was favored by Cinna, and even married his daughter Cornelia. Despite this relationship, he then had the good fortune to be spared by his fellow patrician Sulla, and after Cornelia's death in 69 he married Sulla's granddaughter Pompeia. Eager to gain Pompey's favor, Caesar supported the proposals of both Gabinius and Manilius, and thereafter when

Pompey was out of Rome he also associated himself with Crassus; the potential for mutual advantage in their relationship was obvious to both. Caesar's election as pontifex maximus, as well as his election as praetor for 62, now made him highly prominent.

CATILINE'S RISING (63–62)

The second election of note was for the consulships of 62, a race in which Catiline again competed and again lost. This was a grave blow to him, because he too had been risking bankruptcy in order to distribute more lavish bribes than ever. He owed his failure in part to Cicero, who demonstrated his personal distrust by having a bodyguard escort him to preside on election day in September, and wearing a breastplate visible under his toga. Catiline had already roused widespread alarm by championing the cause of those who were poor, in debt, or dispossessed, and by calling for cancellation of debts and redistribution of land.

In despair at proceeding by legal means, Catiline and his associates now began to gather forces for an armed revolution and other outrages such as arson and murder. However, since not everyone distrusted Catiline as completely as he did, Cicero had to proceed against him with care, and above all secure condemnatory evidence that was unassailable. Once it was confirmed in late November that Catiline, taunted by Cicero and hounded by creditors he could not pay, had left Rome to take command of forces gathered in Etruria, the senate did declare war on him. Finally, at the beginning of December, the evidence that Cicero sought came into his hands from envoys sent to Rome by a Gallic people, the Allobroges. They had been invited to join Catiline and his associates in planning to set fire to Rome later in the month. At a meeting of the senate on December 3 Cicero was able to confront five of the associates, obtain their confessions of guilt, and arrest them. This swung public opinion firmly behind him. Two days later, when he asked the senate what was to be done with the five, the decision after a tense debate was execution, a sentence which Cicero carried out at once.

Public opinion was soon sharply divided over this action, however. To his admirers, Cicero was now *Parens Patriae*, Father of his Country, a new founder of Rome. Opponents, by contrast, saw this summary execution of citizens without trial as illegal and unjustified. Even with the declaration of war against Catiline, there was some force to that argument, and later Cicero would be compelled to confront it. For the moment, he was extravagantly proud of what he had done, and would never waver from the view that he had taken the right course of action. The executions aside, we may agree that his energy and resourcefulness did avert what promised to be a catastrophe for Rome. Meantime, however, he and others ensured that the deeper causes of so much discontent were not remedied.

The debate in the senate on December 5 gave further prominence to Caesar, who took the lead in opposing the execution of Catiline's associates, as well as to Marcus Porcius Cato, who successfully urged this extreme step. Cato was the great-grandson of Cato the Elder, who had been so influential during the first half of the second century. Born in 95, "Young" Cato was still a junior senator—about to become tribune for 62—but was already championing an inflexible devotion to conservative, Optimate principles in the tradition of his great ancestor.

It remains unfortunate that the only accounts we have of Catiline's attempt at revolution are uncompromisingly hostile. At this point, to be sure, with his leading associates in Rome dead, his cause must have seemed hopeless. Early in 62, he and his forces in northern Etruria were trapped between two armies dispatched by the senate and then massacred. Soon afterwards, news arrived from Pompey that his work in the East was completed, and that he and his army were returning home. Suspense over the vital issue of what he would then do was about to reach its climax. Was Rome now about to acquire by violence, or alternative means, another strong leader and reformer on the model of Sulla? Would there be further civil war? Or was the state to remain divided and adrift, as it seemed to have been ever since Sulla's retirement? In this predicament, major threats abroad could be tackled only by resort to extraordinary commands, most conspicuously those created for Pompey himself. Meantime at home, the state was vulnerable to corruption, conspiracy, and rebellion, while little or nothing was done to relieve the miserable plight of the poor.

SUGGESTED READINGS

Badian, Ernst. 1968 (second edition). *Roman Imperialism in the Late Republic*. Ithaca, New York: Cornell University Press.

Lacey, Walter K., and Brian W. J. G. Wilson. 1970. *Respublica: Roman Society and Politics According to Cicero*. Oxford: Oxford University Press. An extensive collection of extracts from Cicero's speeches and writings, with introduction and comments.

Rosenstein, Nathan, and Robert Morstein-Marx (eds.). 2006. *A Companion to the Roman Republic*. Malden, Mass., and Oxford: Blackwell. Essays on a wide range of historical and cultural aspects, with marked attention to the challenges facing the Republic in the first century.

Seager, Robin. 2002 (revised edition). *Pompey the Great*. Oxford: Blackwell.

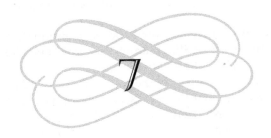

END OF THE REPUBLIC

Caesar's Dictatorship

POMPEY'S RETURN FROM THE EAST (62)

The dazzling wealth and glory with which Pompey returned from the East in 62 outclassed those of all previous Roman conquests. There was truth in his own public boast that he had found Asia a frontier province, and had left it at the heart of the empire. He had been courted by kings and princes, and offered godlike honors. He took possession of Syria and made it a province. He enlarged the province of Cilicia, and reorganized Bithynia and part of Pontus into a single, combined province. Otherwise he entrusted eastern Asia Minor—most notably Cappadocia and Armenia—to rulers sworn to uphold Roman interests; some even paid taxes to Rome. Only with Parthia does no pact seem to have been made, but he left strong Roman garrisons in both Cilicia and Syria to guard against any Parthian incursion there.

The wealth that Pompey brought back from Mithridates' treasure stores and elsewhere was quite simply staggering. Pompey delivered to the treasury 20,000 talents in gold and silver (equal to 480 million sesterces). To each of his soldiers he gave a minimum of 6,000 sesterces (a year's basic pay was 450). Officers were far more lavishly rewarded, and his own personal wealth now dwarfed that of Crassus. For the longer term, his conquests and annexations in the East were reckoned to have raised Rome's annual revenues from 200 million to 340 million sesterces. His achievement there was to be epitomized in the theater complex begun in the Campus Martius after his magnificent triumph in 61, and dedicated six years later in 55 (see Map 7.2). Rome had never seen anything like it. The theater itself was built in stone; linked with it was a vast portico containing a heroic, nude statue of

Pompey himself holding a globe, the symbol of a world conqueror, and surrounded by personifications of the fourteen "nations" he had subdued.

POMPEY AND POLITICAL STALEMATE IN ROME

When Pompey finally reached Brundisium in late 62, he surprised everyone who feared and envied him by simply disbanding his army. It emerged that he had no intention of retaining it to march on Rome and seize power. Such restraint need come as no special surprise. After all, his political involvement had never been deep, he felt no particular attachment to any political group or set of ideas, and he had been away for several years. He might hardly be expected to match Sulla's passion for imposing a fresh political or social blueprint on Rome. It soon became apparent that his sole concerns were to see his arrangements in the East ratified by the senate, and to secure land for the settlement of his veterans. Naturally enough, in view of his prestige, popularity, and achievements, he anticipated no difficulty on either count.

As it turned out, however, he was to be robbed of this hope. One of his former legates was consul in 61 and so was expected to steer the necessary measures through the senate. Unfortunately, however, he proved ineffective, and the main focus of attention during the year turned out to be a frivolous scandal caused by the irresponsible patrician Publius Clodius Pulcher. His father (now dead) had been consul in 79, and he himself had just reached the quaestorship (so he must have been aged about thirty). In December 62, he relished the risk of attending secret nocturnal rites in honor of the *Bona Dea* ("Good Goddess")—dressed as a woman, because males were strictly barred from the ceremony. The special attractions for him were the venue—Caesar's house in Rome—and the hostess, Caesar's wife Pompeia, with whom he allegedly either had, or wanted, an adulterous relationship.

After Clodius was discovered at the rites and prosecuted, Caesar declared Pompeia innocent, but still divorced her on the grounds that his household (that of the *pontifex maximus*, after all) must be above suspicion. He took no action himself against Clodius, whom he regarded as a potentially useful associate for the future. The trial became a sensation, offering extraordinary opportunities for bribery and political intrigue. Cicero displayed rash courage by actually taking the witness stand to break the alibi that formed a vital part of the defense: Clodius claimed to be about ninety miles (145 km) from Rome on the day of the ceremony. In the end, even though Clodius' guilt in trespassing on the sacred rites was patent, massive bribery of the jury

Figure 7.1 *Bust of Pompey.*

determined the verdict, and he was narrowly acquitted. So Cicero's devotion to truth and principle here only served to create a dangerous, implacable enemy for himself.

As it turned out, Pompey had to face the frustration of seeing his requests stalled not just in 61, but also in 60. Lucullus, Cato, and other Optimates took pride in being consistently obstructive. A tribune's proposal for major redistribution of "public" land (of the type made three years earlier in 63) was thwarted, as before, on suspicion that in practice it would serve to benefit the handful of senators placed in charge rather than Pompey's veterans and the mass of poor citizens in need of land. By chance, during 60 two other unrelated requests arose, which Cato took the lead in blocking. First, the syndicate that had won the major contract for collecting Rome's taxes in the province of Asia when this was last auctioned now found itself in difficulties. The amount of its winning bid—which had to be paid to the treasury in advance—was proving far larger than the syndicate found itself able to recoup through tax collection. Because it was now facing a heavy loss, it asked the senate to consider renegotiating the contract and thus, in effect, refunding part of the bid. The plea was hardly a strong one. Even so, Crassus gave it his support. Cato with equal vigor succeeded in blocking it.

The second request was made by Caesar. He had been praetor in 62 and then took up the governorship of Further Spain. He blatantly exploited his year there to recoup what it had cost him to win election as pontifex maximus and praetor. The unprovoked attacks that he launched on peoples in the far west of the Iberian peninsula yielded sufficient loot for him not only to clear his deep debts, but also to make substantial payments to the treasury. By the time that he returned to Rome mid-year in 60, the senate had voted him a triumph. His personal goal now, however, was to stand for election to the consulship of 59, and he had arrived just in time to register as a candidate. But to do so he would have to cross the *pomerium* and enter the city. That step would serve to rob him of his triumph, because a returning commander who was voted one could only cross the pomerium into the city on the day of the ceremony itself, and not before.

So Caesar asked the senate for permission to register as a candidate for the consulship without being physically present. By this means, he anticipated, he would both be able to celebrate his triumph, and still compete for the office without having to wait a further year or more. The concession was one that had been extended—in times of dire crisis—to no less than a member by marriage of Caesar's own family, Marius. In the present political climate, however, to request it was provocative; predictably enough, Cato persuaded the senate to deny it to Caesar. Caesar now surprised his opponents. It was the triumph that he let go; instead, he crossed the pomerium to register as a candidate for the consulship.

The reaction in the senate was one of alarm. Caesar was so popular that he stood an excellent chance of being elected. So now, when it came to determining the provinces for the consuls of 59 (prior to the elections, as required by Gaius Gracchus' law; see Chapter Four), the senate deliberately assigned commissions to police the forests and tracks of Italy—significant tasks in their own way, no doubt, but hardly commensurate with consular prestige, and certainly not with the ambition of someone like Caesar. Moreover, these assignments seemed all the more inappropriate in view of the serious disturbances now affecting Roman interests in Gaul.

PARTNERSHIP OF POMPEY, CRASSUS, AND CAESAR

For all his popularity, Caesar was well aware that it would take money and support in abundance to secure his election as consul for 59. Many senators were contributing to a fund established to ensure the election of a rival candidate, Marcus Calpurnius Bibulus, Cato's son-in-law; Cato himself thought this cause so vital that he was prepared to overlook the widespread bribery that it entailed. Caesar had no such lavish help to hand, but he happened to be on good terms with both Pompey and Crassus, and he was keenly aware of how they too had been thwarted by Cato and the majority of senators. To date, Pompey and Crassus had been too estranged from each other to work together, but Caesar now arranged a reconciliation. He further arranged that the three of them would join to achieve their goals. Pompey and Crassus both had money and influence; Pompey could call upon his veterans, not to mention clients and colonists in most areas of the Roman world; and Caesar could expect to gain a consul's authority. Pompey, the leading partner, stood to gain most at once; Caesar as the junior might hope to gain most in the long term; the potential gains for Crassus in the middle were less predictable.

Before the end of the year the three invited Cicero to join them, but after much anguished soul-searching he declined on grounds of principle. His hopes that all responsible members of society would work in harmony to keep the state stable (as they had rallied briefly against Catiline) were now thoroughly dashed. He was well aware of the significance of the newly formed partnership. It is commonly referred to today as the First Triumvirate, but it was soon branded more appropriately by hostile contemporaries as the "Three-Headed Monster." It was a secret pact at first, and only ever informal, but it could be expected to make a devastating impact.

Figure 7.2 *Bust of Julius Caesar.*

CAESAR'S FIRST CONSULSHIP (59)

Caesar and Bibulus were chosen as consuls for 59. Once in office, Caesar began by striving to be conciliatory, in particular over the proposal for land redistribution, which he put forward first. This deliberately incorporated safeguards designed to overcome senators' objections to the previous schemes advanced by tribunes in 63 and 60. Even so, it was soon clear from the debate in the senate that Bibulus, Cato, and their supporters were not to be placated. They now resorted to filibuster tactics, declaring themselves opposed on principle to *any* land redistribution proposal. In his frustration, Caesar therefore resolved to ignore the senate and to bring the proposal directly to the Tribal assembly for a vote. Since both Caesar and his opponents could call upon tribunes for support, Bibulus believed that it would be more effective for him to give notice that on each day when it was lawful for an assembly to meet, he would be watching the sky for omens, which would automatically invalidate any assembly.

Caesar fixed a day for the vote regardless, and on it ugly scenes unfolded. Not only were the fasces of Bibulus' lictors smashed, but a basket of excrement was also flung over him. A tribune who tried to veto the proceedings was thrown from the platform, and several people were injured in the riot that erupted. Bibulus fled to safety, and Cato was expelled by force when he tried to make a speech. With this opposition removed, and some semblance of order restored, the proposal was voted through—to the benefit of Pompey's veterans, among many others. The following day, Bibulus failed in an attempt to have the vote invalidated by the now frightened senate.

From now onwards Caesar just disregarded Bibulus altogether. His next step was a provocative demand that every senator swear an oath to respect the land distribution measure. This recalled Saturninus' demand during Marius' sixth consulship in 100, but, unlike on that occasion, every senator did eventually swear. Having asserted himself over the senate in this way, Caesar then proceeded to ignore it, and invite no more obstructions, by taking three key proposals directly to the Tribal assembly for voting. All passed. The first refunded to the tax-collecting syndicate for the province of Asia one-third of its overambitious bid; the second formally ratified Pompey's arrangements in the East at last. The third, also of special concern to Pompey, was a comprehensive measure to regulate the conduct of senators who governed provinces, including procedures for hearing charges brought against them and severe penalties for those found guilty.

In these ways Caesar repaid Pompey and Crassus for becoming his partners. All three were still nervous of opposition, however. So when Cicero was rash enough to complain about the current political situation in a lawcourt speech, Caesar took this as the cue to grant Clodius his remarkable wish to change status from patrician to plebeian, thus becoming eligible to stand for a tribunate. The change was made at once, so that Clodius could have the chance of being elected one of the tribunes for 58, which in due course he was, much to Cicero's dismay.

As the year progressed, the Triumvirs made further arrangements for their own benefit and for the continuation of their partnership. Pompey married Julia, Caesar's daughter by his first wife Cornelia, and the only legitimate child he would ever have. On Vatinius' proposal as tribune, Caesar was given a command in Cisalpine Gaul and Illyricum, with three legions, for five years (Map 7.1); the senate's transparent preelection maneuver of assigning supervision of the forests and tracks of Italy was ignored. Then on Pompey's proposal—after the premature death of another commander appointed there—the senate added responsibility for Transalpine Gaul and a fourth legion. Although there was serious trouble to be dealt with in Gaul, it must be doubtful whether this could justify a five-year term instead of the normal one year. Even so, that exceptional term would afford Caesar extended exemption from prosecutions that were sure to be brought against him for his conduct as consul, and the senate may even have felt relief at the prospect of his absence from Rome for so long. Elections for the consulship of 58 were delayed; this time the senate deliberately did not assign provinces in advance. The pair eventually chosen, however, were Aulus Gabinius (Pompey's friend and proposer of his command against the pirates in 67) and Lucius Calpurnius Piso Caesoninus (Caesar's new father-in-law, on his marriage to Calpurnia in 59).

CLODIUS' TRIBUNATE (58)

To all appearances, therefore, it would seem that Pompey, Crassus, and Caesar were satisfied by the outcome of events in 59; the immediate hopes that each had when they formed their pact were broadly fulfilled. How far they could continue to work together was quite another matter. Their pact was now common knowledge, and it was resented not only by fellow senators, but also by many citizens who deplored its use of violence and its contempt for the law. At the same time as the three men experienced this drop in popularity, they began to have doubts about their mutual loyalty to one another. Now, however, if mistrust between Pompey and Crassus were to revive, Caesar would no longer be in Rome to calm them. In addition, all three men felt nervous at the prospect of Clodius as tribune.

True to form, Clodius made a marked impact with two proposals put forward as soon as he entered office. The first was an overhaul of the entire system whereby grain was imported to Rome from the provinces of Sardinia, Sicily, and Africa. At the same time, the monthly ration available to citizens in Rome for a fixed price would now become free. In other words, this grain would no longer just be partly subsidized by the treasury during months when the market price was high, as originally arranged by Gaius Gracchus; it would now be paid for in full by the treasury throughout the year. Needless to say, this was a huge additional burden for the treasury, although the recent steep increase in revenue won by Pompey could only act to reduce it. The second proposal, no less popular with citizens, was a removal of the ban on *collegia* and their activities that the senate had imposed in 64. The ban had been imposed to prevent associations contributing an element of organized violence to political life in the city; the danger that they would now do so again was still present.

So any proposer of these measures might well expect to encounter fierce opposition. But in this case the proposer was Clodius; meantime, neither consul had yet been assigned a province, while Cicero knew what even a murmur of dissent might cost him. So votes passing the proposals went smoothly. Clodius became extremely popular as a result. His aim of becoming the champion of the populace seemed to be fulfilled, and this made him still bolder. He did now arrange "rewards" for the consuls: Gabinius was assigned the governorship of Syria, Piso that of Macedonia. Clodius also succeeded in removing temporarily one senator he loathed: Cato. The opportunity had arisen for Rome to take over from Egypt the wealthy island of Cyprus, and a senator was needed to organize the annexation. What better choice for this special duty than Cato? He could be relied upon to enrich the treasury rather than himself, and above all he would be far from Rome. Fortunately, he accepted the invitation.

For Cicero, however, there was to be none of the consideration shown to Cato. Clodius had a proposal passed reaffirming the ancient principle that no Roman citizen should be executed without trial; anyone guilty of such executions must suffer exile. Although the measure made no reference to any individual or incident, Cicero recognized its purpose; his controversial execution of Catiline's associates in 63 had come back to haunt him. He was hardly surprised that neither consul would offer help, but he was stunned to discover that Pompey would do nothing for him, nor would Crassus, nor Caesar. Feeling deserted and isolated, therefore, Cicero lost his nerve and left Rome for Macedonia rather than await prosecution. Clodius then had a measure passed officially declaring him an exile. It was in fact at this point, in late March 58, that Caesar finally left Rome to take up his command in Gaul.

Clodius' vindictive treatment of Cicero created widespread outrage that was only sharpened by his next moves, both of which suggest that he was now letting his popularity with the mass of citizens in Rome blind him to all other considerations. He provoked Pompey over aspects of Eastern policy, and when Pompey and Gabinius protested, he had the two of them physically assaulted by his supporters, and the consul's fasces smashed. He also called into question the validity of Caesar's acts as consul the previous year, even though one of these had been his own change of status from patrician to plebeian.

CICERO'S RECALL AND THE RENEWAL OF THE TRIUMVIRATE (57–56)

Pompey became so frightened for his personal safety that for a long period from mid-58 onwards he dared not venture out of his house in Rome. But he did encourage two of the tribunes of 57, Titus Annius Milo and Publius Sestius, to recruit gangs to combat those of Clodius. He also supported the senate's persistent efforts in 58, and again in 57, to arrange for Cicero's recall from exile. This issue became the centerpiece of opposition to Clodius. The recall was finally achieved by a vote of the Centuriate assembly at the beginning of August 57.

Cicero reached the city about a month later to find it in the grip of a severe shortage of grain, and the senate deadlocked over how to resolve the problem. It was his motion for yet another extraordinary command that finally won acceptance—that Pompey be given control of grain supplies throughout the Roman world for five years. However, with the onset of winter, even Pompey could not immediately provide relief. By the following spring (56), therefore, Pompey's prestige had suffered, and he was harshly attacked in the senate by Cato, now back in Rome after successfully annexing Cyprus. Pompey suspected Crassus of supporting not only Cato, but also Clodius. Meantime, Cicero felt confident enough to work against the interests of the Triumvirate, and Lucius Domitius Ahenobarbus (who expected to be elected consul for 55) declared that he would press for Caesar's command in Gaul to be terminated.

With their enemies now poised to exploit any rifts emerging between them, the Triumvirs soon resolved to renew their pact with fresh measures for its security. In April 56, Caesar was free to take the lead at a meeting held at Luca (modern Lucca, in Italy), just within the southern border of his province of Cisalpine Gaul. Other senators were invited to attend too, and a strikingly large number of them came. The main item of agreement was that Pompey and Crassus would both stand for the consulship and be elected. Thereafter, with the help of supportive tribunes, Pompey and Crassus would arrange major, long-term commands for themselves and at the same time would extend Caesar's term in Gaul. More immediately, unequivocal loyalty would be demanded of Clodius, and Cicero would be reminded about the pledge of good behavior he had given on return from exile.

A crestfallen Cicero heeded the warning, and the rest of the agreement also took shape according to plan. Pompey and Crassus were elected as the consuls for 55. The Spanish provinces and Syria were assigned to them, each for five years, and Caesar was given the same extension in Gaul through early 49. Because of his responsibility for the city's grain supply, Pompey had always intended to remain in Rome and to administer his province through legates. He was content with Spain, therefore, while Crassus was delighted with Syria. It offered him the prospect of campaigning against Parthia and thus of finally matching the glory, which first Pompey and now Caesar had won by military victories in unknown lands.

Those hopes were not to be fulfilled. When Crassus set off from Syria in 53, his army was soon trapped by the Parthians near Carrhae (modern Altınbaşak, Turkey). Roman losses exceeded 30,000 men, including Crassus himself, along with the legionary standards. It was a final misfortune for a man who after his first consulship in 70 experienced persistent difficulty achieving the further distinction that he craved. He was jealous of Pompey's extraordinary achievements, and despite joining the Triumvirate he never adapted successfully to the changed political atmosphere.

CAESAR'S CAMPAIGNS IN GAUL (58–51)

When Caesar took up his command at the end of March 58, his urgent concern was to forestall the Helvetii, a Celtic people settled on the Swiss plateau, from embarking on a disruptive westward migration. This he soon achieved after major clashes, but his success at once drew him into struggles between peoples farther north. Another battle enabled him to break the control that the Germanic Suebi had been exerting within Gaul and to drive them back across the Rhine River (Latin, Rhenus). By establishing winter quarters for 58–57 in northeast Gaul, Caesar alerted the peoples there to the prospect that he would next try to dominate them. Intertribal tensions led some to seek his friendship, but in 57 others made unsuccessful preemptive strikes, provoking clashes, which brought most of today's northern France and Belgium under his control. Only the far northwest remained insecure, and this—together with the Atlantic coast—was subjugated in 56. So Caesar unexpectedly found himself achieving Roman domination of Gaul's entire vast area. Granted, he had not engaged with the peoples in the center, but they were now surrounded and at this point gave no cause for concern.

Rather, in 55 Caesar looked elsewhere to enhance his military reputation. He first drove more Germanic peoples out of northern Gaul across the Rhine River, marking it once again as the prospective limit of Roman control. Then he crossed to southern England, officially in order to cut off aid sent from there to his Gallic opponents, but no doubt also to gauge the prospects for a full-scale invasion. Although he returned to England in 54, from the following year onwards he was no longer free to do so. Suppression of risings in northern Gaul, by the Eburones and Belgae especially, preoccupied him during 53. A greater challenge followed in 52, however, when a fearsome coalition of peoples from central Gaul led by a prince of the Arverni, Vercingetorix, began a widespread revolt against Roman rule. Its timing was intended to worsen Caesar's political position, and it achieved this by compelling him to postpone the reentry to office in Rome that he had been hoping for. Eventually, however, Caesar's boldness, speed, and inexhaustible energy outwitted Vercingetorix, who was besieged at Alesia (modern Alise–Ste. Reine) and forced to surrender. Such resistance as remained to the imposition of Roman control throughout Gaul was suppressed the following year, 51.

It would be hard to understate the damage shamelessly inflicted upon the entire plundered and devastated region and its peoples. Ancient estimates that one million Gauls were killed in the course of Caesar's campaigns, and another million enslaved, are credible. Caesar meantime developed his taste and talent for supreme command, while his army had no match for experience and fighting quality. There were financial rewards, too; for Caesar himself and his top officers these were so vast that the treasury in Rome received distinctly less than its due.

DEATH OF CLODIUS AND POMPEY'S SOLE CONSULSHIP (52)

Political life at Rome remained violent and disrupted. A climax came in January 52. Magistrates had not been elected for the year ahead of time. Clodius was campaigning to be elected praetor, Milo to be consul. A major clash occurred between their gangs near Bovillae, ten miles (16 km) south of Rome on the Via Appia. Clodius was wounded and captured, and then finished off on Milo's orders. When Clodius' corpse was brought to the city, the populace was so distraught, and their mood so hostile to the senate, that they took up the outrageous suggestion of using the senate house itself as a funeral pyre. The whole structure and its furnishings burned too.

The sense that the city was slipping into anarchy now impelled the senate to pass its "ultimate decree" (SCU), to levy troops throughout Italy, and to adopt the novel expedient of making Pompey sole consul. He quickly introduced measures that would bring to trial those responsible for the worst of the recent instances of bribery and violence—among them Milo, who was condemned and went into exile at the independent Greek city of Massilia (modern Marseille). Pompey also made it the law that after any consul's or praetor's year of office, five years must elapse before he could proceed to a governorship. This interval would allow time for any prosecution of misconduct during office. It would also drastically curtail a senator's opportunity to exploit an immediate governorship as the means of rapid repayment for heavy debts.

By unfortunate coincidence, it was around this time that Caesar first seems to have become seriously anxious about his future. He knew that—after the turmoil of his consulship in 59—the normal procedure for a governor's return would lead to his political ruin. This procedure required him to become a private citizen again on recrossing the pomerium into Rome; were he to seek further office, it would be with this private status that he would have to register in person as a candidate. Caesar fully expected that no matter how short his period as a private citizen, his enemies would use it to bring charges against him. If he were to have any future in Roman public life, he had to contrive that there would be no break between his serving as governor (with exemption from prosecution) and his immediately entering a new office (most naturally a consulship) with continued exemption.

To achieve such a seamless transition, however, Pompey's support would be essential, and at this stage his attitude to the issue of exempting Caesar from one or more of the legal requirements seems to have been ambiguous. The personal link between them provided by Julia, Pompey's wife and Caesar's daughter, had been broken prematurely in 54, when she died in childbirth, aged about nineteen. Since then, Pompey had declined to pursue any proposal by Caesar for a further marriage bond. In all likelihood, there was nothing exceptional about the indecisiveness of Pompey's attitude towards Caesar at this stage. It simply reflected the broader lack of confidence, which his participation in political life had shown ever since his return from the East in 62. That said, the question of his future relationship with Caesar was particularly delicate. On the one hand, less than a decade before, when the Triumvirate was formed, Caesar had been very much its junior member and Pompey indisputably its senior one. Pompey could hardly have relished the prospect that now, by contrast, the upstart Caesar might soon be returning from Gaul not only with his prestige and wealth hugely enhanced, but also with a second consulship. On the other hand, Pompey owed Caesar gratitude for

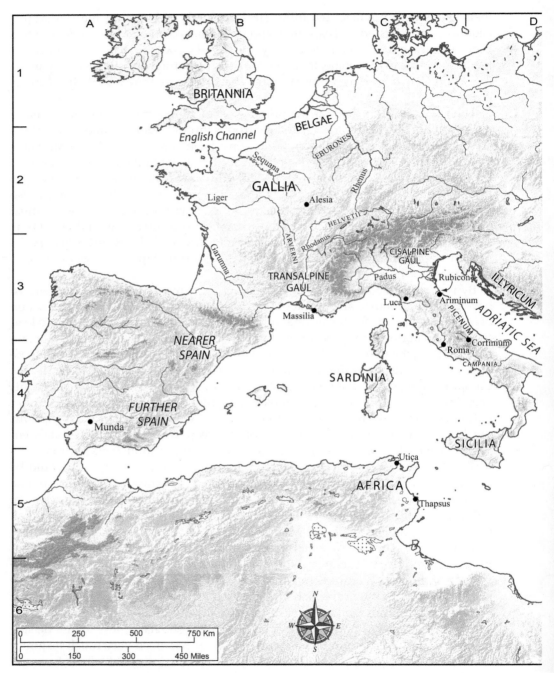

Map 7.1 *Campaigns of Caesar, Crassus, and Pompey, 58–45*

E

F

G

CRIMEA

BLACK SEA

PONTUS

Nicopolis

Zela

Epidamnus/
Dyrrhachium

MACEDONIA

Carrhae

PARTHIA

Brundisium

Euphrates

Pharsalus

ASIA

CILICIA

Amanus Mons

CARIA

SYRIA

CYPRUS

Salamis

JUDAEA

INTERNUM MARE

Cyrene

Alexandria

AEGYPTUS

Nile

Ancient World Mapping Center 2013

vital help in 59. If he were to do nothing in exchange for Caesar now, who else could he turn to for future support except Cato and the inflexible, condescending Optimates? They were not at all a group that he would otherwise choose to associate with. Moreover, they would adopt him not so much as a leader, but as a partner in their own cause. With a choice to be made between two such unpromising alternatives, it need be no wonder that Pompey prevaricated.

PROSPECT OF CIVIL WAR (51–49)

It looked as if Pompey would be forced to clarify his attitude the following year (51), when one of the consuls gave notice that he would raise with the senate the question of replacing Caesar in Gaul. In fact the matter was postponed until September. Pompey's opinion then was that Caesar should relinquish his command in time for his provinces to be reassigned by the senate prior to the next elections for the consulship (in 50). The senate adopted this recommendation (which left Caesar's future open) and accordingly arranged for the matter to be raised again by the consuls in March 50. No resolution was reached then either. Pompey made clear his disapproval of any arrangement whereby Caesar could proceed without a break from governorship to consulship.

Meantime, disturbing news reached Rome in November 51 that two months previously a large Parthian force had crossed the Euphrates River. It was making for the Roman province of Syria, which had been left almost defenseless after Crassus' defeat at Carrhae two years before. It was clear that a senior commander ought to be dispatched there by the following spring, and speculation centered around Pompey and Caesar. But, in the event, the senate left the matter hanging.

With Caesar seeming defiant and Pompey increasingly unsympathetic to him, the alarming prospect of civil war began to loom. Gaius Scribonius Curio, a tribune acting in Caesar's interests, worked to achieve some degree of compromise. In particular, at the beginning of December 50 he proposed to the senate that both Caesar and Pompey should give up their commands (Gaul and Spain, respectively) at a date to be determined. The vote was overwhelmingly in favor: 370 senators for and only 22 against. So in principle, it seemed, the great majority of senators shrank from another bout of civil war. Both consuls, however, thought differently and approached Pompey, authorizing him to raise such other forces as he thought necessary to defend the state against Caesar. Finally pressed in this way to declare himself unequivocally Caesar's opponent, Pompey accepted the consuls' commission.

Even so, the search for compromise continued, and Curio's concern for Caesar's interests was maintained by two of the tribunes for 49, Quintus Cassius Longinus (*not* Caesar's future killer) and Marcus Antonius (better known today as Mark Antony). On January 1, 49, Curio, now acting as Caesar's envoy, read the senate a letter in which Caesar proposed that he and Pompey lay down their commands simultaneously. This plea was ignored. Instead, the consul presiding put to the vote a proposal that Caesar must disband his army by a specified date or be considered an enemy of the state; this vote was at once vetoed by the tribunes Cassius and Antony.

A few days later, other compromises were raised: Caesar should be permitted to try to proceed without a break to a second consulship, retaining in the meantime only Cisalpine Gaul and Illyricum with two legions, or even just Illyricum with a single legion. The degree to which these proposals represented sincere efforts to avoid a clash, rather than mere postures, is impossible to determine. Pompey at least was willing to consider such schemes, but any chance of their adoption was quashed by those senators (like Cato and at least one of the consuls) who were determined to force a confrontation with Caesar. On January 7, it was they who persuaded the senate to pass its "ultimate decree" (SCU) again, instructing all magistrates in this instance "to see to it that the Republic suffers no harm." The tribunes Cassius and Antony were then warned that their safety could no longer be guaranteed if they chose to remain in Rome, so they and Curio fled north to Caesar.

CAUSES AND CONSEQUENCES OF CAESAR CROSSING THE RUBICON (JANUARY 49)

Pompey and his associates were unperturbed by the two tribunes' departure, and because of the winter season they expected no immediate developments. However, this mood of complacency at Rome was soon to be punctured by the shocking news that on or about January 10 Caesar had crossed the Rubicon, north of Ariminum, with one legion. Since this river formed the boundary between his province of Cisalpine Gaul and Italy, it was plain that he had committed himself to civil war, and had done so with characteristic speed: "Let the die be cast," he is supposed to have said as he crossed the river. In part, Caesar justified his resort to civil war as a defense of the constitution, which, he claimed, his opponents had abused by such means as resorting needlessly to the SCU and rejecting the legitimate rights of tribunes. At the same time Caesar did not hide particular concern for his own *dignitas*. In his view, it was disrespectful, petty, and inappropriate for the senate to dictate his future in a way sure to ruin him.

Caesar's opponents naturally disputed his view. They claimed to be safeguarding the constitution against the extreme demands of a rebellious governor. This devotion to constitutional propriety may sound hollow when Pompey, of all people, took a leading role. On the other hand, those who objected to Caesar remaining protected from prosecution did have a valid point. To remain in effect above the law flouted one of the basic principles of the Republic. That said, a case for compromising with Caesar can also be recognized. To this extent, the outbreak of civil war in January 49 under such conditions was by no means inevitable. In view of developments since Sulla's dictatorship, however, compromise now could equally be regarded as just the postponement of a clash over some comparable challenge to the Republic.

Cicero concluded that, in the event, both Pompey and Caesar were prepared to risk civil war because neither wanted to defer to the other; rather, each wanted to be supreme. This was certainly the kind of attitude reflected by many of their associates. Even so, it is important to recognize that at the outset most senators either stood with Pompey and the Optimates against Caesar or had no wish to become involved. In particular, almost no ex-consuls took Caesar's side, and most of his senatorial associates were either young or disreputable or both. In Cicero's view, Caesar's cause had no moral or constitutional basis. At the same time he felt antagonized and disillusioned by the Optimates and Pompey and in the end stayed with them only out of personal devotion to Pompey. How the rest of society throughout Italy would react was hard to predict. In fact the general feeling turned out to be dread of more Sullan-style proscriptions and, in contrast to the 80s, a complete lack of engagement with the issues dividing the senate. The poor in the meantime were for Caesar. They were keenly aware of how little the Optimates had ever cared for their plight, and they certainly did not rush to enlist under Pompey.

With hindsight, the formation, continuation, and then breakup of the First Triumvirate dominate our view of the 50s, and it is easy to conclude that it was the Triumvirate, which "led" to the outbreak of civil war a decade later. Such a view calls for further reflection, however. Potentially there were countless ways in which the Triumvirate might, or might not, have evolved. For years, Caesar in Gaul was even more liable than Crassus to meet his death on campaign. Caesar seems not to have been seriously concerned about preparing a suitable return to Rome until as late as 52, and Pompey wavered still longer over how to react to his requests in this connection. Pompey's eventual stand and Caesar's ultimate defiance did become the trigger for civil war, but this outcome was hardly predictable far in advance. The Republic was already beset by a formidable array of interrelated problems and pressures, both external and internal, at every level of society—issues that those in authority were no longer able or willing to tackle on an adequate scale. Willpower aside, they lacked the machinery, resources, and cohesion for the purpose. By now this highly dangerous predicament was poised to lead to breakdown or conflict. It was largely fortuitous that the fatal clash arose in 49 over no more than a dispute concerning a single senator's future, one from which even many of his fellow members wished to distance themselves.

CIVIL WAR CAMPAIGNS (49–45)

Having crossed the Rubicon River in January 49, Caesar soon dispelled fears that he would be a second Sulla or a vengeful Catiline. As he moved fast down the east coast of Italy, communities went over to him with little or no resistance, including even the entire region of Picenum, Pompey's own home territory. Lucius Domitius Ahenobarbus tried to make a stand with a substantial force at Corfinium, but Caesar quickly gained the advantage, and Ahenobarbus' own men forced him to surrender. The fact that even here Caesar released all captives, executed no one, and declined to take the state funds that came into his hands, made a decisive impression. In mid-January Pompey left Rome for Campania and then in March made for Brundisium, from where he sailed to northern Greece with such forces as he had gathered. Without question, from a military viewpoint his situation in Italy was precarious. Psychologically, on the other hand, to abandon not just Rome, but Italy too, with almost no fight seemed defeatist in the extreme. His plan for subsequent reconquest sounded correspondingly brutal. With all his influence in the East and West, he would recruit massive forces (even barbarians from beyond the Roman empire), control the sea, starve Italy, and then invade. "What Sulla could do, I can do," was his constant refrain, according to Cicero, who was horrified.

Meantime, the entire peninsula was left to Caesar within little more than two months after he had risked crossing the Rubicon. As Cicero in Campania wrote to his friend Atticus at the beginning of March, "But do you see what sort of man this is into whose hands the state has fallen, how clever, alert, well prepared? I truly believe that if he takes no lives and touches no man's property, those who dreaded him most will become his warmest admirers. Both town and country people talk to me a great deal. They really think of nothing except their fields, and their bits of farms" (*To Atticus* 163SB).

After Pompey's departure from Italy, Caesar spent about two weeks in Rome before heading west to tackle the concentration of forces in Pompey's Spanish provinces. Reducing them was an obvious strategic priority, which Caesar achieved by the fall. He next turned almost at once to challenging Pompey himself, who had been assembling troops from all over the East. Even crossing from Brundisium to northern Greece was hazardous for Caesar, because Pompey's fleet dominated the Adriatic. However, by the following year 48, Caesar was able to blockade Pompey's camp at Dyrrhachium (modern Durrës in Albania). Pompey's army then broke out with such vigor that Caesar was forced to flee in order to escape being utterly routed. As he moved southeast, Pompey followed him. In August, under some pressure from his impatient Optimate associates and against his own judgment, Pompey fought a set battle at Pharsalus in Thessaly—the type of major confrontation that he had seldom risked throughout his career. Despite having the larger army, he was defeated and fled.

Caesar offered to forgive any of the enemy who asked for mercy, as many did. Pompey's land and sea forces now dispersed. Cicero, who had remained at Dyrrhachium, returned to Italy. Cato and both of Pompey's sons went to Cyrene in North Africa (annexed by Rome in the late 70s). Pompey himself had evidently made no plan for defeat but now decided to seek refuge in Egypt. In fact, however, the advisors of the young King Ptolemy XIII had him cut down as soon as he landed at the end of September. Caesar in pursuit reached Alexandria, the capital of Egypt, only a few days later. Because contrary winds would prevent him leaving at once, he chose instead to become embroiled in an ongoing war between members of the royal family—a dangerous venture that left him trapped in Alexandria until relieved in March 47. While there, the ambitious royal princess Cleopatra (born in 69) became his mistress. By the time he eventually left Egypt in summer 47, he had established her as ruler of the kingdom; and not long afterwards she gave birth to a son by him, Ptolemy Caesar, nicknamed Caesarion.

While still in the East, Caesar next tackled the threat now posed by King Pharnaces, who in 63 had been confirmed by Pompey as successor to his father, the infamous Mithridates, in the Crimea (see Fig. 6.4). Pharnaces had taken advantage of the turmoil in the Roman world to reclaim his family's ancestral kingdom of Pontus. So Caesar challenged and defeated him at Zela—Roman revenge for Mithridates' surprise victory here twenty years before in 67. This was the battle of which Caesar wrote: "I came, I saw, I conquered." In September 47 Caesar was finally able to return to Italy. By this time, however, his opponents had regrouped in Africa, so he proceeded there at the end of the year and eventually defeated them at Thapsus in mid-46. Utica—at this date the principal city of the Roman province of Africa—then surrendered without a fight. Many of Caesar's prominent surviving opponents—Cato among them—now felt their cause was lost, and committed suicide rather than face the prospect of owing their lives to him.

A few of the leaders, however, including Pompey's two sons, escaped to Spain, where they were able to raise such formidable forces that Caesar recognized the need for him to oppose them personally rather than entrust the campaign to others. He left Rome late in 46, therefore, and was to be in Spain until June 45. He himself acknowledged that the battle fought at Munda (near Urso) in southern Spain proved to be his toughest ever. Even so, it turned into a rout, with 30,000 of the enemy killed and just one of their commanders escaping with his life; he was Pompey's younger son Sextus, in his early twenties. Caesar only reached Rome again in October 45. Altogether, his difficulties in overcoming the Pompeians, and the length of time it took him, are not to be underestimated. He had taken some extraordinary risks and had repeatedly been on the verge of defeat. Just as in Gaul during the 50s, only an astonishing degree of perseverance and good fortune carried him through. Further campaigning lay ahead too. By fall 45 it had already been settled that he would leave Rome on March 18, 44 to lead a major campaign against the Parthians—who were continuing to threaten Syria—and avenge the disastrous defeat at Carrhae in 53. He clearly expected to be away for a considerable time, because by the time of his departure the holders of the annual magistracies for the next three years had been named.

CAESAR'S ACTIVITY AS DICTATOR (49–44)

At least during late 45 and early 44 Caesar had a breathing space in Rome in which to address concerns other than military campaigns. As it turned out, this and the similar intervals between earlier campaigns would prove to be his only opportunities to offer an impression of a longer-term vision for the Roman world, and his own place within it, prior to his assassination on March 15, 44. In reviewing this impression, we should first be aware of how Caesar's official status developed. He held the dictatorship for a few days in fall 49 (on his first return from Spain) in order to preside over elections, in which he himself was made consul for 48; this was his second consulship, after the first in 59. In 48, after the victory at Pharsalus, he was made dictator for a year. It was with this authority that he held elections on his return from the East in fall 47 and was made consul for 46. After the victory at Thapsus that year, the senate voted him annual dictatorships for the next ten years, along with various other lavish and unprecedented honors, including the right to nominate the only candidates for some offices. While remaining dictator, Caesar was also sole consul for much of 45, until he resigned in the fall. In 44 he was consul again (for the fifth time), and from sometime in February he had his dictatorship converted into a perpetual one (Fig. 7.3).

Caesar must surely win praise for his prompt, even-handed attention to pressing social problems. One of the most deep-rooted was that of debt, which had long affected all levels of society, as the widespread support for Catiline's rising demonstrated. An already serious situation was made critical, however, by the outbreak of the civil war. As confidence evaporated, lenders began to demand repayment of their loans, and real estate values collapsed. A serious shortage of coinage for circulation developed, because people hoarded whatever they had; there was in effect no paper money, nor banks as we know them. Desperate borrowers began to agitate for a complete cancellation of debts. Lenders, by contrast, were appalled by the loss they would suffer if such an extreme solution to the crisis were adopted.

By early 48 at the latest, Caesar grasped the seriousness of the situation and both sides' fears. His approach was the moderate one of trying to offer some relief to each. Consequently, he ordered that property must be accepted for repayment at its prewar value, and he reintroduced an old law, which prohibited anyone from holding more than 60,000 sesterces in cash. Even so, his measures were not enough

Figure 7.3 *Julius Caesar as dictator was the first living Roman with the audacity to permit his image to appear on coins. The issue shown here, by the moneyer Lucius (Aemilius) Buca, in 44, dates to the final weeks of his life; it portrays him wearing a crown and describes him as "perpetual dictator." On the reverse, the clasped hands affirm the trust between Caesar and his army, while the globe represents Roman aspirations to world power.*

to placate borrowers, some of whom raised an armed rebellion, which had to be put down by force. Caesar did then act further to help borrowers by canceling interest payments due since early 49, for example, and permitting tenants to pay no rent for a year. Overall, it is true, he came nowhere near to eliminating the problem of debt, but he was responsive and creative enough to alleviate it in a balanced way.

Equally in need of attention was the calendar. The Roman civic year had only 355 days, with provision for an extra month to be inserted from time to time in order to match the solar year. This "intercalation" had been so neglected in the recent past, however, that by the early 40s the Roman year and the solar year were about three months apart. Caesar therefore adapted the Egyptian solar calendar to Roman use. To catch up, the year 46 was lengthened to a unique 445 days, and thereafter each year would have 365 days, with an additional day to be inserted in leap years between February 23 and 24 (as a second February 23; nothing was added at the end of the month). This "Julian" calendar was to be modified again only after another millennium and a half by Pope Gregory XIII in 1582, when it effectively attained the form still in common use today.

Caesar was naturally concerned to settle his veterans and at the same time ready to dispel fears that he would proscribe and confiscate for this purpose as Sulla had done. In fact his attitude towards defeated enemies was typically one of forgiveness (*clementia*), and even though there does appear to have been some confiscation of land in Italy, it must have been on a limited scale. Not many veterans were settled there (15,000 perhaps), and, unlike Sulla's men, they were widely dispersed. Instead, most veterans, along with many of the poor from the city of Rome, were settled overseas—on land that either belonged to the Roman state already or was confiscated from communities, which had joined the fight against Caesar in Spain, Africa, and the East especially. Caesar's two most ambitious settlement projects were perhaps the new colonies founded on the vacant sites of Carthage and Corinth, both destroyed in 146.

Like all Roman colonies, his foundations were certainly intended as centers of Roman strength and culture, but altogether there seems no cause to claim that he had in mind very specific ideas of either garrisoning or romanizing the empire when he selected their sites. Even the number of his colonies is unclear, given that few had developed far by the time of his death; others established later in his name may, or may not, have been among his plans. It may be possible to discern in Caesar's measures a new impetus to raise the status of approved provincials and to make them Rome's partners rather than merely subjects. Even so, to see this as a well-formulated aim, consistently applied, would be excessive. His attitude towards provincial government shows the same ambivalence. In line with his own law of 59 regulating it, he could act considerately. In particular, we know that he abolished the oppressive system whereby a syndicate of *publicani* collected tax in Asia after making the winning bid at an auction in Rome; he now permitted the communities to collect it themselves. On the other hand, there is no sign that he planned any large reform of provincial government.

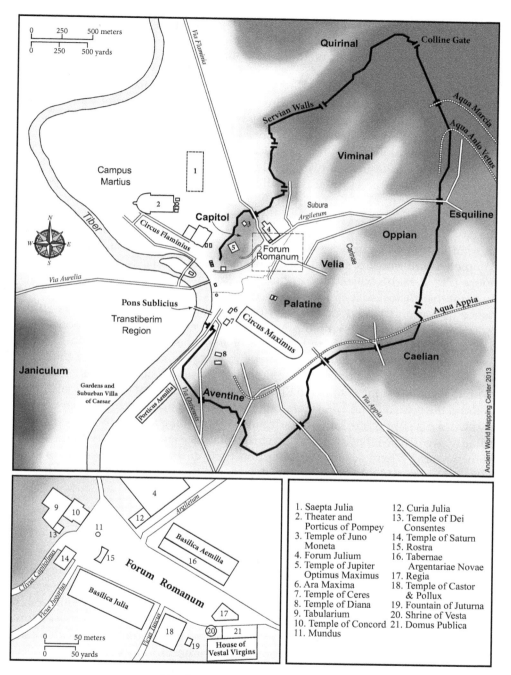

Map 7.2 *Rome in the Late Republic*

1. Saepta Julia
2. Theater and Porticus of Pompey
3. Temple of Juno Moneta
4. Forum Julium
5. Temple of Jupiter Optimus Maximus
6. Ara Maxima
7. Temple of Ceres
8. Temple of Diana
9. Tabularium
10. Temple of Concord
11. Mundus
12. Curia Julia
13. Temple of Dei Consentes
14. Temple of Saturn
15. Rostra
16. Tabernae Argentariae Novae
17. Regia
18. Temple of Castor & Pollux
19. Fountain of Juturna
20. Shrine of Vesta
21. Domus Publica

CAESAR'S IMPACT UPON THE CITY OF ROME

There was much in the city of Rome to claim Caesar's attention (Map 7.2). To reduce unemployment, many of its poor were offered a fresh start in the new colonies overseas. Others who depended on the free grain available monthly to any Roman citizen (as instituted by Clodius in 58) were liable to suffer when Caesar limited these rations to a total of 150,000. If he had contemplated cutting costs further by simply abolishing the free ration, as Sulla had done, he no doubt concluded that the blow to his popularity would be too great. He did arrange for better supervision of the supply of grain to the city, and he is said to have been planning improved access to it generally with a new harbor at Ostia and a canal from Tarracina.

Major new projects for public buildings also acted to reduce unemployment in the city. One of these, the Forum Julium (north of the original Forum Romanum), was sufficiently advanced for Caesar to dedicate it in 46. Others were not to be completed until the 20s, including the Basilica Julia (Plate 1b) and a new senate house (Fig. 7.4a, b), both in the Forum Romanum, as well as the Saepta Julia, a huge marble enclosure for voting situated on the Campus Martius. After his experience of Alexandria, the greatest city of the Mediterranean, Caesar was all the more keenly aware of how unimpressive Rome seemed: he intended both to enhance the city's appearance and to leave his own permanent mark on it. There were said to be other grandiose schemes for a huge temple of Mars, a theater to rival Pompey's, and a library on the model of those in leading Greek cities. It is plain that Caesar wanted to make Rome a center of culture and education.

From the measures he took, therefore, there can be no doubt that Caesar wanted to reward his supporters and to glorify the city of Rome as well as himself. More broadly, we can see that he wanted to bring stability and prosperity to the entire Roman world. There seems little question that, in the limited intervals of time open to him, he did take encouraging steps in the right direction. Even so, there is no knowing how he would have continued.

POLITICAL PROSPECTS FOR ROME AND FOR CAESAR

Caesar's work was cut short by his own closest associates, the senators. He seems not to have appreciated how badly he needed their continued support and respect. He did considerably increase the senate's size. Under him, the total membership of around 600 set by Sulla was expanded to 900. Inevitably, many of the new members were men he wished to reward, and they came from a somewhat wider variety of communities and social backgrounds than hitherto. Of course, traditionalists found fault and exaggerated their grumbles. For certain, the new members must have included men from many Italian communities that had gained Roman citizenship within the past forty years or so and were seeing one of their own become a senator for the first time. There is no question, too, that Caesar did introduce

Figure 7.4a, b *This structure is today a prominent feature of the north side of the Forum Romanum. Once Rome's senate house, in the seventh century it became a church. During the 1930s, however, all the successive accretions were removed. The senate house thus revealed [a] had been erected after a fire in A.D. 283; the conspicuous horizontal openings on either side of the front doors were for medieval tombs. It reproduced the design of the building commissioned by Julius Caesar as dictator and dedicated by Octavian as the Curia Julia in 29 B.C. The interior of the restored structure [b], viewed here from the front doors, is a tall, open chamber measuring 84 × 58 ft (26 × 18 m). Only the floor now offers an impression of the fine marble that originally covered most of the walls too. Along either side are three broad steps where senators sat on benches; at the far end is a dais for the magistrate presiding.*

a few members from Spain and Gaul. To maintain the senate's size, Caesar doubled the number of quaestors set by Sulla from twenty to forty annually, and the number of praetors from eight to sixteen. Elections lost significance after Caesar gained, and used, the right to fill offices by nomination. By the same token, his dictatorships freed him from the need to pay attention to other magistrates, or to consult the senate except as a formality. Hence he poured scorn on Sulla for resigning the dictatorship, mocked the tribunate whose veto could not obstruct him now, and even dismissed the Republic itself as "nothing, a mere name with neither form nor substance."

The senate itself—out of fear, or flattery, or even contempt—encouraged his growing arrogance by voting him a stream of ever more extraordinary powers and honors, most of which he accepted. By the beginning of 44, the image of his head was appearing on coinage, a distinction never before accorded to a living Roman (Fig. 7.3). Antony had also been chosen, though not yet instituted, as priest of a temple authorized by the senate for worship of Caesar as a god. Public worship of a living ruler was a Greek practice (see Chapter Nine), but it had no real precedent at Rome and was completely contrary to the very concept of a republic.

Much the same may be said of kingship. Once again, it is unclear how badly, if at all, Caesar wanted this distinction. The Greek world had indeed had kings, some of whom impressed Romans. Admittedly, too, elements of Rome's own archaic kingship had been carried over into the Republic. For Caesar to go as far as to take the title of *rex*, however, would be a giant leap, certain to offend almost everyone with any regard for the Republic. As it was, he never did actually claim kingship, though he may have toyed with the possibility. Moreover, the fact that Cleopatra and her baby son Caesarion came to Rome in 46 and remained there can only have fueled suspicions that Caesar had it in mind to found a dynasty.

By early 44, there was no further authority that fresh honors could confer on Caesar. He already had absolute power. As he well knew, he was hated for that and for the way he used it. After all, a dangerous consequence of his clemency (*clementia*) was the survival of many of his enemies, plenty of them still in the senate. Even so, to him the Republic was dead, and he could see no secure alternative means of regulating the state's affairs for the future except through himself. His adoption of the title "perpetual dictator" during February 44 confirmed this conclusion. In any event, reform would now have to be put off until his return from Parthia. To many senators, this new title and the prospect of Caesar's long absence marked the end of all hope, the final provocation. They had to act before his departure on March 18, and so determined to kill him publicly in the senate at the last meeting he would attend, on the Ides (fifteenth) of March—just as Romulus had been killed when he became a tyrant, according to one tradition. The leaders of the sixty or so members in the plot were two praetors, Marcus Junius Brutus and his brother-in-law Gaius Cassius Longinus. Both had taken Pompey's side and been pardoned by Caesar. Both claimed descent from ancient families with a tradition of championing Rome's liberty; a celebrated Brutus had led the expulsion of the last king, Tarquinius Superbus.

Caesar fell at the foot of a statue of Pompey. Assassination by his peers was a tragic end for a man who had fought so long and hard to become unrivaled first man in Rome. But along with that insatiable ambition a certain naiveté was detectable. Somehow Caesar always seemed to imagine that, while he must be accorded special rights in deference to his dignitas, the rest of the state can, and will, continue to function around him in the regular, legal way. Eventually it could not. By early 44, even many of his supporters in the senate found it intolerable that they must all remain deprived of their dignitas for the foreseeable future. Hence they concluded that his personal interest could not continue to be so privileged above that of everyone else.

SUGGESTED READINGS

Griffin, Miriam (ed.). 2009. *A Companion to Julius Caesar*. Malden, Mass., and Oxford: Wiley-Blackwell. Thirty essays on Caesar's career, writings, and legacy to the present day.

Millar, Fergus. 1998. *The Crowd in Rome in the Late Republic*. Ann Arbor: University of Michigan Press. This study of citizens' role in Roman politics focuses especially on the period between the dictatorships of Sulla and of Caesar.

Tatum, W. Jeffrey. 1999. *The Patrician Tribune: Publius Clodius Pulcher*. Chapel Hill and London: University of North Carolina Press.

Yavetz, Zwi. 1983. *Julius Caesar and His Public Image*. London: Thames and Hudson.

AUGUSTUS AND THE TRANSFORMATION OF THE ROMAN WORLD

REACTIONS TO THE ASSASSINATION OF CAESAR (44–43)

As soon as they had struck their blows, the senators who had conspired to assassinate Caesar hailed "liberty" and its senatorial embodiment, Cicero. They must have realized, however, that further obstacles to liberty's full return could well emerge. In the immediate confusion and panic, much would obviously depend on the attitude of Antony, Caesar's fellow consul, and of Marcus Aemilius Lepidus, an aristocrat and former consul, who as *magister equitum* commanded the troops in Rome. When Antony summoned the senate on March 17, 44, he gained its support for a compromise whereby no action would be taken against the assassins, but at the same time all of Caesar's measures and appointments would remain valid. The intention was to heal divisions and prevent disruption of the state's management, but the effect was also to diminish the aim of the assassination. The compromise certainly failed to anticipate the mood soon shown by the populace at Caesar's public funeral and the reading of his will, which left them his extensive property across the Tiber and bequeathed each individual 300 sesterces. There was now a mass outcry against the assassins, which Antony himself encouraged. It remained so intense that by mid-April the leaders Brutus and Cassius had been driven from Rome. Cleopatra returned to Egypt with her son without delay. Lepidus, too, left the city to assume command of troops in southern (Narbonese) Gaul and Nearer Spain, where Sextus Pompey was rebuilding his cause after the defeat at Munda in 45 (see Chapter Seven). Before departing, however, Lepidus—with Antony's support—first contrived to have himself made *pontifex maximus* in Caesar's place.

Meantime, as soon as he heard of the assassination from his mother, Caesar's eighteen-year-old grandnephew Gaius Octavius left Apollonia (across the Adriatic from Italy, in Illyricum), where he had been studying, and sailed to Brundisium. He was accompanied by Marcus Vipsanius Agrippa, a friend of about the same age but from an undistinguished family, who was to remain his close, loyal associate. Octavius' mother Atia was the daughter of Caesar's sister, Julia; his father Gaius Octavius was a first-generation senator (*novus homo*) who had been praetor in 61 and died two years later. Their son Gaius Octavius was born in September 63, and had accompanied Caesar on his Spanish campaign in 45 (see Table 8.1). Now, when he reached Brundisium, he learned that Caesar in his will had adopted him and made him his principal heir. Once in Rome, he formally declared his acceptance of the inheritance and took the name Gaius Julius Caesar Octavianus, although he always preferred to omit Octavianus for greater effect. The modern convention, used here, is to refer to him as Octavian.

In view of Octavian's youth and inexperience, Antony at first did not view him as a threat. But it soon became clear that Octavian was succeeding in his attempt to displace Antony as leader of Caesar's friends and supporters, especially among the city populace and the veterans. When asked by Octavian to release Caesar's money, Antony found various reasons not to, and Octavian then won tremendous popularity by selling off his own property in order to pay the bequest of 300 sesterces to each citizen. Thereafter too, amid the turmoil of the next few months, Antony increasingly lost ground to Octavian, who proved adept at attracting support with offers of money and appeals to Caesar's memory. Meantime, in August, Brutus and Cassius decided to take advantage of an official reason to leave Italy altogether, offered by the senate when it made them governors of the minor combined province of Crete and Cyrene. By the end of November, Antony in turn chose to abandon his struggle to deprive Octavian of support in Rome, so he departed with an army to the province of Cisalpine Gaul, which he had arranged to be assigned. He was to find, however, that the governor already in position, Decimus Junius Brutus Albinus (one of the conspirators, but *not* Brutus the leader), was in Mutina (modern Modena) and refused to leave. Accordingly, Antony proceeded to lay siege to the city.

Cicero now seized the initiative in proposing that the senate at last assert itself by eliminating Antony, whom he persistently represented as a would-be dictator. Moreover, urged Cicero, for this purpose the senate could strengthen its own forces—under the command of the two consuls for 43, Aulus Hirtius and Gaius Vibius Pansa Caetronianus—by enlisting the help of Octavian and the large body of troops he had raised privately. Consequently, in January 43 Octavian was offered, and accepted, authority (*imperium*) subordinate to that of the consuls and membership of the senate with the right to be called on to speak among the ex-consuls. Attempts to reach a negotiated settlement with Antony failed, and when the decisive clashes occurred in April he was defeated and Mutina relieved.

Map 8.1 *Roman Campaigns, 44–30*

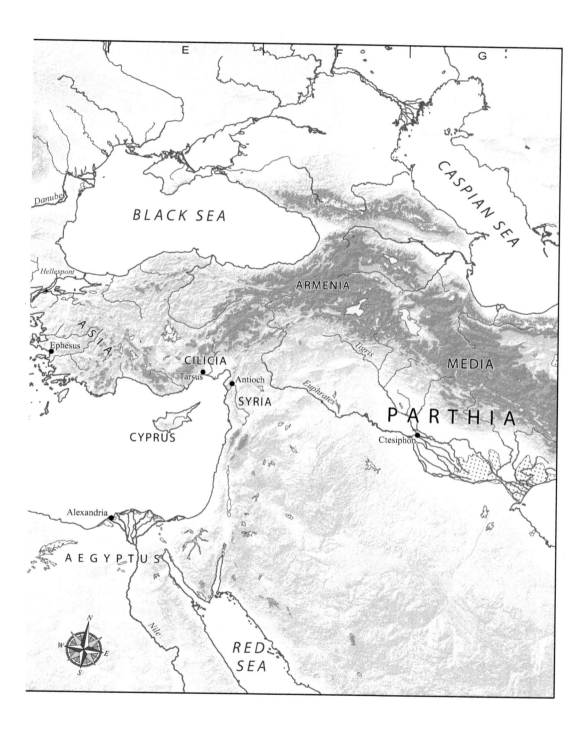

EMERGENCE OF A SECOND TRIUMVIRATE (43)

Unfortunately for Cicero and the senate, however, both consuls were casualties of the fighting. Decimus Brutus and his troops were weak from their long siege and so unable to pursue Antony as he retreated westwards. Decimus Brutus was instructed by the senate to take over the deceased consuls' forces, but he received no support from Octavian, who declined to take orders from him. Octavian appreciated that he, too, had no prospect of eliminating Antony successfully at this stage. So Antony was able to make his way west and join Lepidus, who had so far been assuring the senate of his loyalty but needed little persuasion by his own men and by Antony to switch allegiance. Meantime, Octavian insisted that his priority must be to secure appropriate rewards for his men from the senate; only his election to one of the vacant consulships, he told them, would ensure that these rewards would be forthcoming. Predictably, the senate would not hear of permitting a nineteen year old to stand for that office. Even so, they were forced to rethink in August when Octavian marched on Rome at the head of eight legions. Later that month he duly became consul with his relative Quintus Pedius, Caesar's nephew, who died later the same year.

Octavian now saw to it that Caesar's assassins were all formally condemned and outlawed; so too was Sextus Pompey, despite a settlement with him that the senate had approved in April. With Lepidus' mediation, Octavian also sought a reconciliation with Antony, the successful outcome of which was that the three men became "Triumvirs for the restoration of the state" (*triumviri reipublicae constituendae*) for five years. The arrangements they concluded at a meeting near Bononia (modern Bologna) were made law in Rome in November. Thus this so-called "Second Triumvirate" was formally legal, in marked contrast to its notional forerunner formed in 60–59 (see Chapter Seven). The Triumvirs—dictators in all but name—gained authority to make laws without reference to the senate or the people, to exercise jurisdiction without appeal, and to nominate all magistrates. In practice, however, some formal consultation of the senate or the people did continue, and some elections were held. As for the provinces, Antony was to take responsibility for Gaul, Lepidus for Spain, and Octavian for Africa, Sardinia, and Sicily. The Triumvirate's priority, however, would be to pursue and punish Caesar's assassins, and for this purpose Antony and Octavian were to have twenty legions each—amounting to perhaps two-thirds of the sixty legions under arms across the Roman world at the time.

Even so, the Triumvirs lacked the means to pay such huge numbers of men (a legion comprising between four and five thousand) without rapidly acquiring land and cash on an extensive scale. This they now determined to achieve by resorting to confiscations and proscriptions as Sulla had done (and as Caesar very deliberately had not). The number of victims was perhaps higher than in Sulla's time—supposedly as many as 300 senators and 2,000 *equites*— although it is clear that many of the proscribed escaped either to the East or to Sextus Pompey (see Source 8.1), who now moved with a fleet to Sicily. Antony insisted on proscribing Cicero, who was caught and killed at a villa he owned near Caieta, about seventy miles (112 km) south of Rome, in December 43. Cicero never anticipated the unlikely prospect that Antony would be defeated at Mutina but remain able to escape and join Lepidus. Even worse, he had quite underestimated Octavian's strength and his single-minded pursuit of power. In Cicero's own dismissive words, Octavian was merely a youngster "to be praised, honored, and disposed of." Cicero, in his devotion to Republican principles, had not reckoned with Octavian's ability to switch the allegiance of the senate's own troops to himself, let alone with his demand for a consulship. Still more of a shock was the astonishing turnabout in Octavian's approach, from pursuing Antony as an enemy to making him a partner in a Triumvirate dedicated to the pursuit of Caesar's assassins.

BATTLE OF PHILIPPI (42)

At the beginning of 42 Julius Caesar was deified by the senate, and it was probably now that Quintilis, the month of his birth, was renamed Julius (July). Naturally, Octavian's prestige as "son of a god" (*divi filius*) was enhanced. He and Antony next began to move eastwards against Brutus and Cassius, leaving Lepidus in charge in Italy. Meantime, Brutus had been gathering troops, funds, and other support in Greece and western Asia Minor, while Cassius had been doing likewise farther east. Not until late summer did the two of them cross the Hellespont and jointly advance into Macedonia, where they encountered the forces of Antony and Octavian near Philippi. Each army comprised about twenty legions or 100,000 men, and in two successive battles about three weeks apart during October their fortunes were mixed. In the first battle, Brutus wiped out three of Octavian's legions and captured his camp, while the troops under Cassius' command were so decisively routed by Antony that he committed suicide. The second battle may also have begun well for Brutus, but in the end his entire front broke, and he too killed himself. It is really his death that marks the end of the Republican cause (Fig. 8.1).

Figure 8.1 *What was to prove one of Brutus' last coins (issued by the moneyer Lucius Plaetorius Cestianus in 42) shows his own head on one side, and "Ides of March" on the other, surmounted by two daggers facing a "liberty cap" to symbolize the achievement of that fateful day in 44.*

Antony's bold, skillful generalship was decisive in winning both these battles at Philippi, and his military prestige rose as a result. As a reward, he was now able to assume the more attractive responsibility of remaining behind in the East to settle its affairs. At the same time he retained his responsibility for Gaul, thus also controlling a strategic approach route to Italy from the West. In all likelihood he had not determined how long his stay in the East would be; it is most improbable that at this stage he envisaged staying there permanently.

Octavian by contrast had contributed little to the victories at Philippi, and so he was now obliged to undertake the settlement of discharged veterans in Italy. As it turned out, the land appropriated for this harsh purpose in 43 was nowhere near sufficient, and in the end even more cities suffered confiscations. Every part of the entire settlement process was plagued by injustices and inconsistencies; the misery caused throughout Italy was intense and long-lasting. At the same time Sextus Pompey had now rebuilt enough of a fleet to block grain imports from overseas, and this further pressure led to riots in Rome, which escalated into civil war.

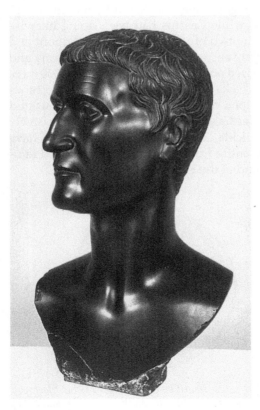

Figure 8.2 *Bust of Mark Antony.*

PERUSINE WAR (41–40)

Discontent against Octavian was co-ordinated by a consul for 41, none other than Lucius Antonius, Antony's brother; he was supported in turn by Antony's wife, Fulvia, the widow of Curio, who had been killed on campaign in 49. By the fall, Octavian had trapped both Antonius and Fulvia in Perusia (modern Perugia), which he besieged and eventually destroyed in spring 40. Antonius was then pardoned by Octavian, and Fulvia was allowed to depart for the East; both in fact soon died. Ironically, Octavian's survival of this severe challenge owed much to indecisiveness on the part of Antony, who reckoned that he had most to gain by inaction. Because he sent no clear directives, therefore, several commanders in the West who were loyal to him chose not to engage their troops. If they had, Octavian's chances of survival would have all but disappeared.

Plate 1a Tomb of the Augurs *In this fresco of around 500 B.C. from the "Tomb of the Augurs" at Tarquinii, two men wrestle over three metal cauldrons, which are probably the prizes of their contest. The cloaked figure to the left carries a curved staff or* lituus, *which was a sign of kingship and, in Rome, a mark of the priests known as augurs, who had charge of the "auspices" (see Chapter Two). One of the chief ways to take the auspices was by defining a field of vision with a lituus, and then observing within it the behavior of birds. Here, the cloaked figure seems to be supervising the contest, while the lituus and the birds flying over the combatants may indicate that he was seeking to foretell the result.*

Plate 1b Forum Romanum *Part of the Roman Forum today, viewed from the Tabularium on the lower slope of the Capitoline hill. The extensive structure to the right, barely preserved above ground level, is the Basilica Julia, begun by Julius Caesar, completed by Augustus, and much used for law court hearings (see Chapter Seven). The trees in the background to the right are up on the Palatine hill.*

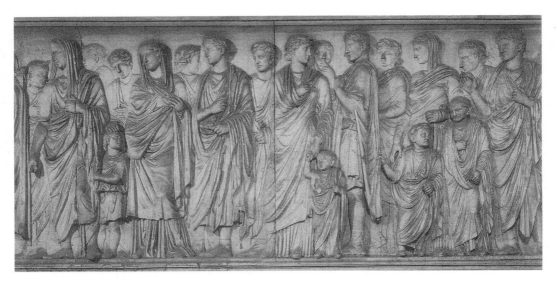

Plate 2a South frieze of the Altar of Augustan Peace (Ara Pacis Augustae), Rome. *This altar was voted by the senate to mark Augustus' return to Rome from Spain and Gaul in 13 (see Chapter Eight). Surrounding it was a walled precinct (38 by 35 ft./12 by 11 m), with reliefs in marble on the two longer sides depicting a religious procession of the imperial family and many other participants (all about three-quarters life-size). The effect is to convey a lasting impression of Augustus' concern for peace, inclusiveness, and religious devotion. Identifications of individual figures should be made with greatest caution. That said, the tall male figure towards the left here is often taken to be Agrippa, accompanied by his young son Gaius.*

Plate 2b Riot at Pompeii fresco *Relatively few surviving frescoes depict historical subjects. This one, from the peristyle garden of Pompeii's House of Actius Anicetus, illustrates a notorious riot in Pompeii's amphitheater (see Figure 6.1 and Chapter Ten). The occasion was a gladiatorial show in A.D. 59, during which Pompeian spectators came to blows with visitors from the nearby rival town of Nuceria. This riot was so injurious that the Roman senate banned gladiatorial shows at Pompeii for ten years. The bird's-eye depiction of the amphitheater shows in addition Pompeii's Large Palestra or exercise ground (with painted inscriptions) and the city walls (with two gates), as well as trees and what seem to be temporary stalls. Only part of the massive linen awning over the amphitheater (to provide shade during shows) is depicted, so as to allow a view into the structure.*

Plate 3a Agrippina as priestess *This grey basalt statue (6 ft/1.8 m tall) depicts Agrippina, wife of Claudius and mother of Nero (see Chapter Nine), in a pose derived from a Greek prototype of the fourth century B.C., and used for women of very high rank. The pose also denotes someone at prayer, especially a priestess. The statue was found in pieces in Rome near the Temple of the Deified Claudius (see Map 10.3), and the likelihood is that it once depicted Agrippina as priestess of the imperial cult for Claudius. The grey basanite stone resembles silver, adding to the luster of the piece.*

Plate 3b Staffordshire (or Ilam) pan *This small bronze vessel, unearthed by a metal detector in England's Midlands during 2003, would seem to be a souvenir produced for a Roman soldier who served on Hadrian's Wall (see Chapter Ten). It is 1.85 ins (4.7 cm) in height, and its diameter extends to 3.7 ins (9.4 cm). The form of the pan is a familiar utilitarian one. Even though it now lacks a handle or base, it could never have been serviceable. Rather, its remarkably well-preserved enamel inlay and inscription are more appropriate to a memento. The pan's entire outer surface is decorated with a band of Celtic-style curvilinear ornament in several colors. Above runs an inscription inlaid with turquoise enamel. The unbroken letter sequence lists four forts at the western end of the Wall, followed by words apparently referring to the Wall itself.*

Plate 4 Thamugadi (modern Timgad, Algeria), a colony established by Trajan in 100. *This view, from the interior of the city towards the west, shows in the foreground a well-paved street, which forms part of the regular checkerboard grid. In the middle distance, dominating the smaller remains of houses and streetside porticoes, stands the triple arch that marks one of the principal entrances to the colony. Like most of the other large and imposing public monuments, this "Arch of Trajan," dating to c. 200, was erected only when the local economy allowed. Although they are not visible in this photograph, Timgad also came to boast a theater (begun c. 160) and, of course, a forum. A temple and city council building both opened onto the forum's central open space, which accommodated public meetings, processions, religious rituals, and other communal events (see Chapter Ten).*

Plate 5a Isis Giminiana *This tomb painting from Ostia shows the loading of grain ("res" here) onto a small, purpose-built river-boat that was hauled (probably by slaves) up the Tiber to Rome. Two longshoremen carrying sacks climb a gangplank onto the deck, where the grain is measured to check for theft during its transfer either from a larger seagoing vessel or from storage in one of the warehouses at the port (see Fig. 11.1). "Master" Farnaces may be the ship's captain. Abascantus, who is depicted larger than the other figures, may be its owner (and the occupant of the tomb); the man to the left of him holds what seems to be a measuring device. "Isis Giminiana," perhaps the boat's name, acknowledges the importance of Egypt to Rome's food supplies by invoking Isis, one of Egypt's most important gods. The boat's prow rises above the water, and its stern even higher; the keel is very curved; sails and oars (except for steering) are absent; a tow-rope would be attached to the mast, set very far forward.*

Plate 5b Septimius Severus, his wife Julia Domna, and their two sons Caracalla and Geta (with Geta defaced). *This painting on wood dates to soon after 198, when Geta was awarded the title "most noble Caesar," and his older brother Caracalla was made Augustus with their father (see Chapter Eleven and Table 11.1). Septimius Severus and Caracalla wear gem-studded gold crowns, and Julia Domna wears a smaller diadem on her head; the three males also carry scepters. This image of a happy, united family is belied by a history of persistent discord between the brothers. Within a year of their father's death (211) and their joint accession, Caracalla had ordered his brother's murder. Geta's name and image were then erased from all public records. As here, however, such erasures themselves were often prominent, a striking reminder of the power of public opinion.*

Plate 6a Scenes from the amphitheater, as shown on a mosaic from Zliten, Libya. *The mosaic formed part of a larger floor, which depicted on its edges numerous scenes from gladiatorial and other shows exhibited in the amphitheater (see Chapter Ten). From left to right, we see condemned criminals' public slaughter in the arena by wild beasts and various wild beast hunts. The mosaic perhaps dates to around 200, and the room from which it came was probably used for banquets or receptions.*

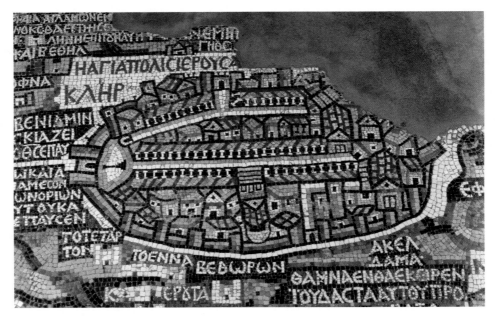

Plate 6b Jerusalem mapped. *This representation of late antique Jerusalem forms part of a mosaic map of the Holy Land found on the floor of a church in Madaba, Jordan. It offers our most detailed, if also very schematic, image of the city that Christian pilgrims were most eager to visit (see Chapters Thirteen and Fourteen). The most obvious features are the long colonnaded main street (cardo) running north–south through the city (left to right on the map), the victory column at the northern end (erected by Hadrian after the Bar Kokhba War; see Chapter Ten), and the imposing Church of the Holy Sepulcher in the lower center. Note its prominent dome over what was thought to be the burial place of Christ.*

Plate 7 Apse mosaic, church of Santa Pudenziana, Rome *From the fourth century onward, emperors, their officials, and private citizens all poured vast wealth into the construction of churches (see Chapter Fourteen). The level of artistic achievement attained can be gauged from this fine apse mosaic installed in the fairly modest church of Santa Pudenziana, Rome, around 390. It depicts Christ enthroned, very much in the manner of an emperor, and surrounded by his apostles. The four winged creatures in the sky above him represent the four evangelists, and the city beneath them is Jerusalem; some scholars have even speculated that the mosaic offers an accurate depiction of the buildings constructed there by Constantine. At either side in the foreground are the apostles, with two female figures (perhaps personifications of the Church and the Synagogue) standing behind them and crowning the martyrs Peter and Paul. Restorations of the mosaic in the sixteenth century removed two apostles on the outer sides and considerably altered the appearance of some of the remaining ten.*

Plate 8 Notitia Dignitatum illustration *The top-level administration for the entire later empire is laid out in schematic form in the* Notitia Dignitatum *(Roster of Offices), a book kept by the emperor's "Chief Notary". It survives only in medieval copies, but these offer a tantalizing reflection of the make-up of the fourth- and fifth-century bureaucracy (see Chapter Twelve). An illustration – like the one here depicting the insignia of the western Count of the Sacred Largesses – accompanies the text of each section, which lists the subordinate officers who worked for each high official. The Count of the Sacred Largesses was charged with the collection of money taxes and the production of coins and other precious metal objects, many of which appear here. On either side of the table, observe gold and silver leaf for appliqué and embossed gold belt-buckles, given as a sign of office and produced in workshops managed by the Count. Below, note plates full of gold coins (marked LAR[G]ITIONES, "largesse", since they were "in the gift of the emperor"); in the foreground, vessels filled with gold coins, a gold coffer, and a locked strong-box. The text that follows (not illustrated) lists eighty-one high-level officials grouped into ten divisions (for example, accountants, treasurers, and mint supervisors); each division could employ hundreds of bureaucrats.*

In summer 40, Octavian gave Antony further cause for concern by taking over Gaul and its garrison, following the death of the governor there who had been loyal to Antony. Antony sought a meeting with Octavian, therefore, which took place at Brundisium in September. The agreement they reached here was sealed by the marriage of Antony and Octavian's elder sister, Octavia; both partners' previous spouses had recently died. Octavian in effect now took responsibility for the West, including Italy, and Antony the East; Lepidus, whose role had become insignificant, was assigned only Africa. Octavian was charged with ending the threat posed by Sextus Pompey, either by defeating him or by making a settlement with him. There was some chance of the latter possibility, insofar as during the summer Octavian had agreed to marry Scribonia, the sister of Sextus Pompey's father-in-law, even though she was considerably older than he. It was her third marriage, and it lasted only a year. But by Scribonia Octavian had his only child, a daughter named Julia.

This agreement reached at Brundisium encouraged Antony to confine his attention to the east of the empire. Meanwhile Sextus Pompey's widespread raids and blockades made a settlement with him the only practical recourse. This was reached at Misenum in summer 39. Sextus Pompey undertook to abandon hostilities. In return, he was to retain control of Corsica, Sardinia, and Sicily and be given the Peloponnese, all for five years. Octavian had Antony to thank for help in reaching this pact, although he had no wish to adhere to its humiliating terms any longer than absolutely necessary.

ELIMINATION OF SEXTUS POMPEY AND LEPIDUS (39–36)

The fragility of the terms agreed at Misenum was soon exposed. Sextus Pompey took offense when Octavian divorced Scribonia in fall 39, and again when Antony delayed handing over the Peloponnese to him. During spring 38 he won two clashes with Octavian's fleet—off Cumae, and in the Straits of Messina—although he then did not dare to follow up his advantage. His hesitation offered Octavian a respite, in which he begged Antony for help. The two met at Tarentum (modern Taranto) in summer 37. They renewed the Triumvirate (probably to the end of 33), and Octavian agreed to send about 20,000 men to the East in return for being permitted to keep 120 of the warships accompanying Antony.

For Octavian, the advantage of this exchange was that the ships were immediately at his disposal, whereas his own commitment to provide men was only a promise for the future—which in fact he never honored properly. As consul in 37, Agrippa now took the lead in delivering Sextus Pompey a knockout blow. Lepidus even agreed to bring help from Africa. In 36, three hundred ships engaged on each side off Naulochus in Sicily, and—thanks to Agrippa's leadership—only seventeen of Sextus Pompey's escaped. He then fled to Asia Minor, where he was pursued and executed in 35. The energy with which he had unflinchingly maintained the cause inherited from his father is remarkable, as is the degree of success that he achieved. With a little more boldness, in 38 especially, he might even have displaced Octavian.

SOURCE 8.1: *This long Latin document, inscribed on stone at Rome, originally had two columns, of which only the second survives, and not all of it. It takes the form of a* laudatio *or eulogy to be delivered at a funeral by an upper-class husband for his wife. We know the name of neither, although scholars have customarily (but erroneously) referred to her as Turia. The wife praised here must have died around the beginning of the Christian era. For her legal position and the nature of* manus *marriage, see "Changes in Roman Society" in Chapter Five.*

You were suddenly left orphaned before the day of our marriage when both your parents were murdered in lonely country. It was mainly due to you that the death of your parents did not remain unavenged, because I had already departed to Macedonia, and your sister's husband Gaius Cluvius likewise to the province of Africa. You put so much effort into performing this sacred duty by insisting upon a prosecution and due punishment that, even had we been available, we should not have been able to do more. Rather, the credit is all yours, in partnership with that most respected of women, your sister. While you were engaged with this duty, and the perpetrators had been punished, you immediately left your family home to safeguard your virtue, and moved to that of my mother, where you awaited my return.

You were then pressured to declare that your father's will, in which you and I were made heirs, was invalid on the grounds that he had taken his wife into a *manus* marriage. . . . This would have required you, and all your father's property, to revert to the guardianship of those pressing the point. . . . Your resolution made them desist and not bring up the issue any further. . . .

It is rare for a marriage to last so long, to be ended by death rather than broken by divorce; ours turned out to last forty-one years without upset. I only wish that it could have been my death which ended it, since it would have been fairer for me as the elder to go first. Why should I mention your personal qualities? You were chaste, obedient, obliging, agreeable, an active woolworker, pious but not to excess, in dress fashionable but not glamorous, and altogether discreetly elegant. Why should I speak of your affection for your relatives and your devotion to the family? You showed the same concern for my mother as for your parents, and provided the same restful retirement for both, displaying overall the countless qualities found in every matron who seeks to be well thought of. . . .

Together we have taken care to preserve the entire inheritance received from your parents. You were not concerned to add to it, since you handed it all over to me. We shared responsibility such that I took care of your property, and you looked after mine. . . . You demonstrated your generosity with regard to very many relatives, and especially in your devotion to the family as a whole. . . . Certain female relatives of yours you brought up in our household, and you equipped them with dowries so that they could attain a status worthy of your family. Gaius Cluvius and I put our heads together about these dowries that you had settled upon. While we approved of them, we did not want you to diminish your own inheritance, so we tapped our resources and used our property to pay them. . . .

You provided the greatest support for my flight [from proscription in 43/42], helping me with your jewelry in particular by handing me all the gold and pearls from your person. . . . You deceived our enemies' guards. . . . Even though your courage kept urging you to try and test the strength of the military, you restrained yourself. . . . Amid all this you had the resolution not to let slip any undignified remark. . . .

Caesar [Octavian] was right when he said that it was you who made it possible for him to restore me to my native land because, but for the arrangements you made for him to save me, even his promises of help would have been in vain. . . .

I will acknowledge, however, that your plight made for the most terrible event of my life. It was when I had been restored to my country—as a useful citizen of it still—by the generous decision of Caesar [Octavian], who remained overseas. His colleague [as Triumvir], Marcus Lepidus, who was in Rome, objected to my reinstatement. When you prostrated yourself on the ground at his feet, he did not just fail to raise you up, but you were caught and dragged along the way slaves are, your body was all bruised. Even so, you reminded him most resolutely about Caesar's edict with its congratulations on my reinstatement. After hearing his response and enduring his abusive, cruel insults, you openly denounced him as the person who should be known as responsible for all my perils. Later he suffered for his behavior. . . .

Once peace returned to the world and the Republic was restored [in the 20s], it was then a time of rest and contentment for us. We did long for the children that already for some time fate had begrudged us. If fortune in its usual caring way had allowed them, what would the two of us have lacked? Advancing age ended our hopes. . . . Doubting your own fertility and distressed at my childlessness, you talked of divorce so that I—by remaining married to you—should not forfeit the hope of having children and be miserable as a result. You said that you would leave and hand over the household to another, fertile, woman. . . . You insisted that you would regard these children-to-be as shared and as if your own. You would not make any division of our property, which to date had been shared, but it would continue to be under my control and, with my consent, administered by you. . . . I must admit to having become furious enough to be out of my mind; I was so aghast at your proposals that I could barely regain self-control. . . . (*ILS* 8393)

Instead, as it turned out, Sextus Pompey's defeat at Naulochus prompted Lepidus to conclude that *his* time to displace the upstart Octavian had arrived. He demanded that Sextus Pompey's land forces surrender to him; but Octavian objected. He brazenly entered Lepidus' camp and invited all the troops—Lepidus' own and Sextus Pompey's—to recognize *him* as their commander. Not for the first time, his audacious personal appeal succeeded. As a result, Octavian was now able to humiliate Lepidus by removing him from the Triumvirate, taking control of Africa from him, and requiring him to live as an exile. In addition, Octavian's victory at Naulochus eliminated doubts about his military ability. For the first time, too, Italy was within his undisputed control, and he could now begin restoring it to stability and prosperity.

ANTONY IN THE EAST (42 ONWARDS)

This is the point for us to go back and trace developments in the East following Antony's victory at Philippi in October 42. Here there was much to occupy him

over a vast expanse of territory. Funds had to be raised urgently for paying troops
and settling veterans; disloyal local rulers had to be replaced; and consideration
also had to be given to resuming the offensive against Parthia that Julius Caesar's
assassination had forestalled. As part of all this activity, it made sound sense for
Antony to establish good relations with the ruler of the richest independent state
of the eastern Mediterranean: Cleopatra, queen of Egypt (Fig. 8.3). The meeting
that he requested at Tarsus in Cilicia in 41 was not their first; they must have met
previously when Cleopatra was in Rome.

Now, however, their relationship soon became personal. Cleopatra gave birth
to twins only a year later, and Antony spent the winter of 41–40 with her in Alexandria. Even so, this is not to say that he abandoned his grip on affairs. He took
various steps to help strengthen Cleopatra's rule (which was to Rome's advantage), and in spring 40 he departed to take the lead in stemming a major Parthian
invasion of Syria and Asia Minor; this had come as a surprise amid Roman plans
to attack Parthia. Very soon, however, Antony felt that instead the activities of
Octavian and Sextus Pompey demanded his presence in Italy; the repulse of the
Parthians was therefore deputed to Publius Ventidius. He in fact achieved this so
effectively over the next two years (through summer 38) that there was little for

a

b

Figure 8.3a, b *Cleopatra's historical importance,
and the inspiration still generated by her memory,
make the quest for an accurate likeness of her only
natural; but a satisfying outcome remains elusive.
Coins minted in Alexandria offer a lifelike profile.
Several three-dimensional portraits have been identified by one expert or another, but in all cases the
figure is not named. Only one is widely thought to be Cleopatra. It is a marble head (with the nose
missing) found in a villa near Rome; the hairstyle and the broad royal diadem match the coin portrait.*

Antony to contribute, even though he did return to the East with his new wife Octavia in fall 39. The spring and summer of 37 saw him back in Italy with a large fleet, however.

Octavia had accompanied Antony back to Italy, but she was left behind when he returned to the East in fall 37; she had already had one daughter by him, and would give birth to another early in 36. In Octavia's absence, Cleopatra now joined Antony in Syria. At this stage he acknowledged paternity of the twins born in 40, and in 36 she had another son by him. The nature of their relationship from now onwards is hard to define. To Egyptians, it was evidently not quite a marriage, although they may have favored it as a sound step by Cleopatra to strengthen her rule. There is no knowing how much Antony was influenced by a desire to help her in this way, nor what private vision she may have had for her own future and that of her kingdom. Most puzzling is Antony's lack of concern for the impression made upon his own wife Octavia, her brother Octavian, and Roman public opinion in general. Moreover, even should he divorce Octavia, as a Roman citizen he could never contract a marriage recognized in Roman law with a non-Roman like Cleopatra.

In 36 Antony set out against Parthia at the head of sixteen legions and many other troops. He did penetrate successfully deep into Media, but then his ally the King of Armenia panicked and withdrew vital cavalry support. So Antony was driven back with the devastating loss of as much as one-third of his army. Roman opinion naturally contrasted his stunning defeat here to Octavian's victories over Sextus Pompey in the same year, an extraordinary reversal of both men's military reputations to date.

CLASH BETWEEN ANTONY AND OCTAVIAN (36–30)

From fall 36, the Roman world had two rulers: Antony in the East and Octavian in the West. The key issue now, we might imagine, was how long this divided rule might continue. There need be no doubt that Octavian saw it only as the prelude to a struggle for sole power, and so he intensified his hostile propaganda against Cleopatra and Antony.

Antony, by contrast, remained preoccupied with the tense situation on the eastern edge of his territory. We have no clue as to why he was so slow to react to the growing threat from Octavian in the West. It was no doubt unwelcome to him, but it was also blatant and dangerous. As it was, he concentrated on subduing Armenia, partly to avenge its king's desertion in 36, partly to establish a bridgehead for a further invasion of Parthia. This he did achieve in 35 and 34, despite being first distracted by an embarrassment of Octavian's devising. Octavian dispatched Octavia with troops in token fulfillment at last of the exchange agreed in 37. Antony accepted this aid, but he instructed Octavia not to proceed beyond Athens, and he spent the winter of 35–34 in Alexandria with Cleopatra. Still, neither he nor Octavia exercised their right to divorce the other.

Antony's behavior on returning to Alexandria in 34 seemed even more cavalier. To celebrate the conquest of Armenia, he staged a Roman-style triumph, and then in an extravagant ceremony—the so-called "Donations of Alexandria"—he distributed eastern lands (some of them Roman provinces) to Cleopatra, her three children by him, and her son by Julius Caesar. To be sure, these actions were only gestures, no doubt designed to gratify the Egyptians, but it is easy to see how a more sinister construction could be placed upon them in Rome.

By the following year, 33, Antony recognized that he must give priority to preparing for a clash with Octavian, and in 32 he finally divorced Octavia. Octavian, for his part, sought further means of justifying his cause. He actually descended to the shameless illegality of seizing Antony's will, which had been deposited with the Vestal virgins, and publicizing its provisions. These supposedly included arrangements for burial in Alexandria and gifts to Antony's three children by Cleopatra. As a more solemn precaution, Octavian took the unusual step of arranging for civilians throughout the West to swear a personal oath of loyalty to him (see Source 8.2) in the war that was declared against Cleopatra. This declaration was made against her alone, not Antony too; all suggestion of civil conflict was studiously avoided.

Once the two sides' large forces encountered each other at Actium in western Greece in 31, the ensuing action proved surprisingly undramatic. Throughout the summer each side had sought to trap and blockade the other. Antony was forced more and more on the defensive. Eventually, at the beginning of September, he ordered a breakout by his fleet. In the brief clash, both he and Cleopatra did burst through with their squadrons, but for some reason they then sailed on—she back to Alexandria directly, he via Libya first. That left the rest of the fleet, and their entire land forces, at Octavian's mercy. All quickly gave up the fight.

The following year, 30, Octavian mounted a full-scale assault on Alexandria, by land from east and west simultaneously. In the event, the city fell at the beginning of August with almost no resistance. Antony's fleet deserted, and he committed suicide, perhaps in reaction to a false report that Cleopatra had done so. In fact she was captured and spared; but then she, too, took her own life nine days later. Caesarion, her son by Julius Caesar, was executed. Egypt's wealth came into Octavian's hands, and the kingdom was annexed as a Roman province.

OCTAVIAN AS SOLE RULER (30 ONWARDS)

So, at the age of only thirty-three, Octavian had finally achieved the undisputed control of the Roman world that had been his unwavering ambition through fourteen years of civil war. To this end, he had been responsible for death, destruction, confiscation, and unbroken misery on a scale quite unmatched in all the previous phases of Roman civil conflict over the past century. Time and again he had returned from the brink of disaster, thanks to his skill as a propagandist, his ability to attract able associates, and his willingness to sacrifice any principle to one overriding purpose. Now, after this utterly amazing outcome, it became his concern to maintain the supremacy he had gained. The fact that he was also to do this successfully over a period of forty-four more years is hardly less miraculous than his elimination of all rivals to date.

Among the challenges of every description facing Octavian after his restoration of peace in 31–30, the nature of his own official position for the future was a particularly delicate and pressing issue. There had been no renewal of the Triumvirate after its lapse, probably at the end of 33. In practice, however, he continued to exercise a Triumvir's sweeping powers, even after beginning to hold a consulship annually from 31 onwards. Nobody was in a position to contest such irregularities, especially after the oath of loyalty had been sworn. Even so, Octavian wanted a more secure footing for the long term. The fundamental question was the nature of the regime that should now rule Rome. Two possibilities were surely to be avoided. The first was Caesar's style of autocracy. The second was some form of sole rule that relied primarily upon the army; Octavian's civil war experience must have warned him against attempting this. Rather, he believed that from the traditional Republican framework itself could emerge a way forward that would both satisfy the upper classes' desire to reestablish the supremacy of the senate and at the same time enable him to keep control.

Octavian signaled his choice of approach in 28 by acknowledging for the first time that he and his partner in the consulship, Agrippa, were coequals. Then, at a carefully staged meeting of the senate in January 27, he handed back all his authority to the senate and people. To calm members in their alarm, he at once consented to remain consul and to take responsibility for Spain, Gaul, Cilicia, Cyprus, Syria, and Egypt for ten years, on the grounds that these areas were in particular danger from invasion or revolt. Clearly, he could not govern all of them personally, still less command the troops stationed there, so he was granted authority to appoint legates to serve for whatever terms he should fix. The expectation was that he would continue to be reelected consul himself. Governors of all other provinces would now once again be chosen by lot from ex-consuls and ex-praetors to serve for one-year terms in the traditional manner.

Along with this grant, often referred to today as the "First Settlement," the senate bestowed upon Octavian the new name Augustus and also renamed the month Sextilis (repeatedly a time of success for him) in the same way. With the sense of "revered," this name has a semireligious connotation, and it was deliberately intended to symbolize Octavian's decisive break with his violent past. The times were now to be normal, with peace and the Republic restored.

"THE REPUBLIC RESTORED"

How genuine is this claim? Certain ancient writers much later, looking back with the advantage of hindsight, represent it as a sham, because they are keenly aware of how authoritarian the rule, which dates from this point would become over time. It is vital to appreciate, however, that contemporaries enjoyed no such insight into the future. Their comparison would be to the past. By this measure, there is no question that the First Settlement allowed the Republic's traditional institutions and offices to function with a degree of independence and stability unknown since, say, the formation of the First Triumvirate in 60–59. Augustus wanted a return to the rule of law and sought a legitimate, regular position within such a framework (Fig. 8.4). Those who had no grasp of constitutional issues might refer to him as *imperator* (hence "emperor"), but he represented himself as no more than *princeps*, a bland, informal term signifying merely "leading figure." Previously there had been many *principes*, whereas now there was to be only one. Hence this new phase in Rome's history is termed the Principate. Even this single Princeps might in time relax his hold further. The First Settlement, after all, was made for no more than ten years. To this extent, there was cause for hope. There was also now the realization, unlike in 44, that another assassination would not of its own accord serve to make the senate supreme again.

For his part, Augustus understood, as Caesar had not, how vital the senate's support was to his control of the Roman world. He further realized from Caesar's experience that an ostentatious display of authority gave offense without bestowing more power. Instead, Augustus believed that the authority he could exercise within the traditional Republican framework was sufficient. He encouraged the senate to determine many matters without reference to him. Even where he had an interest, he typically chose to advance it, not by open exercise of authority, but through his personal, unofficial *auctoritas* or "influence."

Figure 8.4 *This coin is a gold piece, from an issue not known until 1992, probably minted in the province of Asia. It dates to Octavian's sixth consulship (28 B.C.), and its reverse shows him wearing a toga, sitting on his magistrate's chair, holding out a scroll, with the words (in Latin) "he restored to the Roman people their laws and rights." The design reminds us that the changes we term the First Settlement were not all made at a single meeting of the senate in January 27, but instead began in 28 as a series of steps.*

Augustus' *auctoritas* was unmatched, and contemporaries were certainly aware of how the noun and his new name share the same root. His quiet, skillful use of *auctoritas* served as a formidable reinforcement of his official authority. He even used it to extend that authority, however, and this was more disturbing insofar as it undermined his own representation of his position after the First Settlement. In particular, he caused governors outside his own assigned sphere to take steps (even make war), which no individual consul had the right to authorize without consulting his partner in office or the senate. If Augustus wished to act in this way, then he would have to alter the formal basis of his position. At the same time, he shared the growing sense that it would not be truly republican for him to continue holding the consulship year after year; when Marius had done so, after all, it was only under special circumstances in a crisis. Nobles moreover were sure to become increasingly frustrated that from now on they could compete for only one of these prized consulships annually, rather than two. Last among the manifestly unrepublican features of the First Settlement was the sheer size of Augustus' sphere of command. No consul had ever been assigned one so large.

SECOND SETTLEMENT (23)

The First Settlement was unavoidably experimental. Augustus' experience with it convinced him that he needed to make his formal authority more sweeping, as well as less obtrusive. A plot by senators that was fortunately detected at the planning stage may have prompted him to act; a near-fatal illness in mid-23 certainly did. The changes he now made were threefold and are often referred to today as the "Second Settlement." First, on July 1, 23, he resigned the consulship and never held the office again under normal conditions. He had realized that he could just as well retain only its authority. Accordingly, he kept his provinces and the all-important imperium (now of a proconsul, strictly speaking) to govern it. Moreover—the second change—his imperium was made "greater" or *maius* by the senate. In other words, it was now specifically recognized as superior to that of all other officials everywhere and could therefore be the legitimate basis of instructions to them. Third and last, he took a further power without office, that of a tribune (*tribunicia potestas*), and was in fact to renew this annually until his death, so that the years of his rule from 23 can be counted in this way. This power added little to authority he already had, although it did make him sacrosanct, and it conveniently permitted him to summon the senate and to impose a veto, should the need arise. The unique appeal of "tribunician power," however, was its modest, popular image as provider of protection for ordinary citizens. It therefore became the power that Augustus paraded; by contrast, attention was never drawn to his *maius imperium*.

Although the Second Settlement offered every prospect of eliminating the flaws in the First, Augustus evidently did not anticipate the strength of the reaction to his withdrawal from the consulship. The people were bewildered by Augustus' failure to stand for the top office as usual, and feared that as a result they were losing their greatest benefactor. In 22 they evidently begged him to accept a life consulship, which he declined; in both 21 and 20 they rioted and refused to elect more than one candidate. Eventually, in 19, the senate permitted Augustus to wear a consul's insignia when he appeared in public; the fact that he now looked like a consul seems to have soothed widespread fears. Thereafter his official position underwent little further alteration. The only further office he took was the lifetime religious one of pontifex maximus, which finally became vacant on Lepidus' death in 12. The title (rather than office) of *Pater Patriae*, "Father of his Country," bestowed on Augustus in the senate in 2 B.C., was likewise naturally for life.

THE ROMAN FAMILY IN THE AUGUSTAN PERIOD

Augustus felt that Rome, and the upper classes in particular, no longer showed sufficient respect for marriage and its vital role in rearing children to maintain families and the community as a whole. In his view, too many respectable Roman men were choosing to remain bachelors; some men who did marry made unsuitable matches, or condoned adulterous behavior by their wives; and married couples capable of producing children were deliberately remaining childless. We cannot ascertain the accuracy of these perceptions, but there is no doubt about the strength of Augustus' lasting concern to remedy what he considered to be a crisis. He promoted some complex legislation for this purpose in 18/17, and had it revised as late as A.D. 9.

First, penalties were introduced for both men and women who remained unmarried, or who married but for whatever reason failed to have children, between the ages of 25 and 60 for men, and 20 and 50 for women. Second, members of the new senatorial class (see "Senate and *Equites* " below) were debarred from marrying any ex-slave or anyone not regarded as respectable (an entertainer, for example). And third, all validly married couples who did have children were rewarded, on an ascending scale (the more children, the more benefits). A husband who became aware of adultery by his wife now had to divorce her and then prosecute her (the same did not apply in the case of an adulterous husband, but his wife could still divorce him). On conviction for adultery, a woman stood to lose half her dowry and one-third of her other property; she also faced exile to an island, and could never remarry. Her male partner, if still alive, could likewise be prosecuted and punished. These interfering measures regulated by law for the first time a wide variety of spheres that Romans had always regarded as entirely private. There is no sign that they were in fact successful in altering society's behavior or attitudes. Indeed, although Augustus' own daughter Julia had five children with her second husband Agrippa (some twenty-five years her senior), she resented the third marriage expected of her (to Tiberius) within a year of Agrippa's death in 12 (see Table 8.1). Later, in 2 B.C., she was exiled for adultery and treason.

Some women may well have chafed at the pressure to marry and bear children. Wives were held to a higher standard of behavior than husbands. Married men's involvements with other women could largely be tolerated so long as they were not blatant, and not with married women of supposedly respectable background. A wife, by contrast, who became involved with any other man, especially one of lower social status, could not expect the same tolerance, and the Augustan laws outlined above expanded the legal ramifications. Either partner to a marriage, however, could initiate divorce. In Roman law, marriage itself was a purely private act, which required no formal ceremony—although a celebration was often held—nor any certification by the state. Rather, a relationship where both partners were eligible (neither could be a slave, for example), and behaved towards one another as husband and wife, constituted a legally valid marriage. By the same token, either marriage partner could formally mark the termination of the relationship with a divorce by simply informing the other. Once again, this was a purely private matter. A husband contemplating this step would need to consider his obligation to return all (or, in some circumstances, part) of the dowry; he could be sued if he did not. The wife, for her part, if she had borne children, would have to weigh the likelihood that after a divorce they would remain with their father, since they were regarded as belonging to his family, not hers. Typically, little stigma attached to divorce or remarriage. To some wives, however, the ideal was to be *univira*, in other words, never to have more than one husband, even if they were widowed and were in a position to remarry. This traditional ideal— upheld by Cornelia, mother of the Gracchi brothers, for example (see Chapter Four)—seems at odds with Augustan legislation encouraging remarriage and procreation.

How far women could control their childbearing remains unclear. Without question, Roman women shared—mainly just by word of mouth—a rich store of information about both contraception and abortion. The effectiveness of these procedures is hard to determine, but surviving texts show that many were downright dangerous for the woman. The preference of wealthy women to hire wet nurses for their babies could accelerate the birth rate for a fertile woman like Augustus' daughter Julia, who bore Agrippa five children in eight years. On the other hand, maternal mortality was high, and the young age at which an elite woman could be married—in her lower teens—made childbearing even more risky for her in the first years of a marriage. In any event, few women eager to rear children to adulthood would limit their family's size. So many children were likely to die either at birth or as infants (see Fig. 9.4 and Chapter 14) that as many as three out of five might never reach adulthood. Poor understanding of infant nutritional needs, ignorance about germs, and lack of skilled medical help were among the factors limiting family size; the lower the parents' place on the social and economic scale, the less chance there was for a child's survival. Even for those

Table 8.1 The Julio-Claudian Family

This family tree is a deliberately selective one, omitting certain individuals and marriages. The abbreviations b., d., cos. signify respectively born, died, consul (in the year stated). All dates given are certain, or almost certain; dates A.D. are those normally used for the individuals concerned; descriptors in italic (e.g. the younger) offer additional identification. Emperors' names are in CAPITALS. Names bolded are in boldface. Names **bolded** *are those normally used for the individuals concerned; descriptors in italic (e.g. the younger) offer additional identification. Emperors' names are in CAPITALS.*
= signifies a marriage; the figure above = gives the date of the marriage, where known. The figure in parentheses immediately before or after the name of an individual who married more than once specifies this marriage's place in the sequence.

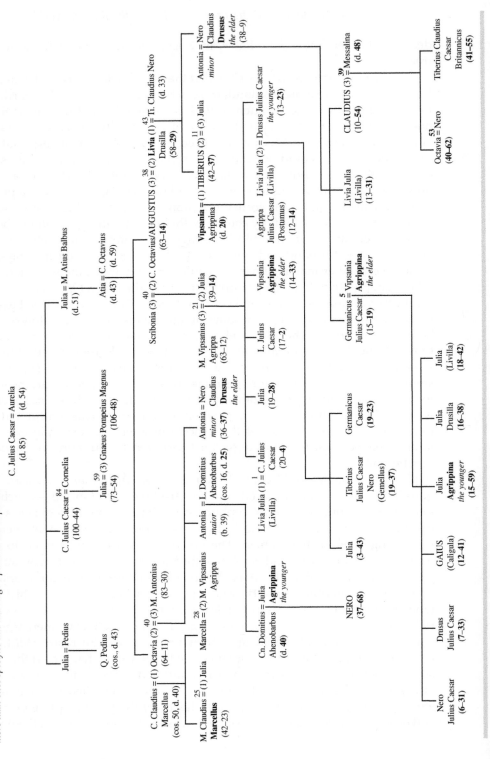

who did reach adulthood, life expectancy remained low. A bride in her late teens would be lucky if she had even one grandparent still alive to attend the wedding; the chance that her mother would still be living was no better than 60 percent, and her father 50 percent. Given the traditional, long-standing importance of family to the Romans, many couples must have wished for as many children as they thought they could raise.

SUCCESSION

From the First Settlement of 27 onwards, despite his claims to have restored Rome's traditional constitution, Augustus in practice infringed a basic principle of any republic by quietly wielding a quite disproportionate amount of personal authority. From an early stage too, he developed another highly unrepublican preoccupation by planning to pass on his position to a capable successor of his own choosing, and if at all possible a blood relative (Source 8.2). To uphold both his family's interests and those of the state for the purpose was certain to prove an extraordinary challenge. But most Romans would surely have agreed that a power struggle after Augustus' death was to be avoided at almost any cost. Moreover, given the depth of family pride in Roman society, his passionate desire to install a successor of his own blood must at least have met with some understanding, even on the part of contemporaries opposed to such a plan.

That said, for him to gain the acceptance of any successor was still extraordinarily delicate, partly on grounds of principle, but also because he had only one child—a daughter Julia, from his short-lived marriage to Scribonia. His wife thereafter, Livia Drusilla, whom he married in 38, never had children by him, despite having produced two sons by her first husband Tiberius Claudius Nero—Tiberius (born in 42) and Drusus (born in 38). Only in 25 was anyone singled out who might seem destined as a successor, when Julia married Marcus Claudius Marcellus (born in 42), son of Augustus' sister Octavia by her first husband. Julia and Marcellus produced no children, however, and he died prematurely in fall 23. Moreover, a few months earlier when Augustus himself had expected to die, it was to his loyal associate Agrippa, not to young Marcellus, that he gave his signet ring. That desperate gesture demonstrated the embarrassing absence of plans for any succession at this stage.

Fortunately, Augustus did not die in 23, and in fact his poor health even improved thereafter. But this crisis now stirred him to make adequate arrangements for the succession. Because he had no remaining male blood relatives, he again turned to Agrippa, prevailing upon him in 21 to divorce Marcella (his second wife, Marcellus' sister) and marry Julia. Agrippa already had imperium bestowed on him for a mission in the East. In 18 this was renewed, and *tribunicia potestas* added. Agrippa was the first person with whom Augustus shared this latter

Figure 8.5 *Bust of Livia.*

power, and it became the mark of a designated successor. Augustus was overjoyed that the marriage of Agrippa and Julia had already produced a son, Gaius, born in 20. A second, Lucius, followed in 17; both were adopted by Augustus as his own sons the same year.

Gaius and Lucius were still only children, however, when Agrippa died unexpectedly in 12, aged about fifty. Augustus now therefore looked to his elder stepson Tiberius for the first time. He in turn was asked to divorce his wife Vipsania Agrippina (Agrippa's daughter by his first wife, Caecilia Attica) and marry his stepsister Julia. He did so with great reluctance, not least because it was only in the previous year that Vipsania had given birth to a son, Drusus. The new marriage became a failure. Tiberius was granted imperium and tribunicia potestas for five years in 6, but soon afterwards he evidently felt so alienated by the efforts to advance Gaius—who was now about to enter public life—that he withdrew to become a recluse on the island of Rhodes. His official position was not renewed, and he only returned to Rome in A.D. 2, still out of favor. Julia by contrast had not left Rome, but in 2 B.C. Augustus felt obliged to exile her for scandalous sexual misconduct.

Augustus suffered further grief when both adopted sons died young, Lucius in A.D. 2 and Gaius two years later. In 5 and 2 B.C., respectively, Augustus had even occupied the consulship to introduce each to public life, the only times he ever took that office after 23. Gaius became consul himself in A.D. 1; his marriage to Livia Julia (Livilla) the previous year remained childless. Augustus had so fervently desired one or both of these young men to succeed him that their deaths were the most cruel blow. By A.D. 4, his only practical option was to turn back without enthusiasm to his elder stepson Tiberius (the younger stepson, Drusus, had died in 9 B.C.). At last, Tiberius was no longer merely a stopgap for others. He was now adopted by Augustus as his son, and had imperium and tribunicia potestas conferred on him for ten years; when those powers were renewed in A.D. 13, his imperium was specifically made equal to that of Augustus.

So against all the odds, when Augustus died the following year 14, there duly occurred the smooth, undisputed transition to a capable new Princeps that he had so long planned. Tiberius was reliable, experienced, and faced no obvious rival (by contrast, what if Gaius and Lucius had both lived? or if Tiberius and Julia had had sons?). Beyond that, a sound foundation was laid for Augustus' broader concern to maintain the regime, which he had developed for the long-term benefit of the Roman world.

SENATE AND *EQUITES*

In a prayer, Augustus once referred to his regime with studied vagueness as the "best condition," *optimus status*. If we now turn to reviewing some of its most important aspects, it is appropriate to begin with the senate and its members. A strong, active senate, comprising an outstanding elite of wealthy statesmen, was at the center of Augustus' vision for the future. To remove unworthy members, he conducted two major reviews—acting like a censor for the purpose, although this office was not revived on a regular basis either now or later. The first review, as early as 29, reduced the senate from about 1,000 to 800, with Octavian placed at the head of the roll as *princeps senatus*. The second review, in 18, removed a further 200. This left a body of about 600 members (the size that Sulla had made it), to which the normal means of entry was by election as one of the twenty quaestors annually. By the time of the second review, Augustus had further elevated the senate as a new, exclusive social class to which members and their families belonged. He also made 1,000,000 sesterces the minimum level of wealth for any senator; previously, none had been specified beyond the 400,000 required of an eques.

Generally speaking, Sulla's regulations for the *cursus honorum* were once again observed. Elections were conducted freely, too, although Augustus did intervene in some key respects. He fixed the number of praetors to be elected each year, and both for this office as well as lower ones he seems to have recommended a certain number of candidates, whose election was thus in effect assured. To what extent, if at all, he acted likewise for the consulship remains obscure. He certainly did introduce an important change for it from 5 B.C. onwards, whereby the pair who entered office on January 1 resigned midyear, thus requiring "suffects" to replace them. Since it was the honor of attaining this magistracy that senators sought—with length of tenure a matter of indifference—this new practice was a brilliant means of satisfying more aristocrats' ambitions, while maintaining the tradition that only a pair of consuls should be in office at any time.

Even if a senator about whom Augustus had reservations did rise through the cursus honorum, that was little cause for alarm; a senior magistrate's scope for action was now severely limited. Rather, the practical value of a praetorship or consulship was the eligibility it conferred for holding the empire's top military or administrative positions. Most such appointments were for the Princeps to make, and he did little to depart from the tradition that senators alone should be chosen to fill them. Hence in practice ambitious senators needed to maintain Augustus' favor. Already in 27, at the time of the First Settlement, most legions were stationed within his provinces, and by his death only one (in Africa) was not. Thus almost all legionary commanders were his legates (typically ex-praetors), as were the governors of the provinces where these forces were stationed (ex-consuls or ex-praetors, corresponding to the significance of the region). Within Rome and Italy, senior senators also came to be given administrative responsibilities in spheres of greater concern to Augustus than they had ever been to the Republican senate. They supervised the distribution of the 200,000 free monthly grain rations in Rome, for example, as well as the upkeep of the city's aqueducts and public buildings, and the main roads of Italy.

It need be no surprise that the morale of the senate seemed generally low throughout the reign. Plenty of old families had faded during the civil war period, many members survived only to be removed, and the remainder had to adjust their outlook. The same applied to new entrants, whom Augustus (himself the son of a novus homo) followed Julius Caesar in cautiously encouraging from Italy and the Latin-speaking West. Now every senator's dilemma was how best to act in an environment where the Princeps' opinion had always to be respected, and nothing that he requested or supported could be denied. Augustus went out of his way to attend the senate, and to consult it respectfully; he even formed a committee of members to determine the agenda in advance of meetings. However, this step only sharpened the sense that the senate's role was merely to approve what had already been decided in private elsewhere, in particular with regard to such key issues as state finances, foreign affairs, and the disposition of the army. Some members were gripped by fear or resentment. Others meanwhile resorted to flattery, and almost all hesitated to articulate opinions. Really, it was not until Tiberius' reign that the senate's morale was boosted by the adoption of some important new functions. Even then, the basic issue of the relationship between Princeps and senate was to remain tense and unresolved.

In contrast to senators, equites had no cause to feel immediately threatened by Augustus. Rather, because the Roman Republic had done almost nothing to tap their particular managerial and financial talents in its service, equites were gratified when he took the novel step of seeking out their assistance. The sphere where Augustus particularly enlisted equites was in managing all the various properties that came under his control, and in representing him in the courts in this connection. Soon enough, no doubt, he must have had such equestrian "procurators" in every province of the empire (the Latin noun *procurator* simply means "agent").

Strictly speaking, they were all just his private staff. Even so, procurators within his own provinces gradually came to be entrusted with assignments in the public domain—handling tax payments, for example, commanding troops, and even governing an entire province. In this latter connection, the outstanding example was Egypt, where, from its annexation in 30, all the top Roman officials and commanders were equites exclusively. Security was surely the reason here—equites would not share senators' political ambitions—and it again must have been what prompted Augustus to place his own guardsmen, the Praetorian Guard, under the command of a pair of equestrian prefects from 2 B.C. onwards. Some years later, in A.D. 6, a disastrous fire in Rome prompted him to form a night patrol of 3,500 "watchmen" (*vigiles*), under the command of an eques. Then soon afterwards, following a severe shortage, he recognized the need for permanent monitoring of the supply of grain to the city (imported mostly from Africa and Egypt; see Plate 5a), and asked another eques to undertake this responsibility.

ARMY

Augustus' bitter experience during the long civil war period had demonstrated the importance of the army to his rule, yet also the many dangers that the army posed. He himself had encouraged disloyalty on the part of his opponents' troops, while also needing to combat it among his own men. Now he had to secure the entire army's unshakable loyalty, as well as to reform the traditional outmoded Republican arrangements for recruitment and discharge.

After his victory at Actium, Augustus' immediate concern was to discharge 140,000 or more men from both sides; Egypt's wealth enabled him to buy them land instead of confiscating it, and to give them a little cash. This left a standing army of twenty-eight legions (each about 5,000 infantrymen), which must represent the size of force that Augustus regarded as strategically adequate for the long term, and at the same time affordable. Not until 13, however, do we hear of new conditions of service. The changes were radical. In principle, henceforth all legionaries would be volunteer citizens who committed to serving for a fixed number of years, at the end of which—if they stayed loyal and survived to be honorably discharged—they would receive a fixed bounty payment. During their service they could not legally be married; Augustus was no doubt eager to keep his forces mobile, and he perhaps wanted to avoid all claims by dependents. In cash, the bounty equaled about thirteen years' pay (thus sufficient to support most veterans to the end of their lives), although in some instances it comprised land with proportionately less cash. Initially, a legionary's term of service was set at fifteen years with a further four as reservist, but various setbacks forced Augustus to raise those figures to twenty and five respectively. To pay such substantial bounties, in A.D. 6 Augustus established a special "military" treasury, the *aerarium militare*, administered by ex-praetors, for this sole purpose. He funded it himself initially, and for the future made the proceeds of a sales tax and an inheritance tax payable to it. For citizens, therefore, from 13 onwards military service became a lifetime career choice, and the army a professional force.

Julius Caesar had already doubled soldiers' pay, and—except in the singular case of his own Praetorian Guard—Augustus did not seek to buy their loyalty by raising it further. Nor was he eager to continue the civil war practice of bribing soldiers with "donatives." He did, however, give a huge boost to the regular pay of centurions (legionary officers), who now received anything from thirteen to over fifty times the basic rate, depending upon rank and seniority (Fig. 8.6). With rare exceptions, all top army officers (senators and equites) were Augustus' own legates, appointed by him and serving for whatever period he might determine. From fear of rivals, he chose not to entrust large groupings of legions to the command of aristocrats, preferring either members of his own family or "new men." More broadly, he ensured that it was now he and his family to whom all soldiers swore their oath of loyalty—not to their officers, who were only his deputies (compare Source 8.2). Mutinies and strikes against

Figure 8.6 *This tomb monument was erected by the brother of a centurion, Marcus Caelius, who died in what is referred to as "Varus' war," in other words the massacre in the Teutoburg Forest in* A.D. *9. He is presented as the model of a successful career officer in Augustus' reshaped professional army. His age (53) and high status as a centurion of the first rank are specified. He wears a very distinguished set of decorations for valor—an oak-leaf "civic crown" (corona civica) for saving a fellow citizen's life, torques hanging from his shoulder straps, medallions on his chest, and bracelets on each wrist. In his right hand he grasps the dreaded stick of vine wood (vitis), with which all centurions maintained discipline. The sense of his proud status is enhanced by the inclusion of a freedman on either side of him.*

SOURCE 8.2: *It was specifically to Augustus and his family that soldiers came to be required to take a regular oath of loyalty. From time to time he also used oath-taking as a means of promoting civilians' loyalty to himself. There follows the text of a Latin oath sworn by the magistrates, senate, and people of Conobaria, not far north of Gades (modern Cádiz) in southern Spain, probably in connection with the introduction of Gaius Caesar to public life in 5 B.C. Note that Marcus Agrippa (Agrippa Julius Caesar), Agrippa's posthumous son by Julia born in 12, is named here among the members of the imperial family; later, however, in A.D. 6 Augustus removed him from the family, allegedly for some mental disability or character flaw.*

In all sincerity I avow my concern for the safety, honor, and victory of imperator Caesar Augustus, son of the Divine Julius [Caesar], pontifex maximus, and of Gaius Caesar, son of Augustus, Leader of Youth, consul designate, pontifex, and of Lucius Caesar, son of Augustus, and of Marcus Agrippa, grandson of Augustus. I shall bear arms, and shall hold as friends and allies the same ones I understand to be theirs. I shall consider as my enemies, too, those whom I observe in opposition to them. And should anyone take action or make plans against them, I shall pursue him to the death by land and by sea. *(AE 1988. 723)*

the regime remained a very real concern throughout Augustus' rule and far beyond. In general, however, his efforts to maintain the army's loyalty were to prove remarkably successful.

THE EMPIRE AND ITS EXPANSION

The army was to be used both to protect Rome's empire and to expand it. Augustus saw no contradiction when he sought praise both for bringing peace and for making conquests even more extensive than those of Pompey or Caesar. In his own words, his peace was one "secured by victories." It is hard to define his various goals for the expansion of Roman power. There is no question that in any case these underwent changes over such a long period of rule, and there were plainly major disappointments and failures too. Moreover, his geographical grasp was nowhere near as complete or accurate as ours. It is possible that for a long time he had "world conquest" somehow in mind, along the lines claimed by his great Republican predecessors. This ambition could certainly account for expeditions ordered in the 20s south from Egypt and far into the Arabian peninsula (Fig. 8.7), as well as for his determination to subdue the huge area between the Rhine and Elbe rivers. To stretch so far in each of these instances proved a failure in practical terms. The image they fostered was still a glorious and exotic one, however, which diplomatic dealings with rulers as far away as Britain and India only reinforced.

Meantime, Augustus was aware after Actium that several areas within the empire were not secure, and that from a strategic viewpoint it was altogether a

Map 8.2 *Expansion of the Empire in the Age of Augustus*

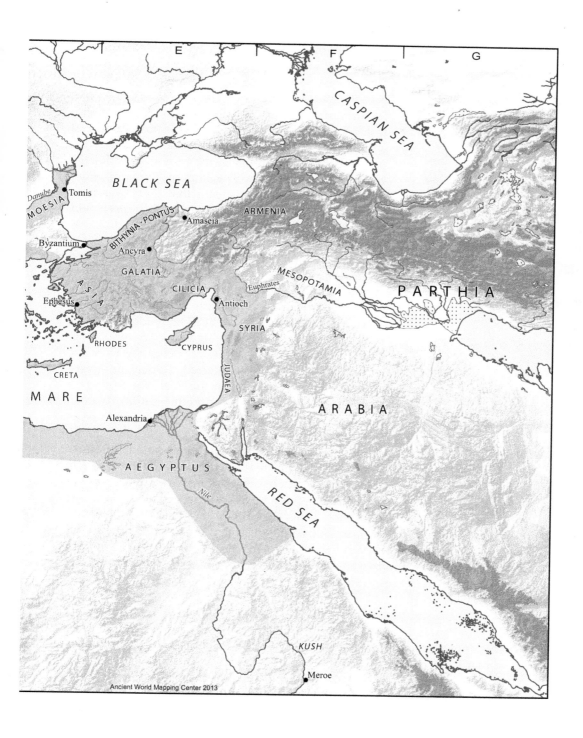

CASPIAN SEA

BLACK SEA

Danube
MOESIA
Tomis

Byzantium

BITHYNIA · PONTUS
Amaseia

Ancyra

GALATIA

ARMENIA

ASIA

Ephesus

CILICIA

Euphrates

MESOPOTAMIA

PARTHIA

Antioch

SYRIA

RHODES

CYPRUS

CRETA

JUDAEA

MARE

ARABIA

Alexandria

AEGYPTUS

Nile

RED SEA

KUSH

Meroe

Ancient World Mapping Center 2013

badly fragmented whole. During the 20s he himself imposed Roman control throughout the Iberian peninsula, especially its rugged northwest, which had never been subjugated previously. At the same time, he authorized others to embark upon the immense task of extending the empire northwards in central and eastern Europe as far as the Danube River. This thrust led to the creation of the provinces of Raetia, Noricum, Dalmatia (an expansion of Illyricum), Pannonia, and Moesia, and meant that there was now Roman territory linking the empire's western and eastern halves. A related initiative, long overdue, was to subdue the entire area of the Alps.

In the East, there was much less campaigning, and in general Antony's administrative reorganization remained in place. Apart from Egypt, the two notable additions to the empire were the large region of Galatia in central Asia Minor in 25, and Judaea in A.D. 6; both were former "client kingdoms." Several other states maintained this status; as such, they were not ruled by Rome, but respected Roman interests. Augustus' major concern in the East was to forge a viable long-term relationship with Parthia. To exact some form of vengeance for the defeats of Crassus and Antony seemed essential. On the other hand, Augustus felt unable to spare substantial forces to guard against Parthian incursions, and he was still less enthusiastic about mounting his own major offensive there. Because he also appreciated that it was the exception rather than the norm for Parthia to act as a well-organized, aggressive military power, he risked

Figure 8.7 This large bronze head excavated in 1910 at Meroe, capital of the independent kingdom of Kush on the Nile River (in modern Sudan), is an outstanding example of the standard, idealized image of Augustus from the 20s. In the years immediately following Rome's annexation of Egypt, relations with Kush to the south were hostile, and the head was no doubt booty from a Meroitic raid into the new province.

relying upon tough diplomacy rather than force. By this means, in 20, he did achieve the return of legionary standards captured from Crassus and Antony, and gained agreement to the principle that the king of Armenia should acknowledge Roman overlordship.

It was in the West that unexpected difficulties arose. In A.D. 6, peoples in Dalmatia and Pannonia raised a major rebellion, which Tiberius had to spend three years suppressing. Immediately afterwards (in A.D. 9), Germans ambushed three Roman legions under the command of Publius Quinctilius Varus as they marched through the "Teutoburg Forest," northwest of modern Osnabrück (see Fig. 8.6). Here, too, Roman rule had not been adequately established, and in fact it never would be. Augustus was devastated by the loss of Varus' legions, as well as by the fact that the German leader responsible, Arminius, chief of the Cherusci, had previously served in the Roman army and had even been awarded Roman citizenship.

It was natural enough that when Augustus died in A.D. 14 he advised Tiberius against any rash further expansion of the empire. By then, too, it had clearly reached various natural boundaries of sea or desert and the three great rivers, the Rhine, Danube, and Euphrates. This said, Augustus' warning to Tiberius need not mean that he would have been opposed to all future attempts at expansion. As it is, he delighted in the glory and respect that he gained for doubling the empire in size. At the same time, by forging a territorially unified whole for the first time, he gave Romans a new conception of empire and their imperial mission.

CITY OF ROME

It was essential that Rome itself be worthy of its status as the empire's capital. As early as the 30s, Augustus began to improve the city's amenities and services, as well as to restore its dozens of temples and public buildings and to construct a stunning array of new ones (compare Maps 7.2 and 8.3). The latter included a basilica and senate house (both begun by Julius Caesar; see Plate 1b and Fig. 7.4), an entire new Forum Augustum dominated by a great temple of Mars the Avenger (vowed at Philippi and dedicated forty years later in 2 B.C.), and extensive development of the Campus Martius. Augustus' mausoleum and the Altar of Augustan Peace (Plate 2a) are among the monuments constructed in the latter area.

There were multiple benefits to these initiatives. All served to glorify Augustus' rule and to boost his popularity; he himself bragged that "he found Rome a city of brick, and left it one of marble." The construction work provided employment for the free poor in huge numbers. Perhaps as many as one million inhabitants were now crammed into the city. Improvements to services were tangible daily reminders of a concern for this population that had been absent during the Republic. For example, thanks to Agrippa's efforts in particular, three new aqueducts were built, and a permanent organization was established to maintain the entire water supply system. No aqueduct had been built since the 120s, when the city's population had been much smaller. Rome became a safer place with the establishment of three "urban cohorts" (perhaps 1,500 men in total) to maintain law and order; their commander, the City Prefect, was a senior senator. They were reinforced first by the three (out of nine) cohorts of Augustus' own guardsmen, the Praetorian Guard, who were regularly stationed in the city (one such cohort comprised at least 500 men); then also, from A.D. 6, by the night patrol (*vigiles*).

Last but not least, Augustus knew the value of providing the people of Rome with memorable entertainment. It need be no surprise that when recording the achievements he wished to be remembered for, he included the shows he had sponsored—eight gladiatorial games, three athletic games, twenty-six beast hunts,

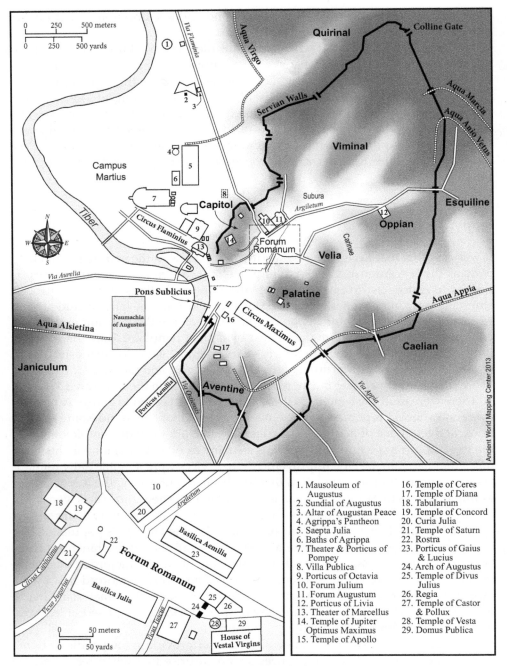

Map 8.3 *Rome at the Death of Augustus*

1. Mausoleum of Augustus
2. Sundial of Augustus
3. Altar of Augustan Peace
4. Agrippa's Pantheon
5. Saepta Julia
6. Baths of Agrippa
7. Theater & Porticus of Pompey
8. Villa Publica
9. Porticus of Octavia
10. Forum Julium
11. Forum Augustum
12. Porticus of Livia
13. Theater of Marcellus
14. Temple of Jupiter Optimus Maximus
15. Temple of Apollo
16. Temple of Ceres
17. Temple of Diana
18. Tabularium
19. Temple of Concord
20. Curia Julia
21. Temple of Saturn
22. Rostra
23. Porticus of Gaius & Lucius
24. Arch of Augustus
25. Temple of Divus Julius
26. Regia
27. Temple of Castor & Pollux
28. Temple of Vesta
29. Domus Publica

one mock naval battle, the special "Secular Games" of 17 B.C. symbolically inaugurating a new age (*saeculum*), and twenty-eight other shows. These events could involve the participation of thousands of people.

ATTITUDES OUTSIDE ROME

In Italy and the provinces, too, Augustus' rule was widely welcomed. He made little change in the established pattern of provincial administration. It may be that his novel step of slowly taking a census of the entire empire region by region increased the burden of Roman taxation. Even so, this was made bearable by the return of peace and stability, as well as by the sense that now, at last, there was a responsible, approachable ruler in control who was concerned to remedy distress and injustice. Moreover, he funded construction work all over the empire, especially the building and repair of roads and the foundation of many colonies.

In the East, the extravagance of the devotion shown by Greeks concerned Augustus from an early stage. Ever since the fourth century, there had been public cults of rulers as benefactors in the Greek world, Alexander the Great especially. After Rome became involved there from the second century, cults sprang up to *Roma* as well as to Roman commanders, including Antony. Augustus welcomed similar devotion to himself with some caution. He stipulated that Roman citizens should worship only "Roma *and* Augustus," thus discouraging any development of a personal cult. On the other hand, he did promote such a cult at Lugdunum (modern Lyon) in Gaul and at Ara Ubiorum (modern Köln/Cologne) in Germany as a means of fostering loyalty, although without marked success.

This selective promotion of what we generally refer to as an "imperial cult" is in fact just one means among many by which Augustus used religion to strengthen his own position. People of widely differing status and wealth were called upon to participate across the entire empire. For example, in each town or city, formation of a group of freedmen was encouraged, who would maintain a cult of Augustus' *genius* or "vital spark." These *Augustales* thereby enjoyed a public role that their slave origin otherwise denied them. At a higher social level, delegates from each community in a province had the honor of forming a "council"—*koinon* in the Greek East, *concilium* in the Latin West—to celebrate the imperial cult.

AUGUSTUS: FINAL ASSESSMENT

Augustus' goal as Princeps was to involve all sections of society and gain their lasting support. In one form or another, his name and image were prominent everywhere, even on coins. There remains the ugly fact that a large measure of his success stemmed from the death and destruction he had previously ordered through fourteen years of civil war. After this ordeal—only the latest of several during the previous half-century—everyone was desperate for peace, stability, and reconciliation. Among the politically active upper classes, many of the most energetic were dead, and there was grudging acknowledgment that some form of monarchy was the only practical safeguard against the recurrence of ruinous personal rivalries, which, among much else, blocked large-scale social or economic change. The rest of society was indifferent to the loss of whatever political role it had ever had, because this had become increasingly meaningless. Augustus did irk the upper classes with his attempts to regulate by law a range of private moral and social matters such as marriage, childbearing, and adultery. On the other hand, the upper classes were gratified by his respect for them, as well as by his continued exclusive reliance on them for commanding the army and administering the empire along traditional lines.

Both Augustus' transformation of the city of Rome and his largely successful desire to expand Roman power by force of arms brought him much popularity. Peace within the empire was counted the greatest blessing, along with the end of any draft for citizens. A "professional" army with a clear focus of loyalty was a development welcomed universally. Welcome, too, were his manifest concern for everyone's welfare, his basic respect for the rule of law, and his reluctance to flaunt supreme authority, let alone exercise it hastily. There is no question that he learned much from the prior experience of Sulla, Pompey, Caesar, Antony, and other leading figures. Gradually he came to appreciate, as they had not, that it was possible for him to retain control *and* at the same time restore the institutions of the Republic along with much of its outlook. Many changes could thus be linked to the past and tradition, and several were represented as an overdue return to neglected past practice. Altogether, by appealing to conservative sentiments, which he shared himself and at the same time instituting a new, personal style of long-term, responsible leadership, Augustus saved and reshaped the Roman world. It was an astonishing achievement, even if it did ultimately value peace and security above freedom. How far his prayers for its endurance would be answered, only time could tell.

SUGGESTED READINGS

Campbell, Brian. 2002. *War and Society in Imperial Rome, 31 B.C.–A.D. 284*. London and New York: Routledge.

Cooley, Alison E. (ed.). 2009. Res Gestae Divi Augusti: *Text, Translation, and Commentary*. Cambridge: Cambridge University Press. This record is Augustus' own crisp presentation of his achievements; the selection and wording shed light on how he wished to be remembered.

Osgood, Josiah. 2006. *Caesar's Legacy: Civil War and the Emergence of the Roman Empire*. Cambridge: Cambridge University Press. Survey of the period from the assassination of Julius Caesar to the deaths of Antony and Cleopatra.

Zanker, Paul. 1988. *The Power of Images in the Age of Augustus*. Ann Arbor: University of Michigan Press.

THE EARLY PRINCIPATE
(A.D. 14—69)

*The Julio-Claudians, the Civil War of 68–69,
and Life in the Early Empire*

THE JULIO-CLAUDIAN EMPERORS:
CIVIL GOVERNMENT AND MILITARY CONCERNS

The relations between each emperor and his subjects encompassed dealings with the highest orders—that is, senators and *equites*—and with the masses comprising the populace of Rome itself and Roman subjects elsewhere. Julius Caesar's assassination had revealed how dangerous it was for a Roman ruler to shame or humiliate his supposed peers in any way. Augustus had deliberately opted to portray himself as a *princeps* who was *primus inter pares*, first among equals, rather than as *rex* or *dictator*, thus emphasizing civil rather than military power. Augustus' immediate successors came from his extended family so that, although the principle was never enunciated, a single dynasty ran the Roman empire from 14 to 68. Yet Augustus' virtues and success were not genetic. The political difficulties of his successors usually stemmed from neglecting civil consensus and from alienating Rome's traditional political and military elite.

Equally significant for success or failure was the emperor's relationship to the army and Rome's military traditions. The emperor was commander-in-chief of all armed forces by virtue of his *maius imperium*. Restriction of the right of a full triumph to him or a member of his family after 19 B.C. underlines his military preeminence. The state's military traditions meant more than armed men loyal to Rome. As its history amply confirms, the military and imperial growth were two of Republican Rome's key elements. Although Augustus is said to have advised in his will that Rome be kept within its boundaries, borders are conceptual rather than hard, and the frontier was permeable everywhere, especially in the north and east. Moreover, borders were constantly renegotiated in Rome's vital yet shifting treaties with kings at its edges, most notably with the kingdom of Armenia that separated the Romans from their most organized enemy, the Parthians (see Map 8.2). The fifty-four years of Julio-Claudian power after Augustus' death witnessed different ways of dealing with the army and with the ideological and practical ramifications of militarism and its renunciation. Mutinies in 14 strikingly underscored the necessity of military support for imperial power. At the end of the Julio-Claudian dynasty, this truth was revealed again by the revolt of Julius Civilis and the wider military dissatisfaction of 68.

TIBERIUS (14–37)

Tiberius had spent much of his adult life away from Rome before becoming Princeps at Augustus' death in 14, and he did not have many personal friends in the city. He spent many years elsewhere serving as a highly successful military commander. His personality only aggravated his sense of isolation as Princeps. From all accounts he seems to have been a secretive, even suspicious soul, introspective, and cautious. Tiberius' interactions with senators only worsened as treason (*maiestas*) trials increased during his rule. By this date—although no formal enactment was ever issued—charges of treason could be made on the grounds of conspiracy against the Princeps' life, libel and slander against him, or adultery with a member of the imperial family; a successful prosecutor received a portion of the convicted person's estate.

Tiberius' general distrust, combined with his military background, led him to rely on the Praetorian Guard. Between 19 and 23, he built it a huge barracks at the edge of Rome itself (see Map 10.3). This ensured that all future emperors would have a personal bodyguard there, and over the next two centuries these troops did often influence the choice of emperors. The prominence of these special troops, underscoring the military basis of imperial power, subverted the value of civil consensus and contributed to the difficulties of Tiberius' Principate. By the early 20s, Lucius Aelius Sejanus was sole Praetorian Prefect, and he exploited Tiberius' trust and confidence to advance himself. Treason trials proliferated. In 23, Sejanus may even have masterminded the death of Tiberius' own son, Drusus the Younger (see Table 8.1). Sejanus' influence increased after Tiberius' move to Capri in 26 (see below), because thereafter it was he who controlled communications with the Princeps. Although Sejanus' unscrupulous intrigues finally brought about his own denunciation and execution in 31, Tiberius looked at the individual and not the weakness of the system. The equally dissembling Quintus Sutorius Macro then took over as Praetorian Prefect.

Tiberius never developed a close relationship with Rome's populace. As Princeps, he proved generally apathetic about providing Rome with monuments and amenities, and seldom attended public spectacles. His restraint may have stemmed from fiscal concern; even so, the change marked an unwelcome break with

Augustan precedent. Tiberius did respond quickly to public calamity, yet he chose not to highlight his generosity, and so failed to improve his reputation by this means. After twelve years as Princeps, in 26 he moved to the island of Capreae (modern Capri) in the Bay of Naples (Map 9.1). He never returned to Rome, not even for the public funeral of his mother, Livia, in 29. His absence meant that he had no direct contact with anyone there, and his relationships with both the elite and the populace remained at a low ebb to his death in 37.

Most of Tiberius' energies went to military and administrative matters. In 14, after Germanicus had quelled the uprising of the troops stationed in Germany, Tiberius ordered him to go on the offensive along and beyond the Rhine. These strikes against the Germans from 14 to 16–17 were ostensibly to avenge the great disaster of 9, when the Germans had cut down Varus' three legions in the Teutoburg Forest, but they also suggest Rome's customary use of external war to encourage internal harmony. Germanicus did not succeed in establishing a new border north of the earlier one at the Rhine, and Tiberius recalled him in 16–17. After a great triumph in Rome, he next sent the young general east with maius imperium (but subordinate to his own), because the Parthian king had just expelled the Roman nominee from the throne of Armenia. Then, in 19, Germanicus sickened mysteriously and died, allegedly poisoned by Gnaeus Calpurnius Piso the Elder, the governor of Syria, who had quarreled repeatedly with him. To display Rome's military might, Tiberius also turned to his own son Drusus, two years younger than Germanicus, as well as to other men of less renown. It was Drusus the Younger who was dispatched to discipline the rebellious legions in Pannonia in 14. Upon returning to Rome he held a consulship in 15, then from 17 to 20 served in Illyricum, another area of Tiberius' own early successes. Drusus continued to receive honors. But his premature death in 23, allegedly by poison at Sejanus' agency, ended his career.

Tiberius' own death at the age of seventy-seven in 37 was generally welcomed in Rome itself. His standing in the provinces is harder to gauge. As Princeps he neither traveled through the empire nor, after Drusus' death in 23, did he send family members out of Italy. Though this lack of mobility spared communities the enormous costs of hosting an imperial visit, at the same time it significantly diminished opportunities for provincials to feel a personal link with the Princeps. Yet his rule did generally better the empire. How perceptible such benefits were, however, is hard for us to discern.

GAIUS (CALIGULA) (37–41)

Tiberius' grandnephew and successor Gaius is known by the nickname Caligula, given him for the miniature military boots (*caliga*) that he wore as a toddler when he lived in military camps with his parents, Germanicus and Agrippina the Elder. He had a glorious lineage, directly descended from Augustus through his mother and from Livia through his father. But he had a difficult childhood and suffered severe bouts of epilepsy throughout his life. When he was seven, his father died amid malicious rumors; as a teenager, he saw the exile and execution of his mother and brothers voted by the senate under apparent pressure from Tiberius. When eighteen, he was summoned to Capri, where his companions were an ill-assorted group. In consequence, Gaius gained no familiarity with his peers from the senatorial and equestrian orders.

At Tiberius' death the Praetorians' favor for Gaius, rather than for Tiberius' grandson Tiberius Gemellus (made co-heir by Tiberius), seemed suspicious to some. But Gaius' arrival in Rome from Capri was celebrated with high hopes, and the senate immediately conferred imperial power on him. After all, he was the son of the wildly popular Germanicus, a connection he paraded. He undertook both to restore senatorial prestige, by granting the senators full authority to make decisions, and to overturn the secrecy of Tiberius' later years, by publishing an imperial budget. Gaius attended races in Rome and showed himself accessible to the people. Yet within a year he fell seriously ill, perhaps with a brain fever, and, although he recovered, his erratic behavior escalated. By 38, he executed Tiberius Gemellus and the Praetorian Prefect Macro. By 39, he had quarreled violently with the senate and was ruling more and more autocratically. His insults ranged from the political, as when he allegedly planned a consulship for his favorite racehorse Incitatus, to the moral and religious, as when in 38 he had his sister Drusilla deified. Gaius appeared in public in the dress of various gods. In Rome he performed as charioteer, gladiator, and singer, pandering to the populace but outraging senators and *equites*.

Yet Gaius also attended to the army and to foreign affairs, though in ways that often appear capricious. He launched small expeditions against Germany and Britain during winter 39–40. In Mauretania, he had the king Ptolemy deposed and executed, thus prompting a revolt and Claudius' later annexation of the region as a province. Otherwise Gaius' attention was directed eastwards. He dethroned the king of Armenia, triggering problems there that lasted through the rule of Nero. Gaius appointed Agrippa I, the grandson of Herod the Great, to rule part of Judaea. For reasons that elude us, he also insisted that his own statue be installed in the Temple in Jerusalem and other synagogues. Although this order was countermanded following his death on January 24, 41, it contributed to the unrest that resulted in the First Jewish Revolt in 66. Gaius' megalomania, unpredictability, and religious arrogance alienated many. His deficient military leadership was the root cause of his assassination by members of the Praetorian Guard, whom he had relentlessly humiliated. Few mourned his passing.

CLAUDIUS (41–54)

Gaius' uncle, Claudius, had been born at Lugdunum (modern Lyon, France) as the youngest son of Drusus the Elder and Antonia; he was Livia's grandson and Tiberius' nephew. In his youth he had endured various illnesses, perhaps including cerebral palsy, and he was deaf in one ear as well as lame. Military and political preference had always gone to Germanicus, his older and more charismatic brother. On the other hand, Claudius had a scholar's mind and training, and the historian Livy was one of his tutors. Before becoming Princeps in 41, Claudius had exercised no real power. He had survived the lethal years of Tiberius and Gaius by playing the fool and keeping out of the public eye. His Principate was due to the Praetorians. After Gaius' assassination he hid in the imperial palace, to be accidentally discovered there by a Guardsman who hailed him as Princeps. The senate had already convened in order to "restore the Republic," but as its deliberations dragged on, the people began to demand Claudius as Princeps. Once in power, however, he reduced his reliance on the Praetorian Guard and loosened its grip by appointing two Praetorian Prefects rather than one. But he had already alienated the senators, and he angered them further when he paid each Praetorian 150 gold pieces (*aurei*).

As Princeps, Claudius took his imperial duties seriously and treated the senate with respect. He consulted it frequently and involved himself actively in military and administrative affairs, even reviving the old Republican office of censor in 47–48. Yet his tone, as it emerges from surviving documents, often appears self-absorbed and almost fussy. He considered it his task as Princeps to take part in all sorts of trials. Senators, however, saw this judicial activity as meddling with their prerogatives and dignity, especially because his judgment was liable to prove erratic. For most advice, Claudius relied on imperial freedmen rather than equites or senators. His choice is understandable in view of his previous situation in the imperial household, but it antagonized Rome's elite, who felt that their power and prestige were being handed to social inferiors.

Claudius also seemed to be susceptible and credulous with women. In 41, he was married to his third wife, Valeria Messalina, a second cousin about thirty years his junior who bore him two children, Octavia and Britannicus. Claudius did not notice or care that she became unfaithful to him. Only with difficulty was Claudius persuaded to denounce her in 48 (leading to her suicide). His own niece Agrippina the Younger then schemed successfully to marry him in 49. Within a year she had greater public visibility than any other woman, and received the honorific title Augusta. By 53, she had secured the succession of her own son, Nero, who married Claudius' thirteen-year-old daughter Octavia and superseded the slightly younger Britannicus.

Claudius was much more active militarily than his two imperial predecessors; rather, he shared Augustus' concern to expand the empire. In 43, he directed the invasion of Britain, emulating Julius Caesar's exploits there and going to the island personally for the climax of the campaign (Fig. 9.1). In 43, he annexed Mauretania as a province, and in 46 Thrace.

Claudius unpretentiously enjoyed races, gaming, and dicing, pleasures that he shared with the majority of Rome's inhabitants (see Chapter Ten). His many celebrations of military achievements created notable festivities for the city. He was particularly alert to Rome's grain supply and devised special inducements for merchants to import grain during the winter. His public buildings and renovations tended to be utilitarian, such as the new aqueduct Aqua Claudia and the new

Figure 9.1 *This marble relief was found at Aphrodisias (modern Geyre, Turkey) in the province of Asia, a city that took pride in its special relationship with Rome in general and the family of Julius Caesar in particular. The relief is one of a series depicting the Julio-Claudian emperors and embellishing a centrally located sanctuary (sebasteion) of the imperial cult, which was begun in the rule of Tiberius and completed early in that of Nero. Here we see Claudius almost life-size, heroically costumed only in helmet, military cloak, and sword belt, about to strike down the female personification of Britain (his sword and most of his right arm are missing). He pins her down with his right knee, and with his left hand draws back her head, exposing her throat. The island's submission is emphasized by rendering Britannia as a woman, unarmed, and with her right breast exposed. The composition evokes earlier Greek models of the slaying of a female Amazon warrior.*

port for Rome north of Ostia (see Fig. 11.1). Claudius seldom traveled far from Rome, but his military activity kept him in the public eye. Even so, his widespread popularity never overcame the resentment felt towards him by senators.

NERO (54–68)

Nero was not yet seventeen when he succeeded Claudius. At his accession in 54, he promised good relations with the senate, equites, and army. At first, without doubt, Nero did heed his two tutors—Lucius Annaeus Seneca, a brilliant philosopher, author, and senator hailing from Corduba (modern Córdoba, in southern Spain), and Sextus Afranius Burrus, a learned eques from Narbonese Gaul, who was one of the Praetorian Prefects. Agrippina also tried to exercise power through her young son, but her behavior was more scandalous than harmful (Fig. 9.2 and Plate 3a). Meantime, Nero's own interests were in the arts and showmanship rather than in government and the military, and he became more headstrong as he grew older.

In 59, Nero staged the Juvenalia festival marking the official shaving of his beard for the first time, and later the same year he had his mother Agrippina killed in an elaborate ruse involving a staged shipwreck. In 62, his unlimited spending, together with protracted military actions in Britain and Armenia, caused him to devalue coinage and to revive the laws of treason. He forced Seneca first into retirement and then to suicide three years later in 65. In 63, Burrus died, supposedly poisoned on Nero's orders; the Praetorian Prefect who succeeded him, Ofonius Tigellinus, seemed as venal and corrupt as Nero himself. Some senators, such as Publius Clodius Thrasea and Publius Helvidius Priscus, were suspect to Nero because they refused to adopt their fellow members' servility towards him and adhered

Figure 9.2 *This gold coin* (aureus) *was struck in the first year of Nero's rule. On the "obverse"—a coin's more important side—are depicted Nero and his mother Agrippina the Younger, face to face and of equal size. This is the first time that anyone had appeared on the obverse of a Roman coin with a current emperor. The surrounding text translates: "Agrippina Augusta, wife of the deified Claudius, mother of Nero Caesar."*

to Stoic philosophical principles. Other senators and equites actively colluded against him. The abortive Pisonian conspiracy of 65 united many at different levels of society in common hatred. In 68, as reports streamed in about revolts in Gaul and Germany, and as Nero vacillated between terror and nonchalance, the senate finally disowned him, declaring him a public enemy (*hostis*). Nero committed suicide, and the Julio-Claudian dynasty ended with him.

Even so, Nero's death was generally mourned by the people of Rome. Both as spectator and as performer he loved exhibitions and performances of all kinds. He considered himself a great actor, charioteer, and singer. As time went on, Nero adapted his public image ever more to Rome's masses and ever less to the senators and equites. His relationship with the populace in Rome was not always smooth, however. In 62, they reacted violently against his divorce and murder of Octavia, Claudius' daughter, and they were hostile to his subsequent marriage with Poppaea. He was rumored to have caused the great fire of 64, which damaged eleven of Rome's fourteen regions, because he then appropriated much of the devastated land for his immense Golden House. The scandal persisted even after he proposed a rational plan for rebuilding the city and let the dispossessed camp in his imperial gardens. When he tried to provide a scapegoat by attacking a new sect, the Christians, his plan backfired because the horrible tortures inflicted on the accused provoked widespread sympathy. By 66, however, when he crowned Tiridates as king of Armenia in Rome, he seems to have regained public favor in the city.

Outside of Italy Nero's reputation was high in Greece, the sole part of the empire that he visited during his fourteen-year rule. During his tour of the Panhellenic sanctuaries in 66–67, he declared the province of Achaia exempt from taxes. But public favor in Rome and Achaia did not help him allay the problems of Judaea, where the First Jewish Revolt broke out in 66. Nor did such popularity secure Nero support against the generals and governors of the western provinces, who began to rebel in 67.

There were many causes for the dissatisfaction. Nero was uninterested in military matters and never visited any Roman troops. Despite being served by some capable commanders, he was unable to solve the provincial and foreign problems created by Gaius' mismanagement and Claudius' expansionism. Britain was still far from secure. Roman rapacity, embezzlement, and cruelty led to a revolt there in 60, headed by the queen of the Iceni, Boudica, and supported by other native leaders. Much of its impetus came from the Druids, dynamic female and male priestly leaders. In 66 the First Jewish Revolt broke out as the combined result of Roman mismanagement and Judaea's internal problems. In February 67, Nero sent Titus Flavius Vespasianus to take command there, a solid military man who had risen from a successful command in Britain under Claudius to a consulship in 51. Vespasian's unpretentious ancestry and relative obscurity may have protected him from Nero's paranoia in the later 50s and 60s. No one suspected that such a first-generation senator would use initial victories against the Jews as a springboard to the Principate.

CIVIL WAR IN 68–69

Gaius Julius Vindex, governor of Gallia Lugdunensis, began a revolt there in 67. Vindex was a senator of Gallic descent, from a family granted Roman citizenship by Julius Caesar. Despite its lack of strength, it was this insurrection that precipitated Nero's downfall and a civil war. Vindex did at least gain the support of Servius Sulpicius Galba, the governor of nearby Hispania Tarraconensis, who promised the single legion under his command. By the time Vindex's modest force was defeated in Gaul, the senate declared Nero a public enemy. In his place, it recognized as Princeps the seventy-one-year-old Galba, who came from a most distinguished patrician family.

The civil war that filled the next eighteen months was particularly devastating both for northern Italy and for Rome itself, the traditional seat of power. Now, however, Nero's neglect had opened the way for any commander with willing troops to bid for the Principate. Two of the four contenders in 68–69 were originally declared emperor by forces outside of Rome—Vitellius, who was supported by eight legions on the Rhine, and Vespasian. Otho, a third contender, was declared emperor by Praetorian Guardsmen in Rome itself. Galba stressed that he had been acclaimed by the senate and people, but his quick downfall at Otho's hands emphasizes the predominance of the military. Accompanied by Otho, Galba slowly made his way to Rome by October 68, but there he openly alienated a significant part of the army and failed to win the favor of the Praetorians or the populace. He proved harsh and refused to pay a donative to the Praetorians, who had deserted Nero for him on their Prefect's promise of money. Perhaps also in misguided anxiety about finances, Galba suspended public games. Worst of all, he did not placate the troops on the Rhine, who felt insufficiently rewarded for their suppression of Vindex's revolt. So on January 1, 69, the four legions of Upper Germany took the oath of allegiance in the name of the senate only, omitting Galba's name. The next day, at the urging of the legionary commanders Aulus Caecina and Fabius Valens, the four legions in Lower Germany declared their new general, Aulus Vitellius, as emperor, and were seconded by the four legions in Upper Germany. Although Vitellius was inexperienced in military and civil positions, his father had acquired great fame and influence in faithful service to the Julio-Claudians.

Galba was by now attempting to strengthen support for himself by adopting a successor. He again misstepped, however, because his choice was the relatively unknown aristocrat Lucius Calpurnius Piso Frugi Licinianus, rather than the more popular Marcus Salvius Otho, who had already rendered him valuable service. Otho's reaction was to seek the Praetorians' backing for himself through bribes and promises. This he quickly achieved, so that on January 15, 69, both Galba and Piso were slaughtered in the Roman Forum in full sight of the populace. Cowed by the Praetorians, the senate and people then declared Otho emperor.

As news of these developments at Rome spread, neither Vitellius nor the troops elsewhere were satisfied. Caecina and Valens had meanwhile been leading Vitellius' forces to Rome. Vitellius himself followed more slowly, indulging in banquets and

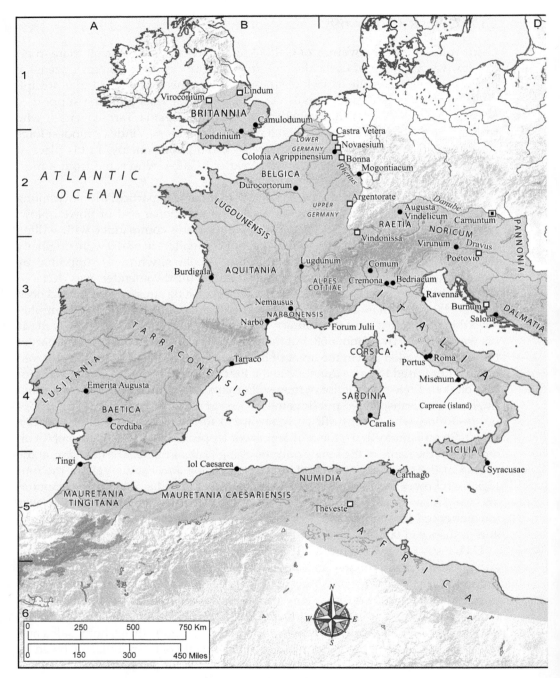

Map 9.1 *Roman Empire in* A.D. *69*

E   F   G

☐ Legionary base (normally a single legion)
◪ Principal settlement with legionary base adjacent
Not all legions' bases are known.

BLACK SEA

Viminacium
☐

Danube
Oescus ☐   ☐ Novae   ● Odessus
MOESIA   ● Amastris

THRACIA   BITHYNIA - PONTUS   CAPPADOCIA

Perinthus   Ancyra   Caesarea (Mazaca)
   Nicomedia   GALATIA

MACEDONIA   COMMAGENE
Thessalonica   Cyrrus ☐

Pergamum   A S I A   Euphrates
     CILICIA

AEGEAN
SEA   Claros   Aphrodisias   Antioch
   Ephesus   SYRIA
A C H A I A   LYCIA   ☐
Corinth   Raphaneae
     Myra

Gythium   RHODES   Paphos   CYPRUS

Gortyn   CRETA   Caesarea
      JUDAEA
INTERNUM MARE   Jerusalem
      Dead Sea
      Masada

     Alexandria
Cyrene   ☐

A E G Y P T U S   RED SEA

Nile

Ancient World Mapping Center 2013

games. In April, the armies of Otho and Vitellius clashed decisively in northern Italy, first at Cremona and then at Bedriacum, where Otho committed suicide. Vitellius was now the first Princeps since Tiberius to gain power without the immediate support of the Praetorian Guard. Once in Rome, however, he seemed incapable of making political or military decisions.

On July 1, 69, the troops in Judaea declared their general Vespasian emperor, seconded by the Syrian legions led by Gaius Licinius Mucianus. Vespasian also won the allegiance of Tiberius Julius Alexander, Prefect of Egypt. The threat of famine in Rome, outrage at the conduct of Vitellius' troops, revulsion at his personal excesses and his ineptitude, and news of Mucianus' approach all bolstered support for Vespasian. The troops in Pannonia declared for him and, led by their commander, Marcus Antonius Primus, marched to Italy. In October, they defeated Vitellius' forces in a second battle at Cremona. By December, Primus' men stormed Rome itself. Vitellius was killed in the fierce fighting that destroyed much of the city, including the temple of Jupiter Optimus Maximus. The senate and people declared Vespasian emperor, although he entered Rome only the following October (70). During the intervening ten months Mucianus took charge of the city, aided by Vespasian's younger son Domitian.

In these eighteen terrible months of 68–69, Roman troops had repeatedly marched on Rome. The civil war destroyed everything in its path, was ruinously expensive, and diverted attention and manpower from more strategic points, particularly in the East. This catastrophe revealed the disunity of the empire in general and of the troops in particular. Much of Gaul had rebelled against Italy, the armies in Germany and then those in the East had threatened Rome, and each side had attacked the other. Who was at the center: the senate, Praetorians, or Roman people? The senate had some authority; when it had declared Nero a public enemy and named Galba emperor, Nero had killed himself in despair. On the other hand, Galba's failure to win support among Rome's populace and the Praetorians undermined the senate's decision. Otho's elevation once again underscores the power of the Praetorians in Rome. Yet this elite corps proved to be no match against more numerous troops from elsewhere. Of the four contenders of 68–69, only Vespasian proved himself enduringly capable once in power, and his bid to gain it was the best prepared. This turmoil made it clearer than ever that the dynastic principle instituted by Augustus was unable to guarantee the best ruler for the Roman world.

ECONOMIC AND SOCIAL CHANGE: ARMY

Archeological and documentary evidence confirms that the Julio-Claudians' continuation of Augustus' Principate is associated with profound changes for the empire. In this time of general peace, the army was maintained more or less steadily at about 150,000 legionaries and an equal number of auxiliaries. These land-based forces were supplemented by marines in naval squadrons stationed at Misenum on the Bay of Naples, Ravenna, Forum Julii (modern Fréjus, France), and other ports to curb piracy and aid military communication.

At this date, thirteen of Rome's twenty-five legions were stationed in the provinces along the Rhine and Danube. Gallia Belgica's two regions along the Rhine, Lower and Upper Germany, each had four legions; Raetia, Noricum, Pannonia, and Moesia held the other five. Wherever they were based, the armed forces changed the economic, social, religious, cultural, and political lives of the areas they occupied, although Roman military groups could and often did also act as societies unto themselves.

Although it was expensive to pay the troops and to offer the discharge bounties instituted by Augustus (see Chapter Eight), these expenses could be foreseen and budgeted for; in the first century legionary pay was 900 sesterces annually, and auxiliary pay was rather less. Creation of a standing, state-funded army, with its requirements of steady pay and supplies, encouraged the monetarization of the Roman state, the production of surplus goods, and trade. Imperial mints were established in Rome and Lugdunum. Local coinage in nonprecious metals continued to be minted in the West until Claudius' time and in the East right up to that of Diocletian in the late third century; this coinage was used only for local, low-level exchanges and not for larger, empire-wide transactions. The establishment of the imperial army helped break down barriers created by Rome's hitherto pervasive subsistence farming economy. An agrarian economy still continued to characterize the Roman world, but a commodity economy also grew up. Towns, military camps, and other centers all needed and wanted finished products like shoes and boots, lamps and other pottery, glassware, cloaks, and other manufactured goods. This demand encouraged some economic mobility, and with it social and political change. Despite reckless spending by certain emperors, there was a general rise in the economy.

"BENEFICIAL IDEOLOGY"

Although peace had been gained by Augustus' elimination of his rivals, it was maintained by the threat of force and by a "beneficial ideology." In other words, the Roman emperors were consciously magnanimous, even if not necessarily to the same degree nor in every sphere. Of the Julio-Claudians, for example, only Claudius followed Augustus' example of funding construction in the provinces, although the range of his building types and their distribution fell far short of those of Augustus. In Rome itself, imperial beneficence was regularly expressed in the provision of cheap food and lavish entertainments for the populace, the "bread and circuses" (*panem et circenses*) made famous by the Roman satirist Juvenal. Emperors also distributed money, food, and other goods. They were typically generous with aid to communities struck by disaster.

The number of equestrian and senatorial offices—the nearest equivalent that Rome had to a bureaucracy—rose in the Julio-Claudian period and faster thereafter, although never to a particularly high level. It is estimated that only between 150 and 350 elite officials oversaw the civilian government in the first century A.D., at most one for every 350,000 to 400,000 subjects. The equestrian and senatorial orders had great prestige, although more respect traditionally went to senators. The imperial freedmen who rose to prominence and extraordinary wealth under Claudius and Nero became the targets of vicious snobbery. Ability and culture were the prerequisites to success, but even these talents could rarely overcome the stigma of a slave or freedman past. In any case, members of the political elite of Rome, whatever their origin, made up only a minuscule fraction of the empire's population.

CITIES AND PROVINCES

As established by Augustus, the empire relied not on bureaucracy imposed by the central government, but on communities' self-administration. Throughout Italy and the provinces, local magistrates and councilors were responsible for the collection of taxes, census registration, supply of men for the army when volunteers were lacking, provision of hospitality and transport animals for travelers on official business, and shelter, equipment, and supplies for any military units passing through. Such obligations to the central government coexisted with a high degree of local autonomy. In general, individual cities were left to oversee their own public buildings and cults, the maintenance of their water supply and baths, local law and order, and embassies to Roman officials, including the Princeps himself.

The empire, which encompassed perhaps fifty to sixty million inhabitants during the first and early second centuries, depended on cities. Achaia, Asia, Crete and Cyrenaica, southern Gaul, and eastern and southern Spain had long been urbanized along their coasts and waterways. Other provinces had different forms of social and political organization. In the interior of Gaul and the Iberian peninsula, for example, warrior elites commanded tribal groups, usually either nomadic or scattered in farmsteads and villages. Between them, Julius Caesar and Augustus established some seventy-five veteran settlements in the provinces and over forty in Italy. They were located primarily in north Italy, southern Spain, north Africa, coastal Illyricum and Greece, and southern Turkey. In Italy they often supplanted communities that had been on the losing side during the Triumviral period; elsewhere, too, they could be just as disruptive to the local inhabitants. In addition, stationing troops on the borders of the empire encouraged the development of towns there, as well as along the roads leading there.

The new foundations and centers, like older cities in the Roman world, consisted of an urban nucleus and dependent agricultural land. The urban centers were quite small by modern standards. Most had a maximum of only five to fifteen thousand inhabitants, comprising local citizens (including freedmen and freedwomen) and their "families" (including slaves); residents from elsewhere, such as traders; and public slaves and other dependent labor. It was essential that cities govern themselves by some version of the tripartite system traditional to Rome: magistrates, advisory council, and citizen body. Magistrates and councilors were required to possess a certain level of wealth, usually held in the form of land. Yet the urban conglomerations themselves offered various possibilities for financial gain and prestige, and the imperial peace encouraged at least limited social mobility. Freedmen and freedwomen could engage in small businesses and gain some wealth and respectability for their children; as we saw in Chapter Eight, freedmen even could hold a priesthood as *Augustales* (note Fig. 9.4 for one such individual). Descendants of former slaves often gained municipal offices and other priesthoods, sometimes even within a generation.

The growing number of cities in the Roman world was made possible not only by peace, but also by the Roman engineering responsible for urban amenities such as a forum, aqueducts, fountains, streets and sidewalks, temples, baths, spectacle buildings like theaters and amphitheaters, and multistoried dwellings. However, what we think of as the "typical" Roman city took time to evolve in the provinces (see Chapter Ten). The urban model was Rome itself, upon which Caesar, Augustus, and many subsequent emperors lavished attention. Although by the early third century the empire had attained a degree of urbanization not to be matched again in the West until the nineteenth century, the limitations of its preindustrial technology and science meant that many areas still remained scarcely urbanized. Cities were mostly found along coasts, rivers, and major inland routes. Inaccessible hinterlands were more desolate and were normally left undisturbed so long as their few inhabitants did not cause problems.

One major type of imperial benefaction initiated by Augustus and resumed by Claudius was the building and maintenance of roads and harbors. Generally speaking, land transport cost at least five times more than water transport, and bulky commodities such as grain, timber, and fine stone were conveyed long distances only for the army or for the city of Rome itself (note Plate 5a). Yet archeology increasingly documents long-distance trade for luxury and semiluxury goods too. The technologies essential to blown glass and to highly polished, molded ceramic bowls, lamps, and other pottery objects had been invented by the end of the Republic. In the Augustan peace such technologies disseminated quickly, spreading the availability of these and similar personal items. One gauge of an area's interface with Rome is the proliferation in its graves of Roman-style goods, such as glass perfume bottles, ceramic lamps, iron objects like needles and strigils (curved scraping instruments used for personal hygiene), worked-bone pieces like combs and even dolls, and similar accessories. Such items were bought and exchanged in towns by increasing numbers of individuals who attained status and prestige through various possible types of service to their own communities or to Rome, or both. This said, we should not forget that, even at its height, Roman urban culture never extended to the great majority of the empire's inhabitants.

DIVERSITY: WOMEN, LOCAL LANGUAGES, AND CULTURE

The material remains from the early Principate demonstrate increasing public visibility for women in Rome and in Italian and provincial cities (Fig. 9.3). Although Roman women had long before gained some financial and legal independence (see Chapter Five), the very institution of the Principate, with its stress on family, thrust the imperial women into the limelight. Augustus' sister Octavia and his wife Livia had unprecedented visibility and patronage. Women in the cities of Italy and adjacent areas of the Latin West now started to hold prestigious religious positions, as they had already long been doing in cities in the Greek East. Priestesses and other women feature on statues, relief sculpture, and inscriptions—never in the numbers attested for men, it is true; even so, this commemoration of women does allow us a glimpse of the rapidly changing social history of the early Principate (see Plates 2a, 3a).

Despite an increasing similarity of material culture, the empire still retained great diversity. Many languages were spoken in the various provinces, even though Latin dominated in the army and official correspondence. In the Greek East—the region where already for centuries the common language of educated people had been Greek—Roman administrative correspondence was written in Greek. Instances of parallel texts in Greek and Latin, especially for records of important decisions, are numerous too. We also find bilingual texts apparently aimed at two different audiences. Even so, indigenous languages and dialects persisted alongside these official languages for a variety of reasons—communities' autonomy in local affairs, the large number of static

Figure 9.3 *This statue from Pompeii depicts a woman in the pose and costume of a respectable matron. She modestly shields her chest with her right hand and covers her head and most of her arms with a heavy cloak. A dedicatory inscription (not shown) reads: "To Eumachia, daughter of Lucius, public priestess of Pompeian Venus, from the fullers." The statue was found in a covered gallery at the back of the "Building of Eumachia," a spacious, opulent building donated by her in the first half of the first century A.D. alongside Pompeii's Forum. We know neither the specific use of the building nor the source of Eumachia's wealth, although her father's family were noted producers of wine, amphoras, jars, and bricks. Both the rendering of Eumachia herself and the decoration of the building reflect the influence of models to be found in the city of Rome; the same may be said of Eumachia's public generosity and visibility.*

rural dwellers on their subsistence farms, the relatively low level of bureaucracy, the uneven spread of the military, and the absence of extensive mass communications. For similar reasons, local cultures remained dynamic and still maintained a hold even when Roman material culture spread to a region.

RELIGIOUS PRACTICES AND PRINCIPLES

Rome's diversity, and its limits, are perhaps reflected most strikingly in the wide array of religious beliefs and practices of the polytheistic empire. Thus the traditional Egyptian zoomorphic gods later decried by Christians as "dog-headed" could be, and were, worshipped with their traditional rites even after Egypt was annexed as a Roman province in 30 B.C. In Gaul, various powerful female deities, often called "mothers," were venerated alongside other gods less alien to the Romans, such as Jupiter sky gods. Silvanus, a god of the woodlands, was worshipped in the heavily forested areas of the northern empire.

Because monuments were often erected to recognize the fulfillment of prayers, the formulaic nature of many of the religious sentiments preserved in literature, inscriptions, and other documents is liable to strike us as calculating. Also conspicuous are the apparent ease with which many individuals participated in disparate religious practices and the wide range of religious dedications, even within a single town or sanctuary (Fig. 9.4). This latter phenomenon was aided by what Romans termed *interpretatio*, the assertion of equivalence between a foreign deity and a Roman one (as with Mars Belena). Romans and their subjects could believe as they pleased, so long as they did not actively reject religious rituals that had been made part of the state religion. The few exceptions to the Romans' generally tolerant polytheism arose when a religion seemed to pose a political threat. For example, because Druidism functioned as a source of resistance to Rome in Gaul and Britain, Claudius and his successors apparently undertook to extirpate it, killing its priests and priestesses and destroying Druid shrines. Judaism, with its exclusively monotheistic belief, posed continuing problems because of the number of its adherents, their spread throughout the Roman world, their strict lifestyle, and the antiquity of their doctrines.

The Christians, who first came to notice under Tiberius, ultimately posed an even more intractable problem. Roman authorities and intellectuals did not know what to make of this new religion. Like Jews, Christians were exclusively monotheistic, and they included the Jewish Old Testament among their sacred books. The earliest Christian adherents came from the Jewish geographical and social world, but Christians distinguished themselves from Jews. Initially, therefore, Romans considered the new religion to be simply a sect of Judaism but without the authority of antiquity, much like the sects documented by the Dead Sea Scrolls or other contemporary evidence. Thus the debate about Jesus Christ was seen as a dispute of merely local concern. According to the earliest accounts of Christ's life and death, the governor of Judaea, Pontius Pilatus, did not know what to do with the man

Figure 9.4 *This votive relief of the late second century or early third century is dedicated to the Nutrices, protective "nursing" deities found in many northern provinces. The relief comes from a well-attested shrine in Poetovio, Pannonia (modern Ptuj, Slovenia), and is damaged on its upper right and lower left corners. On the right is a Nutrix, seated on a low chair; she holds a baby in swaddling clothes to her left breast. To her right is an altar over which a woman holds a naked child; this toddler rests its left leg on the altar and extends its arms towards the Nutrix. At the relief's left edge, a woman (perhaps a servant) in a long dress holds on her head a basket with two ribbons. Below the image, an inscription states in Latin: "Sacred to the Augustan Nutrices. Lucius Fuscinius Exsuperatus, Augustalis of the colony of Poetovio, and Aelia Honorata discharged the vow made for the health of their son, Fuscinius Honoratus." The cult of the Nutrices is apparently Celtic in origin. The description of Poetovio's Nutrices as "Augustan" reflects one means by which local cults were linked to the imperial house. The strength of this cult at Poetovio during the Principate suggests high infant and childhood mortality in the area, an all-too-common phenomenon in antiquity.*

denounced to him as a popular and potentially dangerous religious leader. Following a tumultuous examination rather than a formal trial, Pilate decided to have him executed, apparently capitulating to traditional Roman fears of subversive provincials and to pressure from the Jewish authorities and the crowd. After Christ's death, the religion mostly dropped from Rome's official consciousness.

Christian monotheism, however, was sharply at odds with the polytheism prevalent throughout the empire. Thus Nero fixed on the Christians when he needed a scapegoat after the great fire of Rome of 64. His brutality created some of Christianity's first martyrs, possibly including St. Peter, and unintentionally strengthened the new religion. By around 120, key features of Christianity had taken shape—an organized priesthood; the scriptures or sacred writings; an insistence on revelation (Christ was revealed as God, and the scriptures were revealed to the faithful); initiation at baptism and subsequent stages; and a belief in salvation and the afterlife. The Epistles of Paul and the Gospel of Mark were probably written between 50 and 70, and by 130 the other scriptures were completed. Christianity spread in cities before the countryside, as indicated by the term "pagan" used for non-Christians (*paganus* denotes someone from the countryside). But we should always bear in mind that during the early Principate Christianity was merely one of what may now seem a bewildering number of religions.

IMPERIAL CULT

Christianity, Judaism, and a few other monotheistic religions aside, the imperial cult cut across all of the varied beliefs and practices. This religious and societal phenomenon provided one of the strongest unifying forces for the diverse Roman empire. The imperial cult could be practiced on the personal level. Because the cult was principally public, however, there is much fuller evidence for it at the municipal and provincial levels and at Rome itself.

Roman imperial cult evolved from Hellenistic Greek and Republican Roman precedents and, like them, it was intrinsically tied to military and political power. Beginning with Alexander the Great, dominant kings (and later their queens) had commanded cults with temples or altars, priests, public sacrifices, and games— visible signs, in short, of their unmistakable power over their subjects. As Rome became involved in the Greek East from the end of the third century B.C., certain Roman generals received extraordinary, quasi-divine honors there to mark their popularity or military success. In the West, too, leading figures could find it advantageous to exploit divine associations: Marius had sought guidance from a Syrian prophetess, Martha, and Sertorius allegedly gained inspiration from a white doe (see Chapter Six). In Rome itself, great charisma accrued to triumphing generals, who were dressed like the Capitoline statue of Jupiter Optimus Maximus as they paraded through Rome on a chariot pulled by four white horses. In what was to be the last year of his life, Julius Caesar had a temple for himself authorized by the senate. Later the people of Rome spontaneously established a shrine where his body had been cremated in the Forum; the appearance of a meteor shortly thereafter reinforced the belief that he had ascended to heaven. The authority of the Triumvirs, and of Octavian in particular, was boosted when the senate eventually ratified Caesar's deification early in 42 B.C.

Designation as "son of a god" (*divi filius*) was only one of many divine associations that Octavian assumed over time, despite discouraging any cult that seemed too closely tied to his own person (see Chapter Eight). His position as *pontifex maximus* after 12 B.C. placed him as intermediary between the Roman people and the gods. Thereafter each Princeps until Gratian in the late fourth century took this leading priesthood on accession. The divinity that the senate ratified for Augustus after his death was only one of many such posthumous honors.

The imperial cult spread after Augustus. Although Tiberius refused the organization of any cults to himself and was not deified after his death, Gaius assiduously pursued religious associations, as noted earlier. Claudius promoted Livia's deification by the senate; he in turn was deified. Later the emperor Vespasian was to quip on his deathbed, "Dear me! I must be turning into a god!" Rituals identified with the imperial cult will be discussed in the following chapter. Here, however, it is important to stress Rome's incipient imperial cult as an expression of the ambiguous relationship between the Princeps and his subjects.

SUGGESTED READINGS

Champlin, Edward. 2003. *Nero*. Cambridge, Mass., and London: Harvard University Press.
     A provocative attempt to interpret Nero's extreme behavior as highly intelligent and
     calculated to appeal to widespread social attitudes of the time.
Erdkamp, Paul (ed.). 2007. *A Companion to the Roman Army*. Malden, Mass., and Oxford:
     Blackwell.
Greene, Kevin. 1986. *The Archaeology of the Roman Economy*. Berkeley, Los Angeles, London:
     University of California Press.
Osgood, Josiah. 2011. *Claudius Caesar: Image and Power in the Early Roman Empire*. Cambridge: Cambridge University Press.
Rives, James B. 2007. *Religion in the Roman Empire*. Malden, Mass., and Oxford: Blackwell.

10

MILITARY EXPANSION
AND ITS LIMITS

The Empire and the Provinces (69–138)

INSTITUTIONALIZATION OF THE PRINCIPATE

One of the earliest and starkest signs of the Principate's institutionalization is the law now called the *lex de imperio Vespasiani*, passed some time in 69–70. A substantial part of it—specifying various powers and rights of the emperor—survives on a bronze inscription in Rome's Capitoline Museum. Ratified by the Roman people upon presentation by the senate, this law indicates the continuing significance both of popular support for the Princeps and of concern for Rome's governmental processes. Yet it also makes clear that the emperor's authority was no longer a nebulous *auctoritas* centered on the individual himself (as with Augustus) or on family loyalty (as with the Julio-Claudians). Rather, the document clearly defines various powers and prerogatives, justifying them by specific imperial precedent. Here we may note both Romans' respect for their past and their pragmatism; this law made custom binding. Another sign of the institutionalization of the Principate is the adoption of *Imperator* by Vespasian and subsequent emperors as a first name (*praenomen*).

The Principate's civil underpinnings were reestablished by a greater use of senators and *equites*, rather than freedmen, in the imperial service. This change, perhaps induced by loathing for what were seen as Claudius' presumptuous freedmen and Nero's toadies, sent a clear signal that to rule the Roman world was not the exclusive prerogative of one individual or family. Added involvement of equites and senators in administration began with Vespasian and gained momentum in the second century. Thus more subjects than ever actively participated in their own government, filling a quantity of prestigious positions hierarchically arranged.

This social and political mobility seemed to confirm the Augustan ideal that equestrian and senatorial posts were open to any man of merit, good birth, and the requisite financial standing.

VESPASIAN (69–79)

Vespasian was an unpretentious man from Reate in north-central Italy. His family, the Flavii, had been respectable tax gatherers and customs agents of equestrian rank, with none of its members ever advancing to the senate before his elder brother and himself. Vespasian's special strength was his military acumen, demonstrated outstandingly in Germany, Britain, and Judaea. It was through the army that he came to power. His talents as a civilian leader, on the other hand, were unknown. Yet both aspects of the imperial position were demanded in 70. The Jewish and Germano-Gallic revolts had still to be suppressed, while Rome and Italy meantime needed to regain normalcy after all the destructive civil strife there.

The first problem that Vespasian had to face was the Jewish revolt, also known as the First Jewish War (66–73). This desperate struggle against the Romans was conducted as a kind of guerrilla war, and within the Jewish population there was much dissension, especially between Pharisees and Sadducees. The revolt had not yet been completely crushed when Vespasian, who had been sent to Judaea by Nero, was declared emperor by his troops. Titus, his elder son, was left in charge, and in 70 he stormed Jerusalem (see Map 9.1). To the Romans, the destruction of its great Temple signaled the end of the revolt (Fig. 10.1), although pockets of resistance held out a few years longer. Of these, Masada is the most famous; its Herodian palace-fortress fell only in 73. The revolt decimated Judaea's population, and Jews were prohibited from proselytizing to gain new converts. A few concessions were made, however, in recognition of the antiquity of the Jewish religion. Those born in the faith could worship in it, and Jews were evidently not forced to participate in the imperial cult. The suppression of this Jewish revolt furthered the Jewish diaspora and contributed to the distinction of Christians from Jews.

In 69–70, Vespasian also had to suppress the Germano-Gallic revolt. It had developed from Vindex's revolt against Nero in 68 and the ensuing civil war. The Gallic chieftain Gaius Julius Civilis roused Gallic and German tribes and locally

---

Facing page

Figure 10.1 *The triumphal procession of Vespasian and Titus in 71 was memorialized in various relief panels on the marble Arch of Titus (Map 10.3). Because the arch also contains a panel depicting Titus joining the gods (not shown), its completion must postdate his death in 81. Here we see part of the procession as it goes into Rome through an ornate city gate or arch. Soldiers wearing laurel wreaths (symbols of victory) carry litters on which are displayed some of the booty seized in Jerusalem: (left to right) a menorah, the table of the Shewbread, and the silver trumpets. The placards carried by the soldiers may originally have offered painted identifications of the booty or of the military units responsible for the victory. Such displays would precede the triumphing general himself.*

recruited auxiliary soldiers. Although the insurrection was crushed by spring 70, it plainly demonstrated the perils of recruiting men locally to serve as auxiliary soldiers in their native areas. The Flavian emperors now ended this practice, as well as breaking up large concentrations of troops such as the eight legions stationed in close proximity along the Rhine. In addition, legionary recruitment was extended from Italy alone to Roman citizens in Gaul and Spain. Generally speaking, it now became standard practice to station individuals other than where they had been recruited.

The Flavian emperors attended to Rome's borders and troops by other means too. Under Vespasian and Domitian, and again in the second century, attempts were made to acquire and fortify the reentrant angle between the upper Rhine and the Danube. Roman control of this area, the so-called *Agri Decumates*, would allow troops to move more swiftly between the Rhine and the Danube (Map 10.1). In Gallia Belgica (probably around 90), Domitian differentiated two new provinces along the Rhine—Germania Superior and Germania Inferior (Upper and Lower Germany)—so as to separate this more militarized zone from the civilian populations farther west and south. Also during Domitian's rule, the Romans advanced farther into Britain under the leadership of Gnaeus Julius Agricola. Meantime, the Danube region was not yet fully pacified.

Under the Flavians, a sweeping fresh start was essential. Nero's extravagance, the civil war, and the revolts had all drained the treasury of more funds than booty from Judaea could repay. Vespasian himself declared that he needed at least 400 million sesterces to set the state to rights again, and one of his first acts was to rescind the tax exemption that Nero had granted to Achaia. Flavian public building at Rome demanded even more expenditure. Altogether, Vespasian was highly thought of as emperor. Peace was restored. Although taxes were raised, they were assessed and collected less capriciously than under Nero. In turn, Roman rule dispensed tangible benefactions. Vespasian himself was accessible, hardworking, modest, and diligent. At the same time, the monarchical foundation of the Principate was plainly strengthened.

TITUS (79–81)

Vespasian's elder son and successor, Titus, was to serve as Princeps for no more than two years. He was already popular and well groomed for the position. He had taken a leading role in the suppression of the Jewish revolt, and by 79 he had served as Praetorian Prefect, consul seven times, and censor. His unexpectedly brief tenure of power is marked by two disasters: the eruption of Mt. Vesuvius in 79 and a devastating fire in Rome in 80. In good imperial fashion, Titus worked immediately to mitigate losses. Further, signaling a desire for a smooth relationship with Rome's upper orders, he banished informers from the city and refused to hear maiestas cases. What else he would have accomplished, however, will never be known, because he died prematurely and still unmarried in 81.

DOMITIAN (81–96)

Power passed smoothly to Vespasian's younger son, Domitian. He differed from his father and brother in many ways. He had no military experience, and he had held few positions in Rome. Compared to Titus, he had been ignored; there had been no expectation that he would ever become emperor. Once he was, he somehow never gained the self-confidence or the patience to develop a satisfactory working relationship with the senate. In part, the alienation resulted from his tactless accumulation of offices. From 82 through 88, he held the consulship every year, and in 84–85 he became "perpetual censor." His neglect or contempt for the senate contrasts with his devotion to the army and his concern for the people of Rome and the provinces.

By 93, Domitian apparently insisted on being addressed as *dominus et deus* ("lord and god"). He wore triumphal costume in the senate, offending traditional sensibilities. These actions and others that emphasized his supreme prerogatives shattered any illusion that the Princeps was first among equals. Yet the length of Domitian's rule indicates that he had some support among senators and equites—the senators including the two men who in turn would succeed him as Princeps. His power rested not only on such associates and his family's general popularity, but also on continuing approval by the populace of Rome and the troops. In Rome itself, Domitian intensified the building and reconstruction programs initiated by his father and brother, providing work for many. He raised legionaries' annual pay by as much as one-third (to 1,200 sesterces). Beginning in 83, he embarked on campaigns across the Rhine. Later, he crossed the central Danube to attack the Quadi and Marcomanni to its north; farther east he went into Dacia. As the first emperor since Claudius to go on campaign personally, Domitian reasserted the military character of the Principate. He was generally successful. By 88, despite initial setbacks, Roman forces had defeated the Dacian king Decebalus. Military support, however, did not make Domitian's autocratic style any more acceptable. His increasing paranoia turned him against many senators and finally his own family. The conspiracy that killed him the following year may have involved his wife Domitia as well as the two Praetorian Prefects. Even Rome's city populace was allegedly not stirred by the news of his assassination.

A NEW, BETTER ERA?

Domitian's death in 96 ushered in an era that would last to 180 and later be praised by the eighteenth-century English historian Edward Gibbon as "the period in the history of the world, during which the condition of the human race was most happy and prosperous." All the emperors of this period made a point of deferring to their peers, who gained more marks of status. Ever more responsible administration was linked to peace and prosperity; child-support schemes, seemingly aimed at bettering the lives of those of lower status, were established; urbanization

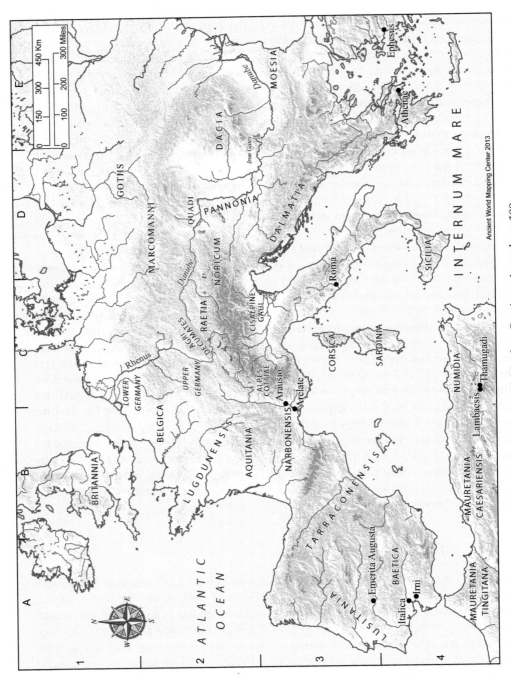

Map 10.1 *Rome's Northern Provinces Around* A.D. *100*

Ancient World Mapping Center 2013

was liberally encouraged; and the judicial system was standardized. The period was free of the searing persecutions of Christians that were to scar the history of the third century, and it also had the good fortune to be spared lengthy warfare with external foes. Even so, we should recognize that poverty and deprivation remained widespread.

NERVA (96–98)

Very few individuals participated in the plot to assassinate Domitian. At all levels of society, there must have been many who recalled with dread the dire aftermath of Nero's death in 68. When the senate met after the assassination, it officially condemned Domitian's memory (*damnatio memoriae*) and chose as his successor Marcus Cocceius Nerva, a senior ex-consul aged sixty-six. His seniority was what counted. Otherwise he lacked military distinction and had passed through perilous times unscathed.

Nerva devoted special attention to Italy during his two years as Princeps. He gave sixty million sesterces to buy land for distribution to citizens who had none, especially those living in Rome. Nerva also seems to have been the emperor who established the so-called *alimenta*. This complex child-support scheme enabled emperors to furnish the principal for low-interest loans to Italian landowners. The interest paid by these borrowers funded monthly distributions to children. More boys are attested as recipients than girls, though this may simply be because only parents without eligible sons would put forward daughters for the scheme, since boys received higher payments. The scheme is often interpreted as an attempt to increase the birthrate in Italy and the amount of land under cultivation there. If so, however, we cannot gauge its effectiveness in either respect, nor can we be sure that these were its ultimate purposes.

Despite these benefactions, Nerva lacked the support of the Praetorians and of the army, who still remembered the favor shown to them by Domitian. By 97, the Praetorians were demanding the execution of Domitian's assassins. Dissatisfaction persisted even after Nerva gave his consent. Worse consequences were precluded only by an unexpected move on his part. In late October 97, he adopted Trajan, the newly appointed governor of Upper Germany (now with a garrison of three legions) and the son of a brilliant soldier-governor. Born and raised at Italica in southern Spain and forty-four years of age at the time of his adoption, Trajan was to be the first emperor from the provinces. Nerva marked him out as successor by conferring the title "Caesar" on him and by securing his election as consul for 98. When Nerva died a natural death on January 25, 98, Trajan's succession as Princeps was ratified despite his absence from Rome. He remained away until October 99, inspecting the frontiers along the Rhine and Danube. The maintenance of consensus at Rome at this time is a remarkable achievement, because it allowed the empire to survive Domitian's assassination without further civil war.

TRAJAN (98–117)

Trajan is one of the few Roman emperors who successfully combined the goodwill of the army and harmony with the senate. He was involved in many civilian initiatives yet was decidedly eager to expand the empire. He has come down in the tradition as *Optimus Princeps*, "Best Princeps," a term appearing on coins and inscriptions beginning in 103. From the start, Trajan acted independently despite conscientious consultation with others. He aimed to strike the note that he was Princeps, not *dominus*, Rome's first among equals and not its monarch. Nevertheless, his accessibility was coupled with an iron will. He expended much energy on civil matters. With his support, the alimenta schemes begun by Nerva were extended in Italy. In addition, some of the last veteran colonies established by Rome were Trajan's initiatives. A prime example is North African Thamugadi (modern Timgad, Algeria), whose orthogonal planning, handsome public monuments, and evident prosperity seem to embody the effects of the "beneficial ideology" at the local level (Plate 4).

In response to local difficulties, Trajan made special appointments to oversee cities and whole regions for limited periods. These troubleshooting caretaker officials (*curatores*)—including Pliny the Younger, dispatched to Bithynia-Pontus in 111–112—reported directly to the emperor (see Source 11.3); how their tasks meshed with those of the regular officials is unclear. At least we can see how this innovation breaks with the traditional principle of cities' autonomy, which all emperors from Augustus onwards had consistently upheld. Yet the work of such caretakers (who had seldom been appointed previously) seems to have been beneficial. Finally in this connection, Trajan was responsible for numerous public works that featured opulent buildings of all types in Rome (see Map 10.3), as well as roads in Italy and the provinces.

Funds for these extensive benefactions came primarily from the Dacian Wars, which Trajan waged in 101–102 and 105–106. From the time of the Late Republic onwards, Rome had dealt intermittently with the Dacians of the Transylvanian plateau and the Carpathian Mountains—rich in gold, silver, and iron mines—above the loop of the lower Danube. Relations had intensified in the late first century, when the Dacian king Decebalus had fought against the Romans until his recognition as a "friendly king" by Domitian in 88. But Decebalus had then in fact renewed his bid for expansion, triggering further war with the Romans. Rome's victories are said to have yielded about 225 tons of gold, double that amount of silver, and 50,000 slaves. These spoils financed the great Forum of Trajan in the heart of Rome and many other monuments in Rome, Italy, and elsewhere (Figs. 10.2 and 11.1). Dacia's mineral wealth also prompted many immigrants to move there. The more exposed location of the new province, beyond the well-defined Danube River boundary, shifted the weight of Rome's garrisons east from the Rhine to the lower Danube and to Dacia itself.

It was possibly the sheer success of the Dacian Wars that spurred Trajan to further expansion. In 105–106, during the second Dacian War, he annexed Arabia

Figure 10.2 *Two bands of the marble relief on the Column of Trajan in Rome, dedicated in 113. This continuous relief portrays events in the Dacian Wars of 101–102 and 105–106. Juxtaposed here are two significant motifs: Roman military superiority, and the farseeing supremacy of Trajan. Below, Romans defend themselves against a Dacian attack on their camp. The bearded Dacians fight bravely, but are no match for the better organized and equipped Romans. Above, Trajan, followed by troops, is reunited with a legionary contingent at a fortified locale (in the background). Soldiers and officers meet him with a bull decorated for sacrifice and attendants for the ritual. Behind them are two bandsmen playing curved horns, and three military standards. These reliefs are sufficiently detailed to distinguish between Roman auxiliary troops, depicted in fringed overshirts and neckcloths (below), and legionaries depicted in their sturdier armor (above right). As always, Trajan appears calm, somewhat larger than other figures, and in full control.*

Petraea, "rocky Arabia," previously called Nabataea (Map 10.2). The new province was wealthy because of its incense, spices, gold, and gems, as well as its active role in Roman trade with India. Almost immediately, Trajan marked the area as Roman by commissioning a great road from the Red Sea to Damascus in Syria. But the creation of the province destabilized an area already unsettled by the death of the king of Parthia to its east (probably in 105). In 110, problems surfaced in Armenia when the new Parthian king replaced the Roman vassal king there with a noble of his own choosing. This action provoked the Parthian War, which was to occupy Trajan until his death in 117.

In October 113, Trajan set off to the East to command the war in person and perhaps to explore the possibilities of advancing beyond Armenia. Mesopotamia, which was ruled by a landowning military aristocracy under a king, was perennially volatile. Its annexation would give Rome a very rich province as well as access to the Persian Gulf. Literary sources also cite Trajan's emulation of Alexander the Great, who had traversed this area on his famous eastern march. By 114, Trajan had captured Armenia and reduced it to a province. As he advanced into Mesopotamia, however, long stretches of desert and semiarid land obstructed communications. The Roman troops were unused to the harsh climate, and supplies were hard to obtain. Disasters, both natural and manmade, exacerbated the difficulties. In winter 114–115 a devastating earthquake hit Syrian Antioch (modern Antakya, Turkey). Although Trajan himself was spared along with his distant relative Publius Aelius Hadrianus (Hadrian) accompanying him, many other men of high rank died, as did soldiers assembling at Antioch for the following year's campaign. In addition, later in 115 the Second Jewish revolt broke out, diverting attention from the expansionist Parthian War to internal discontent. By 116, the unrest had spread to Mesopotamia. The crisis was not finally brought under control everywhere until late in 117; repression of the Jews was especially brutal in Egypt.

In 117, Trajan concluded his Parthian campaigns and embarked on his return journey to Rome. However, in the course of it, he died unexpectedly at the port of Selinus in Cilicia. His final act was to adopt Hadrian as his heir (Table 10.1). Hadrian was aged forty-one at the time and was still in Syria. In his youth, Trajan had been his guardian. Like Trajan, he came from Italica in southern Spain. In 100, he had married Trajan's grandniece, Sabina. Despite these close links, however, Trajan did not clearly mark him out as his successor until the adoption. Hadrian was amply qualified to become Princeps. He had held many administrative and military positions, serving in Pannonia as well as Syria, both of them strategically vital provinces. As a cultured and prominent senator, he combined military and civil talents.

Trajan's rule marks a delicate moment in Roman history, particularly with regard to Rome's traditional imperialism. From some perspectives at least, Trajan's expansion into Dacia can appear glorious and beneficial. Huge amounts of wealth fell into Roman hands, and the emperor and his army performed amazing feats, such as bridging the Danube below the "Iron Gates" rapids. The society created in Dacia after its conquest may seem to demonstrate a constructive type of

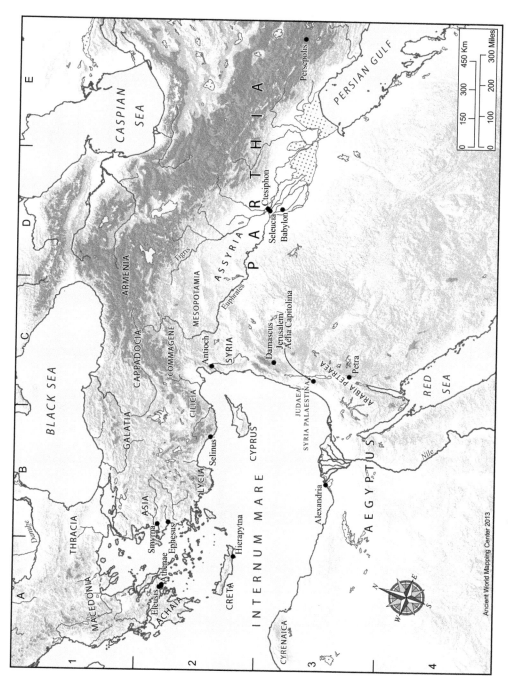

Map 10.2 *Eastern Expansion of the Empire in the Early Second Century*

TABLE 10.1 The Antonine Family *The presentation follows the style of Table 8.1, explained there.*

Ulpia = Aelius Hadrianus Marullinus (?)

M. Ulpius Trajanus = Marcia
(d. before **100**)

C. Salonius Matidius Patruinus = Ulpia Marciana
(d. **78**)   (ca. **50–112**)

TRAJAN = Pompeia Plotina
(**53–117**)   (d. **123**)

P. Aelius Hadrianus Afer = Domitia Paulina
(d. **85**)

L. Vibius Sabinus (1) = Matidia = (2) Rupilius Bonus
(ca. **69/75–119**)

HADRIAN = Vibia Sabina
(**76–138**)   (ca. **83/86–136/137**)

Rupilia Faustina = M. Annius Verus

T. Aurelius Fulvus = Arria Fadilla

ANTONINUS PIUS = Annia Galeria Faustina *the elder*
(**86–161**)   (ca. **100/105–141**)

M. Annius Verus = Domitia Lucilla

L. Aelius Caesar = Avidia Plautia
(**101–138**)

Annia Galeria Faustina *the younger* = MARCUS AURELIUS
(ca. **130–176/177**)   (**121–180**)

LUCIUS VERUS (1) = Annia Aurelia = (2) Ti. Claudius Pompeianus
(**130–169**)   Galeria Lucilla
    (**149–182**)

COMMODUS = Bruttia Crispina
(**161–192**)   (**164–188**)

Romanization. Only one legion and some auxiliary troops were stationed there, and the Romans developed the province's mines. During what was to be a relatively brief period of Roman control—from 106 to 270, when the emperor Aurelian abandoned the area to the Goths—Dacia saw the introduction of the Latin language, Roman religion, and cities in the Roman style. Still today, the Romanian language is heavily Latinate. In short, the new province seems to have been made a flourishing part of the empire, rather than simply remaining territory to be exploited.

There is a strong contrast between Trajan's expansion into Dacia and his involvement with Parthia. The East provided luxury goods for the Romans, and the Parthians were their most organized and formidable foe. Involvements with Parthia predated Roman contact with Dacia, and they had generally not been advantageous; the defeats of Crassus and Antony in the first century B.C. had been particularly severe (see Chapters Seven and Eight). But the rich and exotic East apparently always beckoned. To that extent, it is not hard to see why Trajan decided for a Parthian war. However, this was not as easy to win as to begin. It vastly overextended Roman troops and energy. It diverted Roman attention from provinces elsewhere, opening the way to revolts and invasions. Very soon Trajan's eastern conquests had to be abandoned, and in hindsight we can appreciate the war's negative consequences. The withdrawal is attributed to Hadrian by many authors, because in antiquity's schematic view of Roman history and its leaders, Trajan was unequivocally praised. A large part of his fame was his military achievement, represented as always successful. Hadrian was to acquire a more ambivalent reputation.

HADRIAN (117–138)

With Hadrian's accession in 117, the focus shifted from expansion to consolidation. As it turned out, Hadrian spent more than half of his twenty-one-year rule outside of Rome in travels throughout the empire, visiting cities, natural wonders, and troops along the frontiers. His activity centered on bettering the empire internally. An inward turn is detectable in other ways: Hadrian himself painted, designed buildings, appreciated aesthetics, and wrote poetry as well as speeches and an autobiography. None of these preoccupations would have been possible without widespread peace. Hadrian ruled from 117 to 138. One of his many accomplishments was to settle the succession for the next two generations, although he had no children of his own. Towards the end of his life, in 136, he adopted Lucius Ceionius Commodus (renamed Lucius Aelius Caesar); but when he died within a year, Hadrian turned to others. At the beginning of 138 he adopted Titus Aurelius Fulvus Boionius Arrius Antoninus (later known as Antoninus Pius), and since Antoninus had no son, he had him adopt two younger men. One, the seventeen-year-old Marcus Annius Verus, was to become the emperor Marcus Aurelius. The other, the seven-year-old son of the deceased Lucius Aelius, would later rule as

Lucius Verus jointly with Marcus Aurelius. All three of Hadrian's choices belonged to a circle of friends and relatives with ties to southern Gaul and Spain, typical of the senatorial and equestrian orders in early second-century Rome.

Some innovations can be credited to Hadrian; other changes are not due to him alone. One of his first acts was to complete Rome's decisive withdrawal from Trajan's farthest conquests. Widespread confidence was spurred by Hadrian's travels, during which local notables throughout the empire could meet him. In his first great journey, from 121 to 127, he visited Gaul, the Rhineland regions, Britain (where he began "his" Wall; see Plate 3b), Spain, Asia, Greece, and Sicily. He returned to Rome for less than a year and then visited Africa briefly in 128 (Source 10.1).

After returning to Rome, at the end of 128 he embarked on his second great journey, which lasted until 131. In these years he visited Athens and many regions of Asia, Syria, and Egypt. Sometime during this trip he may have visited Judaea, where his decision to settle a veteran colony at the site of Jerusalem (Colonia Aelia Capitolina), combined with his prohibition of circumcision, set off a major revolt. This Third Jewish revolt, also known as the "Bar Kokhba War" after the Jewish leader Shim'on bar-Cosiba (nicknamed Bar Kokhba, "Son of a Star," by a rabbi), lasted from 132 to 135. It devastated Judaea and exacted a heavy death toll from Jews and Romans alike. Afterwards, in what now seems an attempt to eradicate Judaism, Judaea was renamed Syria Palaestina, and Jews were forbidden entry into Jerusalem (note Plate 6b).

Figure 10.3 *Statue of Hadrian from Hierapytna, Crete. He wears full parade-dress military costume, including a large laurel crown. His magnificent breastplate includes a depiction of Romulus, his twin brother Remus, and the she-wolf (below its central figure) that is said to have rescued and nursed them (see Chapter One). Hadrian triumphantly rests his left foot on the back of a captive barbarian boy, who may be Jewish. The statue—originally set up in an imperial cult shrine—embodies the merciless violence that the Romans inflicted on those who opposed them.*

SOURCE 10.1: *When Hadrian visited North Africa in 128, he reviewed the troops of the province of Numidia at their Lambaesis headquarters (modern Lambèse, Algeria). The garrison later inscribed excerpts from his five addresses to the men. The sections that follow give a flavor both of the troops' mundane tasks and of their military training; they also show Hadrian at work as commander-in-chief.*

[To a cavalry cohort] . . . Defenses which others take several days to construct, you have completed in one. You have completed the lengthy task of building a strong wall—the type typically erected for permanent winter quarters—in not much more time than is needed to build a turf wall. For that type of wall, the turf is cut to a standard size and is easy to carry and to handle; its erection presents no problems because it is naturally pliable and level. But your wall was built of large, heavy, uneven stones which no one can carry or lift or position without them catching on each other because of their uneven surfaces. You cut a trench straight through hard coarse gravel, and made it smooth by leveling it. Once the job had been approved, you entered the camp speedily, and got your rations and your weapons. . . .
[To the cavalry of the Sixth Cohort of Commagenians] It is difficult for cavalry attached to a cohort to make a good impression even on their own, and still harder for them not to incur criticism after a maneuver by auxiliary cavalry—they cover a greater area of the plain; there are more men throwing javelins; they wheel right in close formation; they perform the Cantabrian maneuver in close array; the beauty of their horses and the splendor of their weapons are in keeping with their level of pay. But, despite the heat, you avoided any boredom by doing energetically what had to be done; in addition you fired stones from slings and fought with javelins. On every occasion you mounted briskly. The remarkable care taken by my distinguished legate Catullinus is evident from the fact that he has men like you under his command. . . . (*ILS* 2487, 9133–35)

Hadrian conscientiously consulted senatorial and equestrian advisors and encouraged well-qualified individuals to participate in administration. In addition, he engaged in an enormous program of building and other benefactions throughout the Roman world. His constant travels proclaimed his accessibility and his care for all, and because he journeyed with the apparatus of the central government (still small in this period), important decisions were often made outside of Rome. His military background matches his acute concern for the empire's security. Despite renouncing further expansion, he took a keen interest in the army and military matters. The Second and Third Jewish Revolts marred the beginning and end of his rule (note Fig. 10.3), and further insurrections in Britain and Mauretania occurred around 117. Hadrian may have aimed his provincial benefactions at preventing discontent, but he apparently could not conceive that provincials might reject the Greco-Roman culture he so fervently promoted. Thus his blunders with the Jews in the 130s provoked one of the fiercest revolts that the Romans ever experienced. Hadrian thereafter slowed his activity and became more isolated until his death in 138.

ROMAN CITIES AND THE EMPIRE'S PEOPLES

In size and population the Roman empire was at its peak between the reigns of Vespasian and Hadrian. Its vast expanse—from modern England, the Atlantic Ocean, and Germany across to Syria, Armenia, and the Nile Valley—was studded with cities on the coasts and rivers. There were perhaps fifty to seventy million people living in Roman territory, with probably some 20 percent of these in cities (one million people in Rome itself). This percentage in cities is relatively large. At the end of the twentieth century, 47 percent of the world's people were living in cities, according to United Nations calculations. But this extraordinary proportion is possible only because of recent technological and scientific advances like water purification, refrigeration, heating and cooling, antibiotics, gas-fueled transport, and the like. Of course, none of these advances existed in the Roman world's 2,000 or more cities.

Emperors encouraged cities by both direct and indirect means—through grants of colonial or municipal status, remissions of taxes, personal visits, and funding construction. Better communications and the necessity of supplying the Roman army assisted commerce, agriculture, and the creation of some surplus capital. The provincial cities were above all where social and political mobility could take place. There, freedmen could gain some local prestige and wealth, opening doors for their descendants to rise still higher in the social and economic scale. Soldiers honorably discharged from the legions or auxiliary forces commanded great respect in the towns where they retired, and they often served as town patrons or in some other political capacity. Even working women are documented in Roman cities as greengrocers, midwives, and shopkeepers, besides more traditional but disreputable professions like prostitute or barmaid.

Rome's cities were linked to one another and to Rome itself by roads and harbors, to which the emperors paid much attention. But the Roman world's vast majority, whose horizons were limited to the soil they tilled and to towns within a day's walk, can never have traveled far by land or water. To this vast majority, did it really matter who ruled at Rome? In the early fifth century, Synesius, a cultured bishop and philosopher from the coast of modern Libya, suggested that even educated provincials were indifferent to, perhaps ignorant of, the ruling emperor. Such must always have been the case for the mass of Rome's subjects, struggling to eke out a living from land prone to drought, flood, and other natural disasters. But during times of relative peace and prosperity, those inhabitants of the empire fortunate enough to live in or near a city probably had some inkling of the emperor, perhaps even of some benefaction from him.

THEATERS AND PROCESSIONS

One way that the imperial family affected Roman citizens and subjects was through the demonstration of its images at almost every event. As in the

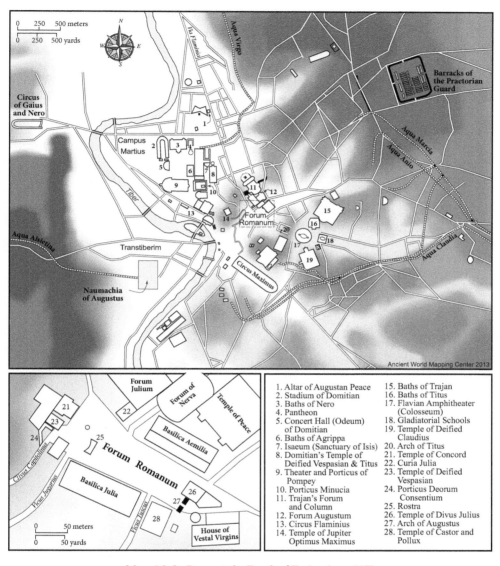

Map 10.3 *Rome at the Death of Trajan (A.D. 117)*

The following place legend appears with the map:

1. Altar of Augustan Peace
2. Stadium of Domitian
3. Baths of Nero
4. Pantheon
5. Concert Hall (Odeum) of Domitian
6. Baths of Agrippa
7. Isaeum (Sanctuary of Isis)
8. Domitian's Temple of Deified Vespasian & Titus
9. Theater and Porticus of Pompey
10. Porticus Minucia
11. Trajan's Forum and Column
12. Forum Augustum
13. Circus Flaminius
14. Temple of Jupiter Optimus Maximus
15. Baths of Trajan
16. Baths of Titus
17. Flavian Amphitheater (Colosseum)
18. Gladiatorial Schools
19. Temple of Deified Claudius
20. Arch of Titus
21. Temple of Concord
22. Curia Julia
23. Temple of Deified Vespasian
24. Porticus Deorum Consentium
25. Rostra
26. Temple of Divus Julius
27. Arch of Augustus
28. Temple of Castor and Pollux

well-preserved theater of Emerita Augusta (modern Mérida, Spain), for example, care was taken to exhibit statues of the emperors and their relatives at public gathering places (Fig. 10.4). Theatergoing was a favorite pastime of the Romans. A later, fourth-century calendar found in Rome designates 102 days a year as "theater days," and there is little reason to think that the total was much less during the three previous centuries. Behind their stages, Roman theaters characteristically exhibited an elaborate and unchanging architectural backdrop (*scaenae frons*), whose many niches were filled with statues of gods, heroes, and the imperial family. Theaters—dating predominantly after the mid-first century A.D.—are found throughout the Roman world. Typically seating some 5,000 spectators, but often much larger than seems warranted by just their city, they must also have accommodated countryfolk and visitors from neighboring towns alongside the local citizens. Spectators included men and women, slave, freed, and free, with the front seats reserved for those with the highest rank. Although theatrical performances differed, invariably each "theater day" opened and closed with sacrifices and prayers on behalf of the Princeps, the imperial family, and Rome.

Theaters in the East staged at least selected parts of the classic Greek plays like *Oedipus Rex*. The Latin West favored performances that could be described as mime or vaudeville, with stock characters in silly situations. Actors usually wore masks. Ironically, given the popularity of theatrical spectacles, professional actors and actresses were considered disreputable; in Roman law they were under certain restrictions, such as not being permitted to receive legacies.

Figure 10.4 *Theater at Emerita Augusta (modern Mérida, Spain), as restored in the early twentieth century. Originally commissioned by Agrippa in 16–15 B.C., this theater was remodeled in the early second century A.D. to include a shrine (sacrarium) for the imperial cult in the lowest part of the seating (the area now lacking seats in the rising semicircle). In the photograph can be seen reproductions of some of the statues originally placed between the columns of the stage's backdrop.*

Religious and civic processions often began or ended at theaters. Such processions were an essential part of the public and official religion of Rome and its cities. On festal days the city's priests and priestesses would parade precious metal images of gods and goddesses, as well as deified emperors and empresses, stopping at various points for public prayer. Often a local notable would pay for a public distribution, feast, or additional performance such as a singing contest, further enhancing the appeal of the day and simultaneously forging a personal link with gods and emperors.

CIRCUSES AND CHARIOT RACING

Such connections also applied to circus races, another favorite diversion of the Romans. Again, the fourth-century calendar from Rome is illuminating. Then, at least, sixty-four days a year were designated for circus races at public expense. The most famous circus is Rome's Circus Maximus (Map 10.3). According to tradition, at its site Romulus and the first Romans had abducted Sabine women from their fathers and brothers. In Augustus' day, after successive rebuildings, it was claimed to hold between 150,000 and 180,000 spectators, men and women, slave and free. Trajan enlarged it to accommodate as many as 250,000, perhaps a quarter of the city's population at the time.

Circus racing remained popular even into Late Roman times. In addition, gatherings at Rome's Circus Maximus, just as those at theaters and amphitheaters, had always allowed the populace to express their opinions to emperors and other figures in authority. This function of the Circus Maximus was reinforced by the location of Augustus' house on the Palatine overlooking it and by the later extension of Domitian's palace towards it. Contemporaries often note interaction between emperor and subject at the races, so that Tiberius' infrequent attendance at the circus only added to his unpopularity. Other features of circus spectacles also remained constant. In the standard arrangement, four-horse chariots lapped at least seven times, for a total distance of 5.25 miles (8.4 km). Each race took about fifteen minutes, and twenty-four races were usually staged in a day. The contenders were traditionally divided into four teams— Reds, Whites, Blues, and Greens. Competition was fierce, and successful charioteers were richly rewarded. Racing—not to mention betting—was extremely popular everywhere, and charioteers were much acclaimed in their communities (Fig. 10.5).

THE AMPHITHEATER AND GLADIATORIAL GAMES

Although spectacles at the amphitheaters are perhaps the most notorious feature of Roman civilization, they were not held as often as is commonly assumed. The

Figure 10.5 *This top of a four-sided marble funerary monument from Hadrian's time shows a Roman charioteer much as he would have been dressed in a race. Over his tunic—which would probably have been painted the color of his team (red, white, blue, or green)—is wrapped a corset of leather cords to provide protection for his rib cage from the jarring ride. The palm tree at the front corner of the monument recalls the palms of victory that were given to the winners. On the side can be seen a racehorse.*

fourth-century calendar from Rome lists only ten days a year devoted to games in the amphitheater. Gladiatorial and beast fights are documented there as early as the third century B.C., but the earliest known permanent amphitheater was built only around 70 B.C. (see Fig. 6.1 and Plate 2b), and the first permanent one in Rome dates to the Augustan Age. Both Roman and modern amphitheaters are commonly called "Colosseum" after the great Flavian structure that rose in place of the lake of Nero's Golden House. The name in fact derives from the adjacent colossal 120-foot-tall (36 m) statue of Nero, which the Flavians then modified to resemble Titus or the sun god, Sol. This amphitheater is a marvel of engineering, harmoniously proportioned, designed to maximize visibility and audibility, and structured so that it could be emptied of its 50,000 or so spectators in five minutes. Its design, which also rendered it fairly impervious to earthquakes, set the standard for all later amphitheaters throughout the Roman world.

Together with mosaics, gems, lamps, and inscriptions commemorating events staged there, these structures attest to a Roman liking for "blood sports" that shocks many modern sensibilities. Spectators watched men fighting against men, almost always in individual pairs except on extraordinary occasions funded by the emperor. Other events pitted men against wild beasts; beasts against men or even women, as when an individual found guilty of a capital crime was condemned to the beasts (*ad bestias*); and various types of beasts against each other (Plate 6a). Gladiatorial costumes and weaponry were standardized, and gladiatorial training schools were usually maintained at public expense. Most gladiators began as slaves; men of good repute and high social standing were to be spectators, not actors, in the amphitheater. Many rich men financed games there in a display of public benefaction as well as a conspicuous sign of their wealth and power. The search for exotic beasts—whose display reflected the extent of Roman rule—contributed to emptying North Africa and other regions of indigenous fauna. Gladiatorial fights were banned only by the emperor Theodosius II in 407, after almost a century of Christian emperors, and wild beast fights continued in Rome's Colosseum until 523.

Recent interpretations of amphitheater spectacles have stressed their use for social control and manipulation; thus the demonizing of gladiators and victims here strengthened the unity of the Roman citizens watching them. Other interpretations have focused on the martial aspects of the gladiatorial fights and on the virtuous bravery that men were expected to show in the very face of death. Because every spectacle day included public prayers to the gods and public homage to the emperor, we again find the same peculiarly Roman amalgam of imperial transcendence, public leisure, and the creation of consensus that was standard in the theater and circus.

OTHER URBAN AMENITIES AND EDUCATION

The culture just described was furthered by the urban amenities of Roman cities. Aqueducts—apparently an essential component of veteran colonies established by emperors and extremely expensive—began to be built in other cities, too, by the end of the first century and the beginning of the second, particularly in the East. Hadrian, for example, sponsored the construction or restoration of at least twelve aqueducts. Thanks to Romans' engineering and the strength of their concrete, remains of many Roman aqueducts can be seen today (Fig. 10.6). Water went first to the public fountains, which either gushed water continuously or let a smaller volume trickle out. After the public fountains, water was supplied to the public baths. Runoff water was channeled to the baths' toilets or neighboring public ones before being carried out of the city through sewers. Only after public

Figure 10.6 *The Pont du Gard. This bridge, 330 ft (49 m) in height, is part of a long aqueduct built with imperial support in the mid-first century to carry water to Colonia Augusta Nemausus (modern Nîmes, France) from a source 31 miles (50 km) away. In fact most of this aqueduct, like others, was underground, which was a safer and more economical method of construction. But because gravity was responsible for water flow, water channels would be carried directly across valleys, often at a considerable height, as here. This aqueduct is estimated to have had a flow of some 30,000 cubic meters a day and to have cost up to 100 million sesterces.*

uses had been satisfied could private individuals pay to have water brought to their houses. Prices were high, and the powerful often tapped into water lines surreptitiously.

Although Roman baths were created by the end of the Republic, their heyday came during the Principate, and particularly from the later first century into the third. Bath design did not become standardized until the time of Nero and his ostentatious public baths in Rome's Campus Martius; the great imperial baths of Rome were created first by Titus and then Trajan. No other city could provide space for a bath of more than forty rooms; local patrons could hardly afford to install and embellish such extensive structures. Smaller and more intimate baths were built in almost every city, however, and many cities boasted more than one: Thamugadi had at least fourteen, Athens twenty. After undressing in a foyer, individual bathgoers would typically go first to the *tepidarium*, then to the *sudatorium* (sweat room), and then to the great cool pool of the *frigidarium*. Some open ground was also provided, where people could roll hoops, throw balls, sprint, or do other exercise. Peddlers hawked their wares in the baths, and teachers and poets often used the larger rooms and courtyards to teach or declaim. Baths were extremely popular.

Pompeii and a few other cities preserve evidence for separate baths catering to each sex. Elsewhere the two sexes may have used the same facilities at different hours. We do not know if individuals bathed in the nude or with some modest covering, although Roman paintings and sculptures suggest a deep-seated aversion to total nudity. Baths were one of the most accessible places that the ordinary individual could go to be surrounded by opulent architecture and embellishment evoking Rome's majesty; statues of the imperial family were frequently displayed in them.

Integral to Roman culture was the Roman system of education. Schooling and literary culture were based on a thorough knowledge of the past and the skill to reshape the past for the present. There was minimal emphasis on innovation of a technological sort. Memorization was essential, and students (mostly boys) had to learn passages by heart. By the second century, girls could also participate in classes offered by publicly funded teachers in certain cities, at least through the basics of reading, writing, and grammar. Nonetheless, there were no publicly funded educational institutions, let alone compulsory school attendance. Students educated to a level of sophistication that enabled them to write nuanced prose or poetry or to speak effectively in public with or without preparation were almost certain to be from a wealthy, privileged background. Libraries offered some limited public access to books (in scroll form). The most famous libraries were those at Rome and Alexandria, but smaller ones were to be found in Athens, Ephesus, Comum, Thamugadi, and other cities.

Thus, at its peak of population, prosperity, external security, administrative efficacy, and local autonomy, the Roman world depended upon cities and advanced them. Within these urban communities, social hierarchies were reproduced and perpetuated, with every level linked to the supreme figure of the emperor.

SUGGESTED READINGS

Bennett, Julian. 2001 (second edition). *Trajan: Optimus Princeps.* London and New York: Routledge.

Birley, Anthony R. 1997. *Hadrian. The Restless Emperor.* London and New York: Routledge.

Boatwright, Mary T. 2012. *Peoples of the Roman World*. Cambridge: Cambridge University Press. Accessible exploration of the tensions that developed between assimilation and distinctiveness, with particular attention to northerners, Greeks, Egyptians, Jews, and Christians.

Fagan, Garrett G. 2011. *The Lure of the Arena. Social Psychology and the Crowd at the Roman Games*. Cambridge: Cambridge University Press.

Potter, David S. (ed.). 2006. *A Companion to the Roman Empire*. Malden, Mass., and Oxford: Blackwell. This large volume's broad scope encompasses the different sources of our knowledge; government; religion; and social, economic, and intellectual life.

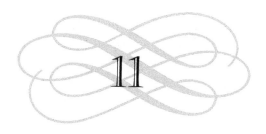

ITALY AND THE PROVINCES

Civil and Military Affairs (138–235)

ANTONINUS PIUS (138–161)

Hadrian's successor Antoninus Pius never left Italy during the twenty-three years of his rule. He was much less involved with the military than were his predecessors and successors. Yet he maintained the appearance of military preparedness and encouraged good officers. A governor of Britain, Quintus Lollius Urbicus, reconquered southern Scotland. This advance was consolidated by the Wall of Antoninus, a turf wall on cobble foundations some eighty miles (128 km) north of Hadrian's Wall; even so, for reasons no longer identifiable, Antoninus' Wall was abandoned not long after his death in 161, and Hadrian's Wall was then regarrisoned (Map 11.1).

No far-reaching legal changes were enacted, nor were there notable administrative changes. Harmony between emperor and senate was a hallmark of Antoninus' Principate. Another characteristic of the time is the firm stress on family and the imperial dynasty, which has meant that the era is often called the "Antonine" Age. Although Antoninus may seem the most unmemorable of emperors, the sheer uneventfulness of his rule reflects both the accomplishments of the preceding half-century and his own capability. Antoninus' time seems to mark the empire's climax as an organized, benevolent, and self-assured form of rule. The diverse forces that would undermine its stability were already present—unrest along the borders, inequities at home—but the vast majority of the empire's inhabitants still accepted their present condition more or less willingly (Source 11.1).

Figure 11.1 *This marble votive relief dates to around 200, and gives pride of place to a ship sailing into the harbor built to the north of Ostia by Claudius and expanded by Trajan. The V and L on the sail probably represent the words V(otum) L(ibens) [S(oluit)] ("He/she repaid the vow willingly"). Meantime, wine-shipping containers are being unloaded from a smaller ship, already moored, at bottom right (compare Plate 5a). So the relief seems to be a dedication from a wine merchant at Ostia's temple of the wine god Liber. To the left, the larger ship has just entered the harbor; at the stern, it is presumably the shipowner and his family who are celebrating a sacrifice for their safe arrival. Duplicated on the sail is the powerful Roman symbol of the she-wolf with Romulus and Remus; nearby an eagle flies through a wreath of victory, a symbol of imperial Rome. To the right of the ship's prow stands Neptune, god of the sea, holding his trident. Behind the prow can be seen the famous four-storied lighthouse; the statue on its third story may represent either Claudius, who began the construction of the harbor, or his successor Nero, who completed it. The two colossal statues with cornucopias and wreaths seem to represent the city of Ostia (the female with the lighthouse on her head) and the harbor itself (her male companion). On the right, an arch bears a chariot drawn by four elephants and driven by an emperor; far right stands Liber, god of wine, with two of his distinctive attributes, a wand (thyrsus) and a panther. The relief conveys both the pervasiveness of religious activity and icons in daily life—note the large "evil eye," believed to avert bad fortune—and the ubiquity of imperial statues and buildings in important cities.*

SOURCE 11.1: *The panegyric* To Rome, *also known as the* Roman Oration, *was written around 144 by Publius Aelius Aristides, a Roman citizen of Greek origin from a town founded by Hadrian in the province of Asia.* To Rome *demonstrates its author's deep engagement with history and philosophy, while placing Roman rule in the most favorable light. It provides an instructive glimpse into the mind-set of wealthy, well-connected provincials during the empire's heyday.*

... You sought the expansion of your Roman citizenship as a worthy aim, and you have caused the word Roman to be the mark, not of membership in a city, but of some common nationality, and this not just one among all, but one balancing all the rest. For the categories into which you now divide the world are Romans and non-Romans. ... Since these are the lines along which the distinction has been made, many in every city are fellow-citizens of yours no less than of their own relatives, though some of them have yet to set eyes on this city [Rome]. There is no need of garrisons to hold their citadels, but the men of greatest standing and influence in every city guard their own fatherlands for you. And you have a double hold upon the cities, both from here [Rome] and from your fellow citizens in each. No envy sets foot in the empire, for you yourselves were the first to disown envy when you placed all opportunities in view of all, and offered those who were capable a chance to be governed no more than they in turn governed. Neither does hatred steal in from those who are not chosen. ... All the masses have as a share in the constitution the permission to take refuge with you from the power of the local magnates. Indignation and punishment from you will come upon these magnates immediately, if they dare to make any unlawful change independently. ... What previously seemed to be impossible has come to pass in your time: maintenance of control over an empire—a vast one, too—and at the same time firmness of rule without severity. (63–66; translation based on that of James H. Oliver, *The Ruling Power. A Study of the Roman Empire in the Second Century after Christ through the Roman Oration of Aelius Aristides.* Philadelphia: American Philosophical Society, 1953)

MARCUS AURELIUS (161–180) AND LUCIUS VERUS (161–169)

Antoninus Pius was deified immediately after his death. Power then passed smoothly to Marcus Aurelius and Lucius Verus, as Hadrian had arranged in 138 by having Antoninus adopt both. Ties among their families had been strengthened further since then (see Table 10.1). The marriage of Marcus Aurelius and Antoninus' daughter, Faustina the Younger, produced perhaps as many as fifteen children—a model demonstration of the importance attached to the family at this period. One of their daughters, Lucilla, was betrothed, aged eleven, to Lucius Verus. The marriage took place at Ephesus in 164, when she was fourteen and he (aged thirty-four) was based at Antioch to prepare for war against the Parthians.

Despite the inevitable difficulty of sharing authority, Marcus Aurelius and Verus ruled from 161 to 169 as joint Augusti with equal powers. Only Marcus

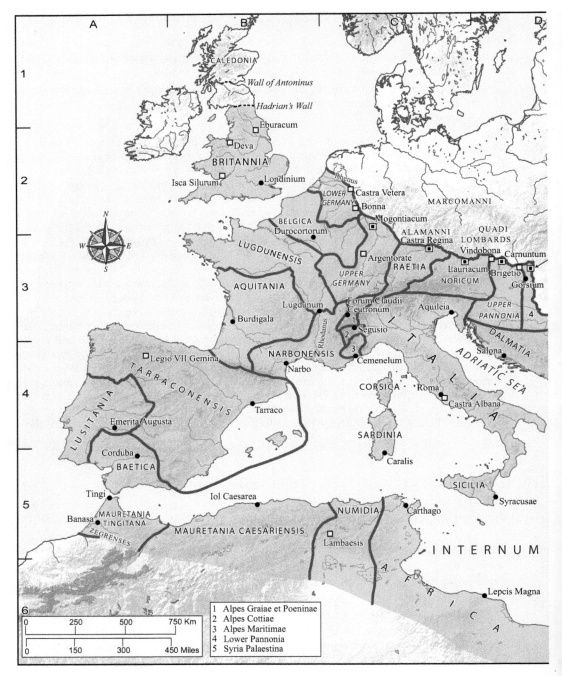

Map 11.1 *Campaigns of Marcus Aurelius and the Severan Emperors*

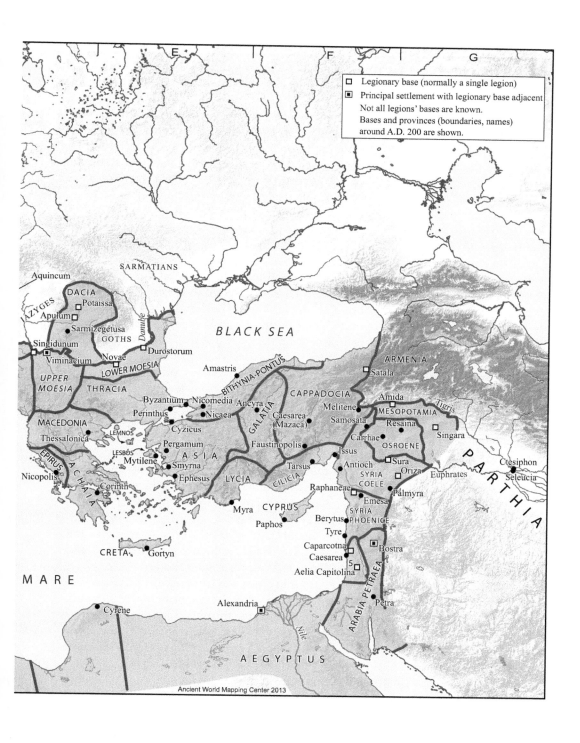

E   F   G

Legionary base (normally a single legion)
Principal settlement with legionary base adjacent
Not all legions' bases are known.
Bases and provinces (boundaries, names)
around A.D. 200 are shown.

SARMATIANS

Aquincum

AZYGES

DACIA

Potaissa

Apulum

Sarmizegetusa

GOTHS

Singidunum

Novae

Viminacium

Durostorum

LOWER MOESIA

UPPER
MOESIA

THRACIA

MACEDONIA

Thessalonica

LEMNOS

EPIRUS

LESBOS

Mytilene

ACHAIA

Nicopolis

Corinth

CRETA   Gortyn

MARE

Cyrene

BLACK SEA

Amastris

Byzantium

Nicomedia

BITHYNIA-PONTUS

Perinthus

Nicaea

Ancyra

Cyzicus

GALATIA

Pergamum

ASIA

Faustinopolis

Smyrna

Ephesus

LYCIA

Myra

CYPRUS

Paphos

CAPPADOCIA

Caesarea
(Mazaca)

Melitene

Samosata

Carrhae

ARMENIA

Satala

Amida

Tigris

MESOPOTAMIA

Resaina

Singara

PARTHIA

Ctesiphon

Seleucia

Tarsus

Issus

Antioch

CILICIA

OSROENE

Sura

Oriza

Euphrates

SYRIA
COELE

Raphaneae

Emesa

Palmyra

Berytus

SYRIA
PHOENICE

Tyre

Caparcotna

Caesarea

5

Aelia Capitolina

Bostra

ARABIA PETRAEA

Petra

Alexandria

Nile

AEGYPTUS

Ancient World Mapping Center 2013

Aurelius' position as *pontifex maximus* marked him as the senior emperor. For much of the time, they divided their energies and attention, Verus commanding in the East against the Parthians from 162 to 166, and Marcus Aurelius ruling in Rome or, after 167, often on the northern frontiers.

Verus' Parthian war was prompted by the Parthians' seizure of Armenia and invasion of Syria in 161. In 162, he went to Antioch to organize the Roman counteroffensive. In 165–166, Gaius Avidius Cassius, then governor of Syria, won conspicuous victories in Mesopotamia, destroyed Seleucia, and razed the Parthian king's palace at neighboring Ctesiphon (near modern Baghdad, Iraq). The Parthians sued for peace, relinquishing part of northern Mesopotamia to Roman control, and Verus celebrated a triumph in Rome jointly with Marcus Aurelius. This brief offensive against Parthia underscores the deadlocked, evenly matched strength of the two empires. Parthian forces were well organized and equipped, and Avidius Cassius' victories would turn out to be short-lived.

Roman troops returning from the East brought back with them a violent infectious disease, perhaps smallpox. After 166, it spread through the empire for some twenty-five years. More than a fifth of the inhabitants of Alexandria are said to have perished, other cities were decimated, and military camps were particularly hard hit. Heavy mobilization of troops for the campaigns against the Marcomanni in the north must have increased the death toll. Even rural areas were afflicted, so that suffering was then exacerbated by ensuing famines. Given the rudimentary understanding of germs and disease, this plague must have been terrifying as well as devastating. It may have contributed to increasing tensions between Christians and the polytheistic majority, which had already led to mob violence against Christians at Smyrna (modern Izmir, Turkey) during the 150s. Another such outbreak, at Lugdunum in Gaul, occurred in 177. The decrease and demoralization of the military and urban populations—that is, the skilled individuals who undertook defense, commerce, and administration—undoubtedly weakened the empire.

Life-threatening epidemic disease was a regular feature of the ancient world. We cannot identify precisely the closest modern equivalent for each "pestilence" reported by our sources, but smallpox, malaria, tuberculosis, typhus, measles, and leprosy were almost certainly common. Ironically, epidemics were spread and made more devastating by the general peace that encouraged travel, long-distance transport, and concentration of populations in cities and military camps (Fig. 11.1). To judge by the limited evidence available, the young were particularly susceptible to disease and ill health. Ample running water brought by aqueducts must have made the Roman cities supplied in this way least vulnerable to water-borne disease. But at the same time, the amenities and opportunities offered by cities must have led to the kind of crowding that admitted more air- and vector-borne disease. Even the rich, who could enjoy the indisputable advantages of roomy living space, a varied, plentiful diet, and clean water, were exposed to ills that have come to be recognized in modern times: lead poisoning both from the water pipes to their residences and from women's cosmetics, and inadvertent poisoning from abortifacients and other medicines.

The Romans' decision to end the Parthian War in 166 coincides with growing problems along the Danube. Beginning in 166, the German Lombards, Marcomanni, and Quadi, as well as the eastern Sarmatians and Iazyges, crossed the middle Danube into the Pannonian provinces and Dacia and then pushed farther south. Both Marcus Aurelius and Verus went north to engage them in 168; when Verus died of a stroke in 169, Marcus Aurelius continued as sole Princeps. In fact he was to spend most of the rest of his life fighting in the north.

Marcus Aurelius' great fame rests not on his military victories but on his frank, and apparently genuine, commitment to Rome's "beneficial ideology." His council of advisors worked well, with its members in Rome handling routine administration while he was far away on campaign. Only one significant civil disturbance marred the general atmosphere of harmony. It occurred in spring and summer 175 and reveals some fundamental tensions in the empire. Avidius Cassius, the general largely responsible for the successful Parthian War of 162–166 and later appointed governor of Egypt, announced to his troops in March 175 that Marcus Aurelius was dead but that he himself was willing to assume imperial power. Duly acclaimed emperor, he ruled in the East for almost four months. He was then killed by a subordinate, just as Marcus Aurelius was making his way to the East with his wife Faustina and the fourteen-year-old Commodus, their sole son to survive childhood.

After personally reestablishing his imperial authority in the East, Marcus Aurelius returned to Rome in 176; Faustina died in Cappadocia on the return journey. Together with Commodus, Marcus Aurelius then celebrated a great triumph over the northern barbarians. Commodus in addition received the consulship and acclamation as Augustus. But by the end of 176, father and son, now joint Augusti, were in Pannonia and Raetia to confront renewed threats from the north. When Marcus Aurelius died of natural causes in early March 180 at Vindobona (modern Vienna, Austria), nineteen-year-old Commodus was acclaimed sole emperor. It is not clear whether he had personally participated in any battles or major military decisions yet, but his father had always surrounded him with the best tutors and a loyal, capable group of advisors. Though some deplored it, his choice was in line with Rome's traditional emphasis on kinship, and even most of the adopted emperors in fact had family links to their predecessors.

COMMODUS (176–192, SOLE AUGUSTUS AFTER 180)

During the first five months of his sole rule, Commodus concluded the Marcomannic wars and abandoned the plans for the prospective new provinces of Marcomannia and Sarmatia. Although his decision allegedly ran counter to his father's aims as well as the opinion of his advisors, some scholars today believe that by now Marcus Aurelius himself had decided to abandon these campaigns to extend Roman control across the Danube. Yet once again—just as in 117 after the abandonment of Trajan's eastern conquests—many observers regarded the preference for peace and the consolidation of borders as inglorious expedients, and so they criticized Commodus. He returned to Rome and another triumph, and the Column of Marcus Aurelius (still a prominent monument today) was erected at Rome to mark the wars' end and Rome's invincibility. Although Commodus did take some initiatives in the provinces, he never came close to matching his father's exceptional concern for the empire. Rather, Commodus' council of advisors was entrusted with much of the administration, and successive Praetorian Prefects exercised great power. Commodus behaved erratically towards the senate, and conspiracies soon began. In 182, his sister Lucilla (once married to Lucius Verus) was implicated in a failed assassination plot. Disorder in Rome itself increased, with the Praetorians lynching their Prefect, Sextus Tigidius Perennis, in 185. Commodus then fell under the influence of Marcus Aurelius Cleander, his freedman servant, whom he promoted to be Praetorian Prefect.

Commodus' own major concerns were his personal gratification and that of Rome's masses. He made many distributions in the city and restructured its grain imports. Like Nero before him, he frequently appeared in untraditional public roles (Fig. 11.2). He fancied himself a great gladiator and wild beast hunter. With his own hands he supposedly killed many thousands of animals, including elephants and ostriches. He is also said to have fought as a gladiator 365 times during his father's rule and over a thousand times during his own Principate.

From 185 to 192, the situation grew grimmer for everyone, the populace included. Cleander's fall from power in 190 was marked by rioting, and authority then passed to Commodus' mistress and one of his servants. In 192, Commodus sponsored two full weeks of gladiatorial games in which he personally performed. He planned to take up the consulship on January 1, 193, dressed as a gladiator rather than in the traditional toga, and to rename Rome "Colonia Commodiana." His dangerous instability finally provoked his assassination on December 31, 192, and the senate then immediately condemned his memory (*damnatio memoriae*).

The chaos that followed stemmed from Rome's lack of constitutional means either to expel unworthy emperors or to ensure an orderly succession. This deficiency was to cause two very serious internal crises

Figure 11.2 *Commodus as Hercules. This bust, dated to around 190, was found in an underground walkway of a luxury garden in Rome. The face is that of the adult Commodus as it is known from other portraits, but here he is portrayed as Hercules. He wears the lion skin over his head and carries a club in his right hand. In his left he holds apples, recalling another of Hercules' legendary labors—taking the apples of the Hesperides. The bust is balanced on an Amazonian shield, whose corners are fashioned as imperial eagles, and on the tops of two cornucopias. All these elements rest on a small globe that symbolizes the entire world. Two Amazons (one now entirely missing) flanked the support, looking upwards in homage to the hero.*

within the next half-century (in 193–197 and 217–221) and ever more frequent ones after 235. From the turmoil of 193 emerged the Severan dynasty (Latin, *Severi*) and an apparent renaissance for the city of Rome, the northern provinces, North Africa, and the East. The Severans are named after Lucius Septimius Severus, who seized power in 193. All subsequent rulers until 235—even the eques Macrinus and his ten-year-old son Diadumenianus, who ruled briefly in 217–218—either were, or claimed to be, related to Septimius Severus or to his wife, Julia Domna (Table 11.1).

SEPTIMIUS SEVERUS (193–211)

Upon Commodus' assassination, various groups vied for power—the senate, the Praetorians, and the army, or rather three different divisions within the army that each promoted its own commander. Each group proved strong enough to bring a candidate to imperial power, but only one of these, Septimius Severus (promoted by the troops along the Danube), was then able to maintain and expand his control.

The first Princeps to be proclaimed in 193 was Lucius Helvius Pertinax. A sixty-six-year-old senator who had loyally served Marcus Aurelius in military and civil positions, Pertinax was the senate's choice. His position as City Prefect in 192 gave him command of the Urban Cohorts in Rome. The Praetorians, however, acclaimed him only reluctantly. At the end of March 193 they murdered him in the palace. The Praetorians then proceeded to auction off the Principate at the gates of their barracks in Rome. Two senators were in the bidding: Titus Flavius Sulpicianus, now City Prefect and father-in-law of Pertinax, and Marcus Didius Severus Julianus. The latter won. Cowed by the Praetorians, the senate ratified their choice.

But the armies outside of Rome, who vastly outnumbered the Praetorians, had already declared emperors of their own. The three legions in Syria declared for Gaius Pescennius Niger, and seven other legions in the East followed their lead. Britain's three legions declared for their commander, Decimus Clodius Albinus. The legion at Carnuntum in Upper Pannonia (modern Petronell, Austria) acclaimed as emperor its commander, Lucius Septimius Severus; his support then spread to the other legions on the Danube and the Rhine, sixteen in all. Severus proved himself the shrewdest of the three claimants. He set off for Rome immediately and reduced the threat from his rivals by appointing Albinus "Caesar" over Britain, Gaul, and Spain. As the Praetorians' loyalty to Didius Julianus began to waver, the senate sentenced him to death and acclaimed Septimius Severus instead. Didius Julianus was killed at the beginning of June 193. A week later, Septimius Severus entered Rome as Princeps.

Septimius Severus was as politically astute as he was militarily brilliant. He had the damnation of Commodus' memory cancelled and had Pertinax deified; the senate confirmed his own assumption of the name Pertinax. In order to break the excessive power of the Praetorians, he dismissed this fickle body of troops and replaced it with legionaries selected for their valor and loyalty. He stationed a legion about thirteen miles (21 km) southeast of Rome at Castra Albana (modern

Albano Laziale), and increased the size of the city's "watchmen" units (*vigiles*) and the Urban Cohorts. No legion had ever been stationed far from a war zone or disturbed area before, let alone in Italy.

With Rome secured and Albinus placated, Septimius Severus next marched east against Niger and seized Antioch, the leading city of Syria; Niger was killed fleeing farther east. The cities that had supported him now had to pay enormous indemnities as well as suffer other punishments. Septimius Severus then divided the large province of Syria into two smaller ones—Syria Coele and Syria Phoenice—thus reducing the number of troops under the command of any single governor.

To boost his image and to deflect attention from civil war, Septimius Severus campaigned against the Parthians in 194–195 and again in 197–199, claiming first that they had offered to help Niger and then that they had seized Roman territory. In these offensives, he annexed northern Mesopotamia as a Roman province (as had Trajan briefly), and also created the province of Osroene. Both campaigns were heralded as glorious triumphs and were celebrated on the Arch of Septimius Severus that is still a prominent feature of the Roman Forum today. Some contemporaries, however, deplored the conquest of Mesopotamia as an overextension of Roman power. It is true that these new provinces did set off a chain of events that weakened the Parthian kingdom, ultimately causing it to fall by 226 to a new group, the Sasanians or Persians. The Sasanian kingdom proved notably more aggressive than its Parthian predecessor, and better able to coordinate the resources of the large area under its control. Moreover, the Sasanians combined their rule with a monotheistic religion, Mazdaism, encouraging fierce loyalty and unity throughout the kingdom.

Between the two Parthian wars, Septimius Severus eliminated his rival Albinus with much carnage at Lugdunum in Gaul (196). He also had himself and his family adopted posthumously into the family of Marcus Aurelius. This was done in 198 to establish a dynastic relationship with the quintessential "good" emperor. When Septimius Severus at the same time renamed his eleven-year-old son Septimius Bassianus as Marcus Aurelius Antoninus and elevated him to the rank of Augustus, he demonstrated yet again the primacy of family at Rome (Plate 5b). This son is better known by his nickname "Caracalla," derived from the Latin word for the long overcoat used by Roman soldiers stationed in the north.

Septimius Severus enjoyed great popularity among the troops. Like Trajan, he fought alongside them and shared their hardships on campaign. He readily engaged in warfare. In addition to his Parthian wars and civil conflict, he fought in Britain from 208 until his death there in 211, trying to deter invasions from the north and perhaps attempting to conquer Caledonia (Scotland). He also enacted many far-reaching military reforms. He further increased the number of legions by three (making a total of thirty-three), stationing one of them near Rome itself, as noted earlier, and the other two in the new province of Mesopotamia. He improved the terms of military service. Around 200, he permitted soldiers to be married while in service, removing the ban on such marriages imposed by Augustus (see Chapter Eight). Soldiers no doubt appreciated this official recognition of the army as a way of life; documentary evidence shows that veterans' sons were already making up a large proportion of recruits. Septimius Severus increased the pay for legionaries from 1,200 to 2,000 sesterces a year, with corresponding increases for auxiliaries. These substantial raises and other military reforms could be seen as blatant attempts to buy the army's favor, but on the other side it is important to recognize that, despite inflation, there had been no increase in military pay since 84, over a century earlier. The personal nature of Septimius Severus' ties to the military is demonstrated by the spread of the title "Mother of the Camp(s)" (*mater castrorum*) for his wife Julia Domna.

Septimius Severus' generosity to the army contrasts with his rough handling of the senate and individual senators. His violent rise to power prompted numerous treason trials in which the sentences handed down were arbitrary and usually harsh. He reduced the number of administrative posts open to senators and gave more prestige and positions to *equites*. Equites now held almost all the great prefectures as well as new salaried positions created specifically for them. Both the City Prefect and Praetorian Prefects extended their administrative and military duties to include judicial ones. All three of Septimius Severus' new legions were placed under equestrian rather than senatorial commanders, and the army's command structure was reformed, making it possible for equites to rise all the way through the ranks. Within a generation, the equestrian officer Macrinus had done precisely this (see Macrinus, below).

Septimius Severus was a Princeps who had a brilliant, wide-ranging mind, and he diligently attended to all the business of Roman government and law. He was closely associated with outstanding jurists like Aemilius Papinianus, who became Praetorian Prefect and perhaps the greatest Roman jurist. Despite his heavy spending, Septimius Severus left a surplus in the treasury. He had a talent for manipulating public opinion. He frequently presented public displays. Meantime, he by no means neglected the empire outside the city of Rome. In the course of his rise to power and his travels as emperor—to Syria and Egypt in 199–202, to North Africa in 202–203, and to Britain in 208–211—he visited most of the Roman world and evidently did so with a genuine sense of duty.

Even when all this is said, the overall picture remains incoherent. Septimius Severus is undeniably one of Rome's great reforming emperors. Like Augustus and Hadrian, he profoundly changed many Roman institutions. Unlike the rule of these two predecessors, however, his was not followed by prosperity and general peace. Instead, his successors were so politically incompetent and militarily inept that their failures damaged Severus himself and his reforms. Further, his years as Princeps—unlike those of Augustus—were not long enough to efface his use of civil war to gain power.

CARACALLA (198–217, SOLE AUGUSTUS AFTER 211)

Caracalla (officially Marcus Aurelius Antoninus) was a less charismatic and more brutal personality than Septimius Severus (see Plate 5b). He followed his father's deathbed advice to show special concern for the military and even raised legionary pay further from two to three thousand sesterces a year. It may have been the need to fund this substantial increase that caused him to issue the *constitutio Antoniniana* in 212. By this decree, he granted Roman citizenship to virtually all the free inhabitants of the empire. One account says that he did this to gain revenue, and various other motives have been advanced too; if the aim really was to raise money, it failed.

Caracalla needed the goodwill of the soldiers, because the empire's borders were increasingly under attack, and he spent most of his Principate on campaign. In 213–214, he campaigned against Alamanni and Goths in Germany, where he defeated some tribes and settled other difficulties by diplomacy. In 215, he moved to Armenia in order to tackle problems caused by his father's Parthian wars. He traveled there through the Danubian regions, and this was where he mobilized his army. By 216, he had successfully battled through Armenia to points farther east and south in Parthia. In 217, however, he was assassinated at Carrhae. His officers feared his erratic paranoia, and his troops were disgruntled at seemingly endless campaigns in desert conditions.

MACRINUS (217–218)

The leader of the coup, now saluted as Augustus by the troops, was Marcus Opellius Macrinus, an *eques* from Mauretania who had held the position of Praetorian Prefect under Caracalla since 212 but had never been made a senator. He thus became the first Roman emperor without senatorial rank. Although he had plotted Caracalla's assassination, he quickly saw the need to associate himself with the Severan family because of its widespread popularity among the military. He adopted the name Severus for himself and added "Antoninus" to the name of his young son Marcus Opellius Diadumenianus, whom he also designated as Caesar. He was unsuccessful in continuing the campaign against the Parthians and caused outrage among his troops when he negotiated a treaty, because this was seen as a cowardly attempt to buy off the enemy. Even more damaging were his decisions to make reductions in army pay and to keep the Danubian troops in the East. In 218, the increasingly dissatisfied troops were approached by Julia Maesa, the sister of Septimius Severus' wife Julia Domna, who claimed that Caracalla was really the father of her fourteen-year-old grandson, Varius Avitus Bassianus (see Table 11.1). As a result, the army eagerly saluted this youngster as Marcus Aurelius Antoninus. Macrinus and Diadumenianus were then hunted down and killed by the same troops who had supported their supplanting Caracalla as emperor only a year before.

ELAGABALUS (218–222)

The four-year rule of Marcus Aurelius Antoninus—or Elagabalus (alternatively Heliogabalus), as he preferred to be called—was one of the strangest that Rome

TABLE 11.1 The Severan Family   *The presentation follows the style of Table 8.1, explained there.*

P. Septimius Geta = Fulvia Pia

Julius Bassianus = Julia Soaemias

P. Septimius Geta
(d. *ca.* **204**)

SEPTIMIUS SEVERUS = (2) Julia Domna
(**146–211**)   (d. **217**)

Julia Maesa = C. Julius Avitus Alexianus
(d. **225**)

C. Fulvius
Plautianus = ?

CARACALLA = Publia Fulvia Plautilla
(*ca.* **186/188–217**)   (d. **212**)

GETA
(**189–211**)

Julia Soaemias Bassiana = Sextus Varius Marcellus
(d. **222**)

Julia Avita Mamaea = Gessius Marcianus
(d. **235**)

ELAGABALUS = (1) Julia Paula
(**204–222**)   (2) Aquilia Severa
(3) Annia Faustina

SEVERUS ALEXANDER = Sallustia Barbia
(**208–235**)   Orbiana

ever experienced. Elagabalus differed from all previous emperors. His advancement resulted not from his own ambitions but from those of his grandmother, Julia Maesa, and his mother, Julia Soaemias Bassiana. His name derived from the god he worshipped as hereditary priest, Elah-Gabal, the sun god of Emesa (modern Homs, Syria). This god was represented not in human form but as a "betel," a sacred black stone. Many Romans were antagonized by the conspicuous orgiastic rites for Elah-Gabal, as well as by Elagabalus' manic promotion of them. When he arrived in Rome a year after his acclamation in 218, it was religious rituals and spaces that preoccupied him, not government.

Senatorial observers, stung by Elagabalus' indifference to administration, depict him as a freakish tyrant and maintain that everything was entrusted to his mother and grandmother. In 221, his grandmother, Julia Maesa, certainly forced him to adopt his cousin, Gessius Alexianus Bassianus, as Caesar. Thereafter the power play intensified. The following year, Julia Avita Mamaea, Elagabalus' aunt and the mother of his cousin, bribed the Praetorians to murder both Elagabalus and his mother, Julia Soaemias, Mamaea's own sister. His cousin Alexianus was then acclaimed emperor as Marcus Aurelius Severus Alexander.

SEVERUS ALEXANDER (222–235)

Although only fourteen years old at his accession, Severus Alexander ruled with some success for the relatively long period of thirteen years. Part of the credit must go to his mother, Julia Mamaea, whose title "Mother of Augustus, and of the Camps, and of the Senate, and of the Fatherland" indicates, however conventionally, that attention was directed to military and civil matters alike. But Severus Alexander also gained by his ostensible deference to the senate. He placed some senators in advisory positions and entrusted the key post of Praetorian Prefect to senators rather than equites. Severus Alexander's rule was a time of great legal advances, the heyday of the outstanding jurists Domitius Ulpianus and Julius Paulus. Severus Alexander was also alert to economic and social concerns, reducing taxes, aiding the grain supply of Rome, and subsidizing teachers and scholars.

His relationship with the military was more problematic. In 223, the Praetorians revolted, killing their Prefect, the jurist Ulpian; Severus Alexander failed to punish this outrage. Nor could the young emperor identify with rank-and-file soldiers in the way that, say, Trajan and Septimius Severus had been able. Soldiers apparently despised him as a weak general, and this disgust led only to further military uprisings. In 231, generalship was demanded of Severus Alexander when the aggressive Sasanians under King Ardashir I—now dominant in the former Parthian empire—invaded Mesopotamia. Accompanied by his mother Julia Mamaea, Severus Alexander went on campaign from Antioch and did recover Mesopotamia by 232. The following year, he returned to Rome to celebrate a triumph, but by 235 he had to go on campaign again, this time against German invaders in Raetia.

When he proved unable to defeat them in battle and began negotiations instead, the army again interpreted this as a cowardly attempt to buy peace. As a result, mutinous soldiers murdered both Severus Alexander and his mother and acclaimed as emperor their ringleader, an equestrian general of Thracian origin, Gaius Julius Verus Maximinus. He was to be the first of the so-called "soldier-emperors," and his rule marks the beginning of a turbulent half-century in which the empire suffered severe pressures on all sides.

ROMAN LAW

The Romans themselves, and subsequent observers, considered law and jurisprudence to be among Rome's crowning achievements. The rationality of Roman law, its firm yet flexible nature, and its public character have all been admired. Its foundation is said to be the Twelve Tables, established in the mid-fifth century to guarantee equal access to the law to all Roman citizens (see Chapter Two). Most of these archaic statutes concerned private law (that is, law dealing with relations between individuals), but a few addressed relations between individuals and the community. Thereafter, to judge from surviving materials, private law and procedure (especially concerning property) continued dominant. The Romans clearly prided themselves on their legal acumen and precision, and statutes were exhibited publicly. Art and literature frequently represented senators and magistrates during the Republic, and later the emperors, deciding cases and enforcing legislation. Beginning in the third century B.C. and peaking in the Severan period, many of Rome's finest minds devoted themselves to jurisprudence ("the science of what is right and wrong" [*Digest* 1.1.10]).

Papyri and numerous inscriptions on stone or bronze preserve statutes and other decisions made by emperors or other magistrates or by the Roman senate, which serve to illuminate Roman social and institutional history. Extant town charters from first-century Spain, for example, document the elevated status enjoyed by magistrates and council members, as well as the gradual assimilation of local to Roman law. The *Corpus Juris Civilis*, or *Collection of Civil Law*, compiled under the emperor Justinian in 528–534, shows the frequent recourse in legal rulings to "what a good man would do." From this million-word digest of earlier laws some scholars have inferred that during the first two and a half centuries of the Principate Roman private law became more liberal and humane, because women gained a degree of legal autonomy, for example, and slaves were increasingly recognized to have some rights. Overall, the evidence confirms a general reluctance to set absolute, unchangeable rules and a willingness to consider mitigating factors. Precedent was consulted, but it was not binding; rather, it assisted the legal reasoning used to decide individual cases (see Trajan's reply to Pliny about the Christians, Source 11.3).

Roman criminal law had no public prosecutor; every case had to be instigated by a male citizen, who took the role of accuser in court if the appropriate judge consented to hear the case. Moreover, by the second century A.D. Roman citizens were in practice divided into two groups. The *honestiores* ("more honorable") comprised senators, equestrians, veterans, town councilors, and other well-educated individuals (and their families); the *humiliores* ("more lowly") were the innumerable others, the great majority of the population. For the honestiores, conviction on a capital charge might bring exile or a fine; for others, the sentence was likely to be assignment to the mines (tantamount to death), hard labor on roads, or being thrown to the beasts in the amphitheater (see Plate 6a). Even so, the distinction between honestiores and humiliores is never explicitly defined in surviving legal texts, and it may have been at the discretion of the court. The use of torture was common in cases involving non-Roman citizens, and it was mandated when a slave was involved. Prison was seldom used as a penalty, but only for briefly holding persons pending trial or execution; Romans were less interested in penitence and rehabilitation than in deterrence and retribution. Despite such harshness, and the persistence of slavery and of legal disabilities for women and some others, Roman jurists and emperors often expressed a belief in basic human equality, and in the rationality and merit of their law. These views resonate with the countless appeals and sheer quantity of legal activity known from the Principate.

ROMAN CITIZENSHIP

The original concept of Roman citizenship was tied to rights (including access to Roman law), duties, and privileges. This tripartite division is common to all ancient societies. A feature peculiar to Rome, however, was the automatic incorporation of freed slaves into the citizen body (albeit with some restrictions in the first generation) and the ease with which individuals and whole communities of outsiders could be admitted. The grant of Roman citizenship to a slave upon manumission by a Roman citizen continued during the Principate. But even before the *constitutio Antoniniana* of 212, this period witnessed three primary ways for free individuals to gain citizenship. Two were connected with military service, which had also been integral to Roman citizenship at its inception; the third reflected the dominant position of the Princeps everywhere.

The first new means to gain citizenship is known primarily through bronze tablets, the *diplomata* that record the grant of citizenship at honorable discharge to provincials who had served in the auxiliary forces; the earliest known diplomata date to the Principate of Claudius. By the early second century, another means had evolved informally and reflects the continued primacy of the soldier-citizen. Because the legions were supposed to be manned by Roman citizens, individuals who enrolled in them were awarded citizenship upon enlistment if they did not already have it. The third means to Roman citizenship was a direct grant by the emperor to individuals and even to whole communities (Source 11.2).

The rights of Roman citizens to vote in elections and on legislation, which caused such great conflict at the end of the Republic, became defunct early in the

> **SOURCE 11.2:** *Inscriptions, such as the following part of a bronze tablet dating to around 168, proudly record imperial grants of citizenship, and allow us to see specific instances of the emperor conferring such benefits. This document comes from Banasa in southwest Mauretania (modern Sidi Ali bou Jenoun, Morocco), where Augustus had settled a veteran colony; the Zegrenses were a local tribe. The last phrase in the wording of the grant is an important warning that a beneficiary's new status as a Roman citizen does not supersede his former civic identity, nor exempt him from local obligations.*
>
> Copy of the letter of our Emperors Marcus Aurelius and Verus, Augusti, to Coiiedius Maximus [governor of Mauretania Tingitana, who had forwarded Julianus' request for citizenship]. We have read the petition of Julianus the Zegrensian attached to your letter, and although it is not usual to give Roman citizenship to men of that tribe except when very great services prompt the emperor to show this kindness, nevertheless since you assert that he is one of the leading men of his people and is very loyal in his readiness to be of help to our affairs, and since we think that there are not many families among the Zegrenses who can make equal boasts about their services—whereas we wish that very many be impelled to emulate Julianus because of the honor conferred by us upon his house—we do not hesitate to grant Roman citizenship, without impairment of the law of the tribe, to himself, his wife Ziddina, likewise to their children Julianus, Maximus, Maximinus, Diogenianus. (*AE* 1971.534)

Principate. Citizen elections for senatorial magistracies were abandoned in Tiberius' time, and assemblies ceased passing laws by the end of the first century. At the same time, on the other hand, the onerous military duty of Roman citizens was greatly lessened by the general shift to a volunteer, professional army. Roman citizens were liable for various taxes, particularly the 5 percent inheritance tax that funded the "military" treasury. Roman citizens in Italy, however, were to remain immune from payment of land taxes until the end of the third century. Most important to the functioning of the empire—since Rome relied so heavily on cities for local administration—Roman citizens as well as all others had to serve their local communities. Each Roman had obligations to his town of origin (*origo*), as well as to Rome itself (see Source 11.2). An origo was an essential part of a Roman's political and social identity. Roman citizens enjoyed extra privileges, however. They could join a legion, or (at the top level) seek equestrian or senatorial status at Rome; altogether, without question, they had the greatest social and political mobility. They might also expect easier access to the emperor—by custom, if not always by law—when appealing a sentence, say, or requesting some exemption from civic obligations. In the early Principate, Roman citizenship seems to have been attractive to non-Romans; it was no doubt seen as the pathway to power and privilege (Fig. 11.3).

However, inscriptions and other evidence suggest that by the end of the second century Roman citizenship was losing its allure. Among municipal elites we find increasing instances of men unable or unwilling to serve their community

Figure 11.3 *Tombstone of the mid-second century from Gorsium, Pannonia (near modern Székesfehérvár, Hungary). This monolithic tombstone combines decoration in the Greco-Roman style—such as the grapevine-spiraled columnnettes—with local elements. The two women portrayed are wearing "native" dress, with heavy turbans, prominent pendant necklaces, and large pins on their shoulders. They are framed, however, by two elegant herm figures. At the foot of the stone, two servants are shown frontally under a curved border characteristic of art from the region, but these plain figures are flanked by sinuous Bacchanalian dancers. The beautifully cut Latin inscription translates, "To the spirits of the dead. Publius Aelius Respectus, city councilor of the municipality, while alive made this for himself and for Ulpia Amasia, his wife. Aelia Materio, their daughter aged ten, is placed here. The parents put up this monument for her memory." The names indicate that the family members are all Roman citizens; the father specifies that he is a city councilor in his community, although without naming it. The unusual "Amasia" and "Materio" apparently maintain the area's indigenous names, as does the woman's dress. This tombstone represents the creative interaction of Roman and provincial cultures.*

politically—participation that by tradition had been seen as an enviable privilege, not a burden. Local political service was essential to the functioning both of individual cities and of the empire as a whole, and by the second century the city councils (whose members are termed "decurions") were the most powerful local political figures. Among other duties, a city's officials were responsible for law and order, public contracts, religious rituals, and entertainment; they also supervised the collection of the tax quota demanded from their community by Rome. Roman, as opposed to local, administration could accordingly be relatively lean (see Chapter Ten). The obligations of a city's council and magistrates were offset by their relative autonomy, an underlying principle of the Principate. But this autonomy would function successfully only so long as the empire's cities were willing and able to regulate themselves. Various developments, such as the appointment of "caretakers" (*curatores*) from Rome, acted to alter the balance between Rome and its cities.

Even by the early second century, some of the distinctive privileges of Roman citizenship had begun to erode, as we saw with the enlistment of non-Romans in the legions. At the lowest levels of Roman society, however, such differences in status were always almost meaningless. Whether someone from the rural poor or urban homeless—who had few or no possessions, and no education—was freeborn, freed, or even slave probably made little difference to the authorities in court or elsewhere, because the elite were so superior in every way to such powerless individuals. The latter themselves were unlikely to be much preoccupied by the question of their legal status, when it was a constant struggle for such poverty-stricken people just to stay alive.

It is against this background that we must set Caracalla's grant of Roman citizenship to virtually all free inhabitants of the empire. What functional and ideological difference did it make? And what constituted being "Roman" at this date? Septimius Severus and his family may illuminate these difficult questions, at least at the top of the social scale. His *origo* was Lepcis Magna, an important city founded by the Carthaginians on the coast of what is now Libya (Fig. 11.4). Although Latin

Figure 11.4 *Lepcis Magna, Tripolitania (75 miles/120 km east of modern Tripoli, Libya), was developed as a Phoenician trading settlement from around 600 B.C., using a harbor at the end of a stream bed, from where a route led far inland to sub-Saharan Africa. Later the settlement also derived prosperity from its rural territory, which produced olive oil in great quantities. By the late first century B.C., Lepcis Magna was shipping three million pounds of olive oil annually to Rome. By the end of the first century A.D., it had become a municipium, and then under Trajan its city status was raised to that of a colony. Later Septimius Severus, who was from Lepcis himself, patronized it lavishly, although it could already boast handsome buildings. He sponsored an enormous forum—whose ruins are prominent here—flanked by a public hall and basilica (behind the high wall on the right); an adjoining, long colonnaded street (partly visible in the right foreground); and a multistoried, elaborate fountain that marked the shift in the city's street grid. The ruins of the magnificent city— preserved by the silting-up of its harbor and subsequent disuse—represent dramatic testimony to emperors' wealth and to the potential power of imperial patronage.*

sources call Septimius Severus "Italic"—descended from Italian emigrants—his Punic background was at least as strong. His grandfather served as chief magistrate of Lepcis Magna, an office that retained its Punic title *sufes* even long after the city had become a Roman municipality. Septimius Severus himself allegedly never lost his provincial accent when speaking Latin, although his Greek was excellent. The origo of his wife, Julia Domna, was Emesa in Syria, and Greek and Syriac were her first languages. Thus what we might consider ethnicity apparently mattered little as a constituent of Roman identity.

On the other hand, those identifying themselves as Romans aspired to adopt Greco-Roman culture and its devotion to, among other tastes, Latin and Greek literature, rhetoric, art, and city life. Although as emperor Septimius Severus never attempted to mask his reliance upon the military, he participated fully in the Greco-Roman cultural ideal. One of his most spectacular accomplishments was the magnificent rebuilding of Lepcis Magna. Julia Domna is said to have regularly met with members of the intelligentsia.

ROME AND CHRISTIANITY

Religion is notoriously difficult to investigate, because it combines practice, or ritual, with belief, or faith. Rituals, which are enacted periodically, are transient even with the best of documentation; participants are caught up in the moment, and observers are disconnected from the experience. As for beliefs, we cannot measure the sincerity of what we read in the stylized literature of the Romans, or even in the public proclamations of belief made in inscriptions, graffiti, or other documents. At the same time, however, we should not dismiss all such declarations as hollow just because they are not statements of Christian or other religious belief as understood today. We should bear in mind that the Roman authorities were to make repeated attempts to eradicate Christianity during the third and early fourth centuries, and that later Christian emperors likewise would seek to obliterate polytheism and Judaism. It is no wonder that the relationship between Rome and Christians was an uneasy one and hard to fathom today.

The close connection between religion and politics in Roman society helps to account for the vehemence of the interchange. As we have seen, religious ceremonies preceded all Roman political activity. The same individuals frequently held political and religious positions at Rome, and minimal specialized training or knowledge was required for most of the latter. At the same time, the Roman state seldom sought to impose any particular religion, concerning itself mainly with the appropriate performance of public cult and the prohibition of any human sacrifice.

But Christian belief demanded absence from polytheistic state rituals. There was a fundamental difference between Christian and polytheistic religious sensibilities. The Christians' religious affiliation provided them, individually and collectively, with an identity distinct from that of city, family, or profession. By contrast, for polytheistic Romans, religious rituals and practices were integral

SOURCE 11.3: *This celebrated exchange between the governor Pliny and the emperor Trajan regarding Christians in Bithynia-Pontus around 112 provides valuable insight into the Roman state's reaction to Christians. It also sheds light on the rituals associated with imperial cult, and on the economic and social ramifications of state religion.*

[Pliny to Trajan] It is my practice, my lord, to refer to you all matters about which I have doubts. For who is better able to resolve my hesitation or to inform my ignorance? I have never been present at trials of Christians. So I do not know what offenses it is the practice to punish or investigate, and to what extent. And I have hesitated considerably over whether there should be any distinction on account of age, or no difference between the very young and the more mature; whether pardon is to be granted for a change of mind, or, if a man has once been a Christian, it does him no good to have ceased to be one; whether the name itself, even without offenses, is to be punished, or only the offenses associated with the name.

Meanwhile, in the case of those who were denounced to me as Christians, I have observed the following procedure: I asked them personally whether they were Christians; those who confessed, I asked a second and a third time, threatening them with punishment; those who persisted, I ordered to be executed. For I had no doubt that, whatever the nature of their admission, their stubbornness and inflexible obstinacy surely deserve to be punished. There were others gripped by the same folly; but because they were Roman citizens, I assigned them to be transferred to Rome.

Soon accusations spread, as usually happens, because of these proceedings, and several incidents occurred. An anonymous document was published containing the names of many persons. My view was that I should discharge those who denied that they were or had been Christians, when they called upon the gods in words dictated by me, offered prayer with incense and wine to your image (which I had ordered to be brought in for this purpose, together with statues of the gods), and in addition cursed Christ—none of which actions those who genuinely are Christians can be made to take, I am told. Others named by an informer declared that they were Christians, but then denied it, asserting that they had been but had ceased to be, some three years before, others many years, some as much as twenty years. All these individuals also worshipped your image and the statues of the gods, and cursed Christ.

They declared, however, that what their fault or error amounted to was that they were accustomed to meet on a fixed day before dawn and sing alternately among themselves a hymn to Christ as to a god, and to bind themselves by oath, not to some crime, but rather not to commit fraud, theft, or adultery, not to commit a breach of trust, nor to deny a deposit when called upon to restore it. After doing this, it was their custom to depart and to reassemble to consume food—but of an ordinary, harmless type. Even this, they said, they had stopped doing after my edict by which, in accordance with your instructions, I had banned associations. Accordingly, I believed it all the more essential to find out what the truth was by torturing two female slaves who were called "attendants." I discovered nothing further except depraved, excessive superstition.

I therefore postponed the trial and hastened to consult you, since I felt the matter warranted consulting you, especially because of the number of people at risk. For many persons of every age, every rank, and also of both sexes are and will be exposed to danger. The contagion of this superstition has spread not only to the cities, but also to the villages and farms. But it seems possible to check and cure it. It is certainly quite clear that the temples, which had been almost deserted, have begun to be thronged again, that religious rites are being resumed after a long interval, and that the meat of sacrificial victims is on sale everywhere, even though up to this point almost nobody could be found to buy it. So it is easy to realize what a mass of people can be reformed if they are given a chance to change their minds.

[Trajan to Pliny] You have observed appropriate procedure, my dear Pliny, in sifting the cases of those denounced to you as Christians. For it is not possible to lay down some general rule to serve as a kind of fixed standard. They are not to be sought out; if they are denounced and proved to be guilty, they are to be punished, with this reservation, that whoever denies that he is a Christian and quite clearly proves it—that is, by worshipping our gods—he shall gain pardon because of his change of mind, despite having been under suspicion in the past. But anonymously posted accusations ought to have no place in any prosecution, since they set the worst precedent and are unworthy of our times. (Pliny, *Letters* 10.96–97)

to all civic and familial activities, and religious roles overlapped with political ones. Romans and their subjects could "believe" as they pleased, so long as they did not actively reject rituals that had been made part of the state religion. Through revolts and legislation, the monotheistic Jews and Rome gradually worked out a compromise over the first two centuries of the Principate, which allowed Jews to be excused from participating in state cult rituals. Initially, the Romans regarded Christianity, too, as a sect of Judaism. But after it became clear that Christians did not accept this identity, they became more problematic for the Roman state.

Widespread incomprehension about Christians in the first century met with a range of reactions in the second. From about 120 to 220, Christians struggled to formulate their own hierarchy and to explain themselves to non-Christians. In part, this attempt came in response to sporadic "persecutions" that were launched spontaneously by non-Christians. We are told of outbreaks of violence against Christians during the rule of Domitian in Rome, under Trajan in Bithynia-Pontus (see Source 11.3), in Smyrna during the 150s, in Lugdunum in 177, and in Carthage and Alexandria at the beginning of the third century. To defend Christianity, "apologists" wrote brilliant tracts that are strikingly sophisticated in their rhetoric and philosophical argument. These authors aimed not so much to convert non-Christians as to persuade them that they had no good cause to fear Christians or persecute them. It is important to note that brutal treatment suffered by Christians during these times was not initiated by the state.

Until the second half of the second century, most Christians lived in cities in Judaea and elsewhere in the Greek East, and in a few large cities such as Rome and Carthage in the West. The increasing sophistication of the church is reflected in the formation of a church hierarchy in Rome, and in the growth of the concepts of heresy and orthodoxy in a debate apparently evolving in the third quarter of the second century. In the Severan period, Christianity evidently gained its first adherents in the equestrian and senatorial orders. These were women. But it remains difficult to say with any certainty who was Christian, and in what numbers, since few publicly professed their adherence.

From the mid-third century into the early fourth, the Roman state actively persecuted Christians. They were labeled a menace to society, and officially sponsored efforts were made to extirpate their cult. In the first state persecution (249–251), an empire-wide requirement of sacrifice to the Roman gods allegedly resulted in thousands of deaths, many at the hands of mobs. All who duly offered sacrifices were issued certificates (*libelli*), which in the case of Christians served to record their renunciation of Christianity. The second state persecution (253–260) initially targeted clergy, but then widened to eliminate upper-class men and women who refused to renounce their faith; their property was to be seized, and they themselves were to suffer execution, exile, and other severe penalties. Christians were fairly easy to identify, because they refused to participate in state cult. As a result, they could not serve in the army, where religious ritual was an integral part of the routine. By the same token, they faced difficulty in taking up municipal or state positions. A major reason for the hostility shown to Christians may well have been their general refusal to assist the community in a civil or military capacity during a period when such help was urgently needed.

The persecutions created a category of persons known as "martyrs" from the Greek word for "witness," because these individuals were considered to have witnessed their faith through their public refusal to deny it. Some Christians bewildered and irked the authorities by presenting themselves voluntarily for martyrdom. Altogether, the persecutions actually strengthened Christianity. They provided inspiring examples of brave Christians whose faith was unshakable, and they encouraged Christian self-perception as a beleaguered, suffering minority. Christianity was appealing in other ways, too. Churches offered aid to widows, orphans, and other marginalized or dispossessed individuals. This form of charity contrasts sharply with the distributions given by the Princeps or by wealthy individuals, which were sporadic and almost invariably directed more towards prestigious recipients. The egalitarian community based on Christian love (*agape*) ignored differences of legal, social, or political status. This alternative approach attracted many individuals excluded from Rome's elites. Women were welcome in the Christian community, too, and they seem to have played important roles as organizers and proselytizers in the early church.

For these and other reasons, there developed the impression that Christians rejected Roman order and society. Their scriptures advocated peace. Many of their rites and customs were misunderstood. Their "eating the body and drinking the blood of their Savior" was called cannibalism, and their habit of addressing one another as "brother" and "sister" was taken to signify incestuous promiscuity. The high proportion of lower-class Christians must have alienated elitist Romans. But Roman society had been changing from the beginning of the Principate. The age-old self-identification according to political and social distinction was shifting. From the second century onwards, it is possible to identify a growing phenomenon, which may be termed "conversion": deliberate and public acts of religious commitment that often acknowledged psychological change. These are mostly associated with what have been termed "mystery" or oriental religions, like those of Isis, *Magna Mater*, and Mithras. Christianity shares some characteristics with these cults insofar as it, too, is based on a revealed doctrine, and features initiation, a dedicated priesthood, the promise of an afterlife, and community on earth. Yet Christianity differs from mystery religions in its greater openness to converts (Mithraism excluded women altogether), its proselytizing, its monotheism, its emphasis on scripture, and its stress on belief and behavior.

SUGGESTED READINGS

Birley, Anthony R. 1987 (revised edition). *Marcus Aurelius: A Biography*. New Haven and London: Yale University Press.

Hekster, Olivier, with Nicholas Zair. 2008. *Rome and Its Empire, AD 193–284*. Edinburgh: Edinburgh University Press. Concise discussion of the period's historical developments, followed by extracts from key sources in translation.

Lendon, Jon E. 1997. *Empire of Honour: The Art of Government in the Roman World*. Oxford: Oxford University Press.

Mattern, Susan P. 1999. *Rome and the Enemy: Imperial Grand Strategy in the Principate*. Berkeley, Los Angeles, London: University of California Press.

Riggsby, Andrew M. 2010. *Roman Law and the Legal World of the Romans*. Cambridge: Cambridge University Press. A clear, wide-ranging introductory treatment.

12

THE THIRD-CENTURY CRISIS AND THE TETRARCHIC RESTABILIZATION

MID-THIRD CENTURY

The years from the assassination of Severus Alexander in 235 to the acclamation of Diocletian in 284 witnessed rapid, often violent political change. In less than fifty years, at least eighteen emperors took power with their legitimacy confirmed or ratified by the Roman senate. Even more men claimed power without such sanction. Most met a violent death. The senate had little power, no longer provided political stability, and must have seemed obsolete when Marcus Aurelius Carus was accepted as emperor in 282 without even applying to it for validation. Though the period is often called the Age of Crisis, there was at the time a strong stress on continuity with the past and the promise of a bright future. The leaders proclaimed the timelessness and transcendence of the empire in coins and inscriptions. For example, despite a devastating loss to Persia, ongoing internal insurrections, and invasions by trans-Danubian Carpi and Goths (Map 12.1), Rome's thousandth anniversary in 248 was celebrated with great pomp by the emperor Philip "the Arab" (who came from the region of Damascus). There seems to have been a greater resistance to innovation, to judge from the empire-wide Christian persecutions by the emperors Decius (249–251) and Valerian (253–260), which were then resumed in the early fourth century.

Just as shortsighted and futile were the efforts of various emperors to assert their supremacy over rivals, rather than to address systematically the problems that the empire faced on its borders. The northern and eastern frontiers were the areas of the greatest external dangers. The jagged northern boundaries—for the most part, the great rivers of the Rhine and Danube—divided the empire from various Germanic and other tribes. But the separation was never complete. Commercial, social, and cultural interaction regularly occurred in times of peace; even during hostilities, the rivers were by no means impenetrable barriers. By the mid-third century, when Rome's river frontiers had been more or less fixed for two centuries, the "barbarian" peoples beyond these frontiers had undergone substantial changes. In large part as a response to their Roman neighbors, they had grown more economically powerful and their societies had coalesced into more complex, hierarchical groupings. Furthermore, new peoples were constantly pushing against the old, creating pressures for borderland groups to enter the empire or to strengthen themselves against threats from both sides by forming coalitions. It is over the course of the third century that we first encounter new confederacies of barbarian groups—not empires like Rome's, but alliances capable of standing up to Roman armies and even defeating them.

By the mid-third century, the Rhine and Danube were being crossed repeatedly by these groups, including Franks, Alamanni and Juthungi, Vandals, and Sarmatians. Franks and Saxons crossed the English Channel to harass Roman Britain, too, which also suffered attacks from the north by tribes in Scotland. The middle Danubian provinces—Noricum, Upper and Lower Pannonia, Dacia, and Upper and Lower Moesia—saw recurrent fighting and military threats. This general region, often termed Illyricum, was famous as a source of fearless soldiers. It provided many of the emperors of the mid-third century. The Roman provinces along the lower Danube were repeatedly attacked by Goths, a Germanic people who by this time had migrated and settled beside the Black Sea. Their coalition achieved some degree of unity under a king named Cniva, who invaded the territory of Thrace in 250 and sacked many Roman cities. When the emperor Decius marched against the Goths the following year, they were able to surround his army at Abrittus (in the marshy territory of northern Moesia) and kill him and his son, whom he had appointed co-emperor. This was the first time Rome had ever lost an emperor in battle against a foreign foe. The Goths later went on to assault Roman provinces in northern Asia Minor, sacking Trapezus (modern Trabzon, Turkey) in 256. Again in 267, Goths and Heruli invaded the Balkans, and sacked Athens, Delphi, and other Greek centers, necessitating the creation of local militias to deal with the problem in the absence of imperial support.

In Persia a new, more aggressive dynasty called the Sasanians had supplanted the Parthians in the 220s and had begun challenging Rome on its eastern border. Under their King of Kings Shapur I (242–272), they reached Antioch (modern Antakya, Turkey) in Syria, sacking it in 253 and again in 260 (Map 12.2). In the latter year, Shapur even captured alive the emperor Valerian at Edessa (modern Urfa, Turkey) (Fig. 12.1). Valerian lived out his remaining days serving as the footstool—literally—of the Persian king, a humiliating blow to Roman pride. This military effectiveness was possible because the government of the Sasanians, centrally controlled under its King of Kings, was strikingly different not just from the less cohesive, shifting groups encountered by the Romans on their borders elsewhere, but even from their Parthian foes of the first century B.C. and following.

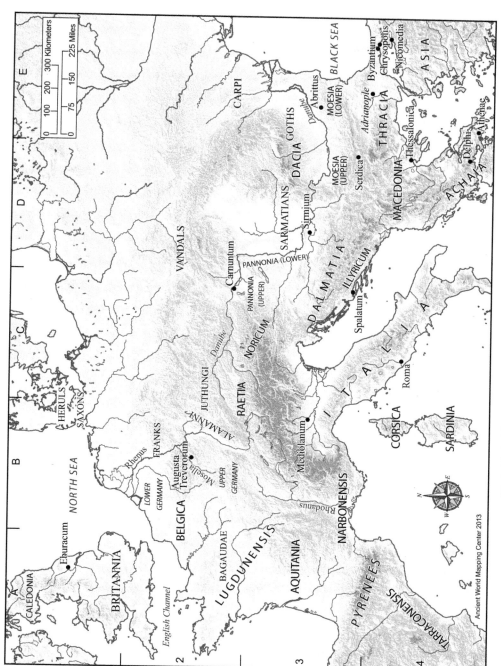

Map 12.1 *The Empire's North and West in the "Age of Crisis"*

Figure 12.1 *The Sasanian King of Kings Shapur I (242–272) took great pride in his many victories over Roman emperors. At Naqsh-i Rustam he described these in a detailed trilingual inscription, across from which he had this monumental relief carved in a cliff face. Here Shapur, seated atop his horse, lords it over two emperors, both shown in military capes (paludamenta) with laurel wreaths as marks of their office. Philip the Arab, who suffered a major defeat near what is today Fallujah (Iraq) and was forced into a humiliating peace, kneels in deference before the King of Kings, and the figure who stands with his upraised hands held by Shapur is almost certainly Valerian, whom Shapur claims in his inscription to have captured "with his own hand" in a battle of 260.*

Foreign invasions and pressure were not the only causes of Rome's political instability. The Principate had never evolved a clear system for the succession. Consequently, when a ruling emperor was assassinated or died on the battlefield—common enough occurrences in the mid-third century—more than one successor could be proclaimed simultaneously in the various provinces, and there was no impartial way to distinguish between claims. Moreover, third-century emperors began systematically excluding senators from military service, and the empire's lack of a professional bureaucracy may have compromised its ability to respond to the turmoil of the period.

The shameful capture of Valerian in 260 surely represented the nadir of Rome's political and military disarray. His son and co-emperor, Gallienus, did not attempt to avenge his father; he faced too many other invasions and revolts elsewhere in the empire. He let others take charge of the East and West unopposed, while he secured Italy, North Africa, Egypt, the Danubian provinces, and Greece. Septimius Odenaethus, a noble from the powerful oasis of Palmyra (modern Tudmur, Syria), received the unusual titles *dux* ("leader") and *corrector totius Orientis* ("overseer of the entire East") in recognition of his protection of the area between the Sasanians and Romans. On his death in 267, his widow Zenobia continued his rule in the name of their young son, Vaballathus, and remained unchallenged until the 270s. Under her leadership, Palmyrene control ultimately extended to Syria, Palestine, Arabia, Egypt, and much of Asia Minor. In the West, the former military commander Postumus controlled Gaul, Spain, Raetia, and Britain as a usurper. From at least 260 to 269, and without official recognition by Gallienus, Postumus collected taxes in these regions, coined money, levied soldiers, and protected the populace from incursions over the Rhine. He thus functioned as a sort of territorial emperor, but in rivalry rather than cooperation with the authority of the emperor in Rome.

In response to ongoing invasions, Gallienus made greater use of Rome's cavalry. This step marks the start of a gradual shift (that continued into the fourth century) to a twofold defensive system relying on a mobile field army and a more stationary frontier force. Gallienus suspended the Christian persecution begun by his father Valerian and attempted other reforms, but in 268 he was killed while trying to suppress a mutiny at Mediolanum (modern Milan, Italy).

Depopulation deepened the empire's problems. The scanty evidence for the mid-third century indicates a twenty-year plague in Italy and cities elsewhere. There were said to have been 5,000 deaths a day at Rome in 262, and two-thirds of the population of Alexandria supposedly perished. Local communities and their resources came under intense pressure. The established pattern of "beneficial ideology" that we have noted in Chapters Nine to Eleven slowed to the point that emperors began legally compelling municipal elites to maintain the services their cities had come to expect. Another manifestation of the instability of the period is the constant debasement of Rome's coinage. One modius of wheat (about 8.6 dry liters) cost two sesterces around A.D. 150 but 400 sesterces around A.D. 300; its nominal price thus increased two hundredfold in a century and a half. A different gauge of inflation can be measured in the debasement of the silver coinage, which sank from 90 percent purity under Nero to just 2 percent by the 260s. This third-century debasement reflects larger economic woes brought on by a perfect storm of problems resulting from a combination of internal and external insecurity; to combat it, ruinous government spending on a cumbersome military was unavoidable.

AURELIAN (270–275)

The emperor Aurelian, an Illyrian commander who was acclaimed by his troops and ruled from 270 to 275 , illustrates the times. His nickname, "Hand-on-Sword," emphasizes the military prowess that was the basis of his accomplishments.

His first step was to defeat northern invaders who had made their way into Italy. He then applied himself to regaining control over those parts of the empire, which had fallen from the dominion of the central state. Zenobia had profited from the assassination of Gallienus to expand Palmyra's control into Egypt and deep into Asia Minor. She had also begun to style herself "Augusta," and her young son Vaballath "Augustus," a clear sign of her growing power and ambitions. In two campaigns conducted in 272–273, Aurelian defeated her and restored all her territory to Roman rule. In 274 he likewise brought an end to what is sometimes called the "Gallic empire" by defeating the last successor of Postumus, who had himself been murdered in 268; as a result, Gaul and other parts of the West once again came under central control after fourteen years of local autonomy.

Aurelian tried to reform Rome's coinage after an eightfold rise in prices between 267 and 274. To tighten the emperor's control, he closed down local mints in the East and abolished the senatorial one at Rome. In their stead he introduced a number of new imperial mints that now struck coins that had a guaranteed silver content, low though it was. He also tried to extend his religious authority by encouraging a monotheism centered on the cult of *Sol Invictus* (the Unconquerable Sun). The god of the sun had long been worshipped, but became particularly popular in the third century. We have already seen that the emperor Elagabalus was a devoted believer in the Syrian version of this deity (See Chapter Eleven). Aurelian built an enormous temple in Rome to Sol Invictus, as well as establishing a new priestly college of Pontiffs and a series of games in honor of the Sun.

Two other steps taken by Aurelian are important. First, he abandoned the province of Dacia, regarding its exposed position north of the Danube as no longer tenable in the face of persistent onslaughts. Regardless of the practicality of this decision, it represented an open acknowledgment that Rome could no longer maintain control of all its territory. Second, in 271 Aurelian ordered a twelve-mile-long (20 km) brick wall to be built around the city of Rome. This was the most uniform set of defenses erected there since as long ago as the fourth century B.C., and the largest ever. The changed conditions to which it was a response seem a far cry from the confidence felt by Aelius Aristides only a century before Aurelian's time, when Aristides praised Rome for not having walls around the city itself—"as if you [Rome] were hiding or fleeing from your subjects"—but only at the edges of the empire (*To Rome* 80; see Chapter Eleven). Like many of his predecessors, Aurelian was killed by his own soldiers. His assassination in 275 ushered in ten more years of political and military strife that ended only in 284 with the acclamation of Diocletian. Apart from the feckless Gallienus, he was to be the first emperor in half a century who would maintain power for more than a few years.

DIOCLETIAN AND THE TETRARCHY (284–305)

Diocletian was a man with no dynastic claims to power. Indeed, the murky history of his early life would indicate that he was either a freedman or, more likely, the son of a freedman. What he lacked in pedigree, however, he made up for in talent and ambition. Like so many third-century emperors, he was born in Illyricum, probably in the Dalmatian town of Spalatum (modern Split, in Croatia). By the time he came to power he had served in several military units in the West and was acting as commander of the *protectores*, a new unit of imperial guardsmen who served at the emperor's side (most of the old Praetorians were now cocooned in Rome as a sort of glorified police force).

Within a year of his accession, Diocletian appointed a co-emperor with the title *Caesar* named Maximian. Diocletian knew well that the empire had grown too large for a single ruler, and Maximian was an old friend and fellow Balkan soldier whom he could trust. Indeed, Maximian, despite his impulsive character, would remain unswervingly faithful to Diocletian for the next twenty years, thus providing the key to the imperial stability that would distinguish Diocletian's reign. To further cement their relationship, the two emperors assumed parts of one another's official nomenclature. They also advertised themselves as "brothers" despite having no blood relationship. Above all, beginning in 287 they each adopted divine protectors in the traditional gods Jupiter/Jove (king of the gods) and Hercules (Jupiter's son, the archetypal strongman), and each began using the additional titles *Jovius* and *Herculius*. These names became ubiquitous—identifying military units and provinces and being featured on artwork and coins.

Immediately after his accession in late 285, Maximian was dispatched to Gaul to deal with an uprising of the Bagaudae, rural insurgents under local, indigenous leadership. His successes there induced Diocletian to promote him to full Augustus in April 286, making the two equals in rank, even if Diocletian remained the dominant ruler. Later that same year Carausius, one of Maximian's commanders, launched a revolt with the North Sea fleet and occupied Britain and northern Gaul. Maximian would struggle with this revolt for the next seven years. Meanwhile, in 285 Diocletian had been able to return eastward to campaign against the Sarmatians—an Indo-Iranian people who inhabited the territory north of the lower Danube—and, in 287, to appoint a new king for Armenia. The following year he returned to the West, where he and Maximian executed a brilliant pincer movement against tribes in Germany. By 290 he was back on the eastern frontier fighting yet another enemy new to Rome, the Saracens. These were Bedouin Arabs who would come to play an increasingly important role along the desert edge of Syria and Palestine.

Diocletian soon realized that even two emperors were not enough to handle Rome's military situation, so he made the decision to expand the leadership to four. On March 1, 293, he appointed a partner named Galerius to support him in the East, and Maximian appointed Constantius in the West. These new partners—both fellow Illyrians—were given the title Caesar rather than Augustus, indicating their subordination to their more senior colleagues, and both also assumed parts of their colleagues' nomenclature. In addition, each was linked by marriage to his respective Augustus: Galerius married Diocletian's daughter Valeria, and Constantius married Theodora, the step-daughter of Maximian, under whom he had already been serving as a general (see Table 13.1).

This four-man system of rulership, which scholars since the nineteenth century have termed the "tetrarchy," has often been characterized as a carefully crafted system of joint rule with two senior emperors exercising authority over two juniors, who were intended to replace them after a period of service (Fig. 12.2). However, the level of forward planning and systematization involved has been questioned. It seems most likely that some degree of conscious planning was indeed present to promote merit and symmetry over the traditional randomness imposed by the old dynastic principle, but traditional elements of dynasty—like intermarriage—were certainly exploited too.

As we might imagine, this system of four-man rule produced dramatic results. Between 293 and 296, Constantius was able to suppress the Gallic insurrection

Figure 12.2 *This group portrait of the four tetrarchs (ca. 300) was originally mounted on a column in Constantinople. In the foreground, the senior Augustus is bearded, and grasps his Caesar with his right arm. Otherwise Augustus and Caesar are identical to each other and to their mirror images, the other two tetrarchs. All four wear the identical military cloak (paludamentum) fastened at the right shoulder; abrasion suggests that a metal brooch or a stone of a different color was fixed here originally. Each man's breastplate is held in place by an elaborate military belt. Each also carries an eagle-headed sword in a rich scabbard, and wears a Pannonian cap, the front of which was originally ornamented with a jewel or stone in its center. In rendering all the tetrarchs alike and positioning them so closely together, this group portrait embodies the unanimity that the four men were resolved to uphold. Their furrowed brows indicate their concern for the empire. But at the same time their elevation above their subjects is conveyed by the gems they wear, as well as by the use of porphyry—a rare, hard, reddish-purple stone reserved by this time exclusively for emperors and their families. During the Middle Ages, this statue was taken from Constantinople to Venice, where it now stands at the southwest corner of St. Mark's Basilica.*

initiated by Carausius and regain control of northern Gaul and Britain. Maximian, meanwhile, passed through Spain and across to Mauretania in North Africa in 297 in order to defeat a dangerous tribal group known as the Quinquegentiani. He then retired to Milan, where he remained while relying on Constantius to continue the defense of the northwestern frontier. In the East, Diocletian remained in Sirmium (modern Sremska Mitrovica, Serbia) near the Danube, while Galerius was sent to the eastern frontier to guard against the new Sasanian King of Kings, Narses. In 296, Narses invaded Armenia, provoking Galerius into a hastily prepared campaign during which the Romans, like Crassus' army long before (see Chapter Seven), were defeated near Carrhae (modern Altınbaşak Turkey) in early 297. Galerius then gathered a new force and surprised Narses by marching into Armenia that same fall. Narses fled, and Galerius captured his baggage train and extensive harem before continuing into Persia and taking its capital Ctesiphon (near modern Baghdad, Iraq) early in 298. Narses was forced into a humiliating peace, which required him to surrender control of northern Mesopotamia in its entirety as well as much of southern Armenia.

Thus Galerius' campaign not only won back for Rome the whole area sacrificed to Persia in the wars of the mid-third century, but it also gained new territory. The tetrarchy had clearly worked, proving itself a system that was at once tightly knit and flexible, with the capacity to respond effectively against all military threats, external and internal. As the tetrarchs would soon learn, however, there remained the problem that, in the absence of a strong leader like Diocletian, old habits of dynasticism and infighting would quickly reappear and once again prevail over the elegant, but also sterile, symmetry that he had imposed.

The one major misstep Diocletian can be said to have taken was a series of persecutions against minority religious groups, and especially the Christians, after he had been ruling for almost twenty years. Since 260 the Christians had largely been left in peace by the imperial administration. A whole generation had grown up in relative calm; the emperor Aurelian had even allowed himself to become involved in settling internal disputes among the Christian clergy. Diocletian, however, was extremely conservative as a religious leader and had little tolerance for this distinctive new cult. As a religion that began in the first century A.D.—and with the public execution of a criminal, its critics argued—Christianity was considered innovative and revolutionary. Diocletian had already expelled Christian soldiers from the army in 299, but a series of failed sacrifices followed by a mysterious fire at his palace in Nicomedia (modern İzmit, Turkey) drove his rage to new heights. On February 23, 303, he ordered his soldiers to destroy the sizeable Christian church of Nicomedia, and on the following day he issued an edict ordering churches across the empire to be pulled down and scriptures confiscated and destroyed. Later in 303 he issued a second edict ordering the arrest of Christian clergy, who could be freed only if they demonstrated their apostasy by offering sacrifice. Two further edicts followed in 304, ordering that all the empire's subjects demonstrate their loyalty by sacrificing in public.

This series of laws and their enactment constitute what modern scholars refer to as the "Great Persecution." The heavier hand of Diocletian's government allowed him to enforce his wishes with more systematic pressure than in any previous state persecution (see Chapter Eleven). While the two western tetrarchs, and particularly Constantius, seem to have enforced the decree only very haltingly, in the East Diocletian demonstrated that the same brutality he had used to pacify the barbarians could also be deployed against Christians. Although the Great Persecution did not stamp out Christianity, it did leave its mark in the form of a heightened Christian ideology of resistance and martyrdom. It also provoked considerable infighting among Christians over their various reactions to the pressure of this attack, including outright apostasy. The rifts caused by such strife were to send shockwaves through the Christian church for the next century and more.

DISSOLUTION OF THE TETRARCHY (305–313) AND THE RISE OF CONSTANTINE (306–324)

Increasingly ill, Diocletian abdicated the throne—the first Roman emperor to do so—and retired in 305 to a palace he had constructed earlier at Split. During the twenty-one years of his rule, he had established what could have seemed a reliable new means of regulating the succession. His abdication presumed that his own Caesar, Galerius, would move up to become Augustus in the East. At the same time he forced retirement upon Maximian, his fellow Augustus in the West, elevating Maximian's Caesar, Constantius, to Augustus there. To Galerius and Constantius were now subordinated new Caesars in the persons of fellow Illyrian soldiers of a younger generation: Maximin Daia for the East, and Severus for the West. Both these men were friends of Galerius, and Maximin Daia was actually his nephew, an indication that family and influence played a role in their selection.

The whiff of patronage and dynasticism behind these appointments no doubt contributed to the almost immediate disintegration of this plan. Maximian's son, Maxentius, had been ignored in the deliberations despite his ambitions to rule. Constantius' son, Constantine, who had once been marked as an imperial favorite, had also been overlooked. The ambitions of both were fed by their knowledge that the empire's subjects, and above all its soldiers, retained a strong preference for dynasty. In 305, an aging Constantius summoned his son, Constantine, then at Galerius' court, to help him fight the Picts in Scotland. When Constantius fell ill and died at Eburacum (modern York, England) in July 306, the troops there promoted Constantine to replace his father. Galerius, the sole remaining Augustus in the tetrarchic system, perceived this seizure of power as a threat to his authority but was forced to sanction Constantine's appointment because he was too far away in the East to challenge it. Constantine was thus able to assume command of his father's troops and during the next few years to use them successfully in the Rhine borderlands.

In no small part as a response to Constantine's appointment, Maxentius himself convinced the Praetorian Guard in Rome to appoint him emperor in October 306. Unlike Constantine, however, he never won recognition from the tetrarchy, which instead sent Severus and in turn Galerius to attack him in 307 and 308 respectively. In both instances Maxentius managed to ward off his foes by remaining behind the city-walls constructed by Aurelian, and he even succeeded in capturing and killing Severus. In November 308 Galerius tried to shore up the faltering tetrarchy by calling a conference at Carnuntum in Upper Pannonia (modern Petronell, Austria). Here Diocletian emerged from retirement briefly to orchestrate a compromise settlement: this reaffirmed Galerius as supreme Augustus and Maximin Daia as his Caesar in the East, but also promoted Galerius' friend, Licinius, to the rank of Augustus to rule alongside Constantine in the West. Maxentius was excluded from these arrangements, which assumed his elimination.

Throughout this period Constantine generally restricted his movements to Gaul, campaigning against the Franks and Alamanni on the Rhine in 309 and 310. Nevertheless, his larger ambitions are indicated by an anonymous speech of praise delivered in 310, which claims that in a vision he saw the gods Apollo and Victory, each of them predicting triumphs and long rule for him. At this time, too, his coins begin to display Sol Invictus, the Unconquerable Sun, Aurelian's favorite deity, suggesting a conscious shift away from the tetrarchic system and its promotion of Jupiter and Hercules (see Fig. 13.3a). Meanwhile Constantine—and indeed Maxentius—had also abandoned Diocletian's religious policy by calling an official halt to the persecution of Christians in the West. This shift was in sharp contrast to the situation in the East, where Galerius and Maximin Daia had revived the persecutions with a vengeance. Only in 311 did Galerius finally come to see that his efforts had failed. Shortly before his death that same year, he issued an Edict of Toleration that revoked the ban on Christian worship and grudgingly granted Christians the right to meet (Source 12.1).

Galerius' death in May 311 could only unsettle whatever stability had been achieved. Rifts opened instantly between Licinius and Maximin Daia over control of Galerius' former territory in Thrace, Greece, and Asia Minor. In summer 311, the two agreed that the Bosporus should divide their realms. Meantime, Constantine concentrated his efforts on eliminating Maxentius, whom he denounced as a "tyrant." In summer 312 he first defeated Maxentius' forces in northern Italy, and then proceeded down the peninsula. For the decisive battle near Rome in October, Maxentius unwisely ventured forth from the protection of the city walls to face Constantine's superior forces. When he attempted to recross the Tiber back into the city after his defeat, he was caught by a booby trap he himself had set on the Milvian Bridge, and drowned in the river along with many of his men. The next day Constantine swept into the city with Maxentius' head on a pike. One of his first measures was to disband forever Rome's Praetorian Guard, whose support had been so vital to Maxentius. These men Constantine replaced with a new special force named the *scholarii* ("staff guards"), who—together with the *protectores*, once commanded by Diocletian himself—accompanied the emperor wherever he went.

Constantine's victory over Maxentius at the battle of the Milvian Bridge has been glorified by Christian historians of the time as the pivotal episode leading to his acceptance of Christianity. Before the battle, we are told, he received an omen

SOURCE 12.1: *Galerius' "Edict of Toleration," issued in April 311, survives in two sources, one Latin (translated here), the other Greek. Although the two are independent, both reproduce the same text with only slight variation. This match attests to the widespread dissemination of the edict made possible by the new tetrarchic bureaucracy.*

Among all the other arrangements which we are always making for the advantage and benefit of the state, we had earlier sought to set everything right in accordance with the ancient laws and public discipline of the Romans, and to ensure that the Christians, too, who had abandoned their ancestors' way of life, should return to a sound frame of mind. For in some way such willfulness had overcome these same Christians, such folly had taken hold of them, that they no longer followed those practices of the ancients which their own ancestors perhaps had first instituted; but simply following their own judgment and pleasure, they were making up for themselves the laws which they were to observe, and were gathering various groups of people together in different places. When finally our order was published that they should devote themselves to the practices of the ancients, many were subjected to danger, many too were struck down. Very many, however, persisted in their determination, and we saw that these same people were neither offering worship and due religious observance to the gods, nor practicing the worship of the god of the Christians. Bearing in mind, therefore, our own most gentle clemency and our perpetual habit of showing lenient pardon to all, we have taken the view that in the case of these people too we should extend our speediest leniency, so that once more they may be Christians and restore their meeting places, provided they do nothing to disturb good order. . . . Consequently, in accordance with this leniency of ours, it will be their duty to pray to their god for our safety and for that of the state and themselves, so that from every side the state may be kept unharmed, and they may be able to live free of worries in their own homes. (Translation based on J. L. Creed, *Lactantius, De Mortibus Persecutorum* [34], Oxford: Oxford University Press, 1984)

of his coming victory. There are two different accounts of its nature—either a dream or an apparition in the sky—but both agree that it was understood as coming from the Christian god. Constantine allegedly saw a cross in the heavens, and heard the militant encouraging words, "Conquer in this sign." Modern scholars, too, are divided over the nature of this vision, although most agree that Constantine's conversion was more of a process, perhaps extending back to his vision of Apollo in 310, rather than a single event. Our sources do agree that in 312 Constantine entered battle after having his men decorate their shields with an emblem resembling a Christogram (✻). This symbol creates a monogram of chi [χ] and rho [ρ], the first two letters of the name "Christ" in Greek (compare Fig. 13.3b). The victory Constantine won outside Rome, and his subsequent successes under the same emblem, persuaded him of the power of the Christian god.

The military and political realities were less straightforward, as reflected in deliberate official vagueness about just what "divinity" had inspired Constantine. Thus, on the arch dedicated to him by the senate and people of Rome in 315 (see Fig. 13.1), the inscription opaquely proclaims that he triumphed over the "tyrant" and all his "faction" by "divine stimulus and greatness of mind." Moreover, although the Christogram features prominently in Christian sources, it rarely appears on official media (coins, art, and inscriptions) before the mid-320s. It is certainly true that already in late 312 Constantine began granting extensive favors to Christians, but outside the Christian community he gave only vague hints of his new religion and often muddled these with continuing nods to his favorite pagan deity, the Sun God.

Although it must have been clear by 312 that the tetrarchy was irretrievably broken, there were still two other claimants to power along with Constantine. He now held Italy, North Africa, and the West; Licinius held Illyricum and the rest of the Balkans; and Maximin Daia held the East. In 313, Constantine and Licinius met at Mediolanum to settle an alliance that included a joint decree—known today as the Edict of Milan—which proclaimed freedom of religious expression and ordered the return of confiscated properties to the Christian church. Meanwhile Maximin Daia had resumed the persecution of Christians in his eastern territories despite Galerius' Edict of Toleration. So Constantine and Licinius had cause to ally against him, and when Maximin attempted an invasion of Licinius' territories, he was roundly defeated in a battle at Adrianople (modern Edirne, Turkey). Thus, by the end of 313, Constantine and Licinius were the only leaders remaining who claimed supreme command. Accordingly, they now divided the empire between them, with Constantine ruling the West and Licinius the East.

The dual rule of Constantine and Licinius as Augusti was to last eleven years (to 324), but it was not a harmonious partnership. The two quarreled repeatedly and even faced one another in open battle in 316. Constantine proved the winner and took the opportunity to expand his territory as far east as the borders of Thrace. Their estrangement widened when Licinius resumed the persecution of Christians in the East around 320. By this time Constantine was expressing his Christianity more openly and had begun to portray himself as a champion of believers—a stance that also provided excellent cover for his political ambitions. When Constantine entered Licinius' territory in 323 to counter an invasion by the Goths, Licinius declared war. In 324 he was defeated in a series of battles culminating at the city of Chrysopolis (modern Üsküdar, Turkey). With Licinius eliminated in this way, Rome's forty years of organized experiments in shared rule were abandoned. Constantine now had sole control of a unified empire.

ADMINISTRATIVE REORGANIZATION UNDER THE DOMINATE

Scholars refer to the period beginning with Diocletian's reign as the "Dominate," a designation, which distinguishes it from the "Principate" established by Augustus. The term is modern, but it traces to Diocletian's use of the designation *dominus* ("lord," or even "master") to reinforce his claims to authority. Such claims filtered

Map 12.2 *Roman Empire of Diocletian and Constantine*

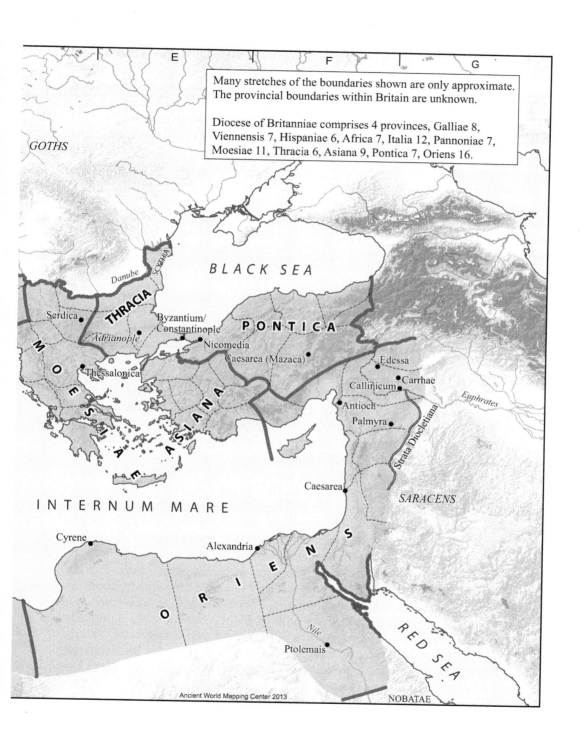

E   F   G

Many stretches of the boundaries shown are only approximate.
The provincial boundaries within Britain are unknown.

Diocese of Britanniae comprises 4 provinces, Galliae 8,
Viennensis 7, Hispaniae 6, Africa 7, Italia 12, Pannoniae 7,
Moesiae 11, Thracia 6, Asiana 9, Pontica 7, Oriens 16.

GOTHS

BLACK SEA

Danube

SCYTHIA

THRACIA

Serdica

Byzantium/
Constantinople

PONTICA

Adrianople

Nicomedia

Caesarea (Mazaca)

Edessa

M O E S I A E

Thessalonica

Callinicum   Carrhae

A S I A N A

Antioch

Euphrates

Palmyra

Strata Diocletiana

INTERNUM MARE

Caesarea

SARACENS

Cyrene

Alexandria

O R I E N S

Ptolemais

Nile

RED SEA

Ancient World Mapping Center 2013

NOBATAE

throughout the central government in ways that show a much stronger desire and ambition on the part of this late Roman ruler and his successors to govern actively. This development was made possible in no small part by Diocletian's increase in the size of the imperial college to four active members. The period also witnessed a change in imperial manners. Numerous sources note that the emperor placed himself above his subjects and began wearing more grandiose trappings such as a purple mantle, a crown, and shoes studded with gems. His subjects were now forced to prostrate themselves in his presence and kiss the hem of his cloak; his court was forced always to stand in his presence, hence its designation as the *consistorium* ("standing room council") rather than the *consilium* ("advisory council") familiar from the Principate. The emperor's appearance also took on a new look, with hair cropped and beard short in the fashion of a soldier. Indeed, the entire court assumed a more military air under these soldier emperors, so much so that even civilian bureaucrats now referred to their offices as *militia* (akin to our word "service," with its double connotations).

With his concern for system and order, Diocletian undertook a number of major reforms in the apparatus of government and the organization of the empire that would essentially lay the foundations for the remainder of its history in the West. The changes he introduced were generally adopted and often elaborated upon by Constantine. In taking stock of them, we should keep in mind that what follows describes developments begun in the 290s but fully realized only over a span of fifty years. Overall, the changes were characterized by an increase in the size of the government, an increase in hierarchy and professionalization, and an increased differentiation between military and civilian functions.

As to size, it has been estimated that the late Roman bureaucracy grew to the point that there were around 30,000 to 35,000 bureaucrats on the imperial payroll, as opposed to the few hundred senatorial and equestrian officials and about 10,000 slaves who administered it in the first century A.D. This increase necessarily demanded a growth in bureaucratic hierarchies, a fact that can be confirmed in the elaborate lists of offices cataloged in the early-fifth-century *Notitia Dignitatum* (see Plate 8). The growth was fueled from the bottom up: most of the new bureaucrats, even those in lofty positions, were not senators but equestrians or even decurions.

One key change occurred in the organization of the imperial court. The late empire's very mobile officials were often referred to as the *comitatus* (retinue) because they traveled in the emperor's company. They consisted of six or more chief officials, many new to the period, each with staffs numbering in the hundreds. Even the traditional offices were significantly restructured. Praetorian Prefects, for example, underwent considerable transformation first under the tetrarchs, who granted them even greater judicial powers, and then especially under Constantine, who stripped them of all military authority and made provisioning the army their primary responsibility. These changes removed the threat that Praetorian Prefects once posed to the emperor's own security and allowed them to act as a check on the ambitions of potentially rebellious generals. By the end of his reign Constantine had also increased the number of Praetorian Prefects from two under the tetrarchs (one for each Augustus) to five, one for each major region of the empire.

The introduction of regional Praetorian Prefectures was made possible by changes to the organization of the provinces that were also initiated by Diocletian (see Map 12.2). First, he divided the fifty or so provinces existing at the beginning of his reign into over one hundred smaller ones. These he put under the charge of governors called *praesides*, whom he also stripped of military power. Later, probably in 313/314, Constantine and Licinius regrouped the newly divided provinces into larger units termed "dioceses" (originally twelve in number). Each diocese was placed under the charge of a new official termed a Vicar (literally "substitute," i.e., for the Praetorian Prefect), whose job it was to ensure the smooth collection of taxes levied in kind. For the first time since the second century B.C., Italy itself was incorporated into the provincial system and forced to pay taxes. Only Rome was left out of the system, for it had its own Urban Prefect who was answerable directly to the emperor. In many ways the change here reflected the reality that, by this date, neither Italy nor even Rome was the center of the empire any longer. The tetrarchs only rarely visited Rome, and the very isolation that shielded the Italian peninsula from invasions also made it unimportant strategically to a new kind of emperor focused primarily on the frontiers. Instead, the tetrarchs introduced the policy of reconstructing the major cities in the provinces frequented by them into "capitals" with elaborate palaces, hippodromes, baths, and even mausolea. Thus Augusta Treverorum (modern Trier, Germany) in Gaul, Sirmium and Thessalonica in the Balkans, and Nicomedia and Antioch in the East were all rebuilt to accommodate the tetrarchs (compare Fig. 12.3).

The Dominate also saw tremendous changes to the army. Just as he did with the provinces, Diocletian carved the old-fashioned legion into much smaller units, averaging around 1,000 men. These were easier to mobilize and better able to respond to the multiple crises so characteristic of the period. Though the units shrank in size, the total size of the army grew to an effective strength of about 600,000 soldiers, perhaps double the size of the first-century army. Because provincial governors no longer controlled troops, a new class of regional generals was invented called *duces* ("dukes") and *comites* ("counts"). These leaders were better equipped to deal with the heightened insecurity of the period because they regularly held authority over territory stretching across multiple provinces, now grouped as security districts.

Diocletian continued the trend initiated by Gallienus of developing units of soldiers not bound to a particular territory—that is, a mobile field army. Nevertheless, it was Constantine who went further by introducing large bodies of *comitatenses* ("retine troops") that followed the emperor or his generals wherever they went. By the mid-fourth century we hear of comitatensian armies numbering upwards of 60,000 men who traveled with the emperor as a massive expeditionary force. To lead them Constantine also developed a new supreme commander called the *magister militum* ("Master of the Soldiers"), who often had his own field army in addition to that of the emperor. These comitatensian troops came to be

Figure 12.3 *The tetrarchic Villa Romuliana. Excavations conducted since the 1950s at modern Gamzigrad, Serbia, have revealed a massive fortified villa complex identified as the luxury palace of the emperor Galerius (293–311). The villa was surrounded by walls outfitted with round towers, and it contained a palace with many rooms, two temples, and two large meeting halls. An inscription and a text attest that Galerius built this villa in honor of his mother Romula; both were buried in twin mausolea found outside the walled perimeter. This style of fortified villa became popular across the empire in the period. Diocletian himself built a similar palace on an even grander scale and retired there after his abdication in 305. Located on the coast of Dalmatia, its walls—which still stand—formed the basis for the construction of the medieval town of Split in modern Croatia.*

distinguished from so-called *limitanei* ("border troops")—generally considered second-class soldiers—who guarded the edges of the empire from stationary emplacements. The limitanei tended to be based in a new type of fortification much smaller in scale, but more abundant in number, than the old legionary fortresses. Diocletian constructed these in great numbers along the river and desert frontiers. His most famous series of such installations was used to fortify a strategic roadway, the Strata Diocletiana, located at the edge of the empire's eastern desert and stretching from Azraq in modern Jordan north to the Euphrates River (see Map 12.2).

Finally, Diocletian also undertook sweeping fiscal and economic measures. By the time he came to power, the empire effectively had no silver coinage, for the old denarius had been reduced to an extremely debased bronze coin. Ever the traditionalist, Diocletian tackled the problem by reintroducing a monetary system that looked very much like that of the Julio-Claudian emperors, with gold, silver, and bronze. Even so, problems with inflation continued, and in an effort to curb this he issued his famous Edict on Maximum Prices in 301. It dictated in minute detail price levels for over a thousand goods and services, and threatened those who overcharged with dire penalties. As might be expected, however, even Diocletian's outsized bureaucracy was in no position to dictate the laws of the marketplace, and the Prices Edict soon failed and was repealed. It fell to Constantine to stabilize the economy further, which he did by introducing a new gold standard.

The currency crisis of the mid-third century had led to a much heavier reliance on taxes paid in kind. The single biggest fiscal expense was always army pay, and because the coinage had inflated so wildly, it made sense to collect taxes in grain, which was then distributed directly to the soldiery. Diocletian preserved this practice but also rationalized it by introducing a new form of tax collection called the *iugatio vel capitatio* ("acreage or headcount"). Where the old system had attempted to collect a percentage of each year's produce, Diocletian's new plan collected fixed amounts based either on the total acreage owned by a taxpayer or on the total number of producers in his household, or both. This rationalized system permitted the government to predict annual revenues more accurately and thus to undertake some sort of advance budgeting. It also led to a much stronger desire on the part of the state to oblige people to remain on the land where they were registered. So Diocletian's new fiscal system contributed to the process whereby tenant farmers (*coloni* in Latin) were eventually "bound" to the land on which they were born, a precursor of medieval serfdom.

For all of his conservatism, Diocletian was thus an innovator on the grand scale. He reinvented the face of government, giving it a more magisterial appearance and feel. He greatly increased the size and complexity of the bureaucracy, and thereby extended the reach of government into the lives of the empire's citizens. He rearranged imperial offices by increasing their responsibilities and separating civilian and military functions. He reorganized the provinces into smaller units, which were subsequently tied to intermediate jurisdictions with the creation of the diocesan system. He also shrank the size of military units but enlarged the army and its command structure. Moreover, he undertook major economic and fiscal reforms that improved the collection of taxes, and he began the process of stabilizing the coinage. These administrative measures made an excellent fit with the new tetrarchic system of government that he devised. By increasing the number of emperors to four, Diocletian was finally able to gain the upper hand in the border crises that had threatened Roman security, as well as in the civil wars that had so weakened the empire during the third century. This stabilization, internal and external, was perhaps his single greatest achievement, because it furnished the empire with a renewed solidity that ensured prosperity for another century to come. Even so, Diocletian's providence as a military leader and administrator was not matched by equal foresight in the realm of religion. By the time the tetrarchy had completely dissolved in 324, the Christian religion that he was so eager to suppress had taken the lead. It is to the credit of his successor, Constantine, that this new religious wave could be absorbed into the powerful state that Diocletian had engineered.

SUGGESTED READINGS

Brown, Peter. 1971. *The World of Late Antiquity from Marcus Aurelius to Muhammad*. London: Thames and Hudson. Classic introduction to the period, emphasizing the cultural transformation that moved society from Antiquity to the Middle Ages.

Dodgeon, Michael H., and Samuel N. C. Lieu. 1991. *The Roman Eastern Frontier and the Persian Wars (AD 226–363)*. London and New York: Routledge. A history of Rome's wars with Persia told through the sources.

Mitchell, Stephen. 2007. *A History of the Later Roman Empire: A.D. 284–641*. Malden, Mass., and Oxford: Blackwell. Comprehensive survey of institutional history with an emphasis on the East.

Potter, David S. 2004. *The Roman Empire at Bay: A.D. 180–395*. London and New York: Routledge. Excellent survey of political and military history.

Rees, Roger. 2004. *Diocletian and the Tetrarchy*. Edinburgh: Edinburgh University Press. Concise discussion of key themes, followed by extracts from sources in translation.

13

THE RISE OF CHRISTIANITY
AND THE GROWTH OF
THE BARBARIAN THREAT
(324–395)

CONSTANTINE: A CHRISTIAN EMPEROR

After gaining sole control of the empire in 324, Constantine modified his style of rule in measurable ways. Up to this point he had given at least nominal consent to the system of shared rule initiated by the tetrarchs, but he had never found it satisfactory since it ignored the long-standing tradition of dynastic succession in favor of a system of power transfers that remained too schematic. As a remedy, Constantine took what was good about the tetrarchy, its principle of shared rule, and grafted it onto the stronger stock of the family tree. In so doing, he devised a hybrid system that would prevail for the rest of the century. Already in early 317 he had proclaimed his two sons Crispus and Constantine II Caesars, in step with Licinius, who did the same with his own son Licinius II (Table 13.1). These promotions resulted in a system of five-man rule with two senior and three junior emperors that mimicked the tetrarchy. With the elimination of Licinius in 324, Constantine promoted his third son, Constantius II, to Caesar and, in 333, his fourth son, Constans. Dynasty was thus used to backstop shared rule, providing the advantage of imperial birth to legitimize anticipated successors, as well as the benefit of family ties to reduce the chances for discord—at least in theory.

Even before his conversion, Constantine projected the image of heavenly rulership, and afterward he modified it only slightly with claims to be the Christian god's representative on earth (Fig. 13.1). This is a role that he had begun to play already in 313 when he granted special exemptions from mandatory government service to Christian clergy and offered Christian churches a share in imperial revenue. Jointly with Licinius he issued the "Edict of Milan," guaranteeing a final end to persecutions in this same year. The "Great Persecution" had been so

Figure 13.1 *South side of the Arch of Constantine. This enormous edifice was built along Rome's triumphal route by the senate and people soon after Constantine's victory over Maxentius in 312 (see Chapter Twelve). It represents the beginning of a trend toward the strategic reuse of earlier material (sometimes called* spolia) *in new monuments in late antiquity. For example, the bearded statues above the columns were taken from Trajan's Forum, and the round reliefs over the side-arches are from a monument of Hadrian's time. The narrow, horizontal reliefs running below the roundels, by contrast, were commissioned under Constantine and represent his battles with Maxentius and his triumphal entry into Rome.*

thoroughgoing in certain parts of the empire that it had opened sizeable rifts in the church itself. In North Africa the persecutions had been particularly harsh and had led some Christians, even those in positions of authority, to lapse from the faith. After the attacks had ceased in 306, those Christians who had remained rigorous in their defense of the faith argued that they should be considered the new leaders of the church, thus driving a wedge between themselves and the more lenient establishment. These Donatists, as they were called, appealed for aid to Constantine, who organized church councils at Rome in 313 and at Arelate (modern Arles, France) in 314 to resolve the controversy. Although both found in favor of the establishment church, the Donatists continued to assert their authority into the mid-fifth century, creating an ongoing rift in church leadership.

Constantine was also pulled directly into ecclesiastical politics in the eastern empire after he gained control there in 324. A priest in Alexandria named Arius had hypothesized that Christ, though truly the son of God the Father, had been created by the Father and was inferior to him in status. Although Arius won many supporters, his superior Alexander, bishop of Alexandria, regarded his theory as rank heresy. The situation grew so heated that in May 325 Constantine had to organize a council at Nicaea (modern İznik, Turkey)—the first "ecumenical," or world, council of the church—at which he essentially dictated that Christ was indeed "one in being with the Father" (in Greek *homoousios*). This wording, part of the Nicene Creed formulated at the council, continues to be repeated in Christian churches today. Here again, however, Constantine's arbitration did little more than fuel further controversy, which lasted down to 381 at least and perhaps even into the sixth century. Meanwhile, Constantine also favored the church in other ways that will be discussed below. To mention just one here, he legislated that Sunday should become an official day of rest each week, another change with repercussions enduring up to the present.

From at least the mid-nineteenth century, and arguably stretching back to antiquity, people have questioned the sincerity of Constantine's conversion. There are good reasons for this doubt. At times Constantine appears downright pagan in his self-presentation, as when he was portrayed side by side with the Sun God on coins and medallions. He is known to have worshipped this deity prior to his conversion, and it was even claimed that he had witnessed an epiphany from the Sun God in 310 (see Chapter Twelve). The same deity appears on his coinage down to 325 with the legend SOLI INVICTO COMITI ("To his Companion the Unconquerable Sun"; Figs. 13.2 and 13.3a). Such a choice of wording might be excused as an appeal to his non-Christian subjects in the period prior to the elimination of Licinius, were it not for the fact that Constantine erected a statue of himself portrayed as that same Sun God on a massive porphyry column in his new capital of Constantinople, dedicated in 330 (see Map 14.2). Indeed, as late as 337 he permitted an imperial cult temple to be built to his family at the Italian city of Hispellum (modern Spello), provided there be no blood sacrifice performed there. While some historians have seen in this ambiguity a crypto-paganism or, worse yet, a cynical willingness to play all sides to his advantage, it seems fairer to say that

Figure 13.2 Immediately after experiencing a vision of the sun-god Apollo-Sol in 310, Constantine began minting images of this deity on his coinage. The most striking example is this gold medallion, which features Constantine's head beside that of the deity, to whom he bears a striking resemblance. The emperor's shield shows the sun god riding his chariot into the heavens. Compare Figure 13.3a.

Constantine was striving to discover what it meant to be the first Christian emperor in a period when it was not yet clear where the lines between old and new religious traditions should be drawn.

Nevertheless, the significance of Constantine's conversion to Christianity is hard to deny in the light of his own statements about his faith, preserved in great abundance, and also by the monumental church-building program he initiated across the empire. This program is most evident in the two cities of Rome and Jerusalem. Probably already in November 312, Constantine began construction in Rome of a massive new purpose-built "basilica," a word formerly used of royal audience halls that now came to designate large churches. Constructed inside Rome's walls on a property called the Lateran, this basilica was meant to serve as the seat of Rome's bishop, the Pope, a role it still plays today. Constantine also founded some nine other churches, most designed to mark the burial sites of martyrs (*martyria*) outside Rome's walls. Among the nine was a church of St. Peter on the far side of the Tiber at the Vatican Hill, a site that came to serve as the Pope's residence in the Middle Ages. Constantine thus established the architecture of Christian Rome, and as such helped bridge the gap between Antiquity and the Middle Ages, for it was as a Christian capital that the city of Rome survived the fall of the empire.

A similar story can be told in the East. Following Titus' sack of Jerusalem in 70, the city had become something of a backwater, but shortly after gaining control of the East, Constantine initiated a project to reestablish its religious identity along Christian lines. Churches were built at the reputed site of Christ's nativity in Bethlehem, and on what was believed to be the site of Christ's tomb, the Church of the Holy Sepulcher (see Plate 6b). Not least because of these new churches, Jerusalem became a destination favored by Christian pilgrims, who began to travel there in substantial numbers already in the 330s, and still do so today.

In other respects, too, the empire's balance was being tilted eastward by Constantine. No single act of his had a greater impact in this respect than his establishment of a new capital on the Bosporus at the site of the city formerly known as Byzantium (see Map 12.2). His new city, dedicated under the name Constantinople in 330, was designed for a population of about 80,000 and was provided with baths, an imperial forum, and a massive palace connected to an extended hippodrome for chariot-racing (Fig. 13.4). The city was established quite consciously as a "Second Rome" with fourteen districts, its own subsidized grain supply, and above all a new senate. Constantine embellished his city with famous marble and bronze statues taken from around the eastern empire—many of them former cult statues, which he then erected in secular contexts. He also confiscated gold and silver cult statues, but rather than rededicate these, he simply melted them down into bullion and reminted them as coinage. This measure served the dual purpose of diminishing the power and wealth of the traditional cults and increasing his money supply.

Upon his death in 337, Constantine left a prosperous empire to his heirs. After a thirty-one-year reign, the longest since Augustus, he had placed the empire on a firm footing and had established his own dynasty solidly enough that it would endure for the next twenty-six years. Already in the final years of his rule, however, there were signs of troubles to come. In 332 he faced a threat from the Goths (Map 13.1). In the last years of his reign the Sasanian Persians began persecuting Christians in their empire, and eventually they invaded the territory of Armenia, long a bone of contention between the two superpowers. Both Goths and Persians would inflict major defeats on the Romans in the decades to come. Thus, when Constantine set off to battle the Persians in 337, he was about to spark a conflict that would endure for the next half-century. Even so, he did not progress far before succumbing to illness on May 22 near Nicomedia. Shortly before dying, he was baptized a Christian. Few other Roman emperors had a more lasting impact on the course of world history. With his conversion to Christianity, his foundation of a new capital and senate, his establishment of the Holy Land as a site of Christian pilgrimage, and his construction of a Christian Rome, Constantine opened the way to a new epoch. Like Augustus, he was a truly revolutionary figure.

THE SONS OF CONSTANTINE (337–361): THE POWER OF DYNASTY

When Constantine died, his dynasty should have been on a sound footing. He had left three sons, previously appointed Caesars, to resume the tradition of joint rule that he had preserved from the tetrarchy. Constantine II, the eldest, was to rule Gaul, Spain, and Britain; Constans, the youngest, held Italy, Africa, and the Balkans; and Constantius II, the middle son, took Asia Minor and the East. But Constantine's growing taste for the grandiose at the end of his life had led him to appoint two further co-rulers, his nephews Dalmatius and Hannibalianus. In the summer of 337 Constantius had these nephews murdered, along with a host of other relatives who might pose dynastic claims. In September 337, the three remaining brothers had themselves promoted to full Augustus and were thus meant to rule in concord as equals. In summer 340, however, Constantine II began laying claims to the territories of his younger brother Constans and eventually invaded northern Italy. As it turned out, Constantine II was himself defeated near Aquileia and killed in battle. In this way Constans became master of the entire western empire.

TABLE 13.1 **The Constantinian Family**   *The presentation follows the style of Table 8.1, explained there.*

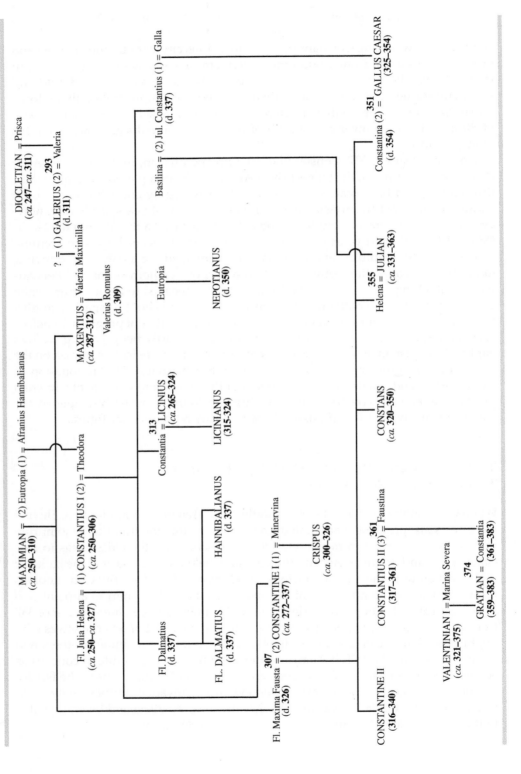

Constans' reign is not well documented, but he is known to have defeated the barbarian Franks in northern Gaul as well as the tribes in Britain. By January 350, however, the army in Gaul turned against him and, proclaiming its own general, Magnentius, in his stead, executed Constans. Meanwhile Constantius II, the lone surviving son of Constantine, had been preoccupied in the East with the aggressive Sasanian ruler Shapur II, who was assaulting Roman fortresses. Rather than come to their rescue, Constantius was forced to return west to fight Magnentius. The usurper was defeated in a bloody struggle at Mursa (Osijek, in modern Croatia) in central Pannonia in September 351, and eventually forced to commit suicide in Gaul in 353.

In fact, the later empire was continuously plagued by civil war. It was large enough, and the foes on its borders were fierce enough, that multiple emperors were required; nevertheless, they often turned on each other, causing Roman armies to slaughter one another. Constantius, thinking to resolve this difficulty using the power of dynasty, appointed his cousin Gallus as Caesar for the East in March 351, while he marched west to suppress Magnentius. Gallus was the son of Constantine I's half-brother, whom Constantius had murdered in the summer of 337. Unsurprisingly, Gallus was less than fully cooperative, and by 354 their relationship had deteriorated to the point that Constantius had Gallus executed. With external troubles continuing to roil in East and West, Constantius felt forced to try a second dynastic appointment. This time he chose Gallus' brilliant half-brother Julian, a man equally resentful toward Constantius, but one whose abilities as a general and devotion to the empire made him a true asset. Julian was proclaimed Caesar in November 355 and sent north to Gaul to regain control of this territory, which had been overrun by barbarians in the aftermath of Magnentius' usurpation. Over the next five years, Julian would systematically travel the Rhine frontier, driving back the Franks in the north and the Alamanni in the south.

Meanwhile Constantius and his generals were also regularly compelled to engage in military campaigns. When he inherited the eastern empire in 337, Constantius had to face the Persian threat stirred up by his father. From then until 350 he based himself in Antioch, parrying the various attacks of the aggressive Shapur II, at Nisibis (modern Nusaybin, Turkey) and Singara in the 340s. During the 350s Constantius shifted his attention to the usurper Magnentius. Toward the end of this decade, however, the Persian threat re-emerged when Shapur launched a massive expedition into Roman territory in 359 and sacked the Roman fortress town of Amida (modern Diyarbakır, Turkey) on the River Tigris. This loss drew Constantius east again and compelled him to request that Julian send detachments from his Gallic armies in support. The request stirred up unrest among Julian's soldiery, who insisted on promoting him to full Augustus in early 360. When Constantius took offense, the two emperors began preparing for yet another civil war. This threat was only narrowly averted when Constantius died in November 361 and left the entire empire to Julian.

Map 13.1 *Major Battle Sites of the Fourth Century*

Legend:
- • Site
- ⊗ Site of civil war
- × Site of external war
- ⊠ Site of both civil and external war

Scale:
0 — 250 — 500 — 750 Km
0 — 150 — 300 — 450 Miles

⊗ Civil wars (dates of battles)
Adrianople A.D. 313, 316, 324
Aquileia 340, 388
Byzantium/Constantinople 324
Chrysopolis 324
Cibalae 316
Cyprus 334
Frigidus River 394
Mursa 351
Nacoleia 366
Parisii 383
Propontis 324
Roma 307, 312, 350
Siscia 316, 388
Susa 312
Turin 312
Verona 312

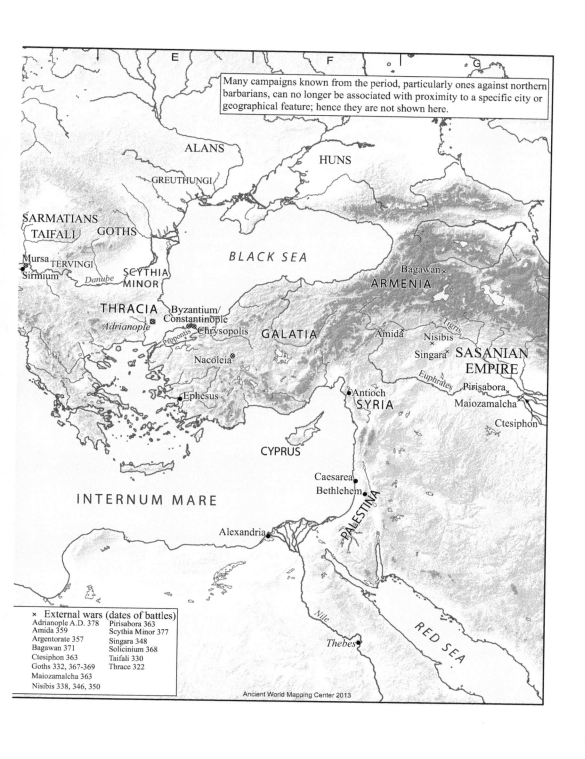

Many campaigns known from the period, particularly ones against northern barbarians, can no longer be associated with proximity to a specific city or geographical feature; hence they are not shown here.

ALANS

HUNS

GREUTHUNGI

SARMATIANS
TAIFALI   GOTHS

Mursa
TERVINGI
Sirmium   *Danube*   SCYTHIA
                               MINOR

BLACK SEA

Bagawan ×

ARMENIA

THRACIA   Byzantium/
               Constantinople   GALATIA
Adrianople   Chrysopolis
               Propontis   Amida   *Tigris*
               Nacoleia   Nisibis
                                                          ×   SASANIAN
                                                   Singara   EMPIRE
                                                          Euphrates   Pirisabora
               Ephesus   Antioch
                                                 SYRIA   Maiozamalcha ×
                                                                          Ctesiphon
                               CYPRUS

INTERNUM MARE   Caesarea
                                                Bethlehem
                                                          PALESTINA

               Alexandria

Thebes

Nile

RED SEA

× External wars (dates of battles)
Adrianople A.D. 378   Pirisabora 363
Amida 359   Scythia Minor 377
Argentorate 357   Singara 348
Bagawan 371   Solicinium 368
Ctesiphon 363   Taifali 330
Goths 332, 367-369   Thrace 322
Maiozamalcha 363
Nisibis 338, 346, 350

Ancient World Mapping Center 2013

JULIAN (361–363): A TEST OF THE CHRISTIAN EMPIRE

As a member of the Constantinian line, Julian had been raised a Christian, but in the course of his formative years he had developed an aversion to the religion of the dynasty, which had wiped out most of his immediate family. At the age of twenty (in 351), he explains in a letter, he abandoned Christianity and "apostatized" to paganism, although he revealed his convictions only to a small inner circle when he was serving as Caesar under Constantius. Earlier, during the period of his education, Julian had been especially influenced by Maximus of Ephesus, who practiced a version of Platonist philosophy that advocated not just contemplation of the divine, but also its worship through ritual, above all sacrifice. From early in 362, Julian invited Maximus and other pagan intellectuals to join his court and began offering blood sacrifice openly. As a symbol of his commitment to philosophical paganism, Julian grew his beard out long, a novelty not seen since the Severan period, after which emperors had worn only short beards or none at all.

Julian's support of traditional paganism and his disdain for Christianity also played out on the practical level (note Fig. 13.3c). He began issuing a series of decrees revoking privileges granted to Christian clergy and even declared that Christians should no longer be allowed to teach classical literature—authors like Homer and Vergil—for the very reason that they did not believe in the gods who featured so prominently in these works. Seeing that Christianity had considerably more appeal than paganism among the masses because of its organizational structure and charitable institutions, Julian diverted imperial resources to build the same sorts of administrative hierarchies and systems of distribution in pagan cult (Source 13.1). Being a philosopher, Julian also undertook an intellectual campaign against Christianity by writing a lengthy tract entitled *Against the Galilaeans*, in which he scorned Christianity as a heretical splinter group from Judaism. To drive the point home, he ordered one of his officials to begin rebuilding the Jewish temple in Jerusalem, which had been in ruins since its destruction by Titus in 70. The project foundered after explosions occurred in the foundations.

Julian also had other motivations to terminate this costly rebuilding effort. He needed all the resources he could muster to fund his most grandiose undertaking yet, a full-scale invasion of Persia. He carefully prepared his expeditionary force—some 65,000 men—at Antioch in winter 362/363. While he was there, rioting broke out, both because of the food shortages caused by the added burden of an imperial army in the vicinity and because of Julian's attempts to restore the shrine of Apollo at Daphne, just outside the city. In response, the Christian populace of the city set the temple ablaze, evidence that Christianity had by now gained the upper hand. Julian left the city in a rage and moved his army into position to invade Persia down the River Euphrates. Initially the Persians offered little resistance, but by the time he reached the capital at Ctesiphon, his fortunes changed. After being forced to abandon a siege, he retreated northward along the River Tigris under constant attack. Ever the impetuous general, he sallied out to engage some skirmishers one day in June 363 without putting on his armor, and a spear pierced his side. He died later that night.

SOURCE 13.1: *The emperor Julian composed this letter (22 [429D–430C]) in 362 to Arsacius, who was serving as high priest in Galatia. It highlights his awareness of the appealing advantages of certain aspects of Christianity, which he disparages as "atheism," over "Hellenism," as he and his contemporaries termed paganism. These advantages included a greater concern with public displays of respectable behavior and, above all, free-handed charity to those in need regardless of their beliefs. With this letter Julian was launching a rearguard action to promote similar behavior among pagan priests, even offering to pay for it out of imperial funds.*

Why then do we not observe that what increases atheism the most is charity toward strangers, concern for the tombs of the dead, and the fiction of holiness in their lives? I think we ought to strive to imitate all of these things. And it should not be sufficient for you alone to behave thus, but literally all the priests in Galatia must do so. Either shame them or persuade them to strive for this, or remove them from priestly service if in visiting the gods along with their wives, children, and servants they should allow these same servants, children, or wives to be impious toward the gods, or even to prefer atheism to piety. Then, too, persuade priests neither to attend the theater, nor to drink in a pub, nor to oversee any craft or labor that is shameful and disreputable. Honor those who obey, and expel those who do not. Establish many hostels in every city in order that vagrants may enjoy hospitality from us, nor just those who are members of our community but also whoever else should be in need of money. I have come up with a plan so that you may have sufficient funds.

Julian was to be Rome's last openly pagan emperor. Had he lived longer, he might actually have succeeded in at least transforming paganism into an effective rival to its new challenger. Ultimately, however, his premature death instead seems to be symbolic of the fate of a religious tradition, which had come to rely too heavily on the support of the ruler.

JOVIAN, VALENTINIAN I, AND VALENS (363–378)

Julian's death while on campaign in the middle of Persian territory put his army in grave danger. The soldiers' reaction was to seize the initiative and elect as his successor an officer from an imperial guard unit, a man from the Balkans named Flavius Jovianus. From the start of his rule, Jovian was faced with the challenge of negotiating a settlement with the Persians that would permit him to extricate the Roman army from their territory. Despite his position of severe disadvantage, he concluded a compromise that ceded only half of the territory formerly held by Rome along the Upper Tigris. The treaty equalized power between Rome and Persia in this strategic region and helped to minimize conflict between the two powers over the next century and a half. Jovian, who unlike Julian was a Christian, died within months of his appointment. In his stead, the court elected another guardsman from the Balkans, Flavius Valentinianus, in February 364. A little over one month later Valentinian made his brother Valens co-emperor with the rank of full Augustus. In so doing, he was continuing the tradition of dynastic corulership perfected by Constantine (Fig. 13.3d). After the two had divided up the army and administration, Valentinian set off to rule the West and left his brother to manage the East.

Valentinian and Valens were promptly faced with barbarian threats on most frontiers. From the first year of his reign, Valentinian struggled against the Alamanni and himself defeated them in a battle at Solicinium (modern Schwetzingen, Germany) in 368. To bolster Roman control in the region, he began an extensive fortification program along the Rhine—the last systematic construction of defensive works along this frontier. His general Theodosius also faced, and subdued, the Picts, Attacotti, and Scots in Britain, and in 373 overcame the usurper Firmus in North Africa. Despite these successes, Valentinian ordered Theodosius' execution in 375 under mysterious circumstances, but Theodosius' son of the same name

Figure 13.3a, b, c, d *Fourth-century coins. These four specimens illustrate the power of coinage to convey imperial messages to the citizens of the empire, who encountered their imagery every day. The first two, minted under Constantine, show the conflicting religious propaganda he disseminated. The reverse of one [a] depicts a nude image of his favored pagan deity "Unconquerable Sun" (SOLI INVICTO), whom Constantine styles his "Companion" (COMITI); compare Figure 13.2. The other [b] shows his new Christian battle standard, the* labarum, *piercing a snake (a symbol of Satan and, by extension, Licinius) and surmounted by a Christogram (an X crossing a P, the first two letters of the name "Christ" in Greek). The third coin [c] shows Julian the Apostate with his long beard, characteristic of pagan philosophers. The reverse features a bull and two stars: Julian's contemporary Christian subjects interpreted this coin as a promotion for animal sacrifice, and they were outraged. The fourth [d] depicts on its reverse Valentinian and his brother Valens enthroned side by side holding a globe with Victory behind them. Below their feet can be read TR for Augusta Treverorum, the city where the coin was minted, and OB for Obryzum ("pure gold"), a quality mark on gold coins after Valentinian's coinage reform.*

quickly replaced his father as the empire's premier general. He first proved himself in 374 against the Sarmatians and Quadi, who had invaded Roman territory along the middle Danube. The following year, Valentinian crossed the Danube and subdued both peoples. In the course of the negotiations that followed, however, he became so enraged that he had a stroke and died at Brigetio (modern Szöny, Hungary) in November 375.

Valentinian's tireless efforts to defend the empire's frontiers are mirrored by his unflagging attention to its administration. He streamlined the imperial bureaucracy, restructured the collection of taxes in order to prevent fraud, and increased the purity of the gold coinage (see Fig. 13.3d). In the east, his brother Valens was equally competent as an administrator, though much less so as a military leader. Already in the second and third years of his reign he had to suppress an attempted usurpation by Procopius, a relative of Julian. After narrowly averting this disaster, he felt compelled to take an army north of the Danube and punish the Goths for having sent military support to Procopius. A three-year war ensued (367–369) that resulted in a stalemate. Valens' forces also attempted to restore territory on the eastern frontier lost to Persia, and by 376 he was preparing to invade the Sasanian empire.

Such ambitions were abandoned, however, in the wake of an uprising by the Goths in the Roman territory of Thrace. These had entered the empire after suffering attacks by the Huns, a nomadic people from the Asian steppe, whose lightning military tactics were to make them almost invincible for nearly a century to come. Unaware of the scale of this threat, Valens permitted a small group of Goths to cross the Danube for resettlement inside the empire in 376. This concession, however, only served to encourage many more Goths and other barbarian peoples, who poured into Thrace and eventually broke into revolt. After failing to contain the uprising in 377, Valens' generals in Thrace urged him to return from the Persian frontier with his army. However, by the time he actually arrived in spring 378, the Gothic forces had gained the upper hand, and they soon defeated the Romans near Adrianople (modern Edirne, Turkey) that August. This disastrous battle cost Valens his life and resulted in the massacre of two-thirds of the eastern field army, about 26,000 of an original 40,000 men. The setback was a grave one. Not only did the eastern empire now lack a fighting force capable of defending it, but it was also encumbered with a large and hostile group of Goths who had no home to which they could return.

GRATIAN, VALENTINIAN II, AND THEODOSIUS I (379–395)

Valens' death did not leave the empire without an emperor. In fact, he had ruled conjointly with not just his brother but also his nephew, Gratian, whom Valentinian had appointed as a second co-emperor in 367, when Gratian was just eight years old (see Table 14.1). Gratian's immediate promotion to full Augustus, rather than to the lesser grade of Caesar, established a precedent of appointing child emperors that endured into the late fifth century. Indeed, the next to follow was Gratian's younger half-brother Valentinian II, who was appointed full Augustus by the armies on the Danube following his father's death in 375. Valentinian II was just four at that point and seven when Valens died in 378. This meant that Gratian was essentially called on to face the rebellious Goths on his own. Emboldened by their victory, they had spread out and gained effective control over the entire central Balkans.

Aware of the challenge posed by the Goths, Gratian resolved to appoint an experienced military commander as co-Augustus. Not surprisingly, he chose Theodosius, who, as we have seen above, had succeeded his homonymous father as the empire's most successful general. Theodosius took office early in 379 and quickly set to work repelling the invaders, who were quite fragmented at this point and could be attacked piecemeal. Although today they are referred to collectively as "Visigoths," they were in fact a multiethnic group of Goths and other barbarian peoples. They had crossed the Danube separately in 376, but in response to Roman hostility they were forced to coalesce around the leadership of the Goths—the strongest group numerically.

After four years of frustrating guerrilla actions, Theodosius made an uneasy compromise peace with the Visigoths in October 382, which required them to fight in Roman armies but also granted them the right to settle under their own leadership in northern Thrace. In effect, therefore, Theodosius had created a semiautonomous barbarian state inside the bounds of the empire; the consequences were to prove devastating (see Chapter Fourteen). Fortunately the eastern frontier was much calmer. The aggressive Sasanian king Shapur II died in 379, and a series of weak successors followed. In 387, during this period of reduced tension, Theodosius and Shapur III reached an agreement to divide control of Armenia between them.

In the absence of serious external threats, two successive usurpation attempts were Theodosius' primary military concern. The first arose in Britain, where the general Magnus Maximus had himself proclaimed emperor in early 383, and then moved into Gaul to defeat Gratian near Paris and kill him. After initially agreeing to stay put in Gaul and leave the child emperor Valentinian II alone, Maximus broke this agreement by marching into Italy and forcing Valentinian to flee to Theodosius. In retaliation Theodosius attacked and defeated Maximus in Pannonia, and eventually captured and executed him at Aquileia in northern Italy in summer 388 (Fig. 13.4).

Theodosius remained in the West down to mid-390, helping Valentinian reestablish his rule. Theodosius' son Arcadius (already appointed Augustus in 383) was left in Constantinople to manage eastern affairs. Theodosius himself returned there in mid-390, but only two years later trouble arose once again in the West. Theodosius had left Valentinian II under the regency of the Frankish general Arbogast—establishing another pattern, regency by barbarian generals, that would recur in the years to come. Arbogast so thoroughly lorded it over Valentinian that the boy eventually committed suicide, whereupon Arbogast proclaimed a court official, Eugenius, as Augustus. Theodosius' reaction was decisive. He proclaimed

Figure 13.4 *Obelisk base from the Hippodrome of Constantinople (see Map 14.2). Following an ancient tradition, Theodosius erected an obelisk in the center of the hippodrome of Constantinople after his victory over Magnus Maximus. On its base, pictured here, he is shown in the imperial box at the racecourse, which was attached directly to the palace. He presides at the circus races, holding a crown for the victor and surrounded by court officials, senators, and bodyguards. Beneath him are the assembled masses, and below them acrobats and musicians, including organ-players. The circus races grew in importance during late antiquity and offered the emperor a powerful symbolic venue for demonstrating his beneficence to his subjects and his rule over them.*

his second son, Honorius, as Augustus in January 393—a sign that there would be no recognition for Eugenius—and in summer 394 he marched west to eliminate the usurper. The two armies met at the River Frigidus (in the foothills of the Tirol, east of Aquileia) and fought for two days. There was stalemate on the first day, but on the second, a tremendous wind came up in the face of the rebel forces and turned the battle in Theodosius' favor. Christian authors portray this as an act of divine intervention, for Eugenius had courted favor from the aristocrats of Rome by allowing them to revive many traditional cults that had been suppressed under Theodosius.

In the aftermath of the battle, Theodosius remained in Italy and even visited Rome in an effort to crush any remaining support for the rebel cause. In January 395 he succumbed to a hard life of campaigning and died in Milan. His death marks the end of an era. He was the last in a long line of emperors—stretching back to the days of Marcus Aurelius—who participated actively in military affairs. For the next century and a half, all western and most eastern emperors would leave military action to their generals and confine themselves to administrative and courtly activities.

NEW ELITES FOR THE EMPIRE

The administrative changes introduced by the tetrarchs, together with the new priorities and values of a Christian world, combined to alter the nature of the ruling elite in the fourth century. In many ways late antiquity represents the period when the multifarious regions of Rome's empire reasserted their unique identities with new vigor; yet at the same time this period witnessed a massive homogenization of elite culture that pulled against fragmentation and served to hold an aging empire together. The growth in the imperial bureaucracy introduced by the tetrarchs and Constantine set the stage for this process. The empire of the second century had functioned with a very bottom-heavy government. At that date there were never more than 600 or so senators, and the senate exercised little practical authority as a governing body, although some individual members had tremendous power. However, their role declined markedly after the Severan period and reached its nadir under the tetrarchs, who favored equestrians and above all military men for appointment to offices.

Constantine, by contrast, began a revival of the senate, which reinvigorated it in the fourth century, yet he did this while making fundamental changes to the senatorial career. His single biggest alteration was the creation of an entirely new senate in Constantinople. By 359 his son Constantius II had increased its membership to nearly 2,000 and had graced the new capital with its own Urban Prefect, an office equal in status to that of Praetorian Prefect. From the time of Constantine the senate in Rome had been increased to a similar size, meaning that the empire now had a senatorial elite about six times larger than what it had been two centuries earlier.

This expansion was made possible because Constantine had drafted primarily men of eastern provincial origin, especially former city councilors, for the Constantinopolitan senate; by this means he opened the way for these formerly low-level aristocrats to come pouring in. In addition, emperors from Constantine onward used senatorial status as the ultimate reward for service in the greatly expanded bureaucracy. By the mid-fourth century, senators were being drawn equally from their traditional ranks, from the new class of bureaucrats, and from high-level military personnel. This expansion gave emperors increased control over access to elite status, especially because two of the channels feeding into it— the army and the bureaucracy—were routed through the imperial hierarchy. The consequent effects on the religious status of the elite were tremendous. With only a single pagan emperor in power from 324 to 395, imperial offices in both the civic and military realm came to be dominated by Christians.

Late Roman administrative reforms also changed the nature of yet another elite structure: the army. By the fourth century its ranks had grown to as large as 600,000 soldiers, a number so high that the Roman authorities needed to turn increasingly to barbarians to fill the ranks. Use of noncitizens in the military was of course nothing new, but the status accorded to barbarian soldiers in the late empire was unheard of even a century earlier. Thus the emperor's elite guard units—the *scholarii*—came to consist primarily of Germanic barbarians, and commanders of barbarian origin also filled nearly half the ranks of officers as well. As their numbers grew, these officers played an increasingly important role in the imperial government. The Vandal Stilicho, who served the emperor Honorius as Master of the Soldiers, was even welcomed into the imperial family when he married Theodosius I's niece Serena. It would be wrong to assume, however, that such "foreign" generals precipitated the "fall of the Roman Empire." Since they had been fully acculturated to Roman military life, they constructed their identities very much along Roman lines and usually remained steadfastly loyal to the empire.

Any description of elite groups in late antiquity must inevitably include a new class of leaders whose power had been minimal in the second century: the bishops. From the beginning, Christianity had developed its own organizational structures independent of the Roman state. At the heart of this system was the bishop. By the early fourth century there were bishops for every major city in Italy and for many minor ones, as well as for areas in heavily Christianized regions like North Africa and parts of Syria and Asia Minor. Thus by 325 Syria had nearly 30 bishops who headed the church in cities like Antioch, Apamea, and Laodicea. The most famous bishop for westerners headed the church in Rome—the Pope. By the fourth century, the bishopric of Rome was an office so sought after that fights would erupt over the succession; on a single day in 366 some 137 people lost their lives in riots over a disputed papal election. Most bishoprics were, of course, considerably less powerful, but with the rapid spread of Christianity during the fourth century the bishop grew in power as the premier local leader.

The bishop's power stemmed not just from the growth of his congregation but also from the many powers and privileges accorded him by the emperors. Constantine, for example, granted bishops the right to receive some revenues generated by imperial estates; he allowed them exemption from taxes and curial service; he regularly allowed them to use the imperial post-horse system; he granted them the right to sit in judgment over civil suits; he also granted them the right to manumit slaves in their churches. These privileges made the bishop into a local powerbroker *par excellence*. His authority is also reflected in the rise of Christian architecture; just as bishops replaced town councilors as civic leaders, so too Christian architecture replaced traditional civic architecture as the standard expression of local prosperity and pride of place (note Plates 6b and 7).

In many ways, however, bishops also assumed the role of a counterweight to imperial power. The ability of bishops to resist imperial authority is attested in numerous instances, and tellingly illustrates how the church was growing into an alternative source of authority. Perhaps the best example comes in the person of Ambrose, who became bishop of Milan in 374. Ambrose squared off against the child emperor Valentinian II and his mother Justina to prevent some powerful pagans of Rome from restoring a beloved altar to the goddess Victory in the senate house. Later he tackled Theodosius I, first by rebuking him for attempting to force a group of Christians who had destroyed a synagogue to rebuild it, and then by punishing him for ordering his soldiers to massacre some 7,000 citizens in the arena of Thessalonica after a senior officer had been killed in a riot. In this last instance Ambrose even compelled Theodosius to do public penance before he was willing to accept the emperor back into communion in his church. Thus, less than eighty years after the close of the Great Persecution, Christian bishops were able to force the emperor to acknowledge their superior authority in religious matters.

PAGANISM AND CHRISTIANITY

Modern scholars use the word "paganism"—cautiously and uncomfortably—to describe the collectivity of practices that characterize ancient non–Judeo-Christian religions. In fact ancient pagans had no one word with which to designate their religion, nor would they have conceived of themselves as a unified group in any period prior to late antiquity. The Latin *paganus* has the sense of "rustic" and was first employed by Christians in the late fourth century as a derogatory designation for those who followed the traditional religious practices. The reason for this ambiguous terminology is that ancient paganism was a fundamentally decentralized phenomenon, best expressed at the local level, with only very weak forces drawing its varied manifestations together into anything that might be recognized today as a single religion. Each community had its own deities, rituals, and festivals—a diversity that emperors generally tolerated, even fostered (see Chapter Nine).

Among the cults to benefit from this tolerance was Christianity. While it endured periods of persecution that grew increasingly intense through the early fourth century, it was largely left alone to develop and spread. During the century after Constantine's death its marginal situation was transformed. It not only gained the ascendency as the religion of the majority and of the state, but it also persecuted, and all but extirpated, paganism. This is not to suggest that paganism was somehow moribund when Constantine converted in 312. On the contrary, pagans in all likelihood represented around 90 percent of the Empire's population, and they still controlled religious practices and politics at the local and imperial levels. By the mid-fourth century, however, Christianity had probably reached a demographic tipping point in cities (the centers of regional power), and it now had the advantage of inertia on its side. Conversion became fashionable in a period during which the emperor himself had converted and was promoting his new faith with the one hand while repressing the old religions with the other. Studies have shown that as early as the 340s emperors began showing preference for Christians in making official appointments. By the 390s very few pagans are attested in office, and by 415 they were legally debarred from holding administrative posts. In this environment, as one can imagine, some conversions were less than sincere, as people trimmed their sails to the prevailing religious winds.

Already under Constantine, Christianity began to inflict some of the same violence on the pagans that it had itself received at the hands of pagan emperors. After assuming control of the East in 324, Constantine ordered the destruction of a handful of temples, and his son Constantius is firmly attested as having banned sacrifice. While Julian repealed all such laws, they were reactivated with a vengeance by Theodosius (Source 13.2), who also began permitting the widespread destruction of pagan temples. One outstanding instance was the destruction of the massive temple of Serapis in Alexandria. After the local bishop Theophilus staged a scene of public mockery against pagan images there in 391, the city's pagans rose up in revolt and barricaded themselves in the temple precinct. Their action ignited a street war between pagans and Christians; many on both sides were killed, and the Christians eventually obliterated the temple. This was just one of many such instances where Christian zealots attacked pagan holy sites with utter impunity.

Paganism had difficulty recovering from these blows. Moreover, the removal of imperial subsidies for local cults from Constantine's reign onward eliminated the means by which rituals could be conducted, as well as severing ties to the communities that had once been fed and feted at civic religious festivals. Once the shrines were closed or destroyed and the festivals discontinued, paganism could survive only in isolated local contexts, especially in the countryside where it had always thrived, and in a limited number of obstinately traditional cities. To be sure, certain pagans did continue to practice their religion well into the sixth century, but only in radically altered form, some by maintaining a very low profile,

SOURCE 13.2: *These two laws illustrate how closely we can trace imperial legislation on religious worship in late antiquity. In the first, Constantius II orders the first firmly attested ban on pagan sacrifice; the law of his father Constantine that he mentions is a matter of dispute. The second law, issued in 391, is more explicit and wide-ranging. It does not just catalog forbidden activities, but also shows how imperial officials were coerced into enforcement. At times, Christians took such laws as motivation to destroy pagan temples, even if this was not the express intent of the legislation.*

(A.D. 341) Constantius Augustus to Madalianus, Vice-Praetorian Prefect. Let superstition cease, let the insanity of sacrifices be abolished. For whoever should dare to celebrate sacrifices in contravention of the law of the divine Emperor my father and of this command of Our Clemency, let a fitting punishment and immediate sentence be passed against him.

(A.D. 391) Gratian, Valentinian, and Theodosius to Albinus the Praetorian Prefect. Let no one pollute himself with sacrificial animals, let no one slaughter innocent victims, let no one approach shrines, visit temples, and admire idols formed by human labor, lest he become subject to divine and human sanctions. This order should also bind governors so that, if any of them is devoted to profane rites and should enter a temple anywhere for purposes of worship, whether along a road or in a city, he should be compelled to pay fifteen pounds of gold immediately, and his staff should pay the same sum with equal speed if they do not resist the governor and report him immediately with a public attestation. (*Theodosian Code* 16.10.2 and 10)

others by intellectualizing their theology and limiting its enactment to an arcane inner circle. Even these, however, were ferreted out after the emperor Justinian closed the Platonic Academy in Athens in 529. By this date paganism was becoming a distant memory, surviving less through active practitioners and more in Christian practices adapted from the ancient pagan forms.

Meanwhile, Christianity had exploited the conversion of the emperor to strengthen the unity that had always been its primary advantage. As a monotheistic religion and a religion of the book, Christianity was also able to develop a more coherent theology. Nevertheless, as a mass movement, it, too, was plagued by division from the beginning. Disputes arose sometimes over leadership (a matter of fundamental concern to the Donatists in North Africa, for example) and at other times over dogma (as in the Arian controversy). The former type of controversy is usually referred to as *schism*, the latter as *heresy*. In both instances the rival Christian communities typically sought the emperor's immediate intervention as mediator, and, from Constantine onward, he readily obliged. Rarely, however, did his authority bring matters to a close, since both sides in any given debate usually regrouped and came back for renewed engagement, with the previous loser sometimes then winning in the end. Engagement persisted because much more was at stake than principled discussion about pious behavior and the nature of God. Theological controversies were often thinly veiled excuses for power plays between the bishops of rival cities or even rival bishops within a single city. The church, after all, was always divided by geography, with each region following its own traditions and each major city—especially Alexandria, Antioch, Ephesus, Constantinople, and Rome—claiming the right to impose its own doctrine and ritual. Thus, although Theodosius theoretically put a stop to ecclesiastical bickering over Arianism at the Council of Constantinople in 381, quarrels soon resumed over other issues, like the role of Mary as mother of God or the admixture of human and divine qualities in the person of Jesus. These questions demanded further ecumenical councils at Ephesus in 431 and Chalcedon in 451, and they continued to create fissures in church unity that persist to the present day.

All of this discord would seem to speak against the unifying power of Christianity as an imperial religion. "No beasts are as harmful to people as most Christians are savage to each other," the pagan historian Ammianus once quipped. But this would be to oversimplify. Christianity had grown up independent of imperial support and had developed its own leadership structures, its own infrastructure, and its own set of values and beliefs, all of which made it what Edward Gibbon in the eighteenth century famously termed "an independent state at the heart of the Roman empire." But once Christianity allied itself with the emperor, it became increasingly intertwined with the state to the point that, by the sixth century, the two formed a seamless web of power. Theological controversies were thus all part of the dynamics of power, providing channels for the expression of rivalries that the emperor himself could control. Christianity also offered a conduit through which he could extend his influence beyond the frontiers. Thus, around the time of Constantine's conversion, the leadership of the kingdoms of Armenia, Georgia, and Axum (Ethiopia) also converted. It is no surprise that the emperors embraced this fortunate situation to widen their political reach. Christianity soon spread—often with active support from the emperor—to the Saracen Arabs, to the Goths, and to other Germanic peoples, and here too it provided common ground. This trend not only boosted the power of the emperor beyond his territorial borders but also remained one of the empire's most lasting legacies.

SUGGESTED READINGS

Curran, John R. 2000. *Pagan City and Christian Capital: Rome in the Fourth Century*. Oxford: Oxford University Press. Surveys the development of Rome's architecture and topography in this period of change.

Lee, A. Douglas. 2000. *Pagans and Christians in Late Antiquity. A Sourcebook*. London and New York: Routledge.

Lenski, Noel (ed.). 2006. *The Cambridge Companion to the Age of Constantine*. Cambridge: Cambridge University Press.

Matthews, John F. 1975. *Western Aristocracies and Imperial Court, A.D. 364–425*. Oxford: Oxford University Press. Invaluable treatment of the ongoing importance of the senatorial aristocracy in late antiquity.

Rapp, Claudia. 2005. *Holy Bishops in Late Antiquity: The Nature of Christian Leadership in an Age of Transition*. Berkeley, Los Angeles, London: University of California Press.

14

THE FINAL YEARS OF
THE WESTERN EMPIRE AND
ROME'S REVIVAL IN THE EAST

THE THEODOSIAN DYNASTY DOWN
TO THE FIRST SACK OF ROME (395–410)

Theodosius I is widely revered for having turned Rome's fortunes around in his sixteen-year reign. He had assumed the throne in the chaotic aftermath of the disastrous battle of Adrianople (378). Using a combination of force and diplomacy, he reached a compromise with the Goths that put them to work in the empire's service. When he died in January 395, there was also hope for continued stability because he left behind two sons as legitimate successors (Table 14.1). Unfortunately, the seeds of trouble were already sown in both of these arrangements. While the Goths had been pacified, they were by no means subdued. Their presence as a semiautonomous group operating inside Roman territory allowed them to build momentum against the empire until they eventually sacked the city of Rome in 410, and went on to secure the surrender of the region of Aquitaine (in Gaul) into their control in 418. All this occurred during the reigns of Theodosius' sons, Arcadius and Honorius, who succeeded to power in 395 at the ages of 18 and 11 respectively. Both had been Augusti since early childhood, but both failed to master the art of rulership in the manner exhibited by their father. They never took to the field on campaign, nor did they become strong managers of affairs at court.

Because of their youth upon accession, and because neither ever grew into a strong leader, both Arcadius and Honorius were controlled by a succession of officials who managed affairs for them. For Honorius, the longest-lasting and most successful of these was Stilicho, the son of a Vandal cavalry officer, who had risen to become Master of the Soldiers in the last year of Theodosius' reign (Fig. 14.1).

TABLE 14.1 The Theodosian Family *The presentation follows the style of Table 8.1, explained there.*

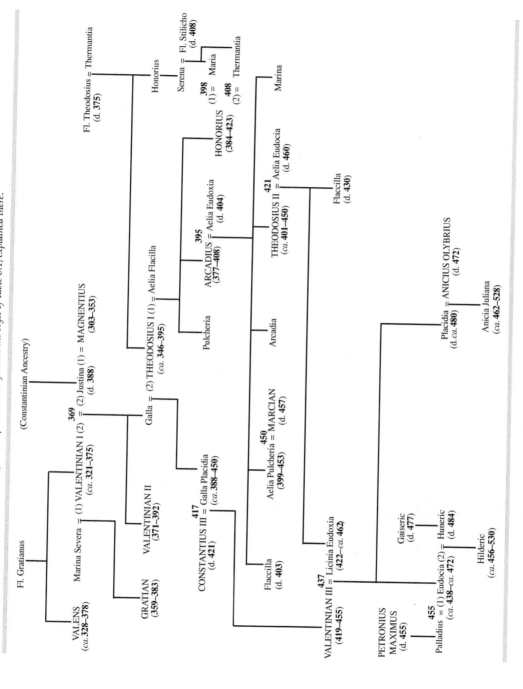

Upon his death in 395, Stilicho gained effective control of both the eastern and the western field armies, which had been united by Theodosius following his victory at the battle of the River Frigidus (394). Theodosius may also have left Stilicho with oversight over both of his youthful sons, but this claim was never recognized by the eastern court. Here, in the eastern capital of Constantinople, Arcadius had been nominal ruler since 392. In effect, however, his Praetorian Prefect Rufinus managed affairs. Tensions arose between Rufinus and Stilicho in 395 after the Visigoths broke into revolt in the Balkans, forcing Stilicho to intervene with soldiers he brought from the West. Arcadius and Rufinus saw his intervention as an encroachment into eastern territory and ordered Stilicho to surrender command of part of his army. He complied, sending the troops to Constantinople under his Count Gainas; but he also ordered Gainas to murder Rufinus upon his arrival.

Figure 14.1 *Late Roman grandees advertised major events in their lives by having commemorative diptychs—two facing writing-tablets—produced in ivory. This example shows the general Stilicho, a man of mixed Vandal and Roman heritage who rose to become Master of the Soldiers under Theodosius I. Stilicho married Theodosius' niece Serena, portrayed on the left together with their son Eucherius, who is dressed as a young Roman noble. The contrast with his father, who styles himself as a barbarian general by wearing a full beard and pants, reflects the intermingling of Roman and Germanic families and customs at this period.*

Rufinus was in turn succeeded by another powerbroker named Eutropius, the chief imperial eunuch. He, too, quarreled with Stilicho for intervening against the Visigoths once again after they invaded Greece in 397. Eutropius helped see to it that Stilicho was declared a public enemy by the senate of Constantinople, and even encouraged Arcadius to respond favorably to a proposal by Gildo, the Count of Africa (part of the western empire), to transfer his territory to the control of the East. Such a transfer would present a tremendous threat to the city of Rome, given its dependence on African grain. Nevertheless, Stilicho again gained the upper hand by eliminating Gildo in 398 and openly questioning Eutropius' authority because of his background as a slave and status as a eunuch.

Eutropius ran into further trouble this same year when a revolt erupted in Phrygia under the leadership of a barbarian general, Tribigild (Map 14.1). He commanded yet another group of Goths settled inside Roman territory, and when Gainas (himself a Goth) was sent against him, the two soon joined forces. Gainas and Tribigild then occupied Constantinople, and demanded Eutropius' removal from power in 400. This they achieved, but the people of the city resented the barbarian force in their midst and expelled it, in the process burning alive a huge number of Goths trapped in a church. In the years that followed, the eastern court became much warier of turning to barbarian generals and troops to fight its battles. In some ways it benefited from circumstances, because in fact it was to be another twenty years before another serious threat arose on the Danube. The Persians too were not disposed to war at this time. However, far from seizing this relative quiet to gain control of political affairs, Arcadius remained a weak figure down to his death in 408.

Arcadius' eastern court to some extent succeeded in avoiding defeat by shifting its barbarian problems westward. This appears to have been the case in 401 and 402, when the Visigoths led by Alaric twice marched into Italy; both times they were driven back by Stilicho, but only at a heavy cost to the western army. During the 402 invasion, Honorius had even felt compelled to withdraw his court from Milan to the city of Ravenna, on Italy's Adriatic coast. Because Ravenna is surrounded by an almost impenetrable swamp, the transfer of the court there was designed to insulate the emperor from threats, but it also had the effect of isolating an already disengaged ruler from action. Once established in Ravenna, the court remained sequestered there for the remainder of the western Empire's history.

The years 405 and 406 saw an unprecedented wave of incursions into the empire. Late in 405 a large multiethnic barbarian coalition under the Ostrogoth Radagaisus crossed the Alps from Pannonia and invaded Italy. Though these barbarians succeeded in overcoming Roman resistance initially, they were eventually cornered in central Italy at Faesulae (modern Fiesole) and massacred in 406. Another multiethnic invasion of Vandals, Alans, and Suebi crossed the lower Rhine on New Year's Eve 405 (or some argue 406), sacked Trier and other cities, and proceeded into southwestern Gaul. Also in 406, groups of Alamanni and Burgundians invaded across the upper Rhine. As a result, by late 406 all of Britain and most of Gaul were outside of Honorius' control.

Meanwhile, closer to Italy, Alaric's Visigoths also began to agitate again. In the wake of a failed plot by Stilicho to use the Visigoths to take back the territory of Epirus from eastern into western control, suspicions arose that Stilicho was favoring the Goths and behaving disloyally to the empire. In mid-408, in a scene of high court intrigue tinged with more than a little ethnic tension, Stilicho was arrested and executed by Honorius. When Honorius then attempted to eliminate Stilicho's remaining barbarian followers, as many as 30,000 of them were driven into the hands of Alaric, whose Visigoths they now joined as allies.

With this swollen force, Alaric grew bolder. In autumn 408 he marched on Rome and besieged it. After an agreement was reached by which Honorius was to pay a massive ransom of 5,000 pounds of gold and 30,000 pounds of silver, Alaric relaxed this first assault. But a second abortive siege followed in 409, and a third the following summer that would prove decisive. On August 24, 410, the Visigoths entered the city and proceeded to loot for three days. During the rampage, Honorius' sister, Galla Placidia, was captured. Although damage was limited and most lives were spared, the symbolic impact of this first "sack of Rome" was massive.

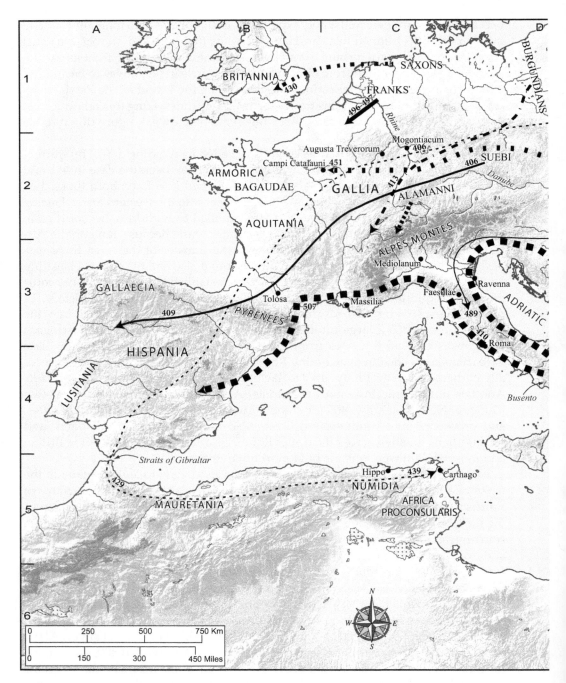

Map 14.1 *The Barbarian Invasions*

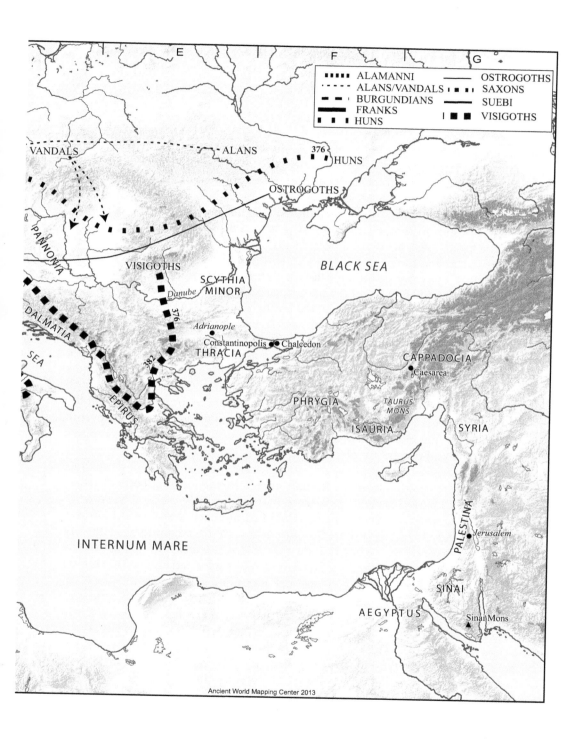

ALAMANNI	OSTROGOTHS
ALANS/VANDALS	SAXONS
BURGUNDIANS	SUEBI
FRANKS	VISIGOTHS
HUNS	

VANDALS · · · ALANS · · 376

HUNS

OSTROGOTHS

PANNONIA

BLACK SEA

VISIGOTHS
SCYTHIA
MINOR

DALMATIA

Danube

376

Adrianople

382
Constantinopolis ● ● Chalcedon

SEA
THRACIA

CAPPADOCIA

● Caesarea

EPIRUS
PHRYGIA
TAURUS
MONS

ISAURIA

SYRIA

PALESTINA

INTERNUM MARE
● Jerusalem

SINAI

AEGYPTUS
Sinai Mons ▲

Ancient World Mapping Center 2013

Jerome, a leading scholar living far away in Palestine (Source 14.1), lamented, "the Roman empire was decapitated, and the whole world perished in one city."

THE FALL OF THE WESTERN EMPIRE (410–476)

After leaving Rome, the Visigoths marched south, hoping to sail on to Sicily and Africa, but storms wrecked their ships. Late in 410 Alaric died. The Goths paused long enough to offer their great leader an elaborate funeral and then headed north out of Italy, now under the leadership of Alaric's brother-in-law, Athaulf. By 412 they crossed into Gaul and then into Spain, both in a state of chaos in this period. They were hoping once again to cross over to North Africa, but were foiled a second time by the destruction of a fleet. In 417, after Honorius' general Constantius succeeded in trapping the Visigoths in southern Spain, they were forced to negotiate a deal. In exchange for supplies and a treaty, they agreed to fight on the emperor's behalf, and even to return the princess Galla Placidia, whom they had held captive since the sack of Rome in 410 (Source 14.1). Their first objective was to attack the coalition of Vandals, Suebi, and Alans who had entered the empire back in 406 and by now controlled Gallaecia and Lusitania (northern Spain and Portugal). As a reward for successes against these groups, and in large part because there was no better solution for their relocation, Honorius granted the Visigoths the right to settle the territory of Aquitania in southwestern Gaul in 418. Although such terms of the treaty as survive leave room for debate, indications are that the Romans agreed to divide up existing estates with the Visigoths, and to permit them the right to rule in this territory even though it was well within the empire's borders—a new and dangerous step.

The same process of settlement was occurring elsewhere around the same time, but with less overt sanction from the Roman state. Information about other barbarian groups at this period is even spottier, so that we can only guess at the precise nature of the ongoing changes; even so, a broad summary is possible. Britain was abandoned already in 410, and thereafter its eastern shores began to be settled by the Germanic Saxons from what is today Denmark. Meanwhile Spain became a battleground between the Vandals, Suebi, and Alans who had entered the region in 407, and a variety of Roman generals and usurpers, at great cost to the local Roman population. Southeastern Gaul (Savoy) was overrun by the Burgundians, who were then settled there on terms similar to those received by the Visigoths in the early fifth century; the Alamanni invaded further to the north (Alsace). At the same time northeastern Gaul, over which the Romans had always had weak control, was beginning to fall under the dominion of the Franks.

Most costly of all was the loss of North Africa. Since the reign of Theodosius it had been subject to usurper generals, and eventually it fell prey to some of the Vandals previously settled in Spain. Under their masterful king Gaiseric, they crossed the Straits of Gibraltar in 429 and proceeded to overrun Mauretania, Numidia (modern Morocco and Algeria), and eventually the prosperous province

SOURCE 14.1: *Paulus Orosius (c. 375–418) was from Spain. Around 417, when living in Palestine, he composed a* History against the Pagans, *in which he argued that the disasters Rome was experiencing in his day paled in comparison to those it had experienced prior to the appearance of Christianity. In this passage, he discusses a conversation between a confidant of the Gothic king Athaulf and Jerome. The passage is striking for the influence it attributes to the captive princess Galla Placidia, whom Athaulf married in Narbo (modern Narbonne) on January 1, 414. It epitomizes the changes afoot in power relations and the adjustments being made in expectations on both sides of the Roman–barbarian divide.*

Athaulf ruled over the Gothic people as king at that time. In the period after the capture of Rome and the death of Alaric [410], as I said, he married Placidia the captive sister of the emperor, and succeeded Alaric as ruler. As rumor had it and even as his own final end proved, he was a quite zealous champion of peace, and preferred to fight faithfully for the emperor Honorius and use the forces of the Goths to defend the Roman state. For I myself even heard a certain man from the province of Narbonensis report [to Jerome] . . . that he was quite close friends with Athaulf at Narbo and that he often heard, under oath to God, what Athaulf used to say when he was still strong in mind, body, and intellect: At first he longed ardently to wipe out the Roman name, and to make all Roman territory into an empire of the Goths, as he would call it; he wanted what used to be "Romania" to become "Gothia," to put it in layman's terms; he wanted Athaulf himself to become what Caesar Augustus used to be. But when he discovered through long experience that the Goths were in no way able to obey laws because of their unrestrained barbarity, and that a state ought not to be deprived of laws (without which a state is simply not a state), he decided that at least he should seek glory for himself by restoring the Roman name to its original condition and by augmenting it using the forces of the Goths, and that he should be considered the originator of Rome's restoration among posterity, since he was not able to be its transformer. For this reason, he strove to avoid war and to pursue peace, being especially softened by the persuasion and advice of his wife Placidia, a woman of incredibly sharp intellect and admirable religion. (7.43)

of Africa Proconsularis with its capital of Carthage, which fell in 439. Gaiseric's power continued to grow as he came to treat the western Mediterranean as a giant hunting ground for his plundering naval forces, giving rise to the modern term "vandalism." In 455 Gaiseric was even able to land a force in Italy and sack Rome a second time, carrying off countless treasures. Already the Vandals had weakened the city immeasurably by depriving it of African grain. Rome's population declined dramatically; by the early sixth century it cannot have been more than about 50,000, one-twentieth of its size during the early empire.

While Gaiseric was overrunning North Africa, the western empire was being ruled by the emperor Valentinian III, who had succeeded to the western throne in 425. He was the son of Honorius' sister Galla Placidia, famous for her long captivity among the Visigoths. Valentinian III had been installed on the western throne in Ravenna by his cousin Theodosius II, ruler in Constantinople. This was only the first in a long series of examples of the eastern court's new primacy over the West; from now onward, the West looked to Constantinople for political support rather than vice versa. At the time of his accession, Valentinian III was only six years old, making him the next in the series of child emperors of the Theodosian dynasty. Like his predecessors, he also turned out to be a weak ruler who was easily manipulated.

The principal power behind his throne was his Master of the Soldiers, Aetius. Relying above all on Hunnic auxiliaries, Aetius won a series of victories over various barbarian peoples in Gaul. Nevertheless, his most glorious moment came against the Huns themselves when he defeated Attila at the battle of the Catalaunian Plains (modern Champagne, France) in 451. After expelling the Gothic leadership from what is today Romania in the 370s, the Huns had gained control of this eastern territory and gradually built a surprisingly centralized and powerful kingdom there. Behind their success lay Attila, who defeated eastern imperial armies again and again. In 450, Attila decided to march west. Skirting the northern edge of the Danube, he crossed the Rhine near Mogontiacum (modern Mainz) and attempted to gain support from the barbarian kingdoms of Gaul. In the event, Aetius was able to convince them that Rome better served their interests than the Huns. In this way he assembled a coalition capable of halting Attila's advance. After this defeat, Attila maneuvered his weakened army back to the Hunnic homeland north of the Danube, but he died in 453, having succumbed to a brain hemorrhage during sex.

In spite of his skill as a general and diplomat, or perhaps because of it, Aetius did not escape resentment from his emperor. In September 454 Valentinian III chose to assassinate him but within six months was himself murdered by Aetius' former bodyguards. The succession dispute that ensued led to the final collapse of Roman imperial control in the West. In the absence of a strong dynastic claimant, the contest for the throne fell to an extensive list of contenders with support from a variety of interested groups: the eastern imperial court, the Roman senate, the Council of Gaul (a group of Romano-Gallic aristocrats who met annually in southern Gaul), the armies of Italy and Dalmatia, and even various barbarian groups all vied to influence the choice of successors. Predictably enough, none lasted long. In the last twenty-one years of the western empire, nine rulers claimed the throne, only three of whom lasted into a third year. Once again the relative weakness of their positions made them reliant on barbarian generals.

Ultimately, however, the western throne was becoming an irrelevancy, for it no longer bestowed much more than titular power. As the West had begun to shed territories to barbarian challengers in the early fifth century, it had simultaneously lost tax revenue, since it no longer controlled the lands and peoples that once filled its coffers. In consequence it was less and less capable of paying for armies and indeed of fielding them, because the loss of territories also diminished the size of its recruiting pool. This reduction in turn led to an ever-growing reliance on barbarian military manpower, which simultaneously strengthened Rome's barbarian contenders and weakened Rome's own capacity for self-defense. This vicious cycle ground down the state to the point that, by the time of Valentinian III's death in

455, the western empire was little more than a rump of what it had been just half a century earlier. In effect it controlled just Italy and a slice of southeastern Gaul.

Thus, when a boy emperor was imposed once again on the rickety western throne in October 475, it took less than a year to topple ruler and throne together. His name was Romulus Augustus (or, in the diminutive, Augustulus). Rome's last emperor thus bore the name of its first king *and* first emperor. When he refused to reward his barbarian auxiliaries, he was deposed and exiled by a general of mixed barbarian race, Odoacer, in September 476. Rather than set up another puppet, Odoacer had the senate of Rome write to the eastern emperor Zeno to report that "they had no need of a separate empire, but a single common emperor would be sufficient for both territories." The statement was of course filled with irony, for Odoacer had no real intention of submitting to eastern authority. The Roman empire had ceased to exist in the West.

THE GROWTH OF A BYZANTINE EMPIRE IN THE EAST (408–491)

Turning now to the eastern court after the death of Arcadius in 408, the first point to note is that, like his father before him, he had the good fortune of a son to succeed him and the bad fortune that this son, Theodosius II, was only a child of seven at the time. Like Arcadius himself, Theodosius II was forever subject to the powerful influence of courtiers. Indeed, in his instance this weakness was compounded by his indifference to politics and his passion for matters intellectual and religious. Theodosius II never participated in military campaigns and is notorious instead for having focused on personal piety. This devotion was encouraged by his older sister Pulcheria, who played an important role in the conduct of state affairs. Following a trend common for pious women of the age, she had dedicated herself to virginity and so helped to foster a court atmosphere, which some contemporaries likened to that of a monastery. It does not follow, however, that Theodosius II was entirely impractical. He did organize the first systematic effort to codify Roman imperial law ever yet undertaken, an effort, which resulted in the appearance of the monumental *Theodosian Code* in 438. He also reorganized the grain supply for Constantinople and equipped the expanded city with a new set of walls, which formed a nearly impregnable bulwark (Fig. 14.2; Map 14.2).

Fortunately for Theodosius II, relations with Persia were relatively stable throughout the forty-two years of his reign. The same atmosphere did not prevail on the Danube, however. Here, as we have seen, during the late fourth century the Huns had come to unite the disparate peoples in what is today Romania, and from the 420s onward they began to pose a serious threat to the empire. Under their king Attila, who came to power in 434, this threat became acute as they made a series of attacks on the Balkans that were calculated to win concessions from the eastern court in the form of annual tribute as high as 2,100 pounds of gold. Theodosius II and his general Aspar gladly paid this tribute rather than face the uncertainty

Figure 14.2 *By the early fifth century Constantinople had more than outgrown the walls built for it by Constantine (Map 14.2). To protect its population (which grew to half a million by the sixth century), Theodosius II ordered a new set of walls to be built between 408 and 413, comprising a taller inner wall with towers separated from a shorter outer wall by a wide terrace. These stretched almost four miles (6.4 km) from north to south along the western edge of the peninsula on which the city was built—the only side from which it could be practicably attacked. This remarkable bulwark, some of which still survives, prevented the city from being overcome by siege down to 1453, when the introduction of gunpowder allowed the Ottomans to take it.*

of battle. To be sure, the eastern empire was not entirely hamstrung on the military front, but it focused its energies on the western empire instead, intervening four times during the course of Theodosius II's reign.

Chief among Theodosius II's concerns was the orthodoxy of his subjects. He was thus easily convinced of the need to call the third ecumenical council in 431, when disputes arose between Nestorius, the bishop of Constantinople, and his rival Cyril, bishop of Alexandria, over the nature of Christ's humanity and, by extension, the proper designation for the Virgin Mary. Today, such disputes seem arcane and often futile, but they constituted the intellectual and cultural spaces within which the ecclesiastical heavyweights of late antiquity wrestled. Theodosius II convened the council at Ephesus, where Nestorius was defeated and exiled. But the issue boiled over again later in the reign, leading to a second council at Ephesus in 449 that devolved into open violence. Although the rival parties agitated for yet another council, Theodosius II resisted down to his death, which occurred in July 450.

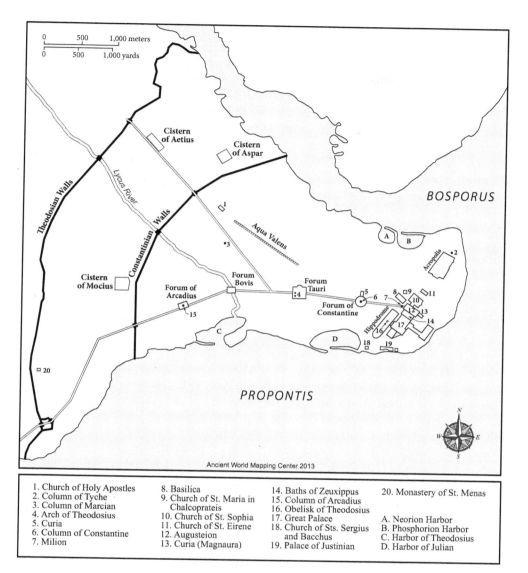

Map 14.2 *Constantinople in Late Antiquity*

1. Church of Holy Apostles
2. Column of Tyche
3. Column of Marcian
4. Arch of Theodosius
5. Curia
6. Column of Constantine
7. Milion

8. Basilica
9. Church of St. Maria in
   Chalcoprateis
10. Church of St. Sophia
11. Church of St. Eirene
12. Augusteion
13. Curia (Magnaura)

14. Baths of Zeuxippus
15. Column of Arcadius
16. Obelisk of Theodosius
17. Great Palace
18. Church of Sts. Sergius
    and Bacchus
19. Palace of Justinian

20. Monastery of St. Menas

A. Neorion Harbor
B. Phosphorion Harbor
C. Harbor of Theodosius
D. Harbor of Julian

Theodosius' successor was a retired general named Marcian, a man of otherwise undistinguished background. To boost his credentials, Marcian felt compelled to marry the empress Pulcheria, by now fifty-one years old and still a committed virgin. Nonetheless, he played his role as emperor well. He benefited from Attila's choice to turn his attacks westward and from Attila's death in 453. This was at once followed by infighting among Attila's sons and then the complete collapse of the Hunnic empire. Marcian added to the Huns' difficulties by withholding any further payments of tribute to them. He also addressed the still-gaping rifts in the church by organizing the fourth ecumenical council at Chalcedon (modern Kadiköy, Turkey) in 451. It issued a new formula describing Christ's nature as consisting of two parts, divine and human, indistinguishably commingled. Although the western church promptly rallied to this new formula, it met a chilly reception in Syria and Egypt. Rather than follow the imperial church, these regions went their own way, forming what came to be called a Monophysite ("one nature") theology that endures in the Christian churches of these regions down to the present.

Marcian died in 457 with no heir. Yet another undistinguished officer, Leo, was chosen to replace him. Leo maintained both the findings of the council of Chalcedon and the eastern interest in managing affairs in the West. He even saw to the imposition of the general Anthemius on the western throne in 467 and coordinated with him a massive expedition against the Vandals the following year. To both men's dismay, it turned into a disaster. The Vandals, using fireships, succeeded in destroying the Roman fleet before it ever reached the coast of Africa. This risky and costly venture underlines the extent to which Constantinople continued to contemplate rebuilding the tattered Roman empire.

Leo's reign also witnessed the rise of a new group of Goths in the Balkans. In the wake of eighty years of ongoing devastation, the provinces of Thrace and Pannonia along the Danube had been left open to barbarian settlement by two separate groups of Ostrogoths. The powerful general Aspar had used the Thracian Ostrogoths as *foederati* —independent peoples bound by treaty (*foedus*) to serve in Roman armies in exchange for payments. Wishing to free himself of Aspar's heavy hand, Leo found an alternative pool of military support in the Isaurians. They were a people living in the Taurus highlands of southern Asia Minor, well within the empire's geographical boundaries. Because of the mountainous inaccessibility of their homeland, however, they had long been able to resist Roman control. Like so many peoples of the period, they could be classed neither as fully Roman nor as entirely independent. Leo tapped the Isaurians as a counterweight against the Thracian Ostrogoths and even went so far as to marry his daughter Ariadne to the Isaurian general Zeno.

Upon his death in 474, Leo was succeeded by the child of this marriage, his grandson Leo II, who died after only ten months in office. But Leo II had appointed his father Zeno as co-Augustus, thus allowing Zeno to continue in power as sole emperor down to 491. Because of his Isaurian background, Zeno was often treated as an outsider in Constantinople and faced no less than three usurpation attempts. To quell the last, he was forced to turn to the other main group of Goths living in

Pannonia and their leader Theodoric. Theodoric proved to be a formidable military and political force, uniting all the Ostrogoths under his authority and eventually marching them west at Zeno's request to retake Italy from Odoacer. After achieving this in 489, Theodoric ruled on as "king of the Romans," in principle holding Italy for Zeno but in practice establishing an independent Ostrogothic state. The Ostrogoths were to maintain control here with Constantinople's consent until the 540s, when the emperor Justinian began a long and bloody war that eventually led to Italy's brief return to "Roman" control.

In a perilous world, Rome's eastern empire had thus developed a formula for survival and prosperity that would serve it well in the centuries to come. Rather than exterminate the peoples who challenged it for power, it put them to work fighting each other or, whenever possible, sent them west. This game was always a dangerous one, but the Byzantines raised diplomacy to a finely tuned art that achieved remarkable results. In no small part their diplomatic skill explains the success of a state, which flourished as the largest empire of Christendom through the Middle Ages.

A CHRISTIAN CULTURE

From the mid-first century, Christian communities had shown a remarkable ability to reproduce themselves with rapidity and relative uniformity. Like an embryonic organism, the church began as a tiny series of cells, which by division and subdivision continuously developed in form and function to suit changing geographical or temporal circumstances, but always retained the same basic genetic code. It was able to achieve its surprising continuity and uniformity in large part because it was a religion of the book. Like its scriptures, Christianity's basic organizational modules were also relatively uniform, consisting of a bishop, a clergy, a *laos* ("congregation" or "people" in Greek, our word "laity"), and a building in which to worship. These were all, of course, subject to local variation, but by the sixth century the basic outlines could be found in communities from as far east as Sogdia in central Asia to as far west as Ireland. Schoolchildren from across this vast expanse studied the same scriptures, clergy preached from the same body of tenets, and all Christians saw themselves as subject to one law and religion. In some regards, then, the most uniform cultural artifact bequeathed to posterity by the Roman empire, and the one that had the greatest worldwide impact, was Christianity.

All Christians believed first and foremost in a message of sin and salvation. They saw themselves as subject to the snares of evil manifested in sins provoked by the devil, but all also assumed that belief in the power of God as manifested in Christ could permit any Christian to overcome these challenges and win eternal life. Although in theory none who had been baptized had any inherently stronger claim to divine access than any other, from the beginning most Christians assumed that some more obviously counted as saved than others. Chief among them were of course the martyrs. After the conversion of the empire and the end of persecutions, however, the surest way to battle sin and guarantee salvation was through *askesis* (literally "practice" in Greek). This involved spiritual and physical training of the body—much like the work of an athlete—in order to overcome sinfulness. During the late fourth and early fifth centuries, asceticism became a significant means to mark off the holiest believers.

This golden age of late antiquity witnessed what one prominent scholar has termed the "rise of the Holy Man." The quintessential representative of this phenomenon is also one of its earliest: St. Antony of Egypt (c. 250–356). He had grown up in a moderately wealthy farming family in the Egyptian Fayyum. At about twenty years of age he was so moved by the scriptural passage exhorting believers to "sell all you have, give it to the poor, and follow me" (*Matthew* 19:21) that he liquidated his estates and moved out to the eastern desert. Over the course of the remainder of his life, Antony lived in this waste practicing *askesis*: living on almost no food, denying himself marriage, sexuality, and family, and doing constant battle with the demons he believed surrounded him. Despite his renunciation of the world, however, Antony was anything but isolated, for he was regularly visited by those seeking healing or advice, and he even attracted the attention of the emperor Constantius and the Alexandrian bishop Athanasius.

Upon this holy man's death, Athanasius composed a *Life of Antony* that became an instant "bestseller" across the empire. Though written in Greek, it was quickly translated into Latin and circulated as far away as Gaul by the early 370s. By then, the story of this social radical was winning converts to a new way of life across the entire spectrum of Christian believers, from the poorest to the richest. This new "philosophy," as they termed their lifestyle, demanded no elaborate education and no comfortable standard of living, but was open to any who could endure self-denial in excruciating doses.

Antony was by no means the first or only holy man of late antiquity. Indeed, by the time of his death a veritable wave of asceticism had swept across the eastern empire, not just in Egypt but also in Syria, where one could witness an even stauncher renunciation of the world and more intensive mortification of the flesh (Fig. 14.3a, b). Nor was Antony's lifestyle as a solitary hermit the only acceptable approach to ascetic living. His contemporary and fellow Egyptian Pachomius (c. 292–347) pioneered a form, which included hierarchy (with a leader and a prescribed rule) and community (with individuals living in a walled complex of rooms termed "cells"). This communitarian style of asceticism also spread rapidly as *monachoi* (solitary ones), from which our word "monk" derives, began to appear across East and West by the late fourth century.

Athanasius' *Life of Antony* was revolutionary not just because of the lifestyle it championed, but also because it represented a new genre of literature, called hagiography—that is, the writing of the lives of saints. The *Life of Antony* was soon followed by a spate of such biographies, which in their turn were promptly translated into the range of languages common in late antiquity—Greek, Latin, Syriac, Coptic—and disseminated throughout the Mediterranean. Such literature brought a wave of travelers to Egypt and Syria to visit the holy men and spread word of their accomplishments. As monasticism spread, increasingly elaborate codes were

a

b

Figure 14.3a, b *Simeon Stylites spent almost forty years (until 459) living in the open air on top of a series of pillars (in Greek,* styloi*) at Telneshe in northern Syria. The tallest was over 40 ft/12 m high. This silver plate [a] shows him on a pillar being tempted by a demonic snake. He became an extremely influential holy man because of his public role in resolving disputes, offering cures, and advising pilgrims and even emperors. Upon Simeon's death, the emperor Zeno constructed an elaborate complex comprising four basilicas placed back to back in the shape of a cross around his last pillar [b]. Today the ruins are referred to in Arabic as Qal'at Sim'an ("the Mansion of Simeon").*

developed and collated, culminating in the sixth-century *Rule of St. Benedict*, which mandated firm governing hierarchies, stern rules of behavior, a regimen of work and prayer, and a strict division of the day according to liturgical "offices" involving set prayers and the singing of psalms. Benedict's rule became the foundation for an institution, which would dominate many aspects of religious practice throughout Christendom in the Middle Ages.

Monasticism was only one major development in Christian culture at this time. Late antiquity also saw the rise of what is now called the cult of the saints. Having begun as care for the corpses of those who had been martyred in the persecutions, this practice grew into a new mode of worship focused on the bodies of those whose life or death marked them off as holy. Yet another development in Christian religion during this period was pilgrimage to the Holy Land. From Constantine's reign onward, it came to be the premier travel destination for Christians, who regarded it as a site of particular spiritual power (Plate 6b). At the same time late antiquity also saw the emergence of new attitudes toward the poor and needy. Roman culture had long advocated the feeding and entertainment of the masses by wealthy members of the elite at public festivals. Christianity, by contrast, removed the civic focus of such benefactions and extended the obligation to give freely much lower down the social ladder (compare Source 13.1).

Many of these developments represent significant departures from earlier Roman practice. Even so, despite its introduction of revolutionary new cultural ideals and practices, in most ways Christianity was a strong force for the preservation of Roman traditions. Indeed, this contradiction is rooted in the Christian gospels, which are by turns both radical and conservative. As a mass movement, Christianity could play to either strain, so that even as Christian radicals introduced an unheard-of new fascination with worldly renunciation, other Christian leaders worked hard to amass power and wealth along more traditional lines. This was particularly true in the West, where the political chaos of the barbarian invasions made the church into something of a refuge for *Romanitas* ("Romanness"). Fifth-century Gaul saw the development of a virtual ecclesiastical aristocracy, in which the office of bishop was passed literally from father to son. Such bishops had at their disposal stores of wealth, landed estates, impressive complexes of buildings, and above all power over cities with walls— bastions for the preservation of life and the continuation of prosperity. These same bishops also had access to education and to Latin texts, which they fastidiously preserved as part of their patrimony from the Roman past. In their hands, and the hands of a growing monastic establishment, Roman culture survived the economic and military turmoil of the barbarian invasions and the early Middle Ages.

A similar story could be told with slavery. Since the nineteenth century some scholars have argued that Christianity had a mitigating effect on this characteristically Greco-Roman institution, which receded in importance in certain parts of the empire in late antiquity. Other researchers, indeed the majority, have denied the influence of Christianity. They have attributed the decline of slavery to a reduction in the slave supply after the end of Rome's wars of conquest and to the rise of alternative modes of bound labor like the "colonate" (see Chapter Twelve), which resembled medieval serfdom. In some sense, both sides of the argument carry conviction. The decline of slavery had multiple causes, and economic factors always played a paramount role. But Christian ideology, which came to permeate all aspects of Mediterranean culture, also had an effect. Christian prohibitions on sexual exploitation and the murder and abuse of slaves, coupled with notions of the equality of all humans before God, eventually led to radical reductions in the freedom of masters to exploit slaves by the sixth century. By the same token, however, Christian injunctions that slaves be obedient to their masters and the notion that slavery was a natural result of human sinfulness helped to perpetuate slavery. Ultimately, the barbarian invasions that split the empire also seem to have resulted in a split in slaveholding practice. In the East, where the central state apparatus remained dominant, agricultural slaveholding on a large scale disappeared by the sixth century. In the West, by contrast, the barbarian peoples who inherited Roman territory introduced new cultural practices, which sustained agricultural slaveholding down to the eighth century. In both instances, Christian principles were used to justify, and equally to condemn, the underpinnings of slavery.

WOMEN'S POWER IN LATE ANTIQUITY

Much of the pattern for women's lives remained in late antiquity as it had been in the early empire. A large part of the reason was the demographics of a world where so few children were likely to reach adulthood (see Chapter Eight). This cruel fact of nature compelled women to endure multiple pregnancies, and also permitted the marriage of girls early in their teens. If anything, marriage commitments occurred at an even younger age in the late empire, for the practice of legally enforceable *sponsalia* (betrothals) at around the age of seven became much more common in this era of heightened sensitivity to sexual morality.

The Christian church, which had always been stricter regarding sexual restraint than Roman or Greek society, also began to exert its influence on ancient law and social practice. In addition to the strictures on sexual behavior laid down by Augustus' legislation, the church began enforcing its own standards of conduct. Abortion and infant exposure were strictly forbidden by the church, and as church and state became increasingly intertwined, the state introduced its own regulations against both practices; it also at times allowed charges of treason to be brought against adulterers. As may be imagined, social practice did not always fall in line with these stricter codes of conduct, but the change in attitude backed up by a stiffening of the laws gradually had the effect of making infidelity seem a serious risk rather than a matter of slight consequence. So too with divorce, which the Roman state had always permitted but the church staunchly condemned, and celibacy, which the Roman state had sought to impede but Christianity encouraged. Already Constantine began issuing laws inverting this dynamic, regulating divorce while removing restrictions on celibacy.

By modern standards it may seem rather shocking that the Church's interest in sexual morality led society to prize the renunciation of things physical and even the mortification of the body. However, this was not how the ancients saw it, and particularly not women. At the very least, the church's official refusal to countenance double standards of sexual behavior put women on a more equal footing in the family. Moreover, the new emphasis on asceticism brought with it an acknowledgement that women were just as capable of this form of virtue as men. In late antiquity asceticism and piety had taken their place alongside martial valor and political achievement as a means to gain status and recognition. Moreover, because asceticism was not a gendered cultural practice (at least not to the degree that warfare and politics were), it was open to women as a way to win status.

It was surely with this prospect at the back of her mind that the empress Pulcheria, older sister of the child emperor Theodosius II, committed herself to virginity as a young woman. This choice offered her an extraordinary claim to power during her brother's administration, not just because she avoided marriage entanglements that might have weakened her personal authority, but also because she exploited the commonly recognized value of asceticism in the period to gain the title Augusta and notable influence in the imperial court. Even after Theodosius II's death, Pulcheria continued to serve as the symbol of empire, so much so that her brother's successor Marcian legitimized his rule by marrying her. Indeed, the marriage itself demonstrated the power of her ascetic vows, for it was agreed to only on the condition that she would be allowed to remain a virgin.

THE "DECLINE AND FALL" OF THE ROMAN EMPIRE

Edward Gibbon, in his lengthy, celebrated study *The Decline and Fall of the Roman Empire*, argued that the empire fell prey to two forces: barbarism and Christianity. From the time of Augustus, he believed, emperors began using the military, and particularly their guard troops, to suppress the Roman people and thus to supplant them as the functional citizen army that had once made Rome great. In his view, emperors increasingly turned to barbarians to man their forces, thus allowing external peoples to grow in strength even as Rome's citizens became effete and weak-willed. Meanwhile Christianity, Gibbon felt, encouraged the Roman people to place their trust in a transcendent otherworld and thus to abandon their concern for the state. The church introduced an attachment to the irrational and created a rival to the state's authority, which undermined Rome's power and further weakened its empire in the face of the barbarian invasions.

From the moment of its publication (beginning in 1776), *The Decline and Fall* provoked strong reactions, positive and negative, and it continues to exercise tremendous influence on the popular imagination of the western world. Although scholars have since set aside many of Gibbon's arguments, his fundamental question still continues to confront those who study Rome's history: "Why did the Roman empire decline and fall?" Historians today are every bit as intent on answering that question as Gibbon was, and they have formulated a wealth of hypotheses: Rome fell victim to invasions by Germanic or Hunnic peoples, or both; it witnessed economic decline due to corruption or depopulation; its leadership classes fell victim to militarism or bureaucratization; it was afflicted with natural disasters like plague, climate change, or environmental destruction. None of these explanations has won anything like universal acceptance. Indeed, more recent studies have tended to marvel less at Rome's eventual decline and more at the very fact that its empire managed to survive as long as it did. Pondering Rome's decline and fall does in fact provoke some reflection about what it accomplished in assembling so large an empire—one larger than the greater Mediterranean region has witnessed ever since—and in holding it together for so long.

It was indeed an epic accomplishment for Rome to have conquered the entire Mediterranean and much of its hinterland, but it was even more remarkable that it was able to hold this territory in a unified empire for 600 years. To do this, Rome needed to develop a powerful ideological framework supporting its claims to dominion, and to disseminate this outlook systematically to its various provinces. In other words, it needed to convince the many peoples living in its many regions that it was operating in their interests and, indeed, that Rome and Romanness were coterminous with their own self-identity. Egyptians and Britons, Africans and Greeks had to want to think of themselves as Romans for Rome's power to prevail. The decline of this sense of community and identity that set in during late antiquity was in many respects concomitant with the collapse of empire.

Even in the West, however, where the Roman state disappeared from 476 onward, Roman identity did not vanish entirely nor even diminish in many communities it no longer directly controlled. The barbarian newcomers who seized power from Rome were by no means averse to the adoption of Roman ways. They were, for example, eager to link their power to the traditional state through the exchange of women in marriage. So, too, the barbarian taste for the titles and trappings of Roman military office confirms an acceptance of the ongoing importance of the Roman state as a source of authority and legitimacy. In Italy, Spain, and Gaul barbarian leaders sought affirmation from local Roman aristocrats in the form of letters and panegyrics, and at various points fairly early in their histories the peoples here began using Latin for official documents and even for vernacular speech.

Naturally, Roman provincials were themselves forced to adapt to new realities that required some degree of assimilation on their part to barbarian ways. Mundane changes in dress provide a telling example. Romans apparently took quite well to wearing barbarian clothes, including furs and pants. The assimilation of Roman to barbarian is also evidenced in instances of intermarriage (extending beyond the level of the nobility), as well as in the appointment of Romans to court offices in the successor kingdoms. Once these new states had introduced their own governmental structures to settle disputes, apportion resources, bestow patronage, and provide for the common defense, it was only natural that the provincials looked to them for support, and gradually began to follow non-Roman social and political customs. In this sense the post-Roman world saw a gradual rapprochement between Romans and barbarians that kept the traditions of the former alive while allowing for their renewal and transformation through the influence of the latter.

Although 476 has been canonized as the year in which Rome fell, in most ways this was a non-event. In reality, Rome's fall from political supremacy in the West was a process that lasted over seventy years, so that this single occurrence represents only one step along a much longer path. It is even more important, however, to recognize that "Rome" continued to live on in the East long after 476. Constantine's new capital of Constantinople, self-consciously styled "the New Rome," came to outshine its older forebear in power and prestige already in the course of the fifth century, and by the sixth the Byzantine emperor Justinian was surely justified in fancying himself the legitimate champion of Roman power across the Mediterranean. In some sense, Rome's loss of power to Constantinople represents the ultimate confirmation of its successful growth far beyond the city itself. Having spread its political, social, and cultural organization so effectively to its provinces, Rome was eventually able to take up residence elsewhere in the empire it had created, and thus to outlive itself.

SUGGESTED READINGS

Brown, Peter R. L. 2013 (second revised edition). *The Rise of Western Christendom: Triumph and Diversity, A.D. 200–1000*. Malden, Mass., and Oxford: Wiley-Blackwell.

Clark, Gillian. 1993. *Women in Late Antiquity: Pagan and Christian Lifestyles*. Oxford: Oxford University Press.

Gregory, Timothy E. 2005. *A History of Byzantium*. Malden, Mass., and Oxford: Blackwell. Coverage spans late antiquity to the end of the Byzantine empire.

Halsall, Guy. 2007. *Barbarian Migrations and the Roman West, 376–568*. Cambridge: Cambridge University Press. Good summary of revisionist approaches to the barbarian migrations, emphasizing fluid identities and consensual, rather than confrontational, models for cultural change.

Heather, Peter. 2006. *The Fall of the Roman Empire: A New History of Rome and the Barbarians*. Oxford: Oxford University Press. Nuanced restatement of the old orthodoxy that waves of barbarian invaders caused the Roman state to fall.

TIMELINE

c. 1000 First undoubted traces of settlement at the site of Rome

900–700 Iron Age; Villanovan and Latial cultures

c. 800 Phoenicians found Carthage

c. 775 Greeks begin to settle in Italy and Sicily

700–400 Etruscan and Greek cities at their height in Italy

753–510 Traditional dates for monarchy at Rome (seven kings in succession)

c. 500 Establishment of the Roman Republic; treaty between Carthage and Rome

c. 500–287 "Struggle of the Orders"

c. 450 Laws of the Twelve Tables are issued

c. 396 Romans take over Veii

c. 387 Warband of Gauls loots Rome

343–290 Samnite Wars: (343–341) First; (326–304) Second; (298–290) Third

c. 280 Rome first issues its own coins

280–275 King Pyrrhus of Epirus campaigns against Rome in southern Italy

264–241 First Punic War, at the end of which Sicily becomes Rome's first "province"

237 Roman takeover of Sardinia from Carthage

218–201 Second Punic War; Romans are defeated by Hannibal at (217) Lake Trasimene and (216) Cannae; (202) final defeat of Carthaginians at Zama

215–205, 200–196, 171–168 First, Second, and Third Macedonian Wars

c. 200–c. 170 Numerous colonies are established in Italy, including the Po Valley

198 Two Roman provinces are formed in Spain (Further, Nearer)

192–189 Rome defeats Antiochus III in the Syrian War

186–183 Suppression of the cult of Bacchus in Italy

mid-150s–130s Roman wars with Lusitanians and Celtiberians, ending (133) with the capture of Numantia

149–146 Third Punic War, ending with the destruction of Carthage

148 Macedon becomes a Roman province, and Corinth is destroyed (146)

136–132 First Slave War in Sicily

133 Tribunate of Tiberius Gracchus

133 Kingdom of Pergamum is bequeathed to Rome and (129) becomes the province of Asia

123, 122 Tribunates of Gaius Gracchus

121 *Senatus Consultum Ultimum* authorizes the elimination of Gaius Gracchus

113–101 Warfare with Cimbri and Teutoni

112–105 War with Jugurtha in Numidia

c. 107–101 Major reform of the Roman army

107, 104, 103, 102, 101 Consulships of Marius

104–100 Second Slave War in Sicily

100 Tribunate of Saturninus and (sixth) consulship of Marius

91 Tribunate of Livius Drusus

91–87 Social War; (90–89) extension of Roman citizenship throughout Italy; (88) tribunate of Sulpicius Rufus and Sulla's first march on Rome

90–85 War with Mithridates in Asia Minor and Greece; Sulla offers peace terms

83–82 Sulla's second march on Rome

82–81 Dictatorship of Sulla; proscriptions

80–73 Sertorius in Spain resists Sullan commanders (Pompey among them) until murdered

74–63 Lucullus, then (from 66) Pompey, resume war against Mithridates

73–71 Slave revolt of Spartacus

70 Consulship of Crassus and Pompey

67 Pompey suppresses piracy in the Mediterranean

64–63 Bithynia/Pontus, Cilicia, and Syria are made provinces by Pompey

63 As consul, Cicero exposes Catiline's conspiracy

60–59 Formation of "First Triumvirate" (Caesar, Crassus, Pompey)

59 Consulship of Julius Caesar

58 Tribunate of Clodius

58–51 Caesar campaigns in Gaul

56 "Triumvirs" meet at Luca to strengthen and extend their partnership

55 Consulship of Crassus and Pompey

53 Crassus' army invades Parthia and is slaughtered at Carrhae

52 Death of Clodius; sole consulship of Pompey

49 (January) Caesar crosses Rubicon River to invade Italy; (March to fall) Caesar campaigns against Pompeians in Spain

48 Pompey is defeated by Caesar at Pharsalus, and killed on arrival in Egypt as fugitive

48–45 Caesar supports Cleopatra in Egypt (48–47), and eliminates Pompeians in Africa (46) and Spain (45)

48–44 Caesar holds consulships and dictatorships; the latter office is made perpetual in February 44, leading to his assassination on March 15

44 (May) Octavian claims his inheritance from Caesar, repulses Antony from Mutina (April 43), and becomes consul (August 43)

43 (November) Antony, Lepidus, and Octavian form the Second Triumvirate; (January 42) the senate deifies Caesar

42 Antony and Octavian defeat Brutus and Cassius at Philippi

41–40 Perusine War

36 Invasion of Parthia by Antony fails badly; but he subdues Armenia (35–34), and stages the "Donations of Alexandria" (34)

36 Sextus Pompey is defeated by Octavian and Lepidus; Lepidus' attempt to eliminate Octavian results in his own exile

31 Octavian defeats Antony and Cleopatra at Actium

30 Octavian captures Alexandria, and makes Egypt a Roman province

27 "First Settlement"; Octavian is renamed Augustus

27–c. 1 B.C. Extension of Roman control in Spain, the Alps, and central Europe to the Danube River

23 "Second Settlement"

20 Parthia returns legionary standards captured from Crassus and Antony

18–17 Augustus introduces legislation affecting marriage, childbearing, and adultery

13 New conditions for army service are introduced

A.D. 6–9 Rebellions in Germany, Dalmatia, Pannonia; (A.D. 9) three Roman legions are massacred in Teutoburg Forest

14 Augustus dies, and is succeeded by Tiberius

17–19 Germanicus is dispatched to the East, and dies in Syria

20 Trial of Piso for the death of Germanicus

26 Tiberius takes up residence on Capri

31 Sejanus (Praetorian Prefect since 14) is denounced and executed

37 Tiberius dies, and is succeeded by Gaius Caligula

41 Assassination of Caligula, who is succeeded by Claudius

40s–50s Claudius constructs a new harbor (Portus) north of Ostia

43–46 Britain (43), Mauretania (43), and Thrace (46) become Roman provinces

54 Claudius dies, and is succeeded by Nero

60 Boudica leads a rebellion in Britain

64 Great Fire of Rome; Christians are persecuted as scapegoats

66–73 First Jewish Revolt; Temple in Jerusalem is destroyed (70), and Masada is captured (73)

67–68 Rising and defeat of Vindex in Gaul

68 (June) Nero commits suicide, and is succeeded by Galba

69 (January) With Praetorians' support, Otho murders Galba and succeeds him; (April) Otho is defeated by the army from Germany under Vitellius, who succeeds him; (July) legions in the East and Pannonia support Vespasian for emperor; Vitellius' army is defeated (October) and he is killed (December); Vespasian succeeds him

70s Vespasian builds the Temple of Peace in Rome, and begins the Colosseum

79 Vespasian dies, and is succeeded by Titus; eruption of Mt. Vesuvius

81 Titus dies, and is succeeded by Domitian

85–92 Domitian campaigns north of the Danube

96 Domitian is assassinated; Nerva succeeds him

96–98 Nerva establishes *alimenta*

97 Nerva adopts Trajan

98 Nerva dies, and is succeeded by Trajan

101–102, 105–106 Dacian Wars; Dacia then becomes a Roman province

105–106 Arabia Petraea (Nabataea) becomes a Roman province

113–117 Trajan campaigns to seize Armenia and Mesopotamia from Parthian control

c. 115 Trajan adds an inner basin to Claudius' harbor at Portus

115–117 Second Jewish Revolt

117 Trajan dies, and is succeeded by Hadrian, who abandons territories seized from Parthia by Trajan

120s Hadrian constructs "his" Wall across northern England

121–127, 128–131 Hadrian makes extended journeys empire-wide

132–135 Third Jewish Revolt (Bar Kokhba War)

138 Hadrian dies, and is succeeded by Antoninus Pius

161 Antoninus Pius dies, and is succeeded by Marcus Aurelius and Lucius Verus

162–166 Lucius Verus campaigns against Parthia

mid-160s–190s Plague sweeps through the empire

166–173, 176–180 First and Second Marcomannic Wars (ended by Commodus)

180 Marcus Aurelius dies, and is succeeded by Commodus

192 (December 31) Commodus is assassinated

193 (January 1) Pertinax becomes emperor, only to be killed in March; the Praetorians make Didius Julianus emperor, but he is killed in June; Septimius Severus, supported by armies on the Rhine and Danube, reaches Rome to replace him

194–197 Septimius Severus eliminates his rivals Pescennius Niger (194) and Clodius Albinus (197)

194–195, 197–199 Septimius Severus campaigns against the Parthians;

northern Mesopotamia and Osroene become Roman provinces

c. 200 Septimius Severus lifts the ban on marriage by soldiers

208–211 Septimius Severus campaigns in northern Britain, where he dies; Caracalla succeeds him

212 Caracalla extends Roman citizenship empire-wide

217 Caracalla is assassinated while on campaign into Armenia and Parthia; Macrinus (first *eques* to be emperor) replaces him

218 Macrinus is assassinated; he is replaced by Elagabalus

222 Elagabalus is murdered, and is succeeded by Severus Alexander

224 Sasanian dynasty takes control of Parthia/Persia

235 On campaign in Raetia, mutinous soldiers assassinate Severus Alexander and Julia Mamaea; their leader Maximinus replaces him

238–284 Age of Crisis

248 Celebration of Rome's thousandth anniversary

249–250, 257–259 Empire-wide persecution of Christians by Emperors Decius and then Valerian

260 Sasanian King Shapur I captures Valerian

260–268 As sole emperor Gallienus seeks to secure the core of the empire

260s–270s Postumus controls "Gallic Empire"; Odenaethus, and then Zenobia, control the East from Palmyra

270–275 Emperor Aurelian abandons the province of Dacia (270), but regains the East from Zenobia (272), as well as Postumus' "Gallic Empire" (274)

284 Diocletian becomes emperor, and (286) makes Maximian co-emperor

293 "Tetrarchy" is formed

290s Provinces are redivided; civil and military positions are separated

301 Edict on Maximum Prices

303 "Great Persecution" of Christians (in the West to 305, in the East to 311)

306 Constantine is proclaimed Augustus in Britain

312 In a battle at the Milvian Bridge, Constantine eliminates Maxentius and wins Rome; he professes Christianity

313–324 Constantine rules the West, Licinius the East; (313) together they issue "Edict of Milan," and unite to defeat Maximin Daia

324 Constantine defeats Licinius, becomes sole emperor, and initiates refoundation of Byzantium as Constantinople (dedicated 330)

325 First Ecumenical Council of Nicaea

337 Constantine dies, and is succeeded by his sons: Constantine II in Gaul and Spain; Constans in Italy, Illyricum, and Africa; Constantius II in East

340 Constantine II is killed in civil war

350 Constans is killed by Magnentius

353 Magnentius is defeated and killed by Constantius II

360 Julian is promoted to Augustus by his troops

361 Constantius II dies; Julian becomes sole emperor

363 Julian is killed in battle with Persians

364 Valentinian I and Valens become joint Augusti in West and East

375 Valentinian I dies, and is succeeded by sons Gratian and Valentinian II

378 Valens is killed by Goths at Battle of Adrianople, and is succeeded by Theodosius I in East (379)

382 Theodosius I makes peace with Goths in Thrace

383–388 Magnus Maximus kills Gratian, and rules in West until defeated by Theodosius I

392–394 Eugenius usurps throne from Valentinian II, but is defeated by Theodosius I

395 Theodosius I dies, and is succeeded by his sons: Honorius in West, Arcadius in East

402 Honorius transfers court from Milan to Ravenna, which becomes western capital

405–406 Ostrogoths invade Italy from Danube; Vandals, Alans, and Suebi invade Gaul and Spain from Rhine

408 Arcadius dies, and is succeeded in East by Theodosius II

410 Visigoths under Alaric sack Rome

418 Settlement of Visigoths in Aquitania

423–425 Honorius dies, and is succeeded in West (425) by Valentinian III

429–439 Vandals gain control of North Africa

438 *Theodosian Code* is issued

450 Theodosius II dies, and is succeeded in East by Marcian

451 Aetius defeats Attila the Hun at Catalaunian Plains (Gaul); Fourth Ecumenical Council of Chalcedon

455 Valentinian III is assassinated; Gaiseric the Vandal sacks Rome

457 Marcian dies, and is succeeded by Leo I

474 Leo I dies, and is succeeded by Zeno

476 Romulus Augustulus, last Western emperor, is deposed

489 Theodoric the Ostrogoth retakes Italy for the East, and rules it as "King of the Romans"

527–565 Justinian rules Byzantine empire; he reconquers (533–534) Africa and (535–554) Italy

GLOSSARY

(Most terms mentioned only once in the text are omitted here.)

aedile—Four annual magistrates in the city of Rome, two of whom had to be plebeian. The office was originally a plebeian one, charged with oversight of the temple (*aedes*) established by the *plebs*. Later, duties came to include general oversight of trade, markets, public buildings, and public games (*ludi*).

aerarium—Roman treasury and depository of documents overseen by *quaestors*, situated in the Temple of Saturn in the Forum. In A.D. 6 Augustus also established the "military treasury" (*aerarium militare*).

ager (*publicus*, *Gallicus*, etc.)—("land") *Ager publicus* ("public land") was property owned by the Roman state that it could assign or lease (for rent), normally through the *censors*.

agger—("mound") A military rampart.

Agri Decumates—Territory that formed a reentrant angle between the upper Rhine and Danube rivers.

ambitio, ambitus—("circuit" or "going round") The quest for public office by promising favors, paying voters, or giving them gifts. Unlike *ambitio* (legal canvassing), *ambitus* was illegal bribery of voters.

amicus, amicitia—("friend," "friendship") *Amicitia* signified a cordial, cooperative relationship in Roman political and social life, although the relationship might only be short-term and the parties to it might not necessarily be on close personal terms otherwise.

amphitheater—Oval-shaped structure (in wood, later stone) designed for gladiatorial and beast fights. The great one built by the Flavian emperors in Rome, and still partially standing today, came to be called the Colosseum in the Middle Ages.

annona—"Food supply," especially the supply of grain to the city of Rome.

Antonines—Line of emperors ruling from the accession of Antoninus Pius (138) through the death of Commodus (192). See Table 10.1.

ara—"Altar," erected in honor of one or more gods, where a sacrifice could be made.

Arians—Christians who accepted the theories of Arius that Christ was created after the beginning of the universe by God the Father and was inferior to him; branded as heresy at the Council of Nicaea in 325.

as (pl. *asses*)—Low-value Roman coin. See *denarius*.

asceticism—(Greek *askesis*, "practice" or "training") Self-denial and mortification for the sake of spiritual improvement, practiced by some pagans and especially by Christians in late antiquity.

atrium (pl. *atria*)—Central entrance and reception room in a Roman house.

auctoritas—Unofficial influence exercised by, and prestige enjoyed by, those individuals or corporate bodies whose advice and recommendations gained special respect.

augur—See *auspicium*.

Augustales—Priests (usually freedmen) who took responsibility for the imperial cult in municipalities; often a group of six, hence the title *seviri* (or *sexviri*) *Augustales*.

Augustus ("revered")—New *cognomen* taken by Octavian in 27 B.C., which later became a regular imperial title. Ancient writers connected it both to *auctoritas* and to augury (see *auspicium*).

aureus (pl. *aurei*)—Gold coin valued at 25 *denarii*.

auspicium—Divination, the search for and interpretation of signs in nature by *augurs*.

auxilia—Auxiliary troops (often cavalry or specialized fighters) who aided the legions.

auxilium—("aid") To aid fellow plebeians was a key function for the tribunes to perform.

Caesar—A *cognomen* (see below), which later became a regular imperial title.

Campus Martius—("Field of Mars") Area at the Tiber River's "bend." During the Republic it lay beyond Rome's *pomerium*. Named after an early altar of Mars located here.

Capitolium (*Mons Capitolinus*)—("Capitoline hill," Capitol) Smallest of Rome's seven hills, and site of the temple of Jupiter Optimus Maximus.

census—In the Republic, the official list of Roman citizens (only; *not* the entire population) drawn up by two *censors* every five years. From Augustus' time, emperors periodically organized censuses of the entire empire and its population.

centuria (pl. *centuriae*)—Voting units or "centuries" (193 total) into which the Roman citizen body was divided in the *comitia centuriata* ("Centuriate assembly").

centurion—Title of the officers responsible for the day-to-day functioning of a Roman legion.

Christianity—Religion inspired by Jesus Christ in the early first century A.D. It sprang from Judaism, but gradually separated from it and developed a more distinct identity. Like Judaism, it required its adherents to be devoted exclusively to its one god.

circus (Circus Maximus, Circus Flaminius)—Long stadium rounded at one end, used mostly for chariot racing in public games (*ludi*) and religious festivals.

clementia—"Clemency," willingness to pardon defeated enemies.

client (*cliens*, pl. *clientes*)—A free man with ties (sometimes hereditary) to an individual of higher standing termed his patron (*patronus*).

client kingdom—A state usually on the fringes of Roman territory, which remained independent but whose ruler agreed to maintain and advance Roman interests; Rome offered protection in return.

cognomen (pl. *cognomina*)—Last component of the typical Roman *trinomina* ("three names"), representing the surname of a Roman family, e.g., Gaius Julius Caesar, who is of the Caesar family. A *cognomen* might also be acquired, and even become hereditary, through military distinction, e.g., Lucius Cornelius Scipio Africanus, following his victories in Africa. Some Roman families never had a *cognomen*; others had more than one. See also *praenomen, nomen*.

cohors—("cohort") A group of one kind or another, frequently a tactical unit within a legion, but also a governor's entourage, for example.

collegium—("group," "association") A recognized group of many kinds (religious, social, commercial, professional), including the groups (or "colleges") of priests.

colonia (pl. *coloniae*)—"Colony" or settlement founded to settle discharged veterans or civilians eager to improve their prospects.

colonus (pl. *coloni*)—1) Farmer (especially a tenant) or country dweller; 2) inhabitant of a Roman *colonia*; 3) in the late empire, farmers bound to cultivate the parcels of land on which they and their ancestors were registered.

Colosseum—See *amphitheater.*

comes (pl. *comites*)—"Companion," "advisor" (especially of the emperor), and (from the tetrarchy onwards) a high-ranking military commander or other official ("count").

comitatenses—("retinue troops") Soldiers in mobile units, considered superior to *limitanei* (see below), who accompanied the emperor or his generals in the large field armies characteristic of the late empire.

comitium (pl. *comitia*)—In all Roman communities, a designated place for citizens to meet when summoned by officials. The plural *comitia* denotes such a citizen assembly itself.

commercium—1) "Business," "commerce"; also 2) the right of a Latin to own Roman land and to make a contract enforceable in a Roman law court.

concilium (pl. *concilia*)—"Assembly," especially that of Rome's plebeian citizens (*concilium plebis*). During the Principate, the term was also used for the provincial assemblies that organized celebrations of the imperial cult. In Greek, *koinon* (pl. *koina*).

consilium—"Advice" and by extension the group that provided it, in particular to the emperor (hence *consilium principis*).

constitutio Antoniniana—The legal enactment (*constitutio*) of A.D. 212 by which Caracalla (Marcus Aurelius Antoninus) extended Roman citizenship to almost all the free inhabitants of the empire.

consul—Chief annual magistrate of the Roman Republic (always one of a pair).

contio (pl. *contiones*)—Public meeting convened by an officeholder to discuss (only) a matter of current concern (legislative, judicial in particular).

conubium—Marriage and the right to enter into a marriage recognized by Roman law.

curator (pl. *curatores*)—General descriptive term for anyone who shouldered a special responsibility, above all in public life. Most notably, from the second century A.D., the term was used for officials dispatched by emperors to intervene at a time of difficulty.

curia (pl. *curiae*)—1) The earliest groups into which Roman citizens were divided; 2) the meeting place of a citizen unit, in particular a senate or town council.

cursus honorum—Literally "succession of offices," the prescribed series of magistracies that Roman senators sought to hold in order to become leading public figures.

damnatio memoriae—("damning of the memory") After the deaths of individuals declared by the senate to be enemies of the state (certain emperors especially), measures taken to blot out their memory.

dea, deus—goddess, god.

decurion—City councilor, the equivalent at a local level to a senator at Rome.

denarius (pl. *denarii*; see also *aureus, sestertius*)—Roman coin made of silver. Initially, during the Second Punic War (218–201), it was valued at 10 bronze *asses*. After this war, however, it was revalued at 16 bronze *asses* or 4 *sesterces* (4 *asses* = 1 *sestertius*).

dictator—Magistrate appointed to take sole control of the state temporarily in order to overcome a crisis.

dignitas—"High rank," and hence the all-important "esteem" due to the holder of it.

dilectus—Levy for choosing men to draft into the army.

diocese—Grouping of provinces controlled by a vicar (*vicarius*), who served as a Praetorian Prefect's (see below) deputy and oversaw primarily fiscal concerns. Initially, Constantine and Licinius divided the empire into twelve dioceses.

diploma (pl. *diplomata*)—Document comprising a pair of folded bronze tablets that certified the holder's privileges on discharge from military or naval service.

divus (pl. *divi*)—"Deified," used only of deceased humans who had been declared deified by the senate.

Dominate (compare *dominus* below)—Period of more openly authoritarian rule instituted by Diocletian after the Principate.

dominus—"Lord," "master."

dux (pl. *duces*)—"General," "leader"; from the tetrarchy onwards, an official title for generals with provincial or regional commands ("dukes").

ecumenical council—"World council" of the church, at which major theological questions were decided. Held at Nicaea (325), Constantinople (381), Ephesus (431), and Chalcedon (451).

eques (pl. *equites*)—("horseman," "knight"; also termed "equestrian") Roman citizens who received the highest rating in a *census* and originally served as cavalrymen. Free birth, respectability, and wealth of at least 400,000 *sesterces* were required.

eunuchs—Castrated males, usually slaves or freedmen. Often employed as chamberlains of the emperor, some became important political figures in the late empire.

fasces—Bundle of rods surmounted by an axhead carried by official attendants (*lictores*) before a Roman magistrate as a symbol of his authority.

fasti—Calendar recording, say, recurrent events (e.g. festivals), or days for conducting different kinds of business (e.g. assembly meetings). Also chronological lists of past holders of an office or honor.

fides—"Good faith," the sense which Romans wished to convey that they were honorable and trustworthy.

flamen, flaminica—"Priest," "priestess."

Flavians—Line of emperors begun by Titus Flavius Vespasianus that ruled from 69 to 96.

forum (pl. *fora*)—In all Roman communities, a designated area for conducting political, judicial, and commercial business, and hence usually a town's focal point.

freedman—Freed (or "manumitted") slave. Almost all slaves freed by Roman owners received not only freedom but also Roman citizenship. Freedmen customarily took the *nomen* of their former owner, who now became their *patronus*.

gens (pl. *gentes*)—Extended family or clan linked by a common ancestor.

gladiator—Participant in armed combat (of various types) staged in an amphitheater. Most gladiators were condemned criminals, slaves, or prisoners of war.

Great Persecution—The final and most extensive persecution against the Christians; initiated on February 23, 303; in the East strictly enforced and continued until Galerius' Edict of Toleration in 311; also enforced in Africa until 305, but much less aggressively elsewhere in the West.

hagiography—Accounts of Christian saints. Such works include accounts of the trial and execution of martyrs, and biographies of other holy men and women.

honestiores ("more honorable people")—From the second century A.D. onwards, those considered by the authorities to merit greater respect and consideration, especially senators, *equites*, town councilors, and veterans, together with their families. The corresponding less privileged category was *humiliores*.

hostis—Any enemy of the Roman state, including a Roman citizen who took up arms against it.

humiliores ("more lowly people")—From the second century A.D., those considered by the authorities to merit only minimal respect, in contrast to *honestiores*.

imago—Portrait (usually made of wax) of a distinguished ancestor; carried by descendants at family funerals and displayed in the *atrium* of the family home.

imperator—Originally, a title for a successful military commander. From Augustus' time it was used of the "emperor" (the English noun derives from the Latin), and from the Flavian period onwards *imperator* was a regular imperial title.

imperium—(from the verb *imperare*, "to command") Supreme authority in Rome's affairs vested in certain officeholders, who alone could command troops and impose the death penalty. The *imperium* of emperors was specifically made *maius* ("greater") so that it outranked that of all other holders.

intercessio—A magistrate's right to halt or "veto" the activity of an equal or lower-ranking magistrate.

interrex—A patrician who was chosen to conduct the election of new consuls when both died or left office without successors during the Republic.

Isis—Egyptian fertility goddess, the focus of a widespread cult.

iugatio vel capitatio— ("acreage or head count") Taxation system initiated under Diocletian that calculated: 1) land tax based on a standard land unit (*iugum* ["yoke"]) and 2) head tax based on the productivity of individuals (*capitatio*).

iugerum (pl. *iugera*)—Unit of land measure. One *iugerum* = 0.25 hectare = 0.625 acre.

ius (pl. *iura*)—Legal right or privilege, legal status.

iustitium—Official temporary suspension of all public business at a time of crisis or mourning.

Judaism—Set of ancient Jewish religious and social practices—most notably, exclusive devotion to one god, male circumcision, observance of the Sabbath, and avoidance of nonkosher meat.

Julio-Claudians—Line of emperors—descended from the Julian and Claudian families— ruling from Augustus in the 20s B.C. to Nero (died A.D. 68). See Table 8.1.

jurist—Expert interpreter of the law.

koinon—See *concilium*.

Lar (pl. *Lares*)—Household or family god, usually worshipped at domestic shrines.

laudatio—Praise of an individual, in prose or verse, or a eulogy at a funeral.

laus—"Praise."

legatus (pl. *legati*; English "legate")—Common term: 1) an envoy; 2) a senior military officer, often the commander of a legion; 3) a high-ranking assistant to a provincial governor; 4) from the time of Augustus, a provincial governor appointed directly by the emperor (as *his* "assistant," therefore).

legion—The standard large Roman military formation, comprising around 5,000 heavily armed infantry. For greater mobility, Diocletian reduced this size to 1,000.

lex (pl. *leges*) ("law")—Statute passed by a citizen assembly or issued by the emperor, and then generally known by the name(s) of its proposer(s): for example, *lex Licinia-Sextia*.

lictor (pl. *lictores*)—Official attendant who carried *fasces* and escorted a Roman magistrate.

limitanei— ("border troops") In the late empire, soldiers stationed in permanent forts along the frontiers. To be distinguished from *comitatenses*.

lituus—Curved stick used by an *augur* (see *auspicium*).

ludi—Public "games" such as beast hunts (*venationes*), gladiatorial shows, chariot races.

magister equitum—("master of cavalry") The deputy of a *dictator*, appointed by him.

Magna Mater ("Great Mother," Cybele)—Goddess introduced to Rome from Asia Minor in 204 B.C.

maiestas—"Treason."

manus ("hand") marriage—A restrictive form of Roman marriage, which placed both the wife's person and property under her husband's absolute control.

monks—(Greek *monachoi*, "solitaries") Practitioners of Christian asceticism who believed in separating themselves from normal society and living lives of sexual and worldly renunciation, whether alone as hermits or in shared communities (monasteries).

Monophysites—Christians, mostly from Syria and Egypt, who refused to follow the findings of the Council of Chalcedon (451) that both human and divine aspects can be distinguished in Christ's nature. Instead, they formed their own group of believers in the "single nature" of Christ.

municipium (pl. *municipia*)—An autonomous city located in Roman territory, but governed by its own laws and city council, while obligated to assist Rome as an ally.

negotiator (pl. *negotiatores*)—"Businessman."

new man—See *novus homo*.

nobilis (pl. *nobiles*) ("nobles")—Rome's governing elite. More specifically, the members of those families with an ancestor who had attained the consulship.

nomen (pl. *nomina*)—("name")—Middle component of the typical Roman "three names," representing an individual's clan (*gens*); see also *cognomen* and *praenomen*.

novus homo (pl. *novi homines*) ("new man")—First member of a family to become a Roman senator.

optimates, *populares*—Terms used to describe the holders of contrasting political attitudes from the late second century B.C. *Optimates* ("the best people") continued to uphold traditional methods of competition among senators. *Populares* ("people's men") sought wider popularity among citizens.

origo—("origin") Line of descent, in particular a Roman citizen's community of origin, to which he owed obligations (in addition to the ones he owed Rome).

papyrus—The equivalent of modern paper; sheets of it were made from strips of the pith of a plant that grew in the marshlands of Egypt's Nile delta.

pater familias—Male head of a family, usually a father or grandfather. In principle, he had complete legal authority (*patria potestas*) over his family, including freedmen and slaves.

pater patriae, also *parens patriae*—("father" or "parent of the fatherland") A special title awarded to an individual (and routinely to emperors) for extraordinary service.

patrician—Member of the more privileged group of Roman citizens (in contrast to the *plebs*, or plebeian group). Patrician status could be gained only by birth (at least, until emperors bestowed it).

patronus ("patron")—See *client*.

pax deorum—("right relationship with the gods") Its maintenance by priests and officeholders was essential to the Roman community's continued well-being.

Penates—Roman spirits connected with the inner part of a private house.

peregrinus ("foreigner")—Any free individual who was not a member of a Roman community.

plebs—The "plebeians," the less privileged group of Roman citizens (in contrast to patricians). The term is also used of the common people anywhere, often dismissively.

pomerium—Sacred boundary of a city ritually marked by a priest.

pontifex (pl. *pontifices*)—("bridge builder," "pontiff") Member of one of the major groups or "colleges" of Roman priests, headed by the *pontifex maximus*.

Populares—See *optimates*.

populus (*Romanus*) ("people," "Roman people")—Collective term for the citizen body of the Roman state, as in the standard formulation "Senate and People of Rome" (*Senatus Populusque Romanus*, SPQR).

praenomen (pl. *praenomina*)—First component of the typical Roman "three names" (see also *nomen* and *cognomen*). The *praenomen* represented an individual's given or "first" name (such as Marcus, Quintus), and distinguished members of the same family.

praetor—Annual magistracy with *imperium*, an important step in the *cursus honorum*.

Praetorian Guard—The emperor's bodyguard, instituted by Augustus, and disbanded by Constantine.

Praetorian Prefect—Commander(s) of the Praetorian Guard (see above), who exercised military and judicial authority second only to that of the emperor. After the disbandment of the Guard by Constantine, Prefects (four or more at a time) were still appointed to serve as high judicial and administrative officials.

princeps (pl. *principes*)—("leading figure") During the Republic, an informal term for those senators who most influenced matters of state. *Princeps* thus appealed to Augustus as best describing the position he developed for himself. Hence, "Principate."

princeps senatus ("leader of the senate")—Informal title used for the senator placed first in the roll of senators.

proconsul—Ex-consul who, at the end of his term in office, accepted an assignment that continued, or "prorogued," his magistrate's authority.

procurator ("agent")—In particular, an individual (often an *eques*) appointed by the emperor to manage property or to represent him in court.

proletarii—Roman citizens whose property at a census was too low to qualify them for military service; all they could offer the state was their children (*proles*).

propraetor—Ex-praetor who, at the end of his term in office, accepted an assignment that continued, or "prorogued," his magistrate's authority.

proscription—Publication of a list of individuals who could be killed with impunity.

provincia ("province")—The sphere of activity which a magistrate was assigned to exercise his authority; hence, in particular, a foreign territory.

publicanus (pl. *publicani*)—Private individual who performed work for the Roman state under contract. Larger contracts might require a group to work together as a "syndicate" (*societas*).

Punic—In Latin usage, Phoenician, hence Carthaginian.

quaestio (pl. *quaestiones*)—Tribunal or court for criminal matters, which could be established permanently or as required in individual instances.

quaestor—Annual magistracy (without *imperium*), the first step in the *cursus honorum*.

Regia—Sacred building in the Roman Forum between the Via Sacra and the Temple of Vesta. Residence of the king, thereafter headquarters of the *pontifex maximus*.

rescript—An official response by the emperor to a legal question or petition. Even though rescripts usually addressed particular cases, they were sometimes held to have the force of general law.

rex—"King."

rostra—Raised platform in the Forum from which speeches were made; named after the prows (*rostra*) of captured enemy ships used for its decoration.

sacrosanctity—Attribute that made it a crime (subject to instant death) on the part of anyone who used violence towards its holder (a tribune of the plebs, for example).

Sasanians—Persian dynasty which seized power from the Parthians in A.D. 224. Reforms to taxation, law, and military organization allowed it to maintain very tight control of Mesopotamia and Iran, and to threaten the Roman and Byzantine empire; it eventually fell to Arab Muslims by 651.

scholarii—("staff guards") Groups of imperial guardsmen newly formed under Constantine to replace the Praetorian Guard (see above).

senatus ("senate")—Advisory council first of Rome's kings, thereafter of the state's senior magistrates.

senatus consultum (SC)—"Resolution" or "decree of the senate."

sestertius (English pl. "sesterces"; see also *denarius*)—Roman coin originally of silver, but from Augustus' time minted in bronze.

Severans—Line of emperors ruling from the accession of Septimius Severus (193) through the death of Severus Alexander (235). See Table 11.1.

socius (pl. *socii*)—"Ally" (of the Roman state).

Sol Invictus—("Unconquerable Sun") A deity worshipped from early in Roman history that became very popular in the third century A.D., especially under Elagabalus, Aurelian, and Constantine.

Struggle of the Orders—Prolonged struggle (early fifth to early third centuries B.C.) by Rome's plebeian citizens to overcome domination of the state's affairs by patricians.

suffect consul (or other officeholder)—Replacement elected to fill the remaining term of office when its original or "ordinary" holder died or resigned.

Tetrarchy—("rule of four") Joint rule established by Diocletian, with an emperor (*Augustus*) in the West and another in the East, each with a deputy (*Caesar*).

toga—The undyed woolen robe that was the distinctive garment of adult Roman civilians.

tribune (*tribunus*, pl. *tribuni*)—From the early fifth century B.C., "tribunes of the plebs" (*tribuni plebis*) with their own authority (*tribunicia potestas*) were recognized as the leaders of the plebeian citizen body (*plebs*). In addition, and quite separately, "military tribunes" (*tribuni militum*) were army officers.

tributum—A tax on property.

triumph—Voted by the senate to honor a general who had soundly defeated a non-Roman enemy; celebrated by a procession through Rome.

triumvir (pl. *triumviri*)—Member of a group, or commission, of three men.

Twelve Tables—Rome's first set of written laws (around 450 B.C.).

Vestal virgins—Prestigious priestesses who performed the rites of Vesta (goddess of the hearth) from her shrine near the Regia in the Forum.

via—"Road."

vigiles ("watchmen")—Paramilitary patrols of freedmen, instituted by Augustus to reduce the danger from outbreaks of fire in the city of Rome.

virtus—"Manly courage," and thus "excellence" or "distinction" as demonstrated in service to Rome.

Zoroastrianism—Dualist religion of Persia, which held that the universe is a manifestation of the battle between the good god Ahura Mazda and his evil counterpart Angra Mainu; it gained particular importance as an imperial religion of the Sasanians (see above).

ART CREDITS

FIGURES

Fig 1.1: after Small, Jocelyn P. 1971. "The Banquet Frieze from Poggio Civitate (Murlo),"
Studi Etruschi 39, p. 28, fig. 1, p. 8. Fig 1.2: Image copyright © The Metropolitan Museum
of Art. Image source: Art Resource, NY, p. 9. Fig 1.3: Deutsches Archäologisches Institut,
Rome, p. 10. Fig 1.4: Warrior, from Umbria, Etruscan, 5th century BC (bronze), Etruscan/
Ashmolean Museum, University of Oxford, UK/The Bridgeman Art Library, p. 11. Fig 1.5:
after Österberg, Carl E. 1975. *Case etrusche di Acquarossa*. Rome: Multigraphica Editrice,
p. 182, p. 12. Fig 1.6: Apollo of Veii, from the Temple of Minerva, c.510 BC (terracotta),
Etruscan, (6th century BC/Museo Archeologico di Villa Giulia, Rome, Italy/The Bridgeman
Art Library, p. 17. Fig 1.7a: Fototeca Unione- American Academy in Rome, p. 22. Fig 1.7b:
Scala/Art Resource, NY, p. 22. Fig 2.1: Fototeca Unione- American Academy in Rome, p. 31.
Fig 2.2: su concessione del Ministero per i Beni e le Attività Culturali - Soprintendenza
Speciale per i Beni Archeologici di Roma, p. 39. Fig 2.3: Alinari/Regione Umbria/Art
Resource, NY, p. 40. Fig 2.4: Scala/Ministero per i Beni e le Attività culturali/Art Resource,
NY, p. 45. Fig 3.1: © Araldo de Luca/Corbis, p. 54. Fig 3.2: © The Trustees of the British
Museum, p. 58. Fig 3.3: © The Trustees of the British Museum, p. 59. Fig 4.1: Fototeca
Unione - American Academy in Rome, p. 78. Fig 4.2: © Vanni Archive/Art Resource, NY,
p. 81. Fig 4.3: after Zanker, Paul. 1998, *Pompeii: Public and Private Life*. Cambridge, MA:
Harvard University Press, p. 36, fig. 5, p. 82. Fig 4.4: *Chiron* 12 (1982) Tafel 7 nos. 12 and
13, p. 84. Fig 5.1: © The Trustees of the British Museum, p. 108. Fig 5.2: Photo courtesy of
Elizabeth Robinson, p. 109. Fig 5.3: after Corarelli, Filippo. 1987.*I Santuari del Lazio in Età
Repubblicana*. Rome: La Nuova Italia Scientifica, p. 39, fig. 10, p. 114. Fig 6.1: Alinari/Art
Resource, NY, p. 119. Fig 6.2: Ny Carlsberg Glyptotek, Denmark, p. 120. Fig 6.3: © The Trus-
tees of the British Museum, p. 127. Fig 6.4: Photo courtesy of Vladimir Kuznetsov, p. 130.
Fig 6.5: Alinari/Art Resource, NY, p. 131. Fig 6.6a: after Potter, Timothy W. 1987. *Roman
Italy*. London: British Museum Publications, p. 132. Fig 6.6b: Photo courtesy of Artelibro,
Firenze, p. 132. Fig 7.1: Ancient Art and Architecture Collection Ltd, p. 137. Fig 7.2: Getty
Images, p. 139. Fig 7.3: © The Trustees of the British Museum, p. 153. Fig 7.4a: Deutsches
Archäologisches Institut, Rome, p. 157. Fig 7.4b: Fototeca Unione - American Academy in
Rome, p. 157. Fig 8.1: © The Trustees of the British Museum, p. 165. Fig 8.2: The National

GAZETTEER

Ancient and modern names are not distinguished. Unless otherwise stated, numbers refer to pages. No more than two appearances of a feature or place are listed, even if it appears on further maps. BP = Back endpaper map, FP = Front endpaper map.

INDEX

Most Roman males are listed by their nomen. Emperors and certain other well known figures are listed by the name usually used for them in English. The maps are indexed in the Gazetteer.

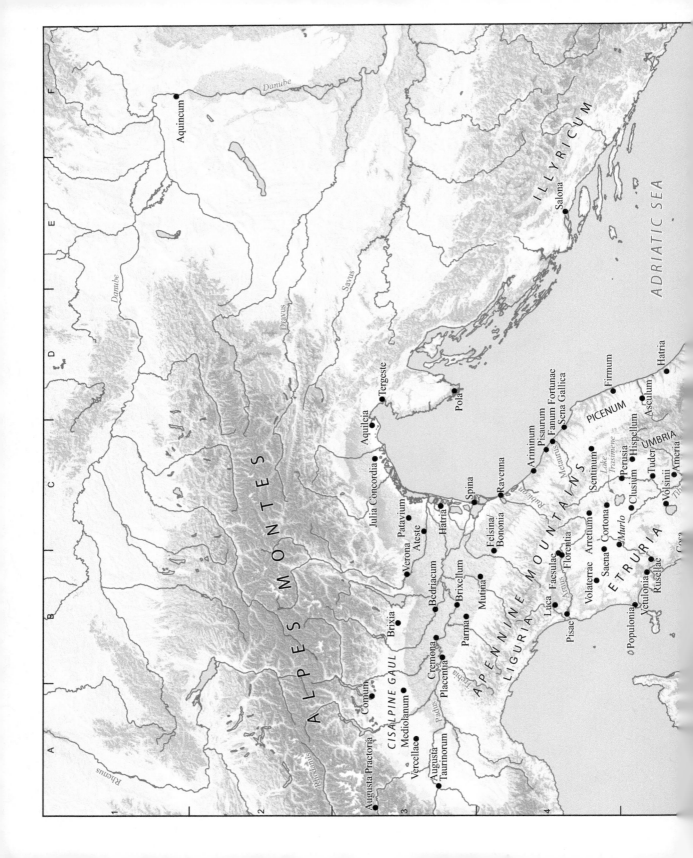